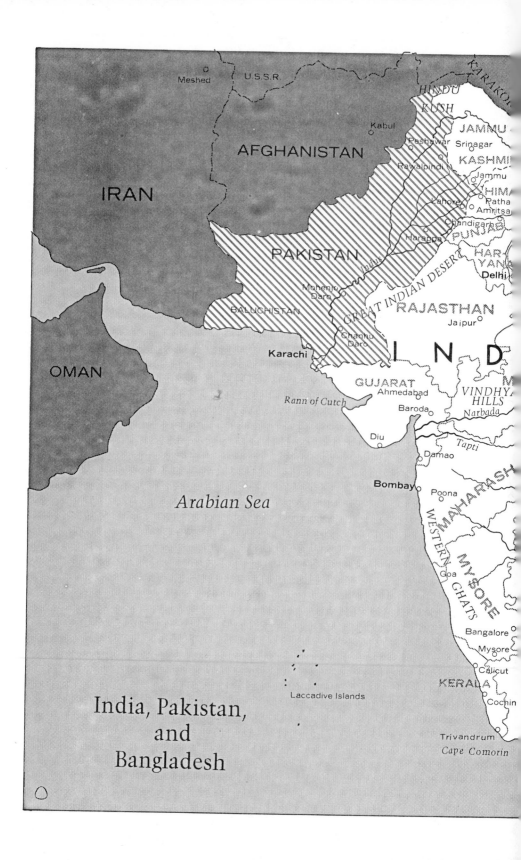

India, Pakistan, and Bangladesh

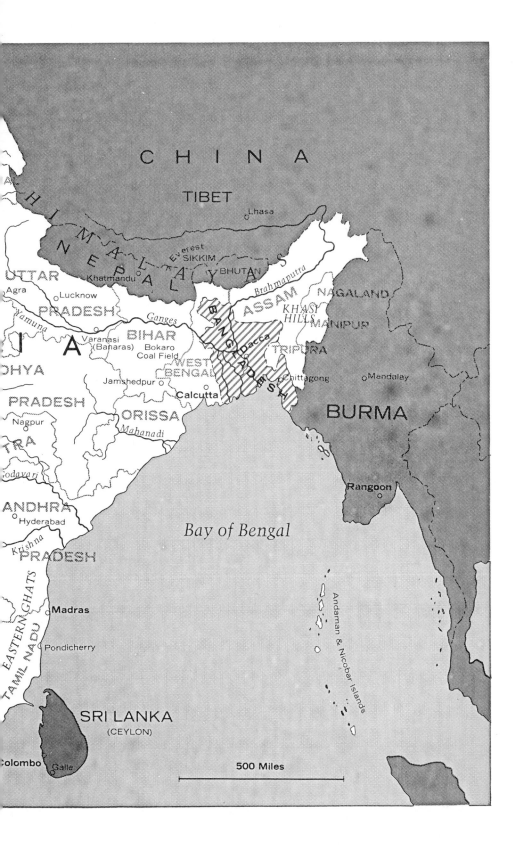

The American Foreign Policy Library

Edwin O. Reischauer, Editor

The United States
and
India, Pakistan, Bangladesh

by W. Norman Brown

Harvard University Press
Cambridge, Massachusetts   1972

This is a third edition of *The United States and India and Pakistan*

Library of Congress Catalog Card Number 72–81270

Printed in the United States of America

Introduction by Edwin O. Reischauer

Of all the major sectors into which the world and its population can rationally be divided, the Indian subcontinent, with its three large nations of India, Pakistan, and Bangladesh, is probably the least well known or understood by Americans. Geographically close to the opposite side of the globe from the United States and screened for long from American attention by the intervening British Empire, it has attracted American interest less than did Europe, Latin America, China, or Japan and, at least in recent years, less than Southeast Asia, the Middle East, or Africa. But geography is no reason for inattention in this day when technology is rapidly making distance irrelevant in the world; nor are historical conditions of a generation or two ago adequate reason for disinterest at this time of constant change in international relations.

The Indian subcontinent is the source of one of the three or, as one might count them, four major streams of ancient civilization that have persisted throughout recorded history. The East Asian stream flowed outward from North China; the Mediterranean later divided into Western Christian and Islamic halves; and the South Asian stream, originating in what is now Pakistan in the northwestern corner of the Indian subcontinent, spread southeastward throughout the rest of South Asia.

The subcontinent thus has a very large place in history, and its present share in the story of mankind is not much smaller. It is today the home of roughly one fifth of the human race. The lives of this vast mass of humanity are in constant flux, as changes of all sorts sweep through the area. The interrelationships of the extraordinarily diverse peoples of the subcontinent are complex and often troubled, and their contacts with the outside world are becoming both more significant and more difficult. The problems of the area are in some ways more intractable than those of any other part of the globe, illustrating in extreme and therefore some· times clearer form the problems that beset mankind everywhere— the deadening hand of past custom, the drag of rural poverty, the desperation of impoverished urban crowding, and the tensions between communities of different language, religion, or social status. On the other hand, the potentialities of this vast quadrant of mankind are immense, even if imponderable. One cannot understand the present world or get much of a glimpse into the world's future unless one knows more than most Americans do about the Indian subcontinent and its peoples.

The dynamic and tumultuous recent history in the subcontinent is illustrated by this present volume and its two predecessors. The first, published in 1953 under the title *The United States and India and Pakistan,* focused on the cataclysmic division of the area six years earlier into these two great but bitterly hostile nations and the tremendous suffering and travail the process of separation produced. The second revised and enlarged edition appeared in 1963, the year after the Sino-Indian border war, by which time the subcontinent had become embroiled in world rivalries and tensions—an interregional rivalry with China and the global tensions between the Soviet Union and the United States. The continuing upheavals of the region are symbolized by the new title for the further revised and enlarged rendition of the story in this present volume, which is being published only months after the violence and bloodshed that accompanied the breaking off of East Pakistan to form the independent nation of Bangladesh.

What was only a generation ago a united area under the British Raj is now three separate states. The huge size of the subcontinent in human terms is illustrated by the fact that one of its three political units—India—stands alone with China as a world colossus of population, some two or three times the size of the Soviet or American giants, while even the two smaller political units each ranks among the nine most populous nations in the world.

When the first edition of *The United States and India and Pakistan* appeared in 1953 it was hailed as unquestionably the best and most balanced account of the history and contemporary conditions of the two nations that then divided the Indian subcontinent. The same high praise can be given this book too. The reason is simple. There is no one better able than W. Norman Brown to write with authority on this area and explain its peoples and their history and culture. A lifetime involvement in the subcontinent and its civilization has prepared him for the task. He lived in British India as a child and learned to speak Hindi. He subsequently entered on the serious study of the classical civilization of India, receiving his doctorate in Sanskrit in 1916. He studied further in India and also taught there and then for many years in the United States. Intelligence work on India during World War II brought him into closer touch with the contemporary political and social scene. All these experiences together with constant travel back and forth between India and the United States for more than seventy years have made him the ideal interpreter of the region.

This revision and expansion of Mr. Brown's now classic work comes at a propitious time. The birth of Bangladesh and the international repercussions of this event have made imperative a reappraisal of the whole situation. So also has the change in the feel of the American relationship with Asia. Great economic growth and social and political development in the subcontinent since Mr. Brown last analyzed conditions there also make necessary a fresh look, for a decade is a long time in an area where change is so constant and also so unpredictable. Without losing any of the value of his solid account of earlier periods, Mr. Brown has given the current situation in the subcontinent the fresh reappraisal it requires. The result is a book that will prove invaluable to anyone who wants to understand the Indian subcontinent—or for that matter the world in which we live.

Preface

This book is the third edition of my *The United States and India and Pakistan* (1953; second edition 1963). The change of title reflects the fact that in 1971 East Pakistan revolted, declared its independence as Bangladesh in 1972, and now seems to be permanently estranged from West Pakistan and destined to continue so.

In the years 1963–1971 the two nations of India and Pakistan made a number of important government, political, economic, and cultural changes. They had to meet crises caused by the forces of nature and crises originating in their own institutions. They had a brief war with each other in 1965 over Kashmir, which was terminated without any change in the status of Kashmir. The short war between India and Pakistan in 1971–72 brought with it renewed hostilities concerning Kashmir, but with no resolution of the quarrel. Religious and linguistic differences within each of the two nations have continued to stir passions. Great leaders have died, especially Jawaharlal Nehru. In this period democratic processes advanced in India; they were repudiated in Pakistan, and the repudiation led to the civil war in East Pakistan and the creation of Bangladesh.

That civil war was fought with the greatest human-made atrocities the subcontinent has known since the invasion of India at the end of the fourteenth century by Amir Timur (Timur-i-lang, Tamerlane). It produced another brief war between India and Pakistan in December 1971, but fortunately did not bring into the hostilities any other nation. The world's three superpowers—China, the Soviet Union, and the United States—succeeded in keeping out of it. The machinery of the United Nations was invoked but without result; the war stopped after India, having defeated Pakistan decisively, proclaimed a cease-fire, which Pakistan quickly accepted.

The hopes, woes, resources, potentialities, and options of India, Pakistan, and now Bangladesh remain concerns of a large part of the rest of the world, certainly of the United States. If this book helps to increase understanding of the problems and difficulties facing those three nations, it will accomplish its purpose.

In preparing this new edition, as in preparing the original and second editions, I have drawn heavily upon the knowledge, wisdom, and writings of many other scholars, and for Bangladesh especially upon the accounts of newspaper reporters, particularly those of the New York *Times*, which have been unflagging and I believe conscientious, objective, and competent.

In preparing this edition I have had highly valued assistance from staff members of the South Asia Regional Studies of the University of Pennsylvania, staff members of the South Asia Library of the same university, and staff members of the American Institute of Indian Studies. I am grateful to Mrs. Panna Naik of the South Asia Library for help in compiling the "Suggested Reading." Mrs. Goldie K. Levin, Executive Officer of the American Institute of Indian Studies, and Mrs. Marjorie Weiler, Miss Parwiz Surati, and Miss Merry Burlingham of the same organization have helped me in checking facts and data and in typing the manuscript. Of course all errors of fact in my text are of my own making.

March 1972   W. N. B

Contents

1 The Indian Subcontinent Today

When the old "British Indian Empire" was partitioned and made into the two nations of India and Pakistan on August 15, 1947, enthusiasts in the two countries celebrated the event in somewhat the spirit of welcoming the arrival of the millennium. In India in 1947 it was thought by many who had been promoting the cause of nationalism that full self-rule (*purna swaraj*), in freeing the country from colonialism, would automatically and quickly lead to progressive release from economic exploitation and bring prosperity and resolution of the country's many problems—economic, social, and political. This was to be effected by Indians themselves on democratic principles through the use of their own government agencies operating secularly. There were, of course, many other Indians, like Jawaharlal Nehru, more sophisticated in outlook and more experienced in public affairs, who knew better. They realized that it would take a long hard uphill pull to achieve even a moderate degree of progress.

In Pakistan the prevailing public expectation about the attainment of national goals through independence was even less realistic than that in India. Partly the difference was due to the fact that the goals were in some important respects less in keeping with twentieth century political aims than India's goals. Pakistan had come into being because the Muslims in prepartition India wanted to live in and have as their own an Islamic state, governed by Muslims and operated for the benefit of Muslims and the fulfillment of Muslim religious ideals. The millennium for them was to be a Muslim one, with a predominantly Muslim population happily released from Hindu—or Christian—dominance. Living in an Islamic state, not only would they enjoy religious preferential treatment but all their economic, social, and political institutions would be informed with Islamic religious principles. The constitution subsequently framed stated at the beginning that the state was to be Islamic. Secularism did not enter into the thinking of the framers of the constitutions which were successively adopted and then abandoned. There were, to be sure, more sophisticated members of the nation, some of them with modern views, but they were generally muted and unheard. In the succeeding years the expectations of the strongly religiously motivated Pakistanis have been only partly fulfilled amid the nation's pressing, and often conflicting, needs and goals. At the same time the economic advance that was hoped for in 1947 has not been met, while the political situation has been unsettled and finally erupted in civil war in 1971, which in 1972 led to the creation of the new nation Bangladesh.

The partition of the Indian Empire had been a disastrous affair. It was accomplished with slaughter of civilians in each of the new nations and migration of large numbers of people in each direction, Muslims fleeing from India to Pakistan, Hindus and Sikhs fleeing from Pakistan to India. Along with this went an effort on the part of Pakistan to take by force the state of Jammu and Kashmir, a predominantly Muslim area, which had the right to accede to whichever of the two nations it wished. Finally its Maharaja, a Hindu, who had the authority to make the decision, chose to accede to India. The quarrel that resulted has never been settled. At all times since 1947 the relations between India and Pakistan have been acrimonious, threatening, and even violent, with war smoldering beneath a thin covering, ready at any moment to burst into flame.

The partition of the British Indian Empire had been made on the basis of assigning to Pakistan, as far as was feasible, predominantly Muslim parts of India that were contiguous. Application of this principle led to the creation of Pakistan as a nation of two parts separated from each other by a distance of 920 miles, with all the intervening territory belonging to India. The old prepartition India, a self-contained subcontinent, well isolated from the rest of the world by difficult land barriers and sea, had about 1,581,410 square miles of territory, less than four ninths the area of the United States. This was divided unequally between India and Pakistan in a ratio of not quite 3.4 to 1, with some regions in dispute, notably Kashmir. Some changes have taken place, such as the annexation by India of the former French and Portuguese holdings in India, and the cession by Muscat and Oman of Gwadar to Pakistan in 1958; in addition, some of India's territory was taken by force by China in 1962 on the ground that the British had occupied and annexed it to India unlawfully in the time of China's weakness. The net result of these changes was that the territorial claims of the two nations slightly exceeded the total area of the old undivided India. Modern India claims 1,261,309 square miles, which is somewhat more than one third the size of the United States. Pakistan claimed 365,529 square miles in 1961, an area larger than that of France, West Germany, East Germany, and Switzerland combined. Of the two parts West Pakistan was much the larger, having 310,403 square miles in 1961 while East Pakistan, which is now the new nation Bangladesh, had only 55,126 square miles in 1961 but was the more populous.

A basic feature of life in the subcontinent since partition has been the growth in population. The first census of the two nations after independence was taken in 1951. At that time the population of India was about 356.9 million and that of Pakistan 75.7 million, making a total for the subcontinent of 432.6 million. Each country had another census in 1961, when the population of India was 439.2 million and that of Pakistan 93.8 million, making a total of 533 million. Each nation had a census scheduled for 1971, but the final figures are not available at this writing. In April 1971, however, the Census Commissioner of India released a preliminary estimate subject to final computation, which gave a figure of 547 million, an increase in twenty years of 190 million (53.5 percent). An official estimate of the Pakistani population for 1970 gave a figure of about 114.2 million persons. Of this, West Pakistan, now all that is left of Pakistan, was estimated to have 53.5 million; East Pakistan, now Bangladesh, 60.7 million. *Bangladesh* (a government publication) in the issue of June 2, 1972, gave an estimate of 75 million. These figures are obviously not final. Bangladesh suffered severe losses of population in 1970–1972 because of natural calamities, slaughter of civilians by (West) Pakistan army forces, and flight of population as refugees from the terror of military repression. But for lack of any better figures we may assume that the total population of the subcontinent is now at least 661 million, which is more than the combined population of the United States, the Soviet Union, Great Britain, East and West Germany, France, Belgium, the Netherlands, and Switzerland. Among the world's nations the population of the subcontinent is exceeded only by that of China, which was estimated in 1969 to be 740 million. The United Nations Bulletin of Statistics for April

1971 estimated that by the year 2000 China would have 1.165 billion persons and India 1.084 billion; the total for the subcontinent as a whole would then presumably exceed that of China. At present there live in the subcontinent between one sixth and one fifth of the world's estimated population, occupying, however, less than 3 percent of the world's land area, excluding the polar regions.

The increase in population, though it shows that the subcontinent has steadily become able to support an ever increasing population, has not yet been accompanied by a satisfactory solution to the problem of providing an adequate food supply. The economy of each nation remains weak. Poverty is general, and sudden disaster can produce a famine, local or widespread according to the circumstances. The subcontinent lives today, as it has always lived, on the basis of agriculture, with relatively little supplement from industry. The imbalance is shown by the small number of industrial workers. The industrial labor force (that is, those employed in registered factories) amounts to around 5.5 million persons. This is probably less than 2 percent of the total labor force.

When traveling in the subcontinent one emerges suddenly from one of the few large cities to proceed for hundreds of miles across open country consisting of fields interspersed with uncultivated, or uncultivable, land, dotted with drab little villages, lightened only by an occasional whitewashed Hindu shrine or a Muslim mosque. Here and there one comes to a small town. There is nowhere any section to compare with the Atlantic coastal stretch in the United States of almost continuous urbanization from Portland, Maine, to Washington, D.C., or with some other American industrial areas, as around Pittsburgh and Chicago. According to official estimates only about 19.87 percent of the Indians, 22 percent of the people in Pakistan, and 13.1 percent in Bangladesh live in cities or town clusters of more than 100,000. (In the United States in 1970 more than two thirds of the population lived in central cities and Standard Metropolitan Statistical Areas.) Just as there are few cities and towns on the subcontinent, so too there are few isolated rural dwellings like the farmhouses of the United States. Most of the people (about two thirds) live in the more than 650,000 villages, which are settlements of generally less than 5,000 population, averaging about 600. Of the villagers much the greater part (about 70 percent of the total population) cultivate the adjacent land; the others supply services or pursue handicrafts (such as weaving, pottery, metal work, oil pressing). The country, as one sees it, consists of clusters or even long stretches of tiny fields, bounded by low mud borders or thorn hedges, streaked with inarable land or jungle. Except at a few centers like Calcutta, Bombay, Madras, Jamshedpur, Asansol, Ahmedabad, Kanpur (Cawnpore), Sholapur, Karachi, and Lahore, factory chimneys are solitary or absent. This is how things are in cultivated sections of "the plains." In the hills and mountains, where agriculture is more difficult, villages are fewer and smaller. In the deserts, as in Rajasthan, they are still scarcer, though sometimes surprisingly large, and even cities are found, as at Bikaner and Jaisalmer.

The water necessary for agriculture is in most parts of the subcontinent of uncertain supply, and getting water is a perennial problem. When the annual monsoons are good the urgency of the problem is reduced, though much human labor is involved in getting the water to the fields. In a region where great rivers can be used for irrigation, as in the Punjab or Sind, the water is impounded by huge dams or barrages and led off through canals. The major outlets are large; from these run off smaller canals, and from these still smaller ones, and so by graduated decrease until the water finally reaches the fields though capillary-like distribution. For part of the year many of these channels must be cut off, to save the water until it is needed later. In dry spells peasants are busy throughout the day opening the sluices leading to their land so as to get the maximum flow during the hours for which they have contracted and to direct the water first to one part of their holdings and then to another. This is the easiest of the subcontinent's ways of using human labor to water the fields, and the most certain. In north India and what was West Pakistan irrigation systems can use rivers fed by the melting snows of the Himalayas and the rain that falls upon their southern ranges during the summer monsoon. River-based irrigation is also practiced in other parts of the subcontinent. Since independence new schemes of irrigation have been inaugurated, many drawing their water from rivers which are not fed by the Himalayan snows. Still other schemes are under construction or are planned. The flow of water in the rivers fluctuates from year to year, but in no year does it cease entirely. Hence, peasants who live in regions where there are river-fed irrigation systems are usually better off and less subject to crop failure and famine than those who must rely upon other sources.

In many areas the farmer gets water for his fields from a well. In the north he may use a great Persian wheel, filling the air with an interminable creaking as it dips an endless chain of earthenware pots into the water, raises them above ground level, and empties them into a trough from which the water flows through runlets to the land. A blindfolded camel or a pair of bullocks operate the mechanism, treading a tiny circle all day long while a man or boy stands by to keep them moving. Elsewhere a peasant may use a buffalo or a pair of bullocks to raise and then lower a leather sack into the water. There is a ramp built up to the well, rising above its mouth some six feet or more. Along it the bullocks tread forward and backward, relaxing the rope to which the sack is tied and so letting it fall, then, when they reverse, raising it to the wooden crossbeam at the high end of the incline, where it is emptied into a channel to flow away. It takes one man to empty the sack, another to drive the bullocks. Very poor peasants who own no bullocks and cannot arrange to use those of a neighbor may operate such a well with only human labor, the subcontinent's cheapest commodity, drawn from the ranks of the family.

In still other areas peasants raise the water with a sweep, like an Egyptian *shaduf*. This is a seesaw-like apparatus with a leather sack or an earthenware pot at one end of the beam and a counterpoise balanced at the other. All day long a man may walk back and forth along the beam, first lowering the container into the well and then raising it to the top, where another man empties it into a runway. Or at the extremity of the sweep there may be a bamboo pole with the vessel fastened to its end. A man stands beside the well forcing the pole down until the vessel is submerged, then letting it go so that the counterpoise can raise it to the surface. In south India one may see a channel or ditch full of water, into which two peasants, often women, jointly dip a shallow scoop, rhythmically swinging it back and forth between them, lifting the water and emptying it into a higher channel through which it flows to the fields.

Throughout most of the land there are hundreds of thousands of "tanks," or artificial ponds, which are filled by the annual rains and serve in the dry season for irrigation, washing, even drinking. It is important to keep these tanks in good working order. Silt must not be left to accumulate; plants, such as the rapidly spreading water chestnut, must be prevented from choking them and absorbing the water supply. A tank has to be cleaned out regularly, and with great care not to dig out the bottom and let the water seep away.

In south India there are myriads of such artificial storage ponds, varying in size from one acre or less to a square mile or more. At the lower end of a gentle slope is an earthen dike, which has to be kept in constant repair; the upper end is a marsh. Seen from the air, the country sparkles with them like the embroidered garments inset with bits of glass that women wear in Cutch. This method of maintaining agriculture appears to have been used since megalithic times.

In every part of the subcontinent where rice is cultivated, from the extreme south to the steep mountains of Kashmir, the peasants have made the cultivable land into series of terraces. These are broad where the slope of the ground is gradual, becoming narrow strips on the steep sides of the lower Himalayas. Around each terrace is a mud wall to retain the water that accumulates during the annual rains or is introduced by some device of irrigation.

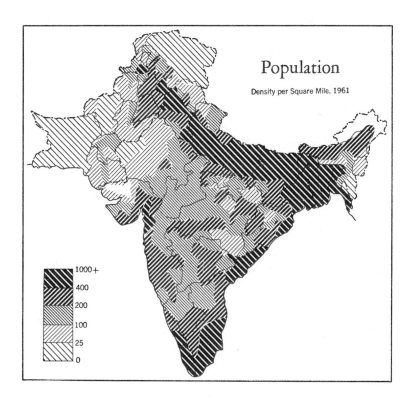

Population

Density per Square Mile, 1961

1000+
400
200
100
25
0

Water brought by river or rainfall has always exercised a decisive influence on the life of the subcontinent. It has been responsible for the population concentrations, for the direction of ethnic invasions, for the development of the arts of civilization. Its importance is certified from the time of India's earliest literature. In the *Rig Veda's* myth of creation the cosmic Waters were at first confined by malevolent inertia and had to be released by a hero-god in fierce battle before a universe could exist and operate. In that same work and in allied literature are charms which priests recited to wake the aestivating frogs so that with the magic spells of their croaking they might summon the needed rain. Fifteen hundred years later the Sanskrit poets were extolling as divine music the peacock's cry, so shrill to our ears, that heralds the approach of the rainy season. In the Rajput and Mughal miniature paintings of the eighteenth and nineteenth centuries the musical mode appropriate to the rolling thunder and serpent-like streaks of lightning that accompany the vitalizing downpour of the moonsoon evokes the artist's most delicate powers of imagination.

What are the facts about the subcontinent's topography, its fertile plains, its river systems, its mountainous areas, its deserts, its basic water supply?

The subcontinent is shaped roughly like a quadrangle—or, more precisely, like a pentagon, though the fifth side is disproportionately short. One long point of the figure is the Deccan peninsula projecting sharply southward into the Indian Ocean, with the Arabian Sea on its west and the Bay of Bengal on its east. The rest is mountainbound. Along the northwestern side, now held by Pakistan, is a protective barrier of hills and desert, generally difficult for armies or peoples on the trek, yet penetrable at various points, and providing the chief means of ingress to the subcontinent by land throughout recorded history. The northern side is a concave arc of lofty mountains, containing the world's highest peaks. It bars both the peoples and the cold winds of the land beyond and at the same time blocks the rainclouds of India from reaching Central Asia, where in consequence large areas remain desert. These ranges are geologically young and they and the nearby plains are disturbed by frequent tremors and occasional disastrous earthquakes, such as those in Bihar in 1934 and Assam in 1950. On the east the short fifth side is the Burma frontier, whose jungle-covered mountains are all but impassable.

Inside the northwestern and northern walls is the great plain of the subcontinent. It extends from the peninsula of Kathiawar in the present Republic of India beside the Arabian Sea, in a direction slightly west of north to Sind in Pakistan; thence a little east of north for about 700 miles to the Himalayas, including all of Pakistan except some mountain areas. From here it turns eastward into India below the curve of the Himalayan chain, across the breadth of the country, coming to an end against the hills of Assam and Bangladesh and the coast of the Bay of Bengal.

This plain varies from 80 to 200 miles in width. In its sweeping extent it contains the greatest of the subcontinent's river systems. In the west is the Indus, which rises on the northern side of the Himalayas, flows westward behind them to round their end, separating them from the Karakoram and Hindu Kush ranges and then drives inside the northwestern frontier down to the sea. The Indus is fed by the five rivers of the Punjab ("Land of Five Streams"), one of which (the Sutlej) also rises north of the Himalayas not far from the source of the Indus, but, unlike it, finds a route directly through them. The four others (Jhelum, Chenab, Ravi, Beas) rise in the range and flow directly to the lowlands. In the upper Punjab the moderate rainfall and the irrigation based upon its rivers support an extensive agriculture. Farther south, in the lower Punjab and Sind, rainfall is scanty, varying from ten to twenty inches annually and in many places being even less. Here agriculture is impossible except with the aid of irrigation. This has been practiced for millennia, but never on a scale to support a large population. Today there are vast systems of irrigation in this region, and others are under construction or planned. East of the long course of the Indus is the Great Indian Desert, which has neither rivers nor rainfall. In form it is an irregular triangle with one side paralleling the river and the others foming an apex which points eastward into Rajasthan in India. Southeast of Sind in India is Kathiawar, a region with moderate rainfall but enough to support a population of medium density.

The northern part of the Great Indian plain, often called Hindustan, contains the Ganges-Yamuna (Jamna or Jumna) river system, which only a low rise of ground separates from the Indus system. The soil of this region is a deep alluvial deposit. Its two main rivers, the Ganges and the Jumna, rise on the lower side of the Himalayas and curve southeast in gradually converging arcs

9

until they unite at Allahabad. From there, absorbing many tributaries, the Ganges continues eastward to Bengal, where it is joined by the Brahmaputra. This last, like the Indus and the Sutlej, rises on the northern side of the Himalayas but, as though to polarize the Indus, flows eastward to turn and circle the eastern end of the mountain chain, where it finds an opening, reverses itself, and flows southwest. It and the Ganges unite and form an immense delta. Their waters reach the Bay of Bengal through many mouths, steadily depositing silt, and today, as for millennia in the past, continually projecting the land area into the bay as low flatland, subject from time to time to floods from the rivers or to tidal waves from the Bay of Bengal created by violent storms.

The part of the northern plain east of the Punjab, favored by its rivers, is in normal years also watered by seasonal rains. It is agriculturally the most desirable part of the subcontinent and has always been the goal of invaders entering from the passages of the northwest. The population density of this region is 800 to the square mile; it contains about two fifths of the subcontinent's inhabitants, although only about one sixth of the total area.

Below the northern plain is a complex highland, the upper end of which is embraced by the two extremes of the plain. Along its northern part are various ranges of low hills, of which the highest peak, Mount Abu, is 5650 feet in elevation. The terrain of central India makes it a difficult area to traverse, and permits it to support only a moderately dense population. Indian literature has for 2500 years spoken fearfully of the wild jungles and the primitive peoples in this area. The largest range of its hills is the Vindhyas, south of which is the Narmada (Narbada, Nerbudda) River. South of this are other ranges (of which the Satpura is the most important), and still farther south is the Tapti River. These two streams run from the center of the Indian peninsula westward to the Arabian Sea and are the only ones of the subcontinent's large rivers flowing in that direction.

Still farther south is the part of the plateau known specifically as the Deccan ("South"), which comprises most of the triangle of peninsular India. This tableland (varying from about 1000 to 2500 feet in elevation) tilts gently from west to east. Its great rivers rise on the western side, flow eastward across it, and empty in the Bay of Bengal. It is not well watered, either by streams or by rainfall, and much of its area is rocky or has soil of inferior quality. Nevertheless it supports around 250 persons to the square mile.

The Deccan is bordered on east and west by low ranges of mountains known as Ghats ("Steps"). The Western Ghats, a kind of seaboard scarp, which have a few peaks of approximately 5000 feet but average round 3000 feet, descend in thickly forested, bold declivities to the alluvial seaboard. The southern part of this shoreline, known as the Malabar coast, is one of the best-watered, most fertile, and most thickly populated parts of India, having around 1300 persons to the square mile, On the other side of the peninsula the discontinuous Eastern Ghats, averaging about 1500 feet in altitude, are less picturesque. They lead down to another well-watered, productive, and thickly inhabited alluvial plain, wider than that on the west and known as the Coromandel coast. The central plateau terminates southward in clusters of hills called the Nilgiris ("Blue Mountains") and Palni, which respectively have peaks as high as 8640 and 8841 feet. Finally, below these, at the extreme south, are the Cardamon Hills. Beyond these last is Cape Comorin, the southernmost point of India, east and south of which lies the fragrant island of Ceylon.

The Deccan highland is geologically old in comparison with the Himalaya; hence its worn appearance and low elevation, though Hindu myth assigns a different reason. The Vindhya mountain, says the great Sanskrit epic *Mahabharata,* became jealous of Himalaya and elevated himself, intending to surpass the latter and to interrupt the circuit of the sun and moon around Mount Meru, the mythical crest peak of the Himalayas and the assembly point of all the divine beings. The gods were alarmed but handled the problem by appealing for help to the renowned sage Agastya. He asked Vindhya to give him passage to the south so that he might carry civilization there, as he is traditionally credited with doing, and Vindhya graciously assented, bowing himself low and promising to remain so until the reverend sage should return. But Agastya never came back, and Vindhya, true to his promise, has never raised himself or even stirred. Being old and settled, Vindhya, unlike the youthful Himalaya, is free of earthquakes; it is not only lowly but resigned as well.

The most important climatic feature of the subcontinent is the annual southwest monsoon, which brings "the rains," and gives

India 90 percent of its heaven-dispensed water. So impressive has this phenomenon been upon India's consciousness that in her languages the commonest words for "year" primarily mean "rain" or "rainy season." The southwest monsoon generally blows during the four months of June through September, when the high sun heats the land rapidly and the hot air rises so that a low-pressure area is created and cool air flows inland from the sea. As it comes in from across the Indian Ocean, it is laden with moisture which it has sucked up. One arm of the monsoon strikes the hills of the lower western (Malabar) coast of India, rises, cools off, and precipitates its water heavily. But by the time it has crossed the Western Ghats, it has lost most of its moisture and has little left to precipitate upon the Deccan behind them. Northerly along this coast the indrawn winds dispense their water in smaller and smaller amounts as the Ghats become lower, until they deposit scarcely any when they reach Cutch (Kach, Kutch) just below the Tropic of Cancer, and Sind, which the clouds hasten across, hoarding their treasure for Kashmir seven hundred miles to the north. Hence Gujarat, which is the region north of Bombay, is productive, rich, and thickly settled, but beyond it Cutch, Sind, Rajasthan, and parts of the Punjab, being almost rainless, are dry and thinly peopled except where irrigated from the Indus system.

The other arm of this monsoon rounds the southern end of India and Ceylon and proceeds north up the Bay of Bengal. It strikes the eastern coast unevenly, but gives fair coverage to the coastal plain lying between the Eastern Ghats and the Bay. When it gets to the head of the Bay of Bengal, it fans out to west, north, and east. The winds which blow westward water the inland areas of eastern India and the long northern plain of Bengal, Bihar, Uttar Pradesh, and the Punjab. They reach also into the center of the country. As they proceed westward, they steadily lose moisture until very little is left for the upper Punjab, especially the part which lies in Pakistan. They beat against the length of the first ranges of the Himalayas, rising and cooling and exhausting their last moisture on the Himalayas' southern side. The rainfall in northern India, in the years when it is sufficiently abundant, soaks the deep alluvial soil and fills the streams, which in the dry season are but thin trickles in wide sandy beds, transforming them into roaring floods. For the time the plain becomes a mass of fertile mud.

The currents of the monsoon which go to the north, northeast, and east drench East Bengal and Assam, especially the hills in Assam, which have the world's heaviest rainfall. Over eight hundred inches have been recorded in a single year at Cherrapunji in the Khasi and Jaintia Hills. This heavy precipitation fits the slopes of the mountains for tea gardens.

Supplementing the monsoon in areas of low elevation is the summer convectional rainfall when the heated earth sends up drafts of warm air, which create cumulus clouds that refresh their parent earth with gentle showers.

Additional rain comes to certain parts of the subcontinent during the months of November and December, when breezes blow inland following the retreating southwest monsoon; sometimes these are called the northeast monsoon. Over most of the country these winds are dry, with only occasional light rainfall known as "mango showers." They make the winter season in northern India a time of cool weather with almost unbroken sunshine and a comfortable temperature, ideal for tourists but of no help to the peasant if the southwest monsoon has been deficient and his crops need water. In South India the case is different. The part of the northeast monsoon which comes inland from across the Bay of Bengal carries moisture which it has absorbed from that body of water. It precipitates and waters the coastal plain and succeeds in carrying some of its charge across the low Eastern Ghats into the rest of Andhra and Tamil Nadu, and into Mysore. With this supplement to the rainfall of the southwest monsoon the area is able to support a good deal of intensive agriculture. Nevertheless, neither monsoon brings the region just east of the Western Ghats very heavy rainfall, and each monsoon is fickle. There is no certainty of adequate annual rain to guarantee full crops, and often there is short supply and the area may be in difficulty.

If "the rains," that "annual gamble" from the southwest, are "normal" and widespread, the subcontinent is prosperous. That is, there is no serious food shortage; the government can collect the land revenue; the peasantry do not have to borrow from the village moneylenders at a ruinous rate of interest and may even do something toward reducing the principal of their debts. But if the rains are scanty in any area or fail, not only do the fields get no direct water from heaven; the sources of irrigation dwindle too. Rivers fall, may even dry up; the village tanks (ponds) are not replenished; the water table is lowered and wells go dry. On the other hand, if in northern India the rains are too full and the rivers flood, as in 1950, 1960, 1971, seed may be washed out, cattle carried off, villages destroyed, and ruin comes upon the area and the peasantry. Where there is irrigation from snow-fed streams, as in the Punjab, the case is not so desperate, for the mountain slopes always get a share of rain, which ultimately collects in the rivers. Elsewhere the inevitable result is poor crops or none at all. Agriculture stops; food is exhausted; there follows a declaration of "shortage," "distress," "scarcity," or "famine," and relief must be brought in from outside. Such conditions have been reported since about the beginning of the third century b.c., when as we are told in the tradition of the Jains, the leaders of their faith left Bihar and went south to Mysore to stay until a twelve-year famine came to an end; this was the way in which Jainism came to south India, where a part of the Jain community still exists and has its monuments. Probably no one can imagine the full horror of a famine-stricken region unless he has seen it. The report of this twelve-year famine comes from shortly after the beginning of documented history in the subcontinent, and famines have been reported ever since. The inevitability of famine, unless provision is made in advance to meet it, is one of the deepest concerns to the subcontinent. After the partition of India the rival claims of India and Pakistan to irrigation waters of the Indus system led to one of the most serious quarrels between the two nations, which was settled only in 1960.

Though the subcontinent is an agricultural area with about 82 percent of its crops in food, it still does not raise all the food it eats. This is true even in a year when the rains are good. In prepartition times it imported from 1½ to 2½ million tons of rice annually from Burma; lack of that rice when the Japanese occupied Burma during World War II was one of the causes of the Bengal famine of 1943. India is more dependent upon food imports than Pakistan, and obtains food grains today under allotments from the Food and Agriculture Organization. Pakistan, on the other hand, is a wheat-growing surplus area, and in most years has a small amount to export.

Complicating the problem of feeding human beings is the presence of a large animal population. The subcontinent in 1945 had 170 million cows and 46 million buffaloes, about 44 million sheep and 56 million goats, and many camels (1.9 million), horses (1.8 million), and donkeys (1.9 million). Postpartition figures are not available for Pakistan, but in 1966 (provisional estimate) India alone had 176 million cattle, 52.9 million buffaloes, 42 million sheep, 64.5 million goats, 1.1 million horses. Orthodox Hindus do not eat the flesh of these, though the unorthodox may eat mutton or goat's flesh, and Muslims eat meat when they can afford it. These animals, therefore, do not relieve India's food needs much, except by providing dairy products. Even this they do only scantily and in poor quality—hence Indians, who at all ages are fond of milk, on visiting the United States exclaim at the abundance and the excellence of the milk everywhere on sale. Fishing is relatively undeveloped in the subcontinent and except in a few areas, such as Bengal, contributes little to food resources.

The chief food crops of the subcontinent and their approximate annual production are: rice, about 47 million metric tons; wheat, about 20 million metric tons; lesser crops of millet, maize, pulses, spices, sugar cane; oilseeds, especially groundnuts (peanuts); also rape, mustard, sesame. Of commercial crops there are produced about 6 million bales (400 lbs. each) of cotton; and 3 million metric tons of jute; 0.4 million tons of tobacco; about 700 million pounds of tea. Both India and Pakistan produce much wool for export.

The bulk of the village population gets only the most meager living in terms of food, clothing, and shelter. Urban factory labor lives no better, possibly worse. Without seeing Indians in their villages, towns, and cities, it is difficult for a westerner to visualize the extent and effect of their poverty. Since 1952 the government of India has operated a Community Development Program to improve village living conditions, and has also done something less ambitiously planned to raise urban living standards. The accomplishments are in many cases impressive to long-time foreign residents in India who remember the conditions of village and urban life before independence, but of course are not noticed by new arrivals. In Pakistan less has been attempted and accomplished. If the average American visitor wants to remain sensitive to the conditions in which the masses of the people live, it is well for him not to stay in the country long. Very quickly the want, the disease, and the misery become only accepted facts.

In 1946 the government's Health Survey and Development Committee (Bhore Committee) reported the average individual diet figure to be 1750 calories a day. The 1958 estimates of the Food and

Agricultural Organization of the United Nations placed the per capita daily caloric intake of the subcontinent at around 2050, well below the 2250 or so which was the minimum requirement cited by the economist M. K. Bennett (*The World's Food*, 1954, especially pp. 189–212). This diet was found to be "ill balanced" as well as low, and it was estimated that 30 percent of India's families were undernourished. Before the Second World War, with food supply at "normal," the director of the Indian Medical Service (Sir John Megaw in 1933) estimated that 41 percent of the people were "poorly nourished," that is, endured continued semistarvation. The government of India in 1952 said that its food deficit was 10 percent. A deficit still continued in 1961 in spite of the completion of two five-year plans of economic development, and the country was obliged to import substantial quantities of food. In 1972 the shortage still continued. Pakistan has also had to import food in spite of her five-year plans. It has always been the case in the subcontinent that when food supply increases in any area, the people breed up to consumption of the total supply at the old subsistence level. Instead of raising living standards, the result has been an increase in the number of people living in the old misery.

For clothing a gauge may lie in the consumption of cotton textiles—almost all clothing on the subcontinent is of cotton. The per capita consumption in India for personal clothing and household purposes combined was about 14.32 yards in 1952; in 1962 it was about 16.26 yards. Figures given for the world consumption of textiles are 42 yards per person per year; for the United States, 64 square yards of cotton textiles alone.

Housing is equally inadequate. In the villages most dwellings are made of mud and wattle or sun-dried brick, crowded together in an irregular huddle, affording little protection from the winter cold, the burning heat of summer, and the torrents of the rainy season. The average floor space per person in the villages is impossible to determine. A survey in 1953–1954 showed that in 53 cities and towns 44 percent of the houses had only one room, 28 percent two rooms, 12 percent three rooms, 16 percent four or more rooms. In the large cities there exist crowded quarters sometimes with six or more persons to a cubicle, while one water spigot may have to provide for a whole neighborhood and latrines may be few and unsanitary. In some sections the quarters were without a chimney or a window, with no lights or water supply, and no sanitary arrangements. Conditions can hardly be much better now, since living costs have gone up more rapidly in intervening years than wages, and the urban population has increased, while little new housing has been erected. In every city there is a large number of people with no housing at all, who sleep each night in the open.

In typical village and urban dwellings furniture scarcely exists. A house, or hut, has a fireplace consisting of a few bricks or stones or molded clay set to form three sides of a rectangle over which a pot or pan can be placed; it usually also contains a few metal cooking vessels and some primitive implements for farming or the pursuit of a handicraft. That is likely to be all. Scavenging is a function of the village dogs. With these basic handicaps to health has gone heavy incidence of disease and paucity of preventive and curative medicine. The various improvement projects have made only little impression on these conditions.

The combined effect of poor diet, insufficient clothing, substandard housing, and paucity of medical resources is a high mortality rate. The 1941 census of (then undivided) India gave a mortality figure of 21.8 per 1000 (against 10.6 in the United States), but some critical studies of the data by competent demographers set it much higher, that is, at 31.2 per 1000. The 1951 census gave the rate in India 14.4 (again possibly too low), and provisionally the estimate for 1957 was 11.0. Figures since then are also unreliable; S. Chandrasekhar says, "officially vital statistics are far from reliable and both the birth and death rates are gross underestimates." For the decade 1951–60, the registered death rate in India is given in *India 1969* as 11, but the estimated rate is 41.7. In the same source the registered birth rate is given as 22 and the estimated rate as 41.7. Nevertheless, the increase of population shows that the death rate has been declining. Life expectation at birth, according to actuarial calculations published in the Indian census reports, averaged 32 years in 1951 (as against approximately 60 for whites and 48 for blacks in the United States at the same time). In 1961 an unofficial Indian calculation based on the 1961 census put it at 42 (figures are not yet calculated for the 1971 census). The brevity and ills of life in India have often been held responsible for her preoccupation with religion, emphasis upon family organization, and intense desire to have progeny and have it early in life, thus conducing to early marriage.

To meet the needs of expanding population both India and Pakistan have ben using two approaches. One is to increase production. Attempts to expand agricultural output have involved developing enlarged irrigation schemes; producing new strains of food grains, which are more resistant to climate and give greater yield; establishing fertilizer factories; adopting improved agricultural techniques through use of better tools and now by introducing machinery as far as is practicable, that is, without displacing more agricultural laborers than the subcontinent can provide with other employment. Each country, and especially India, has also been expanding industry in many fields. In addition to efforts to increase economic production, each nation has been promoting programs of population control by the use of contraception; here, too, India has been having the greater success. More will be said about the means being employed to improve living conditions and to curb the birth rate in Chapter 15.

For some five millennia man in the Indian subcontinent has not merely held his own against the disadvantages which nature puts upon him, but has searched out and utilized means to maintain a life of high achievement in the arts of civilization. If on the spiral of history South Asia once was more accomplished in those arts than the West but now is less so, it may again reach a position of equality. That, at least, is the hope of many citizens of the subcontinent. But the two nations started life after a wearying struggle to achieve independence, and a destructive conflict between Hindus and Muslims, the ill effects of which still continue. With no time granted for recuperation, they have had to attack their critical basic living problems, build new sources of national strength, and assume international responsibilities. Their resources and energy have not yet been equal to the demands, though there has been progress. With the creation of Bangladesh in 1972 the feeding of people became the first problem for three nations.

2 The Traditional Heritage

The principal motive forces for change in the subcontinent during the twentieth century have been nationalism, communalism, and modernization along secular lines. Of these nationalism has been an affirmation of the stream of indigenous Indic civilization against foreign rule. Communalism has been the result, first, of clash between the native Indic ("Hindu") civilization and the imported Islamic; second, of subnational rivalries based upon differences of language, region, or caste. The progress of modernization has come from contact with the West since about the beginning of the nineteenth century. These various forces have all fought a kind of battle royal, with a bewildering sequence of unstable alliances among themselves. To understand these forces, appreciate their present manifestations, and assess them in respect to the future, it is necessary to look, however sketchily, at their origins in the subcontinent's traditional historic heritage and its legacy from Britain. We shall do so in this and the following chapter.

An advanced civilization, most conspicuously appearing in cities of the Indus valley, existed in the subcontinent in the second half of the third millennium B.C. Starting then and coming down to modern times we can observe as a constantly recurring and decisive element in the history of India's civilization the intrusion of new forces from outside, which have almost always entered through the passes of the northwest. We have testimony, sometimes direct in literary works or archaeological remains, later in inscriptions, to the clashes between the new arrivals and those already in the country, and we can observe the slow process of resolving the disharmonies so created. The remaining unresolved disharmonies furnish many of the problems of the present.

The longest standing clash in the subcontinent is that of non-Aryan with Aryan. This may have begun with the first civilization there of which we have record. Starting in the 1920s archaeologists have steadily been uncovering in a number of mounds in the hot and desiccated valley of the Indus and its tributaries more and more data on several cultures, and of related cultures in regions east and southwest of the Indus valley. The most important of these cultures, though not the oldest, is called "Harappa" after the place where it was first found. This was one of the great civilizations of antiquity; its period has been established as the third and second millennia B.C. Well excavated sites are Harappa in southwestern Punjab and Mohenjo-daro and Chanhu-daro in Sind. Other sites are known as far east and northeast as in Bikaner in Rajasthan and near Simla in the Himalayas, and as far south as Kathiawar and Gujarat. Even a seaport has been identified. Houses were built of brick in two and three stories, and copiously supplied with baths. Towns were well laid out; streets were straight; and there was an elaborate drainage system. The people used tools made of copper and bronze, as well as stone. They wore clothing of cotton. They had characteristic painted pottery, decorated with foliage, animal, and geometric designs. They used a system of writing, which unfortunately we cannot read, though we have recovered many seals inscribed with it. The many efforts so far made to decipher it, in several cases including claims to have read it, have so far convinced no one but the authors of those decipherments.

Who the people were who owned the Harappa culture we do not know. The best guess, but it is only a guess, is that they were Dravidians, that is, speakers of languages belonging to the linguistic family called Dravidian, for three thousand years one of India's most important cultural groups. Today Dravidians are found mostly in southern India, but islands of Dravidian speech exist in eastern and central India and one exists within a short distance of Mohenjo-daro, the largest known site of the Harappa culture. Certainly the Harappans were not Aryans (Indo-Europeans), the linguistic kinsmen of most European peoples, who seem to have entered India in the second millennium B.C.

The Indus Valley Harappa civilization contained many elements similar to elements in contemporary nearby Mesopotamian or Iranian cultures, such as the use of seals and of writing or among art motifs the representation of the human hero wrestling erect with one or two lions. Many other items were unparalleled in those cultures, but echoed in later historic Indian civilization. Among these is the pipal tree, shown on seals and pottery as though in religious use; this tree is still sacred to Hindus, and is honored by Buddhists as that under which the Buddha sat when he won enlightenment. Various animals which are revered in later Hinduism are also common on Indus Valley objects in what appears to be a religious environment, for example, the bull. There are figures of a god or man seated in yoga posture, as known in historic Hinduism for the past 2500 years; in one case the figure is flanked by rearing serpents, in another it is surrounded by a group of animals, both of which features recall current Hindu religious notions associated with the god Shiva. Many symbols commonly employed today appeared then, such as the swastika "emblem of well-being," widely used in India's three great native religions, Hinduism, Jainism, and Buddhism, and taken by Buddhists to China and elsewhere. There are evidences of phallic worship and mother goddess worship, both of which are extensive in Hinduism today. There is undoubtedly a large measure of continuity between the pre-Aryan Indus Valley Harappa civilization and the civilization of later Hindu India.

The Harappa culture seems to have continued to the sixteenth century B.C. Who destroyed it we do not know, though suspicion falls upon the Aryans, who entered India from the northwest probably at about 1500–1200 B.C. These Aryans were seminomadic, unlike the urbanized Harappa people. They spoke an archaic form of Sanskrit, which they introduced and maintained in India with modifications. Unfortunately, they have left us only literary records —namely, the four Vedas with ancillary texts, above all the *Rig Veda*—and the dominant interest of these works is the highly ritualistic Vedic religion with its numerous deities, rich mythology, and elaborate fire sacrifice; other topics are treated only indirectly. They have left no remains of cities, burials, arts and crafts; what knowledge we have of their culture beyond religion is largely gleaned by inference.

The early Aryans record their warfare with the people who preceded them. They despised them for their darker color and false religion, and called them *Dasa* and *Dasyu*, as they did also the demonic enemies of their own gods. In the field they had the swift horse to help them—they may have introduced it into India. As social order they recognized three classes of Aryans—the *Brahmans* or priests, the *Kshatriyas* or rulers and warriors, the *Vaishyas* or commons—and a class of serfs called *Shudras* consisting of non-

Aryans accepted on this humble level in the Aryan community. The fourfold structure of Vedic society afterwards became the framework into which the caste system was arbitrarily fitted. But it was not that system; in Vedic times the hierarchical status of the three upper groups was not rigidly fixed; society was mobile. From the time of their first invasion the Aryans have been steadily advancing into non-Aryan territory, whether by force of arms or peacefully, until now their languages occupy about three fourths of the subcontinent.

Though the early Aryans had little of material culture when they arrived, the Aryan invasion was in many respects the most important thing that ever happened to India. It gave the subcontinent its great classical languages. It provided it with a priestly and learned class, the Brahmans, who hold a preeminent though declining position today, even in south India, where Aryan speech does not prevail. Aryanism is in Hindu India the sign of the traditionally elite, and whoever can claim to be Aryan takes pride in doing so. In south India, where Aryanism is least strong, being mostly limited to the Brahman group, the Dravidian elements in the population have in this century used political means to express their resentment of Aryan domination. The Justice party of the 1920s and 1930s made its campaigns on a platform of anti-Brahmanism. In recent decades the Dravida Munnetra Kazhagam (Dravidian Advancement Party) has reacted strongly and successfully against Aryan ascendancy. Today the Dravidian elements are politically dominant and have imposed legal curbs upon the ancient privileges of Brahmans.

Historic indigenous Indian civilization was born out of the union of pre-Aryan and Aryan cultures. The process of fusion and growth to maturity had started by the sixth century B.C., after the Aryans were well established all over northern India. It seems to have begun in Bihar in the eastern part of the Aryan community, where Aryanization was still incomplete and society was headed by landowning rulers who could not rightfully claim Aryan descent. This region was presumably then, as now, one of the most productive agricultural areas in India. In it, too, existed cities with a wealthy merchant class, which wanted a social position commensurate with its wealth, but could not claim it in Brahman-controlled Aryan society. A revolt appeared both in orthodox, that is, Brahmanical, and in heterodox environments. In the orthodox, as shown in the speculative texts called Upanishads, the thinkers acknowledged the Vedas and the Vedic sacrifice as inspired and authoritative, but challenged priestly intellectual superiority based upon mere birth as Brahmans. Heterodox thinking rejected Vedic authority and was expressed most effectively in Buddhism and Jainism, whose founders (the Buddha and Mahavira, the latter following an older but less influential teacher Parshva) lived and preached in Bihar and nearby territory. These two faiths had wide patronage among the rising merchant class and the landowning aristocracy.

For this period, that is, up to the fourth century B.C., our historical records of the Ganges valley are minimal, but from around the end of that century we begin to get fuller data. In about 321 B.C. a king named Chandragupta, belonging to a family called Maurya, established an empire in Magadha in Bihar with a capital at Pataliputra (modern Patna). His grandson, the great Asoka, who reigned probably from 274 to 237 B.C., had an empire covering the greater part of the subcontinent. He is one of modern India's most honored figures. A wheel symbolizing the Buddhist dogma, copied from a monument he erected at Sarnath outside Varanasi (Banaras), is now the emblem on the national flag.

Under the Mauryas and following dynasties, both in the north and the south, during a period of six centuries, Indian civilization assumed its characteristic form. The greatest flowering took place just after this period, under another great wide-ruling dynasty centered at Pataliputra known as the Gupta. This was founded A.D. 318/319 by another Chandragupta, and its greatness lasted until about A.D. 500. In the millennium from the Upanishads to the close of the Gupta supremacy India accepted from non-Aryans or itself evolved from Aryan beginnings—we do not know which—the institution of caste; formulated its legal philosophy; gave classic character to its architecture, sculpture, painting, dance, music. It developed the religion of Hinduism and the classic philosophies. All of this lives today, though in many variations resulting from historic experience and with many modifications coming from contact with the modern world.

After the Gupta brilliance, India entered her medieval period. The country was split politically into a number of small kingdoms; scholarship developed into scholasticism; religion was elaborated into a multitude of complex forms; philosophy, with some notable exceptions, turned from creativity to commentary and dialectic; literature became less creative and more imitative and ornate. This period continued until at least the sixteenth century, and overlaps with the Muslim period.

The greatest achievements of characteristic Indian civilization are in religion and philosophy, and in this field first place possibly belongs to that form of monism known as *advaita*, "non-dualism," described in the Upanishads, systematized by Badarayana, and brilliantly expounded by Shankara about A.D. 800, or possibly earlier. Second only to speculative thought is literature, exemplified in the great epics, the *Mahabharata* and the *Ramayana*, the Sanskrit drama, lyric poetry, and fiction. In sculpture, dancing, and music India developed her own aesthetic theories, styles, and techniques. She erected some of the world's great monuments. As social organization she produced the caste system, which kept Hindu society together when disruptive foreign influences, such as Islam, entered the country. In science, India was preeminent in grammar; it was the European discovery at the end of the eighteenth century of Sanskrit grammatical achievements that led to the development of modern western linguistics. In mathematics, astronomy, and medicine she achieved less distinction. The Indians have produced numerous legal treatises, but have never fully separated civil from religious law. India was weak in the natural sciences, while in history she produced only the fewest of works.

Native Indian—that is, Hindu—religious and philosophical thought has, in general, viewed the world teleologically, as having no end in itself; the end of man is other-worldly. It has put the emphasis on individual duty, rather than on group responsibility. A man acting by himself can accomplish his own greatest ends. Others cannot help him; they can never be more than strangers. The individual must exert himself with all his energy if he is to reach his highest good. His alone is the opportunity and the responsibility, and there are no short cuts. However, on the side of practical living, which is what interests most Indians as it does people of other areas, caste also provided means for unified group action.

One of the most interesting features of indigenous Indian civilization has been its ability to resist rival civilizations coming into conflict with it, though it may accept, modify, and assimilate elements drawn from them. This sort of clash has occurred three times—with the Hellenistic, the Islamic, and the European-Christian cultures. The first of these clashes took place during the formation of characteristic Indian civilization and was long ago finished. The other two are still in progress.

The Hellenistic civilization arose in the old Persian empire after Alexander's conquest and was a blend of Persian with at first Greek, later Roman. It used Greek science, literature, art, and language, but Persian religion. Greek political institutions were a part of it but did not flourish in Persia. About a century and a half after Alexander's invasion of the Punjab, at the time when the Maurya dynasty collapsed (180 B.C.), some Hellenized kings in Bactria (modern Afghanistan) penetrated Gandhara, in the region called the North-West Frontier Province under the British and by Pakistan until 1954. In the first century in our era certain Central Asian peoples named Kushana, of not very advanced culture, reached India by way of Bactria, becoming Hellenized on the way. They overran Gandhara, and went as far east as Mathura (Muttra —between Delhi and Agra), which was then one of India's most important cities. There they established a capital, and from it extended their empire still farther east. These Bactrian and Kushana kings patronized both Indian and Hellenistic institutions. They used the Greek language in their courts, struck their coins in Greek on one side and an Indian language on the other, erected buildings and ordered much of their sculpture in Hellenistic style. But they also adopted much that was Indic. They were Buddhist in religion; they used Indian languages for literature; they employed the local Indian art of Mathura in sculpture. India eventually repudiated Hellenism in favor of her own civilization. Only the scholar finds vestiges of it there today.

The clash of traditional Indic civilization with Islamic began in A.D. 711, less than eighty years after the death of Muhammad, when Arabs invaded Sind and the lower Punjab. At almost exactly the year 1000 Islamic penetration began from the kingdom of Ghazni in modern Afghanistan. From that time on India was invaded by Muslim Turks, Afghans, Mughals. Muslims reached the Deccan and Bengal at the end of the twelfth century. The zenith of Islam in India was under the Mughal emperors in the sixteenth and seventeenth centuries. Every part of India with a few relatively small exceptions, at one time or other fell under Muslim political control, but the central and southern parts of the country have had the least.

Islamic civilization came to India not only with military power but with the accumulated tradition of all Near Eastern culture. It had behind it the cosmopolitanism that flourished under the Caliphate and united the western Muslim world starting with Persia and stretching across the Near East, Asia Minor, and North Africa until it reached Spain. It had all the art and literature of Persia at its command. It inherited and developed Greek astronomy, mathematics, and medicine. It had its own legal institutions and produced some of India's greatest government administrators, such as the Mughal emperor Akbar. Noble and beautiful buildings adorned its cities. Intensely and uncompromisingly monotheistic it was, but within that limitation it fostered philosophy. In India it promoted its own egalitarian social system, developed new schools of thought, and produced an extensive and often scintillating literature. At an Islamic court was cultivated the celebrated Mughal school of painting. The Muslims cherished their own music, which has come to dominate much of northern and northwestern India.

While the clash between Indic and Islamic civilizations was in progress, Europeanism entered, gained political power, and in so doing clashed with its two great predecessors.

In the framework of cultural history as sketched above, race, language, and religion have been dynamic forces and we should note the basic facts about them.

The subcontinent contains today representatives of two of the major human races, namely, the mongoloid or yellow-skinned, and the caucasoid or white-skinned. The mongoloids live only on the northern and eastern edges of the subcontinent, and include the Gurkhas of Nepal, whom the British used to recruit as soldiers; the people of the states of Sikkim and Bhutan, in the eastern Himalayas; many tribes living in the Assam Hills; some of the people of Kashmir; and a few groups scattered along the base of the Himalayas. The common physical type of Bengal may also contain a mongoloid element. The caucasoids, as a group, are darker than those of Europe, but otherwise they are "Whites." They are of three varieties. One of these is tall, often blue- or gray-eyed, and lightish in skin color. This type is found among the Pathans of the northwest frontier; the Kashmiris, whose women are celebrated for their beauty; the Punjabis, including the Sikhs; and occasionally elsewhere in the subcontinent. It is usually considered by anthropologists to be a variety of the "Nordics." Like the mongoloid this somewhat infrequent type seems to be a relatively late arrival in the subcontinent, having been preceded by the other varieties of caucasoids, who provide the characteristic physical types of the subcontinent and are grouped under the wider classification of "Mediterranean." There are two of these: one is long-headed, medium in stature, slight, with skin color ranging from light to rather dark brown; the other type is broad-headed, generally shorter, and varies in skin color from light brown to virtually black. Besides these four physical types there are traces of Negrito in the Andaman islands and some scattered places in south India. Finally, proto-Australoid characteristics have been identified among some Indian tribal peoples in the south.

Color difference has not in general been the basis of political and social discrimination in the subcontinent, though fairness is esteemed. Light color is an asset, always mentioned, in marriage negotiations, and is nowadays often valued even when—as is becoming ever more frequent—caste is not of concern. Yet speaking more broadly, race, in the sense of distinction based upon physical characteristics, such as skin color or facial structure, though apparently a criterion of social differentiation during the Vedic period— Aryans being higher in the social scale than non-Aryans—has now become almost negligible. A number of tribes living in remote areas on a low economic level have in traditional Sanskrit literature been mentioned with fear and loathing. Some are still mentioned slightingly. But the population of the subcontinent is not seriously divided into separate self-conscious groups differentiated by such criteria. Nor do the distinctions of indigenous physical types correlate with distinctions of language, religion, occupation, social status, or any other cultural phenomenon.

Perhaps because they do not harbor prejudice based upon physical differences, the people of the subcontinent are particularly sensitive to white western racial intolerance. Resentment of British color prejudice contributed importantly to the growth of nationalism. It now has an international significance. To these people the widespread western phenomenon of racism appears baseless and unreasonable. They do not comprehend the common attitude of many white Americans toward the blacks. They cannot understand why citizens of India and Pakistan, on emigrating to South Africa, Canada, or the United States, should have been and in some places should still be subjected to discriminatory laws of entry or denied citizenship or deprived of normal human rights primarily because of difference in skin color. Removal of racial discrimination has been for both India and Pakistan a major point of foreign policy and will surely be so with Bangladesh.

Language difference has been recorded in the literature of India as a source of group antipathy since about the middle of the first millennium B.C. At that time speakers of "standard" Sanskrit expressed scorn for those whose pronunciation was inferior, for example, in sounding *l* for *r*. This corresponds to the strong linguistic consciousness and high development of scientific language study in ancient India. Linguistically, the people of the subcontinent are today distributed among five speech groups. In the descending order of number of speakers, these are Aryan, Dravidian, Munda, Tibeto-Chinese, and Khasi (in Assam). The most arable regions are occupied by Aryans and Dravidians; speakers of the other languages and some speakers of Dravidian occupy the less desirable areas, which are on the fringes of the subcontinent or in the interior hills.

The Munda languages may have been the first of the five groups to reach India, perhaps coming in from the east. They are now restricted to hilly and inferior areas in Bengal, Bihar, Orissa, and Madhya Pradesh ("Central Province"). They consist of so-called "tribal" groups, with a comparatively low economic culture. They may have been a substratum of the population in areas where speakers of other languages are now in full possession. There is today a strongly self-conscious movement among them as Adibasis ("first inhabitants") which seeks to establish their equality with the economically more advanced peoples.

The Dravidian languages constitute the second most important group in the subcontinent. They were certainly there before the Aryan, and may once have occupied nearly all the country. They dominate south India today below an irregular line starting south of Goa on the west coast, running roughly northeast, then east, and then about east-southeast, and then northeast again to the Bay of Bengal, more or less following the northern boundaries of the Mysore and Andhra states. Small scattered preliterate groups speaking Dravidian tongues are found in some areas where Aryan speech prevails.

The most important Dravidian tongues are four which have well-developed literatures. These are Tamil, covering most of Tamil Nadu; Telugu, spoken in Andhra Pradesh; Kanara (or Kannada or

Kanarese), prevalent in the state of Mysore; and Malayalam, used in Kerala.

The Dravidians, whether or not they can claim the Harappa culture, have long had a high civilization. Most of their literature is secondary to Aryan Sanskrit literature, but they possess an independent and ancient literary tradition going back a century or more before the Christian era, and have a pride in their peculiar cultural achievements.

The largest and most important language group in India is the Aryan, to which the European languages are cousins. To the Indian branch of Aryan belongs Sanskrit, the chief classical language of Hindu India, in which are expressed its intellectual canons. As the common language of culture, Sanskrit was in ancient and medieval times the tongue through which the learned of all parts of the country communicated with one another, whether their native tongues were Aryan or Dravidian. In this way it was the cement that bound together diverse linguistic groups in a cultural unity, and though the Aryan language complex is an immigrant in India, we commonly call the country's culture Aryan; but frequently now, since Dravidian cultural consciousness has grown so strong, we refer to the culture of south India as specifically Dravidian.

The preeminence of Sanskrit as a medium of educated communication throughout India was impaired by the Muslims as they spread over the country. The languages they honored were Arabic as the vehicle of religion and Persian as the tongue of palace, courts, and polite letters. In the period of their power the position of Sanskrit declined. The British in the nineteenth century made English the main subject of instruction in Indian high schools and colleges and the preferred official language.

Modern Aryan languages in the subcontinent are many. The most widely used has been for some centuries a group of dialects broadly called Hindi, which is native in the Indian state of Uttar Pradesh ("Northern Province"; formerly called United Provinces) and regions west and south. It has several spoken varieties; one of them under the name of Hindustani serves as a lingua franca over northern and central India and has spotty usage in south India. Hindustani has two literary forms, of which one is known as Hindi, in a narrow sense of that term, while the other is called Urdu. Hindi draws its high literary vocabulary from Sanskrit; Urdu draws its from Persian and Arabic. The next most commonly spoken Aryan language is Bengali, current in both Indian and Bangladeshi Bengal. Others are Marathi, spoken east and south of Bombay, throughout the Maharashtra state, and in parts of Gujarat and Hyderbad adjacent to Maharashtra, and even sparingly in Mysore; Gujarati, spoken north of Bombay and in Bombay city, in the state of Gujarat, and in the neighboring part of Rajasthan; Punjabi (Panjabi); Sindhi; Rajasthani; Balochi, used in Baluchistan; Pashtu, spoken in the northwestern frontier of Pakistan; Bihari; Oriya, the principal language of Orissa; Pahari, "Mountain language," spoken in the Himalayan regions; Kashmiri; and Assamese. Out of the language diversity have grown a variety of social and political conflicts in modern times.

By far the most effective force in separating Indian communities from one another and so producing national disunity has been religion. At the same time religion, at least in the case of Hinduism, contributed to the formation, growth, and power of nationalism.

Hinduism is the most numerously followed religion of India. At the last census (1941) of undivided India, out of a total of 389 million, Hindus numbered 225 million. The corrected figure after adding Hindu "tribals," that is, adherents belonging to preliterate "backward" groups, would be about 270 million. In postpartition India Hindus have comprised about 75 percent of the population, counting all tribals as Hindus; according to the 1961 census Hindus constituted 11 percent of the population of Pakistan. This faith, as now practiced, contains elements drawn from all known periods of Indian history, including the pre-Aryan. It is a complex of vegetation and fertility cults, sun cults, and hero cults, mostly derived from non-Aryan sources but blended with Aryan ideas and practices, and to a greater or less degree transfigured by Aryan philosophic speculation. It countenances every shade of intellectual belief from the crudest animism to the most profoundly metaphysical monism, and it does so by taking a relative, but realistic, view of human intellectual capacity. All but the smallest fraction of mankind, it is held, is incapable of comprehending pure and absolute truth. The rest can only approach it according to their limited intellectual and spiritual capacity. The degree of truth that a man can attain is the truth for him and all he can reasonably be expected to hold.

In its most intellectual and spiritual form Hinduism recognizes the Absolute under the terms *atman* "Self" or *brahman* "Holy Power." It is eternal, unbound by time, space, and causality, consisting of pure existence, consciousness, and bliss. Realization of absolute truth is hard; the most esteemed aid in the search for it is the cultivation of Yoga techniques and the practice of meditation.

To men of lesser capacity Hinduism operates as sectarian religion, and contains cults centering about the god Shiva, his wife Parvati, who is the universal Mother, their sons Ganesha (Ganesa), who removes obstacles and is the patron of success, and Karttikeya, god of war, and some ancillary gods; or about Vishnu, his wives, especially Lakshmi, the goddess of prosperity, and himself in various incarnations. Among these last, one of the most important is Krishna, the bucolic hero of the land near Mathura (Muttra) beside the river Yamuna (or Jumna), the lover of the milkmaids, who are interpreted as symbolic of human souls. It was he who, just before the epic battle of the Mahabharata, addressing Arjuna, general of the forces of righteousness, recited his teachings in the well-loved mystic poem called *Bhagavad Gita* ("Song of the Blessed One"). Another incarnation of Vishnu is Rama, hero of the great epic Ramayana, whose wife Sita was abducted to Ceylon by a demon Ravana. Rama, with the aid of animal allies, led by the monkey general Hanuman, killed Ravana and rescued Sita. She is the Hindu pattern of wifehood, and he of kingship. The "Rule of Rama" is the mythical golden age, for the return of which pious Hindus pray.

On its lowest levels Hinduism admits worship of spirits and godlings of the forest, rivers, mountains, disease, and much else. It fosters many holy men or ascetics, conspicuous for their bodily mortifications, endured, even inflicted upon themselves, as a means to win moral and spiritual advancement. Vows and pilgrimages are a part of its practice, taking devotees to the sacred rivers, mountains, and other shrines of India, of which the most renowned is the city of Varanasi (Banaras) on the Ganges. At these the pilgrims gain an auspicious view, if only by the eye of faith, of the great being or beings honored at the place–as in other spheres people conceive that they are benefited if they can only so much as see the bodily form of a great leader like Gandhi or Nehru. Hinduism makes wide use of images, which the intellectually perceptive recognize as symbols, but the unsophisticated may take for deity itself. It is a faith that is highly imaginative and has inspired a rich art. Its ethics center around the principle of *ahinsa*, noninjury of living creatures, especially the cow, which it holds sacred.

The characteristics of so amorphous a faith are hard to define. It has no formal creed. But there are two almost invariable requirements. One is acceptance as revealed literature of the mass of ancient texts known collectively as the Veda and including the four Vedas—Rig, Yajur, Sama, and Atharva—coming from the earliest Aryan times in India, and a number of other somewhat later texts subsidiary to these, of which the philosophic treatises called Upanishads are intellectually the most important. Almost as great veneration is given to certain still later works dealing with religious and civil law and practice, the Shastras; to the two long epic poems *Mahabharata* and *Ramayana;* and somewhat less to a still later body of religious works known by the term *Purana* ("Ancient Text").

The other requirement of Hinduism is the acceptance of the caste system as the structure of society. Every Hindu is in traditional theory born to a caste, in which he must remain for life, and he is bound to live by its rules, subject to severe consequences for failure. A caste is a hereditary, endogamous group, which has a name of its own and some special traits of occupation, cult, or custom, giving it a separate place in the system. Traditionally a man had to take his wife from his caste—there were a few well-defined exceptions—usually could eat only with caste fellows, and was ranked in the social scale by the nature of the traditional customs of his caste. No individual can in accepted theory become a Hindu and enter a caste, though under certain conditions a group may. Hence Hinduism has been a nonproselyting faith.

Caste stratifies Hindus into more than two thousand mutually exclusive groups, most of which, however, have limited geographical extent, so that no more than fifty to a couple of hundred may exist in any single locality. At the top of the caste hierarchy are the Brahmans, whose various castes included about 6.4 percent of the Hindus in 1941 (no figure available since then); at the bottom are the Untouchables, known also as the Scheduled Castes, Exterior Castes, Paraiyas, Fifths, and by Gandhi as *Harijan* (God's folk), amounting to about 12.5 percent according to an estimate in 1968. In Pakistan they amounted to 5.7 percent of the population in 1961. With these are sometimes counted the Scheduled Tribes, primitive folk living on a low cultural level, constituting in 1951 another 6.2 percent of the total population. The Brahmans define social position, officiate in religious ceremonies, have custody of sacred lore, and enjoy marked social privileges.

The Hindus associate the caste system with the four classes into which Vedic society was divided three thousand years ago, and a fifth class developed since. In the three upper groups boys undergo an initiation ceremony at which they are invested with a sacred cord, and hence are "twice born" (*dvija*), but the boys of the fourth, non-Aryan, Shudra (*Sudra*) group, descended from pre-Aryan aboriginal peoples who had been made into serfs, have no second birth. Nevertheless, in south India the position of Shudras is in general good. Orthodox Hindus consider that every caste (*jati*)—which they sometimes call a "subcaste"—belongs to one of these four major groups, which they call the "castes."

Below these four main groups are now, and have been for at least eighteen hundred years, the Untouchables, whom orthodox Hindus regard as without caste and call *Panchamas* ("Fifths"). Actually they, too, are subdivided into castes, with their own hierarchical gradations. They do the most degrading work, and for centuries, if not millennia, have suffered humiliating disabilities, such as denial of the use of village wells or limitation of approach to members of higher castes. Among them are leather workers, scavengers, and others pursuing unclean occupations. They, like the Shudras, are descended from non-Aryans, but having been accepted more recently by Aryan society are lower in the social and economic scale, weaker than the Shudras, and tolerated only on more shameful terms. Their case has been quite different from that of certain other non-Aryans who entered India as conquerors and afterwards, by reason of their military and political position, were brought into the Hindu community in a noble status. Many Rajput (Kshatriya) families of today are descendants of Central Asians who won Kingdoms and position by force of arms. Brahmans have conveniently found them a genealogy leading back to the Sun or the Moon, from which all Rajputs are traditionally sprung.

The lower castes continually struggle to gain higher rank, for the hierarchy of the caste system, though immutable in theory, is variable in practice. If a caste which has been too degraded to have Brahman priests can bribe or otherwise persuade Brahmans to officiate at its ceremonies, it achieves thereby a victory and elevates its status. The rank of castes is not settled by law, only by social convention. A caste, or section of a caste, therefore, may in one way or another come to consider its origin nobler than it once did, and in successive censuses may move, on its own nomination, from a lower one of the five major groups into a higher; only the limits of what public opinion will countenance can check the advance. This aspect of the human will to rise has a corollary in that every caste, however lowly, knows of at least one other which it considers lower than itself and discriminates against.

Though in orthodox Hindu theory nearly every caste has a traditional occupation, it frequently happens that some or even most of its members may not follow it. This is especially true in urban communities. Brahmans, for example, may be lawyers, messengers, clerks, cooks. Some ruling princes may not be Kshatriyas, but members of herdsmen or Brahman or merchant or other castes.

The sanction for caste lies in the Hindu belief in the joint doctrine of Rebirth and *Karma* ("Act"). When a person dies, as we say, the Hindu thinks that he merely passes from one state of existence to another. This process continues indefinitely until a rare individual, by realizing the truth about the identity of the human soul with the Absolute Soul (Brahman), succeeds in saving himself from further rebirth to attain a state of pure bliss in association with Brahman. But while still in the cycle of rebirth every creature lives in a state that has been determined by his past actions in previous existences. Correspondingly, what a human being is doing now determines the status he will have in future existences. Everyone, therefore, is living in exactly the state that he deserves in consequence of his previous actions. If he is born in a high caste, it is because he has lived righteously. If he belongs to a low caste, he is suffering now for previous misdeeds. But let not the high caste man be complacent; if he is a sinner in this life, or even only negligent of duty, he will pay a penalty in future lives. And let not the low caste man despair. He has the hope, if he endures with fortitude and virtue, of enjoying a happier state in the next birth. This doctrine in a rough way tends to divide Hindus into two categories: the submissive, who fasten their gaze upon the present as the inescapable result of the past, "fatalists" in other words; and those courageous striving men who rely upon the power of the human will to win them a better lot in the future.

Caste, as an institution under the intellectual leadership of the Brahmans, gave Hinduism in the past the toughness to withstand social attack. It is uncongenial to a democratic West and is now in disfavor with modern advanced Indian opinion, but it has given a framework to traditional Hindu society for twenty-five hundred years. Undeniable as is its unfairness to the lowly, it has had advantages as well; for example, caste councils institute and enforce much of minor law and order. Further, as Gandhi pointed out, it has prevented a great deal of the social competition and excessive individualism of western society.

During the long history of Hinduism many, like Gandhi in our own time, have denounced as sin the imposition of exaggerated disabilities upon the lowest castes, the Untouchables; it was not the aim of the eternal powers, they have held, to inflict pain upon living beings. So too, conditions of life in the world today are not adapted to the preservation of many established caste customs. Rival religions to Hinduism, which deny the validity of caste, especially Islam and Christianity, and recently Buddhism, welcome the depressed as converts and ease their social and economic lot. Finally, the Untouchables themselves have grown conscious of their potential strength as a political group, and at times have formed political parties. Since they comprise so large a part of India's population, their vote under any system of universal adult suffrage is an important consideration in politics.

Within the caste the traditional unit has been the "joint family," which consists of a man, his wife (or, before polygamy became illegal for Hindus, wives), all his descendants except the married females, and the descendants' wives, living in a common household, the earnings of each member being in some measure the property of all. When the patriarch dies, the eldest son may assume the headship, or the sons may separate, dividing the father's inherited property among themselves. This system has been breaking down in modern India as the economic structure has been changing.

Other ancient indigenous religions of the subcontinent are Buddhism, in India about 3.3 million strong in the 1961 census, and Jainism, which had 2 million in 1961. Jainism had its origin in the eighth century B.C. and Buddhism in the sixth century, but both had their significant development in the sixth, and had a steady growth in succeeding centuries, with a great access of power. They both have been in decline since the Muslims struck them in the centuries from A.D. 1000 on, and their followers began to be reabsorbed in Hinduism. These religions taught the ethical principle of *ahinsa* (nonviolence) and perhaps popularized that doctrine so that it eventually came to be adopted by Hinduism as well. Though Buddhism and Jainism have a small following in the subcontinent today, and Jainism, unlike Buddhism, does not exist outside, each of them has produced a voluminous literature and an important art.

The imported religion of Islam (often miscalled Mohammedanism, a term repugnant to Muslims on the ground that Muhammad was not God but was God's prophet) had in 1941—in the then undivided country—a following of about 94.4 million, which was about one fourth of the total population and over one fourth of all the world's Muslims. In 1961 it had 46.9 million adherents in India, 40.9 million in West Pakistan, and 41.7 in East Pakistan (now Bangladesh). Like Judaism and Christianity, it originated among the Semitic peoples, and like its sister religions it is monotheistic, iconoclastic, and dogmatic, and has been proselyting and aggressive. Though it demands credal conformity, it has its "two and seventy jarring sects," and a major differentiation between the Sunnites, who are generally considered orthodox because they accept traditional Muslim law, and the Shiites, whose center is in Persia. About one Muslim in eleven or twelve in the subcontinent is a Shiah. Religion is the dominant feature of Islamic civilization.

Before partition the Muslims were in a majority in the provinces of Bengal, the Punjab, Sind, the North-West Frontier, Baluchistan. The first criterion in drawing the dividing line in 1947 was to separate from the rest of India, as far as feasible, and constitute as the new nation Pakistan, contiguous areas in which the population was predominantly Muslim. At that time there were a number of the old Indian States in which the Muslims were the largest group; of these the most important was Kashmir, where, however, the ruling family was Hindu. There were also Indian states in which Hindus were the most numerous but the ruling family Muslim, such as Hyderabad then the premier princely state of India.

Sikhism, which originated as a compromise religion between Hinduism and Islam, had about 5.7 million adherents in unpartitioned India in 1941 and about 8 million in 1961 (no figures for Pakistan in 1961, and possibly no Sikhs there at that time). It was founded in the northeastern Punjab in the fifteenth century by

Nanak. It has a simple dogma accompanied by a rigorous discipline of life, is monotheistic, and rejects the use of images. It
reverences a holy book known as the *Granth Sahib* and the memory
of its *gurus* (teachers), several of whom were persecuted by the
Muslims. In recent decades it has been approaching Hinduism.
The Sikhs have increased rapidly in the past sixty years—they
numbered only 1.8 million in 1881. The reason lies partly in their
standard of living, which averages better than that of Hindus and
Muslims, partly in their social practices—they permit widow remarriage and profess to deny caste—and partly in their acceptance
of proselytes. Most of them are cultivators, though many are
soldiers. Two thirds of the community were living in the Punjab
at the time of partition and the dividing line put some of them in
India and some in Pakistan. In the disorders following partition
the most bloody conflict was between Sikhs and Muslims. The
Sikhs had long agitated for a Sikh state (Sikhistan), which was
never created as such, but in 1966 India carved out a predominantly Sikh state called Haryana, with its capital at Chandigarh,
an admirable example of modern city planning and architectural
distinction.

Zoroastrianism exists in India among the Parsis, a community
of about 112,000 in 1951, around one half of whom were living
in Bombay. These were originally Persians who began to leave their
native land in the eighth century under pressure from the Muslim
Arabs. On coming to India, they settled in Gujarat, north of Bombay, and stayed there until the seventeenth century, when they
moved south. The Parsis are a wealthy urban community, which
has an importance far beyond its size. Much of India's biggest
business, particularly in steel and other industries, is in Parsi
hands.

Christianity came to India early: legend, unconfirmable, says
that the Apostle Thomas atoned for his doubt by becoming a missionary to that land. By the fourth or fifth century a community
of Nestorian (Syrian) Christians existed at Cochin in Kerala far
down the western coast, and it still survives, though now the
greater part of it is affiliated with the Church of Rome. Roman
Catholicism came to western India with the Portuguese, who
established themselves at Goa in 1510. In the year 1542 St. Francis
Xavier went to Portuguese India to preach. The Inquisition was
established at Goa in 1560. Protestant missions entered south India

in the seventeenth century. They became vigorous in Bengal in the eighteenth century, at first against British opposition, which was removed later, so that in the nineteenth century they expanded rapidly. The total Christian population according to the 1941 census was about 6.3 million (the corrected figure to include Christian "tribals," that is, converted preliterates belonging to tribes not assimilated to Hindu culture, would be 7.4 million), of whom about 60 percent live in south India. In 1961 the number in India was 10.7 million; in West Pakistan, 149,000; and in East Pakistan (now Bangladesh), about 584,000. *The Catholic Directory for India* in 1962 claimed that Roman Catholics in India numbered 6.2 million.

The Jews were only about 27,000 in number in 1961; they also are considered to have been in Cochin in the fourth or fifth century of this era; a community still exists there, though most Indian Jews live today in the large modern cities, especially Bombay.

The religions practiced by "tribals" outside the orbits of Hinduism, Islam, Buddhism, or Christianity are characterized as "primitive" forms of spirit or nature worship. These aboriginal groups live in hilly regions and speak Munda or Dravidian languages. They are economically the most backward of India's peoples and the most helpless and inarticulate. The government has treated them essentially as wards and under the constitution of the Republic of India the policy is to be continued for a period of years.

All religious groups in the subcontinent have been acutely self-conscious, and all minority religions have viewed themselves as being in greater or less competition with Hinduism. Sikhism, in addition, contrasted itself sharply with Islam. The greatest social and political conflict in prepartition India was that between Hindus and Muslims, and it was responsible for partition.

3 Effects of British Rule

The chief preparation of the subcontinent for modernization has
come from the association with Britain. This gave prepartition
India political unity, administrative and judicial efficiency, inner
economic coherence, a fairly modern system of education, a public
health service, and an acquaintance with western industrialism,
scientific research, technical accomplishment, and social thinking.
Perhaps most of all it gave the subcontinent the English language
as a means of communication in place of the many Indian tongues
not mutually intelligible, and as a means of access to modern
science, technology, thought, political institutions. With the aid of
these, undivided India, on attaining independence in 1947, had
progressed further into modern life than any other large or medium-sized Asian country except Japan and possibly China. Most of
this advance followed from the utilitarian ideology common in
nineteenth century Britain leading to administrative efficiency,
social reform, and political liberalism.

This result came about, however, not from a primary intent of
the British. The British purpose in first coming to India in the
early seventeenth century was the simple one of conducting profitable foreign trade, which, under the mercantilist economic theory
then current in Europe, was to be pursued as a monopoly subject
to state regulation. It was therefore, appropriate that under pressure of circumstances European merchants journeying to India
should be supported by arms, whether to check their European
rivals, or to defend themselves from the Arab traders in the Indian
Ocean, or to maintain their interests against local powers in India.

The English interest in India crystallized on December 31, 1600,
when the London East India Company received a charter from
Queen Elizabeth. The first voyages were to Sumatra, Java, and
other islands east of India, but trade began with India after several
Englishmen had called to make "contacts" at the court of the

Mughal emperor Jahangir—Captain William Hawkins in 1609, William Edwards in 1615, and Sir Thomas Roe as ambassador of James I in 1615. The English got permission in 1612 to open trading posts called "factories" at several ports in the Gulf of Cambay, now no longer important, and at Ahmedabad. The principal factory was Surat; another was at Cambay. The Portuguese and the Dutch had come to the East Indies before the British, setting up trading posts with armed support in the Persian Gulf, India, and the Spice Islands. The British had had to fight with the Portuguese to establish themselves at Surat, which became a presidency of the East India Company. The Surat Presidency did not flourish, and in 1687 Bombay was made the new headquarters. Bombay had been ceded by the Portuguese to King Charles II in 1661 as a part of the wedding portion of Catherine of Braganza and had become a base of the first importance, largely because of its splendid harbor. King Charles had not foreseen the possibilities of Bombay and had granted the island to the East India Company in 1668, in consideration of a temporary loan of £50,000 at 6 percent and a quitrent of £10 per annum (a bargain which may remind Americans of Peter Minuit's purchase of the island of Manhattan from the Indians for $24 worth of junk jewelry in 1626). Not long after entering Surat the British established themselves in southern India at Armagaon, Masulipatam, and Madras, concluding an agreement with the local Indian authorities in 1639 to erect fortifications at Madras and share the revenues of the region with the local nayak (ruler). This was the first English proprietary holding in India. The fort erected was named Fort St. George and the English occupation of Madras was known as the Presidency of Fort St. George. Later it was called simply the Presidency of Madras.

In 1690 the English established themselves at the head of the Bay of Bengal when Job Charnock, "always a faithful man to the Company," on invitation from the local nawab, took possession of a mud flat assigned to him and with a guard of thirty soldiers set to work to fortify it. This became Fort William, so named after King William III, and after varying vicissitudes, Calcutta (as it later came to be called) became the seat of the Presidency of Fort William or Bengal. By the Regulating Act of 1773 Parliament gave the Bengal Presidency supremacy over the other two, and provided for a governor general and four councillors, naming Warren Hastings as the governor general. The Act also empowered the

Crown to establish a Supreme Court of Judicature at Fort William.

Thus the British Indian Empire, which we might say was conceived in Surat in the seventeenth century, was born in Bengal in the latter part of the eighteenth century. It did not attain its majority until 1858, after the Sepoy (Indian soldiers) Mutiny of 1857. This crisis was stimulated by the disaffection of various Indian rulers whose power had been severely curtailed. The titular Mughal emperor and family were without power; the Nawab of Oudh and others, who had not produced male heirs, found the British government refusing to recognize adopted heirs in a number of cases. The heirs of the great Maratha rulers found themselves stripped of much of their power and felt humiliated. The sepoys were aroused by various rumors and grievances, which appear to have had little substantial or rational basis. The mutiny broke out in Meerut in January 1857, spread to Delhi, Cawnpore (Kanpur), Lucknow, Jhansi, and other centers, but was crushed in 1858. Later in that same year Parliament passed a bill to abolish the East India Company, which had been an intermediary between Parliament and the Indian people, and instead to put the government of India directly under the Crown. By a proclamation of Queen Victoria dated November 1, 1858, the rule of the East India Company was displaced.

In 1876 Queen Victoria by an Act of Parliament took the title of Empress of India. On the following New Year's day a darbar (durbar, convocation) was held at Delhi to celebrate the assumption of the imperial dignity. In December 1911 King George V and Queen Mary, at another darbar in Delhi, were crowned Emperor and Empress of India. At the same time announcement was made that the capital of India was to be transferred from Calcutta to Delhi, the old seat of the Mughals. In July 1947 the British Parliament passed the Indian Independence Act, to take effect on the following August. Thus the British Indian Empire came to the end of its life, 335 years after its conception, 174 years after its birth, and 89 years after attaining its majority. But the influence of British rule upon India is today one of the most important elements in the life of the subcontinent.

The growth of British power in India had been made possible—in the British view necessary—by the wars among Indian rulers in various parts of the country and by the efforts of the French to establish themselves in India. When the British first came to

India the Mughal dynasty was in the ascendancy. But a little less than a century later, after the death in 1707 of the last great Mughal emperor, Aurangzeb, the Mughal power disintegrated, though a series of successors held nominal authority in Delhi until 1858 at the end of the Sepoy Mutiny. Other Indian regimes arose, including the Marathas in western and central India and Muslim dynasties in the south. Local rulers who wanted to widen their holdings or defend themselves against Indian rivals or foreign intruders drew the Europeans into their quarrels, desiring their superior military equipment, while Britain and France, fighting in India the same wars they were waging in Europe and North America, made alliances with Indian potentates. In this way European holdings and responsibility expanded. The British were able to break French power because they had control of the seas and superior financial resources in India; thus they could win control partly by battle and partly by treaty terms, which sometimes reversed field successes. In so doing they gained wide territory and then found themselves obliged to administer it.

The weakness of the Mughal authority was demonstrated in 1757, when Robert Clive in the strange battle of Plassey, following skillful intrigue and with the aid of treachery on the other side, won the great province of Bengal. In 1765, with the formal consent of the Mughal emperor in Delhi, the British East India Company assumed the revenue collection and administration of Bengal. As Englishmen acquired more political authority in India, they also secured more opportunity for corruption, dishonesty in dealings with the Company, graft in supplying Indian princes, and oppression of Indians. Many became fabulously rich. Such conditions under Clive showed the British Parliament the great importance of India as a source of wealth which should belong to the Crown but was being diverted into private possession, and it began to deal more strictly with the Company, regulating its affairs more thoroughly and limiting its powers.

Warren Hastings, who ruled from 1772 to 1785, constructed the framework of the Empire. He tightened the administrative machine and by his conquests in north and south and his diplomacy made the name of Britain respected everywhere in the subcontinent. The conquests were extended by Richard Wellesley Lord Mornington (later Marquis Wellesley), Governor General from 1798 to 1805, who won the rest of south India and shook the

Maratha power so that it was afterwards easily destroyed. In
1842–44 the British took Sind following their disastrous first
Afghan War (1838–1842), which had been inspired by fear of
Russian expansion in Central Asia. In campaigns during 1845–49
they annihilated the Sikh kingdom in the Punjab, and in 1856
they annexed Oudh, now a part of Uttar Pradesh. Little remained
to round out the Indian Empire but to consolidate gains and fill
in a few corners, and this the British did after the Sepoy Mutiny.
The English who had obsequiously knocked at India's side door at
the beginning of the seventeenth century, happy to do only a little
buying and selling, had stepped inside and remained to take over
India itself, ruling the occupants with a strong hand and maintaining a monopolistic control over all outside relations.

In the eighteenth century, British dealings with Indians were
stern and direct. Troublesome rulers and men of wealth were
mulcted of immense sums of money and ruined, or their lands
seized, or in some cases executed on grounds that today
appear inadequate. From the imperialistic point of view these
methods could be condoned as necessary for empire-building, and
to Warren Hastings, the most severely blamed and the defendant
in one of England's most noted trials, more than to any other man
were due the decisive British conquests. The more ruthless form of
imperialism that existed under him began to pass away with his
successor, Lord Cornwallis (known to Americans from Yorktown),
who was Governor General from 1786 to 1793. From then on,
British policy allowed India a government that increasingly concerned itself with the welfare of the country. It gradually acquired
rigorous standards of honest administration and by degrees became
more and more concerned with India's agriculture, education,
public health, and industry. A protective tariff instituted in the
1920s showed the government's inclination to look upon India's
financial problem as distinct from Britain's. Indeed, by the beginning of the twentieth century the government of India was often
in sharp disagreement with the home government.

Under the British, India was divided into two kinds of political
units: the provinces or British India, which were directly under
British rule; and the Indian (princely or "native") States, which
were under hereditary rulers, bound to Britain by treaty or other
form of agreement and owing allegiance to the King of Great
Britain as Emperor of India. They had varying degrees of autonomy

depending upon the terms of their agreements, but all recognized the government of India as the paramount power in the country.

In surveying British control we may start with political and administrative policies. These were framed primarily with the twofold purpose of promoting profitable trade and collecting adequate revenue to operate the civil and military establishments. The basic need was that the country be secure from internal disorder and external aggression, free from the warring that in the eighteenth century had compelled European merchants to arm and had damaged trade by keeping the country in that anarchic condition described by classical Hindu political theorists as "the way of the fishes."

The first step was to reform and strengthen the Company's administration, and this was begun in 1773 when Parliament in Lord North's Regulating Act asserted its supervisory rights, and instituted a governor generalship over the three established presidencies, with the seat of government at Calcutta. In 1784 Parliament passed Pitt's India Act whereby it vested all political power and the power to recall any British official from India in a Board of Control appointed by the Crown, but left commercial patronage and commercial administration to the Company's Court of Directors. By the Regulating Act Parliament was to renew the Company's charter for only twenty years at a time, and before each renewal was to subject the administration of India to a parliamentary inquiry; by the Act of 1784 it made provision for substantial reform in the administration.

Lord Cornwallis, who went to India to inaugurate reforms under the Act of 1784, made one of the first objects of his governorship the purification of the civil service. The old methods of the Company were discarded, and appointees to administrative positions were paid adequate, in fact large, salaries; corruption, jobbery, and private enrichment were sternly discouraged. Officers were at first nominated under the old Company system of patronage, but from 1853 they were selected on the basis of competitive examinations. Thus there came into being the elite Indian Civil Service, a socially elect corps of picked officers, almost universally capable and honest, which probably gave India the most just and efficient administration it has ever known. Under Lord Cornwallis it was the practice to restrict admission to the British, although minor posts were filled by hundreds, literally thousands, of Indians. It was not until 1833 that the Civil Service was thrown open to Indians at all, and then only with many limitations, excluding them from the upper grades, to which they were finally admitted in 1854. The framework of the Civil Service still remains the framework of both the Indian and the Pakistani administrative systems. Its ideals still exist, though admittedly in both India and Pakistan they are conspicuously impaired in practice.

During the nineteenth century Parliament steadily encroached upon the prerogatives of the Company. In 1813 it abolished the monopoly of trade; in 1831 it asserted authority over all Indian territories owned by the Company; and in 1833 it enacted a demand that all laws made in India should be laid before it. It was then that it abolished the Company's right to trade at all, though the Company continued to exist and influence legislation until it was dissolved in 1858.

By this time, too, Mughal authority was only a fiction, for the power of the Mughals had long since departed. The Company had at first nominally operated under it, though the real source of power was Parliament and through that body the British electorate. Parliament, therefore, destroyed even this fiction. The India Act of 1858 created in the British cabinet the position of secretary of state for India, with full control over India. To the secretary of state was made responsible the governor general (viceroy), and to the latter alone were responsible, until late in the period of British rule, the provincial governments and through them every government officer in India.

In assuming larger powers over India during the days of the East India Company, Parliament granted to its agents in India the right of making many changes to assist in the better execution of the British purposes. New legal institutions were developed comprising a body of Anglo-Indian law administered through courts established in general on British models, using British procedures. Codes were enacted over a period of many years including an Indian Penal Code (1860), Indian Succession Act (1865), Indian Contract Act (1872), Indian Trusts Act (1882), Transfer of Property Act (1882), Code of Civil Procedure (1908), Code of Criminal Procedure (1898). In family and religious matters the different communities—Hindu, Muslim, Parsi, Christian—had separate statutory provisions based upon their respective customary law. Hindu law, based upon the old Hindu texts with a tradition extending back to at least early in the Christian era, was subjected to a certain amount of modification and modernization. This has been extended since independence especially by the piecemeal adoption of a Hindu Code, which is still incomplete. The language of all but the lowest courts was and still is English, and the body of Indian legal precedents exists in English; any other language would scarcely be workable without many decades of gradual application and the cultivation of a modern legal vocabulary.

A police system was established, and public education was instituted. After the Sepoy Mutiny, Parliament made other reforms. It defined the status of the Indian (princely) States and guaranteed their autonomy subject to certain restrictions. It provided for local district boards and subordinate bodies in 1883–85 to take an interest in local education, sanitation, famine relief, and roads, and extended the power of municipal boards. It reorganized the army to make the land safer for British occupation and to preclude another mutiny. It devised a plan of defense for the northwest frontier and the seacoast. The total result of all these various reforms was in the direction of internal peace and safety from invasion.

Under Britain India gained inner unity. It had a single rule everywhere unchallenged, which brought the whole subcontinent for the only time in its 2500 years of known history to the traditional ideal of living "under one royal parasol." This rule, again for the first time in the subcontinent's history, was secular, favoring no religion. India consisted in the nineteenth and twentieth centuries of many units, diverse in political character and often of mutually contradictory political aims, yet all were unified at the center. All owed common allegiance to the British crown; all respected its representatives and its courts, police, army, and administration. Even the conflicting social groups in the population, which were never really homogenized but only shaken together in unstable union like oil and vinegar, were formally synthesized at the highest level of government and usually at that level were decently civil to one another.

Throughout all parts of British India and generally in the princely States as well, law and order and the processes of justice came to be good. On the lower police levels there was always much petty oppression and corruption, not dissimilar in spirit from that often reported of American municipal police, but on the upper levels administration was efficient and, with only rare exceptions, free of abuses.

The means used by Britain to hold India included a good deal of the "divide and rule" philosophy, whether by design, as nationalists used to charge, or because of the inner nature of imperialism operating automatically and unconsciously. The Indian States were allowed to lag politically behind the provinces comprising British India, so that the two kinds of political units stood side by side physically but philosophically were in contradiction. Large social divisions of the population, especially the Muslims, were permitted—in effect encouraged—to develop and express their fear and hostility toward the Hindu majority and to stand apart as a divisive group.

For a century and a quarter after Hastings no legislative function of any sort lay with the Indian people or any part of them acting through their elected representatives. Indian legislative reform proceeded slowly by stages which at the beginning were minute and infrequent.

A major reform came in 1833 when Parliament added a law member to the governor general's council, and so differentiated the council's legislative functions from the executive. Thereby it inadvertently created the institution that afterwards grew into the Central Legislative Assembly—the thought of this later body would doubtless have horrified the authors of the 1833 action. Thus, before 1833 the governor general of Bengal with his council exercised executive supervision over Madras and Bombay. From 1833 his title was "Governor General of India," and the "Governor General of India in Council" was the supreme executive and legislative authority for India. The governors in council at Madras and Bombay were henceforth more completely subordinate than before.

In 1861 Parliament enacted a statute enabling the governor general to nominate to his council for advisory assistance in framing legislation not less than six or more than twelve Indians. Again the proposers of the statute did not foresee the future growth of similarly designed councils in the Bombay and Madras presidencies into provincial representative legislative bodies.

This revolutionary outcome started under Lord Dufferin, Governor General, 1884–1886. At that time middle class Indian opinion was expressing itself strongly enough to produce in 1885 the

Indian National Congress. Dufferin announced, of course with the authorization of the Secretary of State for India in London, that it was his wish "to give a still wider share in the administration of public affairs to such Indian gentlemen as by their influence, their acquirements, and the confidence they inspire in their fellow-countrymen are marked out as fitted to assist with their counsels the responsible rulers of the country." During the next governor generalship (Lord Lansdowne's) the Act of 1892 was passed directing the Governor General and the governors of the provinces to nominate the nonofficial members of the councils after consulting important bodies in India. In theory and in law this was not election by those bodies, but it was equivalent to election in fact, for their recommendations were accepted. At this time the councils were granted the right to question the government and discuss the budget, important concessions, for they made clear that the councils were more than merely advisory.

The development of representative institutions from this time on is closely associated with the growth of nationalism. By successive demands Indians won concessions through the Morley-Minto reforms of 1909, the Montagu-Chelmsford reforms of 1919, the constitution of 1935, and the Indian Independence Act of 1947. In the end Britain gave nationalism its full demand, not so much from generosity, as is frequently stated, as from recognizing that government of India as a British dependency was no longer either possible or desirable under the greatly changed conditions that followed World War II. The constitution and administrative machinery Britain had provided gave to India and Pakistan when they attained nationhood an operating political structure with which they were able to carry on government and start an attack upon many of their unsolved problems.

During the British occupation notable changes occurred in Indian society and economic life. An obvious basic fact is growth in population. It has been estimated by W. H. Moreland that in 1600, during the reign of Akbar, the country had 100 million inhabitants. It is further estimated that by 1750 the population had increased to 130 million. When the first complete census of India was taken in 1881 (there was a partial and less satisfactory census in 1872), the area corresponding approximately to the present nations of India, Pakistan, and Bangladesh had more than 250 million. In 1941 (the last census of undivided India) the same area had a little less than 390 million, showing an increment of about 56 percent in sixty years. The increase came from a lowering of the mortality rate through elimination of internal warfare, curb of banditry, control of famine, and check of disease. With these went increase of agricultural production, both of food crops and commercial crops.

In furthering trade, the government of india gave the subcontinent much that is today economically important. One of the largest items is the railway system, which was begun about the middle of the nineteenth century. Besides opening up India economically, the railways had a strategic purpose. For example, a good deal of track mileage, economically unproductive and expensive to maintain, was constructed along the vulnerable northwest frontier, now lying in Pakistan. The railways connected the agricultural areas with the inland urban centers and the seaports, promoted export and import trade, helped to mitigate the ravages of famine, and provided work for more than 800,000 persons. At the time of independence in 1947 they were the greatest single instrument available in the subcontinent for further economic expansion.

Other kinds of economic development that took place during the period of British occupation include, in the way of agricultural aids, first, expansion of the irrigation system, especially in the Punjab and Sind. Extensive areas were opened to new settlement and cultivation through large projects for storing and utilizing the waters of the Indus and its tributaries. The government fostered agricultural experimentation and animal husbandry, and extended credit to agriculturists through credit cooperatives and otherwise. Forestry research was modestly fostered under the British control. Some road-building took place, of which a part, as in the case of the railways, was for strategic rather than economic purposes. A banking system was developed under government control.

The most fundamental change in the economic structure of India was that in agriculture; this has seriously affected the village and, therefore, the basic social structure. The country's economy for as far back in the past as we have records has been based upon its villages. Though statistical information does not exist from before the successive censuses starting in 1872, it can scarcely be doubted that somewhere around 80 to 90 percent of the population has always consisted of village inhabitants. These were of two sorts: agriculturists, who cultivated the surrounding land; and the various kinds of artisans and menials, such as weavers, blacksmiths, potters, oilpressers, barbers, washermen, sweepers, and other nonagriculturists, who provided the village with services. A rural tract, bounded at random and containing a dozen or so villages, normally encompassed a population with sufficient occupational diversity to be virtually self-sufficient. The tract raised its own food, supplied most of its other needs by its own products, and imported only a few commodities, such as salt or metal. Frequently local periodic markets within such an area provided a facility for interchanging products. Cultivators, artisans, local officials and functionaries, and the Brahman priests lived an interdependent life, based upon transfer in kind. The village paid the governing authority a tax or land rent, again almost always in kind, consisting of a portion of the annual crops, and this constituted the bulk of the state's revenue. It also usually furnished labor to the overlord. Land was used by families on a hereditary basis; the artisans, again, inherited their crafts and their positions in the community. Land when transmitted from one generation to another was often subdivided, frequently ending up, after several stages of inheritance, in uneconomic fragments which would in time, by some form of redistribution, be assembled again in larger tracts. Then division and subdivision would occur again. The process was iterative and cyclical. Within the village most of the functions of government lay in the hands of village elders. Petty rulers passed part of their returns from the village to higher rulers, and they to others, and so to the top, at whatever number of levels it might be removed from the village. Sometimes an overruler, disliking the system of collecting the land revenue in his realm through a series of subordinates, might try to bypass them and collect directly from the peasants through the agency of tax farmers or his own revenue officers.

Living conditions in the villages were far from idyllic, but at least they had shaken down to a pattern, which might be interrupted by pestilence, crop failure followed by famine, and war, yet gave the villages modest food reserves for a little resilience under minor misfortune. Within the relative stability of such life society was defined by the caste system, which gave every person status from birth often accompanied by inherited and nontransferable specialization of occupation.

The village or agrarian community was the state's chief source of income. For the British, as for their predecessors, the collection of the land revenue was the most important feature of administration; they needed the revenue to finance their rule and conquests. The method of collection had been to make a periodic revenue assessment and "settlement," but when the British assumed the collection in Bengal, administration was in chaos and collection was inadequate. The British desired the land revenue to be paid in money, not in kind. For this purpose they established new types of land ownership. Under Lord Cornwallis in 1793 they instituted the *zamindari* system, by which they converted the old tax farmers and revenue collectors into landlords, called *zamindars,* who were given proprietary rights in the land including sale and purchase on the understanding that they would procure larger revenue returns for the government, while the agriculturists were made tenants, their old hereditary rights were ignored, and they were left helpless before the landlords. The landlords, unable to carry the legal burdens imposed by new judicial processes, in many cases sold their rights to businessmen of one sort or another, who became absentee landlords. Thus both the peasantry and the resident tax collectors lost ownership.

Cornwallis, in establishing this system, permanently fixed the assessment on the landlords at £3 million annually. This was a serious mistake because as the country's economy expanded, it came about that the landlords could get increased rent from the peasants, until in the last period of British control the total amount was reaching figures of from £12 million to £20 million, yet the government's portion remained the same. The difference went to support a series of intervening renters or speculators.

In some other parts of India, notably in Madras under Sir Thomas Munro, 1820–1827, another system called *ryotwari* was employed. By it the peasant (*ryot*) dealt with the government not through the old commune or through a newly created landlord class, but individually and directly. However, his tax also was now collected in money. The ryot had rights of private ownership, could sell or lease his land, and could be evicted or sold out for nonpayment of taxes.

Under both systems the village economy was changed from one of self-reliance based upon exchanges in kind to a money economy, which stimulated the planting of cash crops as well as subsistence crops, and the individual inhabitants of the village lost that measure of security which they had enjoyed in the commune. The emphasis now placed on money in all parts of British India permitted the rise of a moneylender class which could get control of the land under the revised terms of ownership. The evils of land tenancy became obvious in the nineteenth century and the British in various provinces legislated to produce reform, bringing about some measure of improvement but never solving the problem as a whole. Land tenancy has been a major problem since independence and both India and Pakistan have labored to alleviate it. It will presumably remain a problem for Bangladesh.

When European nations first engaged in trade with India, they came for pepper and spices, and also undertook commerce in the handiwork manufactures of the land. Often, their ships came out chiefly in ballast since there was little market in the East for European goods. In India they had to purchase their homeward cargoes of raw and finished products, especially the wonderfully handwoven cotton fabrics, with hard Spanish dollars and silver bullion brought from Europe or with products brought to India from other parts of Asia. India was at that time an exporter of manufactured goods. But during the latter part of the eighteenth century, with the achievement of the Industrial Revolution in Britain, the situation changed. The cotton and silk textiles of India competed with the growing textile industry of Europe, especially that of Britain, which dreaded a rival and was seeking a larger market. A profitable business grew up of exporting textiles to India; the railways, when they were built, helped to reach the large inland market. Before long definite efforts were made to discourage the Indian textile industries. More important, the machine-made goods of the West undersold the handmade goods of the Orient, and the handicrafts of necessity declined. India became a great consuming nation. Thousands, possibly millions, of her skilled artisans were ruined and a source of wealth was taken from the people. Large numbers of landless agriculturists and unemployed weavers had no recourse but to fall back upon the land as laborers.

All these changes led to impoverishment of the villagers, destruction of their independence, instability of their social system. In the opinion of many economic historians they lowered the standard of living. The great increase of national wealth during the British period did not raise the level of individual consumption, they maintain; it was more than absorbed by the increase of population living at the subsistence level, and the end result was that India merely harbored more people living in greater misery than before.

To take up the increase in population and provide it a living, new forms of productive employment were needed. In another Asian country, Japan, the population more than doubled between 1870 (35 million) and 1940 (73 million) but the increase was absorbed in the cities, where a large industrial growth was in progress. In India no parallel development took place. The reason was in part that capital in India was shy of investment in large modern industry and preferred such economically unproductive enterprises as land speculation and the buying and selling of agricultural products. It was also partly that in the nineteenth century the British managing agencies in India, operating with British capital, functioned in many economic fields, including banking, mines, jute factories, and tea and coffee plantations, and were able to check Indian enterprise. In addition, the government did not exploit natural resources for the country's benefit, and there were no protective tariffs for infant industry until the 1920s. On the contrary, after the destruction of India's handicrafts by the flood of cheap British manufactures in the nineteenth century, when India developed a cotton textile industry, all Indian textile factory products were until the year 1926 subject to a countervailing excise duty to equalize the market for Lancashire products. Currency was manipulated also to British advantage. It was only with difficulty that the subcontinent built up a heavy steel industry at Jamshedpur in Bihar and at Asansol in Bengal, its jute manufacturing mills near Calcutta, its cotton spinning and weaving industry located in a number of cities, its sugar mills, cement works, paper factories. The failure to develop industry during the British period was a serious drawback to the subcontinent when it got self-government in 1947, and its effects still continue today. The latest available Indian figures, which are for 1967, put the total number of factory workers at 4.743 million. The government of India's program of increase as part of the successive Five Year plans must have raised this total considerably since 1967. Figures for Pakistan from 1963–1964 show that manufacturing employed 9.23 percent of the total number of employed persons.

The impact of western ideas upon the Indian subcontinent may be considered to have begun with the establishment of British paramountcy during the governor generalship (1798–1805) of the first Marquis of Wellesley (Lord Mornington). The advance of British power before Wellesley's time had meant little to India intellectually. But by 1800 the great intellectual activity of Europe in the eighteenth century had culminated in the French Revolution, and the Industrial Revolution was well launched in England. With the consolidation of a large part of India under British rule, Indian intellectuals began to acqaint themselves with the ideas that were transforming Europe. Throughout the following century western thinking came to India with ever accelerating speed and effect, and as society altered in Britain, the changes there had a cumulative effect upon India as well. In the latter part of the nineteenth century and throughout the first half of the twentieth century India came increasingly into contact with still other dynamic societies and felt their influence too.

Education was the principal means by which new western ideas were spread among Indians. In the eighteenth century education in India was offered in Muslim *madrassahs* and Hindu *tols* and was still entirely traditional. Being a predominantly agricultural area, India did not have a system of publicly supported education nor was private education general. A limited number of people could read and write, and they were likely to belong to just a few social groups: among Hindus these would be certain castes; among Muslims they would be administrators, merchants, divines. Instruction might be given at home or in schools conducted by Brahmans or mullahs, and was mostly confined to religious subjects. With Hindus, astronomy and astrology, law, medicine, mathematics, geography, Sanskrit grammar, the sciences of metals, elephants, horses, or others, the arts—in short, all fields—were considered to have a religious sanction and so were fit subjects of instruction, along with the study of ritual texts and mythology. With Muslims, subjects other than religion, philosophy, and law (*shari'ah*) might be left to guilds as unworthy of a place in the universities, which were meant for educating divines. This situation in both cases tended to freeze the content of any science and perpetuate it from century to century in a traditional form with only minor changes. Hence, for example, traditional medicine, whether Hindu (Ayurvedic) or Muslim (Yunani or Unani), uses today textbooks composed in medieval times, and except as occasionally touched by western medicine does not practice such an innovation as dissection, is unaware of antisepsis, and employs a pharmacopoeia unaffected by scientific research. In recent years, however, modern medical science and therapy have gone very far in diminishing popular reliance upon the traditional systems.

The British on accepting the duties of government had not at first faced the need to modernize education. Western education was introduced in the late eighteenth century by Charles Grant (1746–1823), an East India Company servant, who became a friend of William Wilberforce and other members of the "Clapham Sect"; and by Baptist missionary contemporaries of his—William Carey, Joshua Marshman, and William Ward—who founded a college in 1799 at Serampore, a Danish settlement north of Calcutta; and by other private individuals. Its chief center was at Calcutta, where in 1817 a college was formally opened under the management of a representative group of Indians and Europeans. Forty years later this became the nucleus of the University of Calcutta (1857). The prime mover in establishing the college was David Hare (1775–1842), a watchmaker and an agnostic, who despised western and eastern superstition equally and looked to western science as an antidote to both. He worked in the first stages of planning with the great reformer and liberal Ram Mohun Roy (1772–1833), often called "the father of modern India," who later had to step aside when many orthodox Hindu supporters of the college objected to being associated with him.

When pressure was put upon the government to inaugurate a public system of education there was a controversy between those Europeans who were students of Oriental learning and wanted to use traditional material for literary and cultural content and other Europeans, like the missionaries and T. B. Macaulay, and some Indians, like Ram Mohun Roy, who wanted to employ western learning alone. In England, after the Reform Bill of 1832, the Whigs, then in power, sided with the missionaries and Macaulay, who wrote a decisive minute in 1835 containing passages hostile to Hindu traditional learning that afterwards became notorious in India.

The decision, made by Governor General Lord William Bentinck in 1835, to make western learning the subject of study and the English language the medium of instruction opened the way for modernization, but at the cost to Indians of their own cultural tradition. Classical oriental languages—Sanskrit, Arabic, Persian— were discouraged, though at a later time they acquired an honorable though unequal place among the offerings as elective subjects secondary to English. India received in English a common means of communication throughout the country but students got no introduction to their own cultural heritage, while the English cultural material which they were offered was so remote from their experience that they could not understand and profit from it. They came out of college culturally impoverished.

Public elementary education, already preceded by private missionary enterprise, was instituted following a dispatch to Governor General Lord Dalhousie by Charles Wood (Lord Halifax), President of the Board of Control (of Indian Affairs), in 1854, according to which it was to be given in the local vernaculars. The government, besides maintaining its own schools, provided financial assistance to private schools that met its standards. Public lower (primary and secondary) education, however, was not stressed as was higher education, which was disproportionately large in the system. Since independence lower education and higher education have both been greatly expanded in India, less so in Pakistan.

Three universities were founded in 1857 at Calcutta, Madras, and Bombay. These were examining and degree-awarding institutions modeled on the University of London as it then functioned; instruction was given at colleges affiliated with them. Later other universities were established, as well as technical and professional schools.

An attitude of modernism among Hindus may be considered to have appeared in the nineteenth century in Bengal, when Ram Mohun Roy began to challenge current Hindu religious beliefs and opposed a variety of social evils, such as the rite of suttee (*sati,* immolation of a widow on her husband's funeral pyre), by which his sister-in-law had died. He became an advocate of English education though he learned English only at the age of about thirty. A great believer in British institutions, he nevertheless favored vernaculars as a medium of instruction. He wanted freedom for India. He was the first great progressive in Bengal, which became the intellectual leader of India. A modern approach to life was embraced by the Bengali Hindus, who had been the subject group before the rise of the British power, rather than by the Muslims, the unhappy dispossessed rulers, who would not accept English education. This was a germ of the modern Hindu-Muslim separation and hostility.

Progress in raising literacy during the British period was not outstanding. The country was too poor to give education to any large number of pupils, and most families could not, and still cannot, afford the economic burden of sending sons to school when they might be working. Estimates made by Kingsley Davis on the basis of sample figures in the 1941 census (the last census before partition) give 15.1 percent of the population aged ten and above as literate (27.4 percent of the males, 6.9 percent of the females). The Indian census of 1961 showed a total of 24 percent (males 34.5, females 13.0). The 1961 Pakistan census gave overall literacy as 15.3 percent. The 1971 census figures for India give a literacy rate for the entire population of 29.34 percent. An estimate for Pakistan for 1970 gave a literacy rate of 20 percent.

Modern education in the nineteenth century introduced some measure of western science, technology, history, philosophy, and political, social, and economic ideas. India acquired enough acquaintance with modern scientific achievement to appreciate its usefulness and enough teaching of it to be the basis for enlarged offerings as instructional personnel and financial support became available. The new learning taught the democratic political and social philosophies of the West, stimulated nationalism, and encouraged an international viewpoint. In English India gained a language of educated communication, such as it had not had since the Muslims in their spread had shattered the importance of Sanskrit.

If to the West, during the period of British rule, must go credit for bringing India into touch with new ideas and a stimulating civilization from abroad, so, too, the West was responsible for directing India's attention to certain aspects of its own past. Not that India had completely lost touch with its past, as had Egypt and Mesopotamia. It still had the literature and the religion; but the history and art were obscured, and the ancient cultural connection with regions outside India. The European discovery at the end of the eighteenth century that Sanskrit, the classical language of India, was kindred to the languages of Europe, and the promulgation of the facts of that connection, marked the beginning of modern linguistic science. And the transportation to the West of Indian literature and philosophy made a profound impression upon poets, such as Schlegel and Goethe, and upon philosophers, such as Schopenhauer and Emerson. To India these discoveries were of even greater importance. They showed India its relationship, as of an elder brother, to the cultured nations of Europe, and the power of its literature to make an appeal that was universal. India was at least in the same world if not of it.

Even more important for India was the fact that these first discoveries invited a large number of European investigators to the study of India's antiquities, some working in Europe and some in India, and following them Indians trained in western methods of scholarship. They deciphered India's inscriptions and thus restored its history; they uncovered archaeological sites and found the ancient art; they presented to the West and East alike a scientific inspection of India's great religions, annihilating many of the myths of Hindu tradition but making clear that nowhere has the human race made more splendid achievements in religion than in India. The liberating influence of these studies upon the mind of the West was no greater than it was upon that of India. In India the studies had the additional value of giving to a people then at one of the lowest depths of its political history the example of the past as an inspiration for the present.

It was natural that this revival of interest in the past should lead to a revival in the creative arts. This is illustrated in the case of the dance. The classical Indian dance requires intensive training for competent performance, no matter what the style, whether the highly formalized Bharata Natya common in south India, with its limitless capacity for expression by gestures, or the Kathakali of Kerala, in which another kind of conventionalization is used to depict the battles of the epic, or the sharp quick movements of the Kathak style of north India, or the soft motions of the Manipuri style in east Bengal. There were strict canons, governing pose, movement, and the significance of gesture. To be a work of art, rather than just a series of graceful movements, a dance must evoke in the spectator one of the nine "sentiments" or "flavors" (*rasa*), and the whole subject of aesthetics is focused on these sentiments. This fact led in the history of the Indian dance to a need for ever more professional training until, at some time in the centuries contemporary with the Middle Ages and the Reformation in Europe, respectable women ceased to be trained as amateurs of the dance, and the art was practiced professionally by women dedicated to temple service as *devadasis* (servants of the god) and available as prostitutes. So the dance remained in social disrepute until, with the direction of attention to the ancient arts and the rise of nationalism, the classical dance was rediscovered, cultivated, and restored to a place of honor through the efforts of such sponsors as the poets Vallathol in the south and Rabindranath Tagore in the north. By the 1930s the study and practice of the ancient dance forms by girls of respectable family had spread to all parts of India, and the Indian motion picture industry, responding to the popularity of traditional mythological and legendary themes, had given both the dance and music a new field of expression. Some of this was in the development of new adaptations of old forms, some in a blending of the classical styles with Javanese, Siamese, and Cambodian styles. Some of it, especially in the motion picture environment, became just a degradation of both music and dance as art forms, because the producers could not wait for artists to be trained. But cultivated appreciation of the classical art spread widely and has continued to spread since the attainment of independence.

In painting there was an analogous development. The British in the nineteenth century as a rule had no understanding of Indian art, but at the end of the century E. B. Havell, who was sensitive to its qualities, was appointed principal of the Calcutta School of Art. One of its pupils, Abanindranath Tagore, a member of the celebrated family to which Rabindranath Tagore belongs, was greatly influenced by the Mughal miniatures which Havell showed him. In the twentieth century, Nanda Lal Bose was influenced by the wall paintings of Ajanta and other Indian schools. For about fifty years there arose, flourished, and now has decayed a romantic, imitative body of painting in India, popular and widely practiced, which was a blend of pride in ancient art and a form of cultural nationalist expression. This was aided by the art historian and critic Ananda K. Coomaraswamy (1877–1947). Today there are in India, and to a lesser extent in Pakistan, many artists—painters and sculptors—who are familiar with modern western art and have been influenced by it, blending its forms with those which they know from their own traditions.

New forms of literature developed also under the influence of European examples. This was illustrated first in Bengali in the blank verse of Michael Madhusudan Dutt, who was writing about the middle of the nineteenth century, and in the novels of Bankim Chandra Chatterji (1838–1894), who dealt with historical, social, and religious themes in a romantic and sentimental strain reminiscent to Europeans of Sir Walter Scott. Realism was approached by Rabindranath Tagore (1861–1941) and cultivated more consistently in the novels of Sarat Chandra Chatterji (1876–1938). This was to lead later to a body of fiction with a distinctly proletarian point of view stimulated by Russian literature. The Bengali drama had a somewhat similar evolution. Other vernaculars followed Bengali in exploiting new types of literature. In the middle of the nineteenth century Bharatendu Harishchandra translated Bengali dramas into Hindi, adapted plays of Shakespeare, and wrote original plays and stories, including a very popular drama with a nationalist slant called *Bharat Durdasha,* "India's Distress." In the first part of the twentieth century a number of Hindi novelists and short-story writers dealt with social problems, especially Prem Chand (1880–1936), who wrote forcefully of village life, his best-known work being the novel *Godan.* In other parts of India these new types of fiction were cultivated in the local languages. There was also a considerable number of such works written by Indians in English. Among Muslims the greatest figure was Muhammad Iqbal (1876–1938), poet and philosopher, who wrote in Urdu and Persian. There exists now in the subcontinent a large number of poets, novelists, essayists, and other men of letters who use modern approaches as well as those of their own past.

It seems fair to characterize this activity in the arts and literature as a renaissance. It was wide-ranging, appearing in all parts of the country and in all the principal languages. It represented the urge in India toward new directions, using Indian subject matter and adapting new media drawn from the West to the needs and realities of the scene. It was a form of nationalism in the cultural sphere, blending with the developing political nationalism that was growing simultaneously.

The British made an important contribution to India's well-being in the form of a public health system, which helped to lower the mortality rate and increase the population. Sometimes it had to work against religious opposition, as in administering smallpox vaccine, which, being made from the sacred cow, is liable in the eyes of orthodox Hindus to involve sacrilege. The greatest victory in dealing with epidemic diseases was in reducing the incidence of bubonic plague. Little, unfortunately, was done in providing adequate sanitation for large cities and nothing for the villages. Though the public health service of India under the British was far from sufficient, it furnished a practical working basis for the present services, and for the great success in this century in controlling malaria.

The policies pursued by the British permitted them, in the nineteenth century, firm control of India and economic profits, but did not generate among Indians a desire to stay within the Empire. Perhaps no form of imperialism could have achieved so paradoxical a result. Rather, the policies both aroused the demand for self-government and unwittingly provided nationalism with many of the instruments it used to satisfy the demand. British policies also fostered a desire in India for commercial relations with other nations, and the volume of British trade with India in terms of percentage declined during the twentieth century. What Britain now gets from the subcontinent she gets through goodwill. In this situation it must be said that the British have been amazingly adaptable. British business representatives now say "sir" without self-consciousness to the kind of Indians from whom seventy years ago their predecessors would have demanded obsequiousness. A concomitant of the Indian goodwill toward Britain is an apparently unconscious feeling there today that Britain is India's best and most understanding friend. To a less extent a similar feeling also exists in Pakistan. Bangladesh is likely to be warm toward Britain, which was early in recognizing the new nation and had good cultural relations with Bengal.

Throughout the subcontinent one of the most striking of general effects during the British period was the accelerating secularization of life. With both Hindus and Muslims religion and magic were contracting into narrower and more sharply defined boundaries. The traffic to traditional pilgrim points might illustrate the point. Varanasi (Banaras), for example, in the prewar decades of this century used to support its municipal budget by a pilgrim tax of one anna (equivalent then to about U.S. two cents) a head, which was included in the price of all railway tickets to its stations. By 1948 the number of pilgrims had been greatly reduced from the figures of twenty years before, the railway stations were receiving but a fraction of their former throngs, and the pilgrim tax had become insufficient for the city's needs. By 1971 the number of pilgrims was even smaller than it had been in 1948; food restriction and the need to use a rationing card in the place where issued had served to reduce pilgrim traffic, but the people also appeared to be less interested. We may think that they saw less spiritual profit for themselves in visiting and bathing at the holy spots. Brahman priests at pilgrimage points in various parts of India—north, south, east—when talking today to visitors from America or Europe confirm this impression. They complain that their business has fallen off. Fewer members of the families for which their families had stood vicar for centuries have been arriving and paying fees for their services. Within the cities Brahmans are being called upon less frequently for prayers and ceremonies in times of illness and misfortune. Brahmans add that in the cities witchcraft has come to hold fewer terrors for the populace, magicians are less patronized, and their own antidotes are less in demand. Muslims say that charm-workers have fewer customers than fifty or even ten years ago. In 1948 and 1950, and still more so in the 1960s, urban temples and shrines seemed less frequented than in 1922 or 1928 or 1935. By 1971 the decline had become still greater.

There are no statistics on this point, but the traveler who visits India periodically cannot fail to be impressed. Contrariwise, the number of apothecary shops, drug stores, professional signboards of homeopathic, Hindu Ayurvedic, and Muslim Yanani physicians. seem to have multiplied in the same period. It is probable that much of the diagnosis, prognosis, and medication dispensed by these practitioners and in these shops is useless if not actually injurious, but the interesting point is that people are more and more relying upon physical means to cure physical ills rather than upon deities, devils, demons and magic devices. All these remarks apply to cities and towns; less change has taken place in the villages.

Another aspect of secularization during the latter part of the British period appears in the weakening of Brahman prestige. That "god on earth" came to suffer restriction in Madras, once his firmest stronghold, where the number of seats in colleges open to his sons was less in the 1950s and 1960s than the number wishing a college education. Lower castes in control of the legislature had lost their fear of the formerly privileged Brahmans, and allowed them only their numerical proportion of public advantages. In the Maratha country in and near Poona anti-Brahmanism has long existed; after Gandhi's assassination in 1948 by a fanatical Brahman from that area there were violent attacks upon the houses and persons of Brahmans in many villages. All over India the Brahman has been facing competition from every caste down to the Untouchables in seeking posts that a century before would have seemed his by rightful monopoly. The ridicule of the poor and not-too-bright Brahman, which has appeared throughout Indian fiction for over fifteen hundred years, now has a somewhat more serious tone. His sacrosanct position is hardly being conceded anywhere without an argument. Much of the change in attitude has been due to Brahmans themselves; Nehru and many other Brahmans have repudiated the doctrine of position by birth and have encouraged the process of social leveling. In many areas Brahmans are today, and for many decades have been, leaders in social advance.

Certain features of the caste system were coming to be ignored in a number of quarters during the British period. One of these was limitation of occupation. For example, merchants, who in ancient India hardly aspired to political power—except among Jains and Buddhists—during the British period, under the influence of the British example, became eager politicians and ardent nationalists. Caste customs too changed. Physical contact between members of different castes, formerly forbidden, became a commonplace. In railroad trains and buses high and low became accustomed to sitting side by side without a qualm; in factories they learned to work beside or with one another; they were comrades in labor unions. Such situations had not existed in the agrarian society where caste had originated and developed; therefore the situations were not covered by the inherited rules of caste behavior. Among the socially elite in cities it has now become common for members of different castes to dine at the same table; the practice is even appearing in villages. Some persons who in the 1920s strictly avoided it are practicing it today, quite unaware that their mores have changed.

Marriages across caste lines, which fifty years before independence would have raised a public scandal in the Hindu community, are still not common but they do not in the 1970s produce newspaper comment. Participants seem to have little difficulty with family or fellow caste members. Castes that regarded it as a disgrace for a girl to be still unmarried at the start of menstruation were not seriously disgruntled in conforming to the law concerning age of consent (sixteen years for girls, eighteen for boys) enacted in 1930. In Cochin at a Hindu-controlled Sanskrit school in 1948 an Untouchable was teaching Sanskrit to Brahman boys. In Trivandrum at a Hindu girls' orphanage operated by Hindus, Brahman, Shudra, and

Untouchable girls slept in the same dormitory, played and worked together, ate in the same small room, sitting intermingled and being served from common dishes with food prepared in the same kitchen, all directly contrary to traditional rules. Discrimination did not exist until time of marriage, when husbands were found for the girls in their own caste groups. The association with Untouchables did not impair the Brahman girls' eligibility. Throughout India there are today numerous other instances of similar relaxation of caste requirements.

Such changes must not be assumed to mean that the caste system has withered, though some good Hindus talk as though it has. In Uttar Pradesh in 1950 there were Hindus who predicted that the system would be finished in fifteen years; in Bengal a Brahman said it would last only ten years; in Mysore another set its limit a twenty years. These were somewhat rash predictions, hardly the judgments of sociologists, and cannot be taken to indicate more than skepticism about some features of the institution. Caste is merely being modified in what, except for marriage, seem to be superficial features.

In education, secularism now appears in the fact that the Hindu and Muslim classical languages—Sanskrit, Arabic, Persian—and the literatures composed in them are attracting ever fewer students. The fairly distinguished position which those subjects had achieved in the public education system by the late nineteenth century and continued to hold for some decades had by 1948 contracted disastrously in the eyes of Sanskrit, Arabic, and Persian scholars. Instead students were flocking to the natural sciences and technological subjects. By 1970 the shift had become even greater.

The secularization that began during the British period has advanced since independence. It is embodied in the 1950 constitution of India, which develops the principle that state and religion should be separate. Thus it implements the secular motivation of the Indian National Congress, which was organized to promote secular ends, has aimed to represent all Indian communities, and, though it has sometimes been led by strongly partisan communalists and religious enthusiasts, has always returned to the secular position. Secularism of government is still being attacked in India by Hindu communal groups, but the highest echelon of government supports it faithfully. Speaking before the All-India Congress Committee on July 13, 1951, Prime Minister Nehru said concerning the secular character of the state, "On this subject there can be no compromise of any kind; we must be prepared to stand or fall bv it." The secular state was a platform of the Congress Party in 1951–52 in the first general elections, wherein it won a sweeping victory. As an aim of government it was not seriously questioned in the second general elections in 1957, nor in the third in 1962, nor in the fourth and fifth in 1967 and 1971.

The status of political secularism is not yet established so clearly in Pakistan. The Pakistan constitution of 1956 declared that Pakistan was to be an Islamic state. But on October 7, 1958, Major General Iskander Mirza, then president, lost patience with parliamentary procedures and abrogated the constitution, and many of the religious principles were discarded with it. Nor were they restored by General Ayub Khan, who assumed power at Mirza's invitation— and promptly (October 27, 1958) sent Mirza into exile. The Pakistan constitution of March 1, 1962, has only a few lapses from secularism. But such secularism is strongly opposed by large Muslim groups. In 1971, in suppressing the revolt in East Pakistan that led to the establishment of Bangladesh, much of the fury of the West Pakistanis, according to accounts in eminently reliable newspapers, was directed against Hindus. After achieving independence the leaders of Bangladesh announced that their nation would be a strictly secular state.

4 The Will To Be Free

Nationalism was preindependence India's expression of confidence that it could match in the present its greatness of the past. The immediate provocation and most of the specific aims came from living under British rule. The techniques of revolt were partly shaped by western patterns, but in their most effective forms by traditional Hindu ideas.

The early organizations nurturing nationalism were mostly religious; one, the Indian National Congress, which ultimately had almost a monopoly in furthering it, was secular. For some decades the movement was strictly a middle class phenomenon, promoted by intellectuals, manufacturers, entrepreneurs, newspaper owners and editors, lawyers, religious reformers and revivalists, and other professional persons. It remained so until Gandhi won it mass support in 1920. The purpose in its early phase was to replace British control of the country with middle class Indian control. The issues it agitated were, first, that of political structure; second, those of economic relations between India and Britain; and, third, certain social questions. The aristocracy of the country, which consisted of the Indian princes ruling the Indian (native) States and the great landlords, almost to a man opposed the nationalist movement. Peasants, other villagers, and industrial workers, when they came to support the movement, sometimes did so because of economic discontent and sometimes on religious grounds.

Indian nationalism was primarily supported by Hindus, that is, the nearly two thirds of the total population living by the Hindu way of life. It drew only slightly from the minority communities, of which the largest was the Muslim, comprising something less than one fourth of the population. The will of India at first to be a self-governing dominion within the British Empire, and later to be an independent nation, was the will of Hindu India. Though the

66

Hindu religion, in the narrower sense, or Hinduism, in the broader cultural sense, provided scarcely an issue which Indian nationalism contested with British imperialism, it did the more basic job of defining the group which struggled to win self-rule.

Before identifying elements of the historic culture that supported nationalism, we may first note a few features of India in the early twentieth century which often used to be cited as blocking national unity; some of these still operate to prevent achievement of full national strength.

One of these lay in the political structure; many students and government officers believed that the autocratic rulers of the Indian States would never consent to an intimate political association with the democratizing provinces of British India. The Indian States were 562 in number, comprised about 45 percent of undivided India's area, and in 1941 contained a little more than one fourth of the population (93 out of 389 million). Mapmakers in Britain and India used to show British India in pink and the Indian States in yellow, and the two colors were mixed in a patternless jumble like a New England country flower garden gone wild. But in the outcome the Indian states furnished no serious obstruction to national independence. They were weaker than had been supposed; nationalism took them over in its stride.

The social institution of caste was often named as a sure preventive of any unified nationalistic action, and in the first decade of the twentieth century Sir Herbert Hope Risley, a celebrated civil servant and anthropologist, predicted that political divisions would follow caste lines. In general this was not the case. The Indian National Congress, which was the efficient organ of nationalism, drew from all castes. Though the lower caste groups were often suspicious of Congress, it generally succeeded in retaining them; at the most critical junctures it was able to do so because of dramatic gestures toward social reform made by Gandhi, who knew that the Hindu community needed the support of its lowest segments if India was to win national independence. In the 1950s, however, caste became one of the perils to democracy in India.

The large number of languages was also cited as a hindrance to nationalism, and the separatist effect of language continues to this day to be an internal plague. But the language divisions turned out to be a less serious handicap in the struggle for independence than

67

they had seemed, because English had become the common speech of the educated throughout the country and as such was a tool for nationalism.

Another aspect of Indian life which was expected to thwart nationalism was religious rivalry. Its effect in setting Muslims and Hindus against each other has already been mentioned and will be discussed in later chapters dealing with communalism and partition. But though religion in this way served as a brake on nationalism it also provided, through the dynamic quality of native Indian faiths, the principal driving power for several decades. The adherents to native Indian Hindu culture have a distinctive body of belief and practice and in consequence a special kind of social cohesion which facilitated the growth of nationalist sentiment. This common feeling was, and still is, aided, to a marked degree, by the literature of Hinduism, especially the Sanskrit epics, the *Mahabharata* and the *Ramayana,* and their literary successors, the *Puranas,* read by the learned, heard in recitation by the illiterate. In the *Puranas* are found the stories of Rama, the national ideal of manhood and kingship, and his wife Sita, the ideal of womanhood; of the five Pandavas, who waged the war of righteousness against their wicked cousins; of Krishna, god become man, who was charioteer to the Pandavas' great general Arjuna and taught him the *Bhagavad Gita;* of all the human beings who most affect the Hindu imagination. These heroes and heroines are of the soil of India itself; their lives moved in India; their names are associated with India's mountains, rivers, forests, and cities. Their tales are told with Indian phraseology and with Indian figures of speech. Their hold upon the people's mind is primary and unrivaled.

Hence the religious element in Hindu culture became the heart of Indian nationality, and so various reform sects of Hinduism preaching against actively proselytizing Islam and Christianity promoted a religious nationalism. Hence, too, Gandhi, the most influential political leader of the land in our times, was first of all a man of religion. The life of sainthood which he embodied was a national ideal; the book which he quoted most often and with the most effect was the *Bhagavad Gita.*

It used to be said that nationalism in India could draw no strength from a national historical sense; for there are few works of history in India's abundant literature, and most of these make little distinction between myth and fact. But this judgment must be modified. Important for nurturing nationalism was the fact that in the late nineteenth and the twentieth centuries a historical sense was growing in India and growing in a way to flatter the national self-esteem. Archaeological excavation and study revealed to Indians the extent, quality, and age of their ancient civilization, and its influence upon the rest of Asia. National imagination was stimulated by discoveries which showed that ancient India had a culture in the Indus Valley rivaling those of Mesopotamia and Egypt and in special points surpassing them. Increased knowledge of Asian history contributed to national pride. Indians were stirred when they learned that their religions, literature, languages, art, and law had migrated to central, eastern, and southeastern Asia, to help build civilization there.

In other cultural fields the Hindu ego was being enlarged. A number of Indians were winning intellectual successes in the West, of whom perhaps the most appealing to Hindu imagination was Swami Vivekananda (born Narendranath Datta, 1862–1902). At the Parliament of Religions held in Chicago during the World's Fair of 1892–1893 the vigor and brilliance of his mind and corresponding qualities of presence and eloquence raised him from complete obscurity to a position of dominance over the whole Parliament, and brought India a special prestige in America. Vivekananda became a legendary figure in India as the Hindu who could equal and excel in intellect the thinkers of the otherwise dominant West. Later there were Indian scientists, such as J. C. Bose and C. V. Raman, mathematicians, such as Ramanujan, and literary artists, such as Rabindranath Tagore, who received recognition of the highest order in the West.

When to the national self-assurance so generated was added in the latter decades of the nineteenth century the achievements of orientals in modern warfare, culminating in the Japanese victory over Russia in 1904–1905, Indians began to acquire confidence that they could compete militarily with Europeans. They came to hope that perhaps in some new epoch of history their nation might again have a place with the world's greatest.

It should also be said that Indian national aspirations received aid and comfort from liberal sentiment in Britain and from some highly placed British officials in India. For example, Gladstone published a vigorous claim for the principle of Indian self-government in the *Hindoo Patriot* in 1878. In 1888 Lord Dufferin, Governor

General of India, wrote a minute recognizing the need to satisfy Indian aspirations, and his successor, Lord Lansdowne, continued to support the policy.

Two sections of India were the principal seats of nationalist activity during the nineteenth century. These were Bengal in the east, and Poona and the nearby Maratha country in the west. In the twentieth century other areas of activity were the Punjab, Gujarat, and south India.

In Bengal the immediate source of nationalism lay in an intellectual renaissance, springing partly from the introduction of new ideas from the West and partly from a revival of indigenous Bengali literature. It was in Bengal that western education had first taken hold. There was located Calcutta, the chief European city of India and the most important channel for the influx of western ideas. During the nineteenth century Bengal effervesced with literary activity, which got special point from the aspirations of the Hindu Bengalis to win equality with the Muslims who had ruled them before the British came, and with the British who were ruling them then. Bengal was intellectually the most advanced region of India; the Bengalis were the most sensitive to white arrogance and the most articulate in expressing their resentment. The most influential writer was Bankim Chandra Chatterji (1838–1894), who voiced the sentimental attachment that was growing up among Hindus for India as the mystic Mother threatened by non-Hindu aggression and needing the defense of her sons. From one of his novels (*Ananda Math*) comes the song "Bande Mataram" ("I worship the Mother"), which has an anti-Muslim motivation in its context, but until superseded after independence by Rabindranath Tagore's "Jana-gana-mana" was the anthem of Indian nationalism, and as such was given an anti-British application. Pride of race was stirred by the writings of Bankim and similar, though lesser, authors, and a purpose was evolved which rapidly took form as Hindu nationalism.

Whereas in Bengal nationalism arose largely from intellectual stirrings and expressed itself chiefly in speech and writing, in Poona and the Maratha country it derived from religious dogmatism coupled with the suppressed ambition of a warlike people, and its expression was marked from the beginning by violence.

The Marathas were from the seventeenth to the nineteenth centuries one of India's most martial peoples. They were the most important foes of the crumbling Mughal empire, and they have never since lost their anti-Muslim zeal. Their first great leader Sivaji (1630–1680) harassed the Muslim kingdoms, and became the acknowledged champion of Hinduism; for he patronized Brahmans, honored the gods, and protected cows. When the Mughal empire started to break up at the death of Aurangzeb (1707), the Marathas began to sweep over western, central, and northern India, overthrowing Muslim and Hindu alike, and establishing their own dynasties, which ruled some of the most important Indian states (Baroda, Indore, Gwalior). The central authority of the Maratha states during the eighteenth century was at Poona, and they constituted a loose confederacy which the British finally shattered in 1818. Poona then became the radiation point of Maratha frustration.

Here there came into prominence during the 1890s a fiery Brahman named Bal Gangadhar Tilak (1856–1920) who in the 1900s was the dominant figure in the Indian National Congress. His first interest was the preservation of the Hindu religion, which he saw doubly imperiled, on the one hand by westernized Indians preaching social change and collaborating with the even more subversive government which enacted such religiously dangerous innovations as an Age of Consent Bill (1890) setting a minimum marriage age, and on the other hand by foreigners who themselves engaged in sin and defied Hinduism by eating the flesh of the sacred cow. Second to religious grievances were certain economic complaints which he championed. During the famine of 1896 he tried to launch a "no-rent" campaign among the impoverished peasants, urging them to withhold from the government the land rent (tax). He published a newspaper which advocated violence as a means of political protest, and political murder followed. Political violence still has a home in Maratha country. From there came Gandhi's assassin, who acted in protest against Gandhi's program of peace with Muslims.

Of a different character was Tilak's caste fellow Gopal Krishna Gokhale (1866–1915), also from Poona. Tilak had emphasized the ceremonial side of Hinduism; Gokhale's interest was in the social values of his religion and the wider application of its ethics to life. Where Tilak was provocative and conservative, Gokhale was persuasive and liberal. He represented the tolerant, expansive, compromising side of Hinduism. He waged a long fight with the government for social ends, rather than political. He welcomed instruction from the West on social problems, and was especially an advocate of general popular education, which he felt was necessary for the progress of India. He founded the Servants of India Society, a constructive social agency, to work for the improvement of all Indians, without restriction of caste, race, or creed. He came to believe that India would obtain the necessary social changes only if Indians themselves had a greater share in legislation and administration, and here was the basis for his political propaganda. To him, more than to anyone else of his generation, Indian nationalism was indebted for forward-looking purpose. While Tilak gave passion and fighting vigor to nationalism in its early stages, Gokhale gave it secular objectives and statesmanship.

In the Punjab nationalism developed among the Sikhs, who had been unwavering supporters of the British. Though the British had destroyed the Sikh kingdom in the 1840s, the Sikhs, in the next decade, at the time of the Sepoy Mutiny, had sided with the British and clashed with the Mughals, who for over two centuries had been the Sikhs' oppressors and enemies. Punjab nationalism arose partly because of discrimination against Indians in other parts of the British Empire, partly in consequence of economic dislocations —as when in 1907 the government's policies concerning irrigation canals were compelling the peasants to make economic readjustments—and partly in consequence of religious disputes among the Sikhs themselves, accompanied by bloodshed and death, in which the government became involved.

Gujarat, in the west of India, where Gandhi long had his home, became vigorously and actively nationalist only in 1918. There nationalism was inspired partly by the presence of Gandhi, partly by economic distress of the peasants, partly by disaffection of the mill owners in Ahmedabad—after Bombay the largest city of western India—who wanted to drive out British textile imports and gain the Indian cotton-goods market for their own products.

In southern India nationalism was also of comparatively late growth. Its development was aided by sectional desires of linguistic groups, especially the Telugu speakers in the Andhra region, for separation from the larger province of Madras, and by the desires of the non-Brahmans to get the government of the provinces away from the Brahmans and into their own hands.

In the beginning the various nationalist organizations were weak and mutually antipathetic. Few of them were primarily political. There were religious societies which, as a corollary to their main purpose of establishing true doctrine, engaged in activities with nationalist implications. There were commercial bodies with interests that led to nationalism as their natural expression. Some of the parties came to be primarily political in purpose after the granting of the constitution in 1919, which provided for partly elected legislative bodies.

Of those organizations which proceeded to nationalism through religion, two, though now negligible, were politically influential in their time. These were the occult-slanted Theosophical Society and the revivalist Arya Samaj. It was evident, according to Theosophical reasoning, that the Hindus were unexcelled in religion, and, since religion is the highest phase of human activity, they were unexcelled as a people. The logical conclusion was that they should be subject to no other people, but should have political freedom. The chief leader of the Theosophical Society in the twentieth century was Mrs. Annie Besant (1847–1933), who believed in self-rule for a "Commonwealth of India" as a member of the British Empire. To promote this she and B. G. Tilak founded in 1915–1916 the all-India Home Rule League, which cooperated with the Indian National Congress and lasted until the 1920s. She was president of Congress in 1917.

The Arya Samaj, which was strong chiefly in northern and northwestern India, looked upon all existing forms of native Indian religions as left-handed corruptions of a pure faith taught in a mythically distant past and preserved in the *Rig* and other Vedas. This forsaken religion it aimed to revive. The founder of the Arya Samaj was Pandit Dayanand Sarasvati (1824–1883), who after some years of preaching organized his society in 1875, meaning to save India for Hinduism from the encroachments of Islam and Christianity, and to lead Hinduism back from the "left-hand" to the "right-hand" path. His methods were combative and sophistical, but he had a social program against the rigidity of caste, child marriage, enforced widowhood, the seclusion of women. He aggressively promoted "cow protection," which through his inflammatory propaganda came to be a constant source of trouble between Hindus and Muslims. He had a method of interpreting Vedic texts by which he found mentioned in them all the scientific discoveries and technological inventions of his own day, thereby proving to his own satisfaction that modern civilization was only a deterioration from the perfect civilization of the ancient Hindu seers. The natural conclusion was that India should revert to the glorious past, and to do so she must first become self-governing, free of all non-Hindu elements. The great political leader of this society in the twentieth century was Lajpat Rai (1865–1928). The Arya Samaj was especially strong in the Punjab, where before World War I it provided nationalism with many recruits. In the interval between the wars it contributed to the hostility between Hindus and Muslims.

With a somewhat different twist to events, the Theosophical Society, or the Arya Samaj, or the Servants of India Society, or some one of several other organizations not primarily political in purpose might have been captured by politicians and turned into a political body. Instead each became increasingly less political during the 1920s and 1930s and transferred its political support to the Indian National Congress, which had become the unrivaled spokesman of nationalism.

The Indian National Congress, also commonly known as Congress, was founded in Bombay during Christmas week, 1885, by Allan Octavian Hume (1829–1912), who was a retired Civil Service official, a few other Europeans, and some Indians who had westernized sociological notions. At that time, political discontent, largely focused on the Vernacular Press Act of 1878 (which was repealed four years later), was inspiring the formation of various political organizations, and Hume hoped that Congress would be a constructive political force rather than merely one to agitate grievances. Congress had no religious motivation; rather, its philosophy was secular. Its purpose was to discuss social reform. The first presidential address by W. C. Bonnerjee contained expressions of gratitude to Britain for the good government she had given India, the railways, the new education from the West. The second president, Dadabhai Naoroji (1825–1917), a celebrated man in modern Indian annals, spoke feelingly of "the blessings of British rule," which he characterized as "numberless," and stated his belief that events showed that "the peoples of England were sincere in the declaration made more than a half century ago that India was a sacred charge entrusted to their care by Providence, and that they were bound to administer it for the good of India, to the glory of their own name, and the satisfaction of God."

The change of Congress to an actively nationalist attitude was due, primarily, to the disappointment of Indians in not finding its reasonably presented proposals more sympathetically considered by the government. It objected to the "home charges," which consisted of payments on public debt owed by India in London, certain expenses of administration of India incurred in London, and pensions of British who had served in India; it complained of unduly large military expenditure, of the failure to separate the judicial and executive branches of government, of the lack of equal opportunity for Indians as officers in the army, of the neglect of general primary education. By 1900 it was severely questioning the sincerity of the British professions it had accepted so enthusiastically in 1885. In 1904 a "radical" element began to struggle with conservatives for dominance of Congress, being weary of the failure of the moderates to achieve results by their methods of persuasion. In 1907, under the pressure of continued grievances, including the partition of Bengal during the governor generalship of Lord Curzon, Congress split for a few years between the extremists led by Tilak and the old-fashioned moderates. The next year it adopted a "creed" calling for political rights. From then on it never ceased to be a political body first and a social reform body second.

After World War I Congress attained a commanding position among nationalists under the leadership of Gandhi. In 1916 the "radicals" gained control, and it came to stand for reform by revolution (though without violence) rather than by constitutional evolution. After Gandhi went to jail in 1922 there followed a period of uncertainty and confusion, largely because of dissension among Indian politicians as to what course they should pursue in connection with the constitution of 1919. By 1929 Congress was again united and extremely popular. It led a fight against the Simon Commission which had been appointed by the British government in 1927 to devise constitutional reform. It adopted a goal of full self-government at the end of 1929 and set the next January 26 as Independence Day, a day which since then it, and now the Republic of India, has celebrated annually. It persisted in its campaign during World War II, though harried and declared illegal by the Churchill government. After the war Congress emerged again as the leading Indian political party. It rightfully takes the credit for winning independence.

The growth of nationalist sentiment and activity in the nineteenth and early twentieth centuries is marked, as if with milestones, by a series of crises, developing from a longer or shorter series of political, economic, or social experiences, and significant steps of political reform associated with these critical situations.

The first serious expressions came at about the time of the Sepoy Mutiny (1857–1858). Those Indians who already felt that they had an inherent right to share in governing India were shocked by the brutal vengeance which the British inflicted upon the vanquished mutineers. After the Mutiny, in spite of a general British policy of consideration for the persons of Indians, there continued to be ruthless lapses into militaristic violence, each of which easily undid in the minds of Indians the effect laboriously achieved through many preceding years of moderation. British officials felt the need to become acquainted with Indian opinion, and in 1861 an Indian Councils Act was passed by Parliament authorizing the Governor General to enlarge his executive council from four to five, to devise rules for transacting business, and for legislative purposes to add not less than six nor more than twelve "additional" members. The Governor General nominated Indians as some of these additional members. Similar provisions were enacted for the provinces.

The means used to quell the Mutiny had revolted and alienated the Indian press, which professed to see a potential helper in Russia, then advancing in Central Asia. At about this time came economic difficulties also. There was a crash in Indian cotton in 1865, following the temporary boom during the American Civil War, and in 1866 there was a severe famine, which brought widespread discontent. The press was violent in criticism of the government on this matter too.

Following the Mutiny there arose an acute racial problem which had scarcely existed previously. The mutineers had inflicted atrocities upon Europeans, including women, as at Cawnpore (Kanpur), and this fact aroused in the whites a hatred of Indians. They described their former enemies as cowardly, weak, treacherous, bestial, and symbolized those qualities by the darkness of the Indian skin. A "mutiny complex" arose among European women fearful of rape, a mental state prevalent until well into the twentieth century. The Indians developed a stereotype of the whites as brutal, bullying, arrogant. The British now disdained intermarriage, which in the eighteenth and early nineteenth centuries had been frequent, and looked down upon the Anglo-Indians (formerly called Eurasians), who were sprung from mixed unions. They sent their children back to Britain to school. Some would remain in India as long as thirty years without learning to speak any Indian language. Almost all took advantage of their prerogatives as members of the ruling group to exercise social discrimination in railway trains and other public places. From about 1917 on these features were curbed, but they were never fully eliminated until 1947. The extreme form of anti-Indianism was sometimes openly expressed and usually implicit in the utterances of Britons, sometimes of prominent Britons, to the effect that the Indians were of a different and inferior "race," were a "conquered people," and were unworthy of self-rule and treatment as social equals. This conflict in the relations between Indian and Briton has been considered by some observers, like the late C. F. Andrews, to be the most important element in hardening nationalist sentiment.

The racial antipathy first came to a head in 1883 when the Ilbert Bill was introduced. At this time the Indians who had entered the Indian Civil Service when the higher ranks were opened to them in 1854 were reaching senior grades, and those in judicial service were due to attain posts where they would have had the status to try Europeans had not the right been denied them as Indians. Indians resented the restriction, and the bill was aimed to remove it. The Europeans protested heatedly; Indian feeling also was intense. The government finally withdrew the bill and substituted another granting European defendants the right of trial by jury of which 50 percent should be European. Indians, however, received no corresponding right.

In 1892 Parliament passed another Indian Councils Act, enlarging both the Indian and provincial councils, and prescribing that the nonofficial "additional" members (such as were provided in the Indian Councils Act of 1861) should be filled on the recommendation of municipalities, district boards, chambers of commerce, universities, and others. This was not "election," though in fact it amounted to it. The councils could not vote upon the budget, though they could ask questions and discuss it.

The next events to strike the popular imagination came in 1896–1900. At that time fierce famines, some of the severest on record, swept large sections of central and northern India. It was then that Tilak and his followers, feeling that the government was dilatory in relieving the peasants, organized a "no-rent" campaign.

It had no marked success, but it was dramatic, and it introduced into modern India a weapon that the peasants had used in pre-British times and were to employ later under nationalist leadership. Accompanying this famine was a plague epidemic. In segregating patients so as to control the disease and in disinfecting and evacuating houses, the government was not tactful in handling ignorant and suspicious Indians, with the result that India had its first political murder in modern times, when two British officers were killed at Poona in 1897. The introduction of violence into the political struggle made a profound impression upon the public.

In 1899 Lord Curzon (1859–1925) became Governor General (Viceroy), reigning until 1905. He was a man of commanding intelligence, tremendous industry, strong will, great courage, and an overwhelming consciousness of his imperial mission. It is probably true that no other Viceroy ever accomplished so much of material benefit to India. It is also probably true that no other ever so severely lacerated the feelings of Indians. Two of his actions were sufficiently unpopular to become symbols to the educated classes. One of these was his Universities Act (1904), by which he greatly improved those institutions, but did so at the price of ruthlessly overriding Indian feeling. The trouble lay in the fact that he reduced the number of members of the various senates, the ruling bodies of the universities, and at the same time increased the number of members nominated by the chancellors of the universities, who were always the governors of the provinces in which the universities were located. In this way the government-nominated members came to be in the majority. The Bengalis greatly resented this action in its application to the University of Calcutta. This had become to them the emblem of their intellectual life and cultural renaissance, and they opposed the act violently on the ground that the government was taking over control of the university out of hostility to the vigorous and independent Bengali intellectual development that was showing marked nationalist tendencies.

The second of Lord Curzon's inflammatory actions was the "partition of Bengal," announced in the year 1905. At that time the Bengal Presidency contained not only the two Bengals now belonging to India and Bangladesh, but also the area included in the present states of Bihar and Orissa, and had a population of about 78 million people, far too many for efficient administration. To give relief Lord Curzon decreed that the eastern part of the province, containing nearly one third of the population, should be cut off and combined with Assam as a separate province called East Bengal and Assam, an arrangement which administrative experts recommended as the most efficient way of handling the problem. But the Hindu Bengalis regarded the scheme as destroying their ethnic integrity. The line of division went through a linguistic entity, and they took it as intended to divide them and remove their effective solidarity.

The Muslims in India, and especially those in Bengal, welcomed the change, for the new province, which contained most of what was until 1972 East Pakistan as well as all of Assam, was predominantly of their faith and would be taken out from under potential Hindu control. This feature especially incensed the Hindu portion of the Presidency. Protests of many sorts were made; all India took an interest in the fight. Bomb outrages were perpetrated beginning with 1906 after the Earl of Minto had succeeded Lord Curzon. Terrorism accompanied the use of bombs, consisting of robbery by armed gangs for political purposes, and other forms of violence; a revolutionary movement was the result. Meanwhile Muslims in 1906, to protect their interests, had organized the Muslim League, which afterwards became the organ of Muslim political aspirations and eventually accomplished the partition of India.

At last in 1911, after six years, while still another Viceroy (Lord Hardinge) was in office, King George himself announced that the partition of Bengal was nullified and Bengal was reunited. In 1912 a different partition of Bengal following linguistic boundaries was put into effect taking away Bihar and Orissa and making them into a new province, which in 1935 was itself separated into two provinces. The British had pleased no one—the Muslims, the Hindus, themselves.

The partition of Bengal brought the Indian National Congress unequivocally into politics in 1908. Before then it had been little more than a society for social reform; afterwards its primary object was to advance Indian self-rule. It was also the occasion for the first use of the economic boycott or *swadeshi* ("[buy] home goods") movement, a weapon later used by Gandhi in his long-continuing campaign for *khaddar,* that is, home-spun and home-woven cloth

Under Governor General Minto a new departure was made in

Indian political structure. He and Lord Morley, Secretary of State for India, desiring to allay the unrest, formulated the Indian Councils Act of 1909, known as the "Morley-Minto Reforms," which established executive councils in other provinces than the (then) presidencies of Bombay and Madras, greatly enlarged the imperial (governor general's) and provincial legislative councils, and provided that nearly all the nonofficial members should be elected— by a narrowly circumscribed electorate—leaving the government only a small nominated official majority in the imperial legislative councils. This was a step toward self-rule which in retrospect seems comparatively slight but when announced was impressive.

The Indian Councils Act, however, had another feature which inaugurated political communalism. While the proposals for reform were being considered, Minto received a deputation of Indian Muslims headed by the Agha Khan, which asked that the Indian Muslim community be given separate electoral representation. There had long been a view among British officials that India would some day have to have communal electorates, and Minto promptly acceded to the Muslim position. The reforms when enacted instituted communal electorates as a system and instituted it not on the basis of Muslim numerical strength or property holdings, but of Muslim "political importance," a subjective criterion. Now began a corroding process that thereafter ate its way steadily into public life.

Lord Morley denied that he ever looked forward to parliamentary institutions in India; like most other Britons of his time he thought them unsuitable to the country. He had no hope of gaining the goodwill of irreconcilable extremists with "fantastic dreams that some day they will drive us out of India." Rather his hope was to win as willing cooperators the reasonable proponents of self-rule who sought only a larger part in the government. He did not foresee that the councils he had fashioned would be the means used later for making parliamentary experiments. The reforms did not seem to shake British autocratic rule, since ultimate power rested with the Governor General in (executive) council and the governors of the provinces, who could do as they wished without being bound by the opinions of the legislative councils. It was, nevertheless, portentous that the councils could discuss many subjects, ask questions, and criticize. It was inescapable that they would also want the accompanying power of action.

Hardly had India reflected upon these reforms, when the country received another shock. King George V and Queen Mary had come to India in December 1911 to be crowned as Emperor and Empress of India at Delhi. On this visit the King-Emperor made two announcements. One, calculated to be conciliatory, was that the partition of Bengal was to be reversed. The other, which proved remarkably provocative, was that the capital was to be transferred from Calcutta to Delhi, the old seat of the Mughals. There were certain advantages to be gained from setting the capital in a more central and more historic spot, but the people of Bengal viewed the matter differently. They saw a close connection between the subjects of the two announcements. They felt that the removal of the capital from their province was intended to diminish the importance of Bengal and to punish it for its successful contumacy in opposing the Bengal partition. All the goodwill created by the Morley-Minto reforms vanished; Bengal never forgave her demotion.

Several months before the Delhi Darbar, a dispatch of Lord Hardinge's government to the Secretary of State (August 25, 1911) had enunciated the principle that "the just demands of Indians for a larger share in the government of the country will have to be satisfied, and the question will be how this devolution of power can be conceded without impairing the supreme authority of the Governor-General in Council." The Liberal government in Britain repudiated the principle but it was a kind of forecast of the inevitable.

A few years later national feeling burst out in the Punjab. In May 1914 a shipload of 351 Sikhs and 21 Punjabi Muslims recruited in Hongkong, Shanghai, Moji (a port on the Japanese island of Kyushu), and Tokyo was denied admission into Canada under the immigration laws and all the prospective immigrants were returned to India, where they arrived at the end of September. In their disappointment they saw precisely two things: that they were British subjects; that they had been denied entrance to a part of the British Empire. Here, they felt, was racial discrimination, and if that had to exist within the Empire, then they did not want India to remain in it. When they landed in Calcutta, 300 of the Sikhs tried to march on the city, were turned back forcibly with 18 deaths, then scattered throughout northern India, making their way to the Punjab, preaching hatred and violence, and strengthening the hand of the already existing Ghadr (mutiny) party, which had been organized in America in 1913. Many were arrested and tried; 28 were hanged; a number were transported to the penal colony in the Andaman Islands. Other Sikhs were returned to India from various British Dominions to a total number of about 8000, and they all fomented discontent.

Political terrorism was now rife, supplemented by robbery with occasional murder to raise money for alleged political use, especially in Bengal. There is no reason to believe that the Indian National Congress instigated any of this terrorism, though members of Congress may have participated.

During the period from 1906 to 1914 Indians had increasingly felt that the British Dominions were unfair to Indians living within their borders. The chief region then concerned was South Africa, especially Natal. Indians had been migrating there since 1860 to work as indentured laborers. So long as the immigrants were serving their terms, they were a welcome convenience to the whites, but when the terms were at an end and they became free, they constituted a menace, for their lower standard of living made them competitors endangering the economic security of their former masters. The European community used many weapons to curb the Indians, such as the imposition of a heavy poll tax, limitation of residence on "sanitary" grounds, restriction of travel within the various South African colonies, denial of franchise, hindrance of trading, imposition of educational tests. In 1906 the Black Act was enacted, by which all Asiatics, male and female, were to register and take out a certificate accompanied by fingerprints and detailed personal information ordinarily required of no civilians except criminals. Failure in any respect to comply with the law was punishable by fine, imprisonment, or deportation. The despairing Indians found a leader in Mohandas Karamchand Gandhi, who had gone to South Africa as a lawyer, and under him they waged a long struggle against the governments of the various colonies, and finally against the South African Union. The weapon they used was that of nonviolent resistance—the use of violence would have been hopeless—and at last in 1914 they seemed successful, though actually they were not, and the contest in South Africa has continued periodically ever since. It showed itself in the 1950s in the political principle of apartheid which, because of censure from other Commonwealth nations, led in 1961 to the withdrawal of South Africa from that federation.

India had watched the struggle in South Africa before World War I with a twofold interest. It had, for one thing, been moved at seeing Indians subjected to racial discrimination. It had, for another, been thrilled to see the development of a successful means for offering resistance. The Indian imagination was kindled; Gandhi, author of the new weapon, became a name of power in his homeland. Neither he nor anyone else suspected the important part he was soon to play there.

During World War I, Britain had two problems to solve in India. One was to check the strong and rising antagonism to British rule; the other was to get men and money from India for use against the enemy. The British did not complain that India failed them. Recruitments were many; funds were raised to equip the troops; both Congress and the Muslim League supported the war effort; the princes were loyal; the people as a whole gave their support, making the cause of their foreign rulers their own. Yet at the same time the anti-British agitation did not cease in Bengal and the Punjab. Congress hoped that Britain, in identifying her war role as the defense of democracy, would inaugurate democratic institutions in India, and wanted action accordingly.

While the war continued, two policies appeared as Britain's joint program for controlling India. One was persuasive, leading to constitutional liberalization. The other was repressive, directed against extreme nationalism.

The persuasive policy was initiated by a celebrated announcement which Edwin Samuel Montagu, Secretary of State for India, after due consultation with Lord Chelmsford's government in India, made in Parliament on August 20, 1917, when he said that His Majesty's government would provide for "the increasing association of Indians in every branch of Indian administration, and for the gradual development of self-governing institutions, with a view to the progressive realization of responsible government in British India as an integral part of the Empire." Thus ended an epoch, for this was a definite promise, though undated for fulfillment. Parliament followed it up by passing the Government of India Act of 1919 (the "Montagu-Chelmsford Reforms"), giving India a constitution with a new system of government more liberalized than that which it then had under the 1909 constitution or than anything that would have been imaginable three decades before in the early years of the Indian National Congress. Yet now it fell far short of nationalist demands. British and Indians alike regarded it as temporary, to precede a transition to further self-government.

Under the 1919 constitution decentralization of authority was instituted. The natural tendency of the strong autocratic British power in India was toward centralization, and this the nationalists had attacked. Now the division of function between the central and the provincial governments of British India was more sharply drawn, and many subjects of administration were assigned to the provinces. The central government retained control of certain matters like defense and customs; the provinces got control of law and order, education, agriculture, public health, and certain classes of revenue.

The central government consisted of the governor general (the viceroy) with his appointive executive council, an upper legislative chamber called the Council of State with a life of five years, and a lower chamber called the Legislative Assembly with a life of three years. In each chamber a large number of seats were filled by government nomination—27 out of 60 in the upper, 40 out of 146 in the lower. There was also a Chamber of Princes, where these rulers could meet—with due pomp and ceremony and flashing of jewels—and talk but take no legislative action. There were then ten "Governor's Provinces" (including Burma, which in 1937 was separated from India by the 1935 constitution; also in 1935 two new provinces, Sind and Orissa, were created). Each governor's province had an appointed governor with his executive council, and a legislature. The governor general and the provincial governors were not responsible to the legislative bodies but to the British Parliament. There were also five "Chief Commissioner's Provinces" without legislatures, covering a very small portion of the whole of British India.

In the governor's provinces government was by a system called dyarchy. Some subjects considered to be of first importance, such as law and order, the land revenue, canals, finance, were "reserved" for control by the governor in council, who was responsible to the British Parliament, while others considered to be of second importance, such as education, agriculture, public health, were "transferred" to the legislative councils for control by the governor through ministers responsible to the councils and thus to the Indian electorate. In the case of the central government all subjects could be treated by the Legislative Assembly except the army—which had claim to a sum not liable to discussion or refusal by any body in India—but a final veto rested with the governor general in council (the governor of a province had similar rights), as well as a power of "certification," which he could employ to enact legislation refused by the Legislative Assembly and Council of State but in his opinion vital. This self-contradictory system, which gave representation but denied responsibility, was difficult to make function and was not acceptable to most nationalists. The constitution of 1919 was the target against which nationalism directed its attack, and as it did so it gained the strength it needed for its ultimate victory.

In 1919 communal representation was extended beyond the provisions of the Indian Councils Act of 1909 and beyond the Lucknow Pact of 1916 between the Indian National Congress and the Muslim League, by which Muslims were allotted specified percentages of the elected Indian members in the provincial legislative assemblies of seven provinces, the election to be by separate Muslim electorates. The India Act of 1919 gave separate electorates also to Sikhs in the Punjab, and generally to Europeans, Anglo-Indians, and Indian Christians. In Madras it reserved a definite proportion of non-Muslim seats for non-Brahmans, and in Bombay a proportion of non-Muslim seats for Marathas.

Elections were held by the very limited electorate, and on February 9, 1921, the new government machine began to operate, when the Duke of Connaught, acting in the name of the King-Emperor, opened with pageant and pomp the Chamber of Princes, the Council of State, and the Legislative Assembly.

But all the Indian nationalist goodwill necessary to make the liberalized scheme effective had been killed by the second, the repressive policy. This was epitomized in the two Rowlatt Acts (1918), named after the English justice who framed them. These were intended to crush the extensive terrorism then existing, and they provided for summary procedure. There were to be secret trials before three judges, without the right of counsel, jury, and appeal even from sentences of death, and suspects could be interned without trial. The nationalists were enraged. Parliament would not dare, they claimed, to impose such measures in England; in India the government meant to use them not only against criminals but against any political agitator it might wish to quiet; they were designed, they said, not to preserve law and order but to repress anti-British sentiment. Riots followed, and violence. One act was never passed, and when the other was enacted neither the nationalists nor the government foresaw that it would be too unpopular ever to be employed. These acts, however, further fomented anti-British feeling, particularly in Bengal, where they were primarily meant to be used.

While the resentment against the Rowlatt Acts was at its height, the Muslim community adopted an anti-government attitude over the *Khilafat* (Caliphate) question. This concerned the temporal power of the Caliph, or spiritual ruler of Islam, a position vested in the Sultan of Turkey. Many Muslims in India considered the destruction of the Turkish Empire after the war by the Treaty of Sèvres (1920) and the extinction of the Sultan's position as Caliph to be part of a general conspiracy among the Allied Christian nations to dismember Muslim unity and scotch pan-Islamism. The Muslims, who had been hard to arouse in the interests of nationalism, who had favored the partition of Bengal which had inflamed the Hindus, whose chief organ of expression, the All-India Muslim League, was generally in opposition to the Indian National Congress, who in 1916 had extracted from an unwilling Congress the Lucknow Pact conceding their separate electorate and giving it specified weight, were now at the prompting of the Ali brothers (Mohammed and Shaukat) at last falling into line with Congress against Britain. The Khilafat movement was entirely hollow; even the Turks, after their republic was established, repudiated it; but it increased the number of Britain's enemies in India.

For Gandhi seized upon that discontent as a means of uniting the mutually hostile Hindu and Muslim communities against the British. He openly espoused the Khilafat movement, and got Congress to do so as well. This mixture of oil and water could not endure, but the excited agitation of nationalism kept the two in apparent union for a brief period. Gandhi led the joint forces in demonstrations meant by him to be nonviolent and to consist of protest by *hartal*, that is, cessation of business activity. But not all those connected with his cause were sufficiently convinced that his nonviolent method was effective, and there were riots and blood-shed; the country was in a state of tension.

The scene of the most dramatic episode was in the Punjab. There agitation led to disorder; the situation was complicated by the third Afghan war; and the civil government felt constrained to call out the military in some regions. At the city of Amritsar in that province, the center of the Sikh community, five Englishmen were killed and an Englishwoman injured, and there was other bloodshed. Leaders were deported and assemblage was strictly prohibited. But on April 13, 1919, a crowd variously estimated at from 6,000 to 12,000, disregarding the order, assembled inside the city in a garden known as Jallianwala Bagh where it was listening to speeches. It was here that the fatal event occurred.

The Jallianwala Bagh was a small square of perhaps four or five acres, surrounded solidly by the bare unpierced sides of brick houses and high walls, prohibiting any egress except by one narrow opening, which was also the entrance. The ground inside was level but for a slight elevation just at the left of the entrance. About halfway down the left-hand side near the wall was a large well, perhaps twenty feet in diameter, the only bit of cover in the entire garden.

General Reginald Dyer, the officer in command, acting on his own responsibility, though the civil administration was in charge, hastened there with fifty infantry to control the situation. When he arrived he marched his soldiers through the entrance, deployed them on the low eminence beside it, and with no word or signal to the crowd ordered them to open fire. "The targets," he said after-wards, were "good." There was no escape; the walls were too high to scale; those who leaped into the well only exchanged the bullet for the water. After ten minutes, when 1650 rounds had been fired and the ammunition was exhausted, he marched his men out, leaving the dead and dying without attention. The casualties, according to the government report issued after long delay, were 379 killed and 1200 wounded; nonofficial estimates set them higher.

There is no doubt that in consequence of the third Afghan war then in progress and the proximity of the Punjab to the frontier passes, the situation from a military point of view was dangerous. General Dyer claimed that, "It was no longer a question of merely dispersing the crowd, but one of producing a sufficient moral effect, from a military point of view, not merely on those who were present, but more especially throughout the Punjab. There could be no question of undue severity." A "moral effect" was indeed produced throughout all India, but not of a sort he had forseen. Amritsar became for India a symbol, and the Jallianwala Bagh is now a public memorial to her sons who died there.

Events following the Amritsar tragedy accentuated the ill feeling. Martial law was proclaimed two days later throughout the affected districts. The section of the street where the Englishwoman had been attacked was roped off, and for eight days all Indians who wanted to pass along it had to do so by crawling. Floggings in public were frequent; roll calls were enforced upon students; arrests were many; weapons of war were turned against villages.

The British were slow in calling General Dyer to account for his handling of the situation, and when they did so, Indians felt that the case had been unduly postponed and the investigation instituted unwillingly. He was finally censured in a dispatch from the British government to the government of India, but any effect this action might have had in mollifying Indian sentiment was obviated by the fact that a large sum of money was raised by public subscription in England and among Europeans in India, and presented to General Dyer with a sword of honor as the "Saviour of the Punjab." In 1924, when the matter was aired in England in a libel suit against Sir Sankaran Nair, a distinguished Indian lawyer, presiding justice McCardie in his opinion absolved General Dyer of blame, and again Indian sentiment was inflamed; nor could the Labour government, then in power, counteract the feeling by its conciliatory statement that the learned judge was not in full possession of the facts.

There was another effect of the Amritsar affair that General Dyer had not foreseen: the influence upon public opinion throughout the world, and more precisely in England. At a time when the esteem of other nations had come to be an object of great concern to every country, and Britain was beginning to feel the advisability of a "good press" in Europe and America, the harshness at Amritsar did more in a day in the West to discredit her occupation of India than could have been effected by a century of economic wrong and a decade of nationalist propaganda. In England itself it shook the confidence of many people in the imperialism that held India, and divided public opinion on future policy. The proponents of firmness and imperialistic self-assurance were ever afterwards periodically balked by the doubters, and the treatment of India continued to fluctuate between conciliation and repression, first trying to soothe nationalism with concessions, then irritating it with severity.

It was to the accompaniment of Amritsar that Britain presented India with her new constitution. Its provisions, far more liberal than those of 1909, sure of a welcome reception in an India that had not yet known the Punjab terrorism, now were rejected. India was not satisfied with a scheme that gave the new legislatures control over only relatively unimportant subjects and reserved the most important for final decision by the governor general and the governors of the provinces, that allowed the government the right to nominate large numbers of members to these legislatures, and above all that withheld from India all control of the army, which was responsible only to London. Amritsar had made her want the power to protect herself from her own instrument of defense. It was a dramatic climax to sixty years of accelerating nationalist activity that made firm the will of India to be a fully self-governing nation. If any single event can be said to have destroyed the possibility that Britain might hold India, it was Amritsar. From this time on, under the leadership of Gandhi, sometimes as field commander of the nationalist struggle, sometimes as strategist in the planning room, India marched toward her goal of self-rule, which was later to be conceived as full independence. She had made that fixed resolve which for Hindus is the first and essential step in accomplishing any sacrificial purpose.

5 The Leader of Revolt

India today considers Gandhi the author of her independence. He
had her confidence more than any other of her leaders; he organized the resistance to the imperialist government; he swayed to his
will politicians who had no belief in his mystical theories; he is the
Master whom all public figures profess to follow. His saintly life
won for him the courtesy title of *Mahatma,* "the Great-Souled."
And his warmth, humor, kindliness, and wisdom gained him the
devotion of India's masses as their personal refuge. This they acknowledged by another title, *Bapu* or *Bapuji,* "Father," which was
affectionately applied during his lifetime and after his death was
used by the government of India on a commemorative stamp. The
night he died Jawaharlal Nehru in a moving broadcast said, "the
light has gone out of our lives and there is darkness everywhere."
His death rites were celebrated in every corner of India and wherever Indians lived abroad. His ashes were minutely divided and
sent to all parts of the country to be scattered in the rivers and
lakes and so to be mingled with that sacred water by which the
whole land lives. No man in these times, if ever, has commanded
so much affection in India, nor has anyone's death been so deeply
grieved. He was to his countrymen patriot and prophet in one;
after he died it was a fear of his closest associates that he might
be translated into a deity.

Mohandas Karamchand Gandhi was born in 1869. His father
was an officer in a small seaside state in the peninsula of Kathiawar, about 300 miles north of Bombay. His education was frag-
mentary, but had its climax when he went to England, where he
studied law and was admitted to the bar. On his return to India
he spent several years in an unsuccessful effort to launch a practice, then suddenly went to South Africa on business. He at once
became interested in the social problems of the Indians living there,
who suffered from severe disabilities imposed by the whites, and

he led a strong struggle in their behalf, which in 1914 had at last, but misleadingly, seemed to be successful.

When World War I broke out, he returned to India. He at first helped the government in recruiting, then was disappointed by the government's indifference to Indian rights as he conceived them. He was horrified by the Amritsar tragedy in 1919, and from that time on was the unrelenting opponent of British imperialism in India. He led the Indian National Congress in the civil disobedience, or mass noncooperation, movement in 1920–1922, and ultimately went to jail. In 1924, following an operation for appendicitis, he was released. For several years afterwards he had relatively little part in politics, but in 1928, when the appointment of the Simon Commission on Indian constitutional reform had aroused India, he again took the lead in Congress. In 1930 he organized and directed a second civil disobedience movement, which lasted formally until 1934, and at the beginning of the campaign he dramatized this political protest by organizing and leading a march from his *ashram* (retreat) at Sabarmati to the sea to manufacture salt in violation of the government monopoly and tax. In May of that year he was again arrested. He was released in 1931 to go to London for the Second Round Table Conference on constitutional reform. Within a few days' time after his return to India, he was once more thrown into jail. While in prison in September 1932, he entered upon a "fast unto death" against Prime Minister Ramsay MacDonald's award of separate electorates to the depressed classes and gained his objective. He remained in prison until May 1933, when on the first day of a three weeks' fast meant for his own and his followers' purification he was released. He did not at this time take direct control of Congress again; instead he remained in the background, but his was the dominant voice in Congress affairs.

When World War II broke out, he still did not assume the leadership of Congress. But in September 1940, Congress began another campaign of civil disobedience—this time on an "individual" rather than mass basis—which he led. He was the consultant of Congress negotiators concerning the British war cabinet's proposals of March 9, 1942, known as the "Cripps Offer," which Congress rejected. On August 9, 1942, the day after Congress passed a "Quit India" resolution, he was again put in jail, and was held until May 6, 1944, when, seriously ill, he was released. He was after this time the chief figure on the Congress side in the negotiations between it, the Muslim League, and the British government, leading finally to the grant of independence and the partition of India in August 1947. In the riots between Hindus and Muslims preceding this double event he endeavored to restore harmony and peace, especially by visiting the most disturbed areas in Bengal. After independence, when killings and other violence took place in both India and Pakistan, he pleaded for mutual tolerance. In January 1948 he engaged in a fast for the cessation of communal hostility, and, many people also believe, to persuade the government of India to pay to Pakistan sums due it, according to agreement, from the balances of the government of undivided India. A few days later, on January 30, 1948, he was assassinated by a fanatical champion of orthodox Hinduism.

Like many another great man, Gandhi had an easy simplicity. Spare of body, thin of leg and arm, with shaven head, his features plain, wearing no clothes but a simple white lower garment that set off strongly the dark brown of his skin, seated crosslegged on the low platform of a bare, whitewashed hall, lecturing in monotonous tones to middle-aged peasants on fertilizers and animal husbandry; or sitting in his tiny workroom before a spinning wheel, which he would turn with one hand while he fed the cotton with the other, its scratchy whir now rasping across the conversation, now jarring as with irregular and irritating frequency the thread would break and the turning stop—he was not a personally impressive figure. Nor did he try to be; farmer and weaver he called himself. And he denied that he was worthy of the title Mahatma.

A biographer trying to appraise Gandhi's character can find a wealth of significant detail in the revelations he makes of his sex life and his statements concerning sex problems, in his love of abasing himself as a scavenger, and his guilt feeling for comparatively trivial lapses from his standards, in his early fear of ghosts, of the dark, and of other bugaboos, in his susceptibility as a young man to social disapproval. One can easily relate these to the vows of celibacy, the self-mortification through fasts, the renunciation of worldly pleasures, which he imposed upon himself and the inmates of his retreat. Or, again, one may see a connection between his youthful experiences with whites, when his all too sensitive spirit was injured by their arrogance, and his difficulty in later life in coming to an understanding with British officials. So, too, one may study closely the inconsistencies in his personality, as when he recruited for the British army, though he was an avowed opponent of even the mildest violence, let alone the bloodshed a soldier must cause; or as when in 1920 he stated in an open letter to the Englishmen in India that the unarmed Indians must adopt the weapon of nonviolence because of "our incapacity to fight in open and honorable battle," though at other times he spoke constantly of nonviolence as the only weapon he could ever conscientiously advocate.

Gandhi was first of all a religious genius, and his basic objectives were morally oriented. When he led the struggle for self-rule (*swaraj*) and later preached universal uplift (*sarvodaya*) as the social ideal, and land gift (*bhudan, bhoodan*) by the rich to the landless, he did so that India might achieve her moral destiny. Every kind of human activity, social, political, commercial, or other, he felt should spring from a religious motive, no sanctions were ultimately valid except those of religion. The religion he professed was undeviatingly Hinduism, yet that type of Hinduism which tolerates all shades of opinion in others and is relativistic in its attitude toward human ability to comprehend truth: we are all, except for the rare one in ten million—or a billion—only seekers of truth; we have not found it, and dogmatic certainty is becoming to no one. He said, "Personally I do not regard any of the great religions of the world as false," and he frequently spoke in the highest terms of the Sermon on the Mount. What he asked was that he might draw from other faiths provided he did not have to submit to proselytism. Thus there was much in his personal belief that had parallels in western creeds along with much that had not, as when with his monotheism, faith in mystical realization of God, belief in the moral spiritual value of physical suffering, and reliance upon the human will, he clung staunchly to the doctrines of rebirth, of *karma* that gives scope to the human will and thus determines the conditions of rebirth, of caste that allots a man his proper status in life, of protection for the sacred cow, that "poem of pity," wherein man recognizes his eternal kinship with the animal creation.

His great strength in religion lay on the practical side, in applied ethics, the principles of conduct which he advocated and the means of fulfilling them. There, too, he was profoundly Hindu and humanitarian. The vows of those who came to live in his retreat,

always known as an *ashram,* included truthfulness; *ahinsa,* that is
noninjury of living creatures, whether by word, deed, or thought;
the practice of labor; celibacy; restraint of desire for savory food;
nonthieving, carried to the extreme of not owning more than one
can use; patronage of one's native industries to the exclusion of
foreign; fearlessness; amelioration of the lot of the Untouchables·
the use of native Indian languages for education; the wearing of
homespun cloth. These practices were to cleanse and enlarge the
lives of those observing them and to be a guide to other Indians.
Their combined purpose was to work the regeneration of India, a
return to a golden, if mythical, past.

In the application of these principles he long labored with an
unswerving intensity and he contributed much to India's social
improvement. The campaign he waged against untouchability,
which reached its climax in his "fast unto death" in September
1932, was the most spectacular of the many efforts made by Indians in that direction and should be regarded as the most influential force in producing in India's present constitution the
clause which says "untouchability is abolished." He was deeply
concerned with the conditions of India's peasantry. Cottage spinning and weaving, advocated by him, have, where tried, at times
been mildly helpful in temporarily alleviating rural economic
misery. He taught a "new system of education" (*nai talim*) for
India in which learning was coupled with the practice of a trade,
and this had some practical advantage to his country. He was not,
it happened, very sophisticated in respect to exploitation of labor
in modern industry, but took an ideal mid-Victorian attitude on
relations of employer and employees. Subsidiary items of his pro
gram, such as prohibition of alcohol and narcotics, are today parts
of the law, in one form or another, of many large states in India.

Some phases of this program seemed strange to non-Indians, for
example, patronage of home industries to the degree he advocated.
If you live in Madras, and "a man comes from Bombay and offers
you wares, you are not justified in supporting the Bombay merchant so long as you have got a merchant at your very door, born
and bred in Madras." The quality of the goods offered does not
signify. "In your village you are bound to support your village
barber to the exclusion of the finished barber who may come to
you from Madras."

The underlying basis of Gandhi's social and political program was simple. "My uniform experience," he says in his autobiography, "has convinced me that there is no other God than Truth. And if every page of these chapters does not proclaim that the only means for the realization of Truth is Ahinsa, I shall deem all my pains in writing these chapters to have been in vain." And again, "To see the universal and all-pervading Spirit of Truth face to face one must be able to love the meanest of creatures as oneself. And a man who aspires after that cannot afford to keep out of any field of life. That is why my devotion to truth has drawn me into the field of politics; and I can say without the slightest hesitation and yet in all humility that those who say that religion has nothing to do with politics do not know what religion means."

The application of these principles was as follows. India, and for that matter the world at large, was in bondage to evil as the result of departure from the pure teachings of religion. In India the disease, he said, showed itself in many symptoms, of which subservience to a foreign power was only one; others of major importance were the Hindu-Muslim antipathy, the social crime of untouchability, the poverty of the masses. The cure was to be spiritual regeneration, religious reform; if this were accomplished, all the unhappy features of modern Indian life would automatically vanish. What remained, then, was to determine what things were false and what were true, and it was here that "nonviolence," that is, noninjury of other creatures, came into association with truth. Says the Sanskrit, *ahinsa paramo dharmah* (nonviolence is the highest religion), adding that on this point the scriptures, though frequently at variance in other respects, are unanimous. Gandhi agreed fully when he remarked, "I am fascinated by the law of love. It is the philosopher's stone for me. I know Ahinsa alone can provide a remedy for our ills."

It was the preoccupation with *ahinsa* that was primarily responsible for Indians' esteem for Gandhi. It was not so much his acceptance of bare poverty, weighty as that was—others who had done so had not the same popularity; and one who had not accepted such poverty, Jawaharlal Nehru, was second only to Gandhi in the affections of India. Neither was it his individual political, social, and economic views, with which large numbers of his ardent admirers were in greater or less disagreement. Nor was it the mere fact that he was sincerely devoted to religion, for so were many other Indians. But it was his precise interpretation of the essence of religion that won response from his fellow countrymen, and the fact that he provided a channel for action in keeping with traditional Hindu ideals. The Hindu really believes in the doctrine of *ahinsa,* though through poverty, custom, lack of imagination, or mere human frailty he may often fail to practice it, and in making an idol of Mahatma Gandhi he revealed his own deepest self.

Being a man of strong feelings and deep concern for life about him, Gandhi was no slavish logician. The doctrine of noninjury as enunciated by him should lead to an absolute refusal to harm any creature for the sake of one's own interest, and this is the conclusion of that doctrine in Buddhist and Jain scripture. Gandhi, more practical, drove monkeys from his retreat in Sabarmati, though only after painful soul-searching, and had a suffering calf killed.

That India trusted Gandhi was due, next to his promulgation of *ahinsa,* to the completeness of his ascetic and religious life. If nothing else would have gripped the imagination of Indians, his fasts and his hunger strikes would, being ancient and honored Indian practices. Similarly the habit of silence, which he observed every Monday, is true to the equally ancient Hindu notion that a sage seeking truth can find it only through concentrated silent meditation: a common Sanskrit word for "silence" is *mauna,* which means literally "quality of an ascetic" (*muni*). At the same time Gandhi did not strain the intellect of the masses with ideas that were difficult to comprehend or were revolutionary of the Hindu tradition. He accepted the old dogmas in principle; he wanted only to modify them in application. The terms designating them were symbols for the old forms of the ideas, which the people at large felt to be valid, and also for the new forms, which he gave them, and thus the folk and he had a measure of mutual understanding. And lacking the freedom of the artist that so often arouses distrust in the general public, he had the self-confident strength of the puritan. He spoke to the people simply, forcefully, and on issues of prime importance, while his sincerity was coupled with a personal charm that made his propagandizing a work of genius.

So much freedom from conservatism and traditional prejudice was offensive to strict orthodox upper-caste Hinduism. Throughout his career Gandhi was subject to denunciation from such elements. At various times and in different parts of India he was met on his travels with open hostility and sometimes violence from those who disapproved of him. It was finally one such person, belonging to disaffected orthodoxy, who assassinated him.

Possibly the greatest contribution which Gandhi gave to nationalism, greater even than his convincing justification of its aims, was a philosophy of resistance on which he developed a practical technique of revolution. This was his political mass use of nonviolence. Though this abstract principle had an ancient and honorable tradition in India, it had never before been applied on a concrete national scale to achieve a broad political end. He persuaded Congress to adopt it, in spite of misgivings and disbelief among many Congressmen. To see how it operated we may look at a simple, uncomplicated average case of a sort that attracted no special notice in the press when it occurred but shows nonviolent resistance in typical application.

At Jubbulpore (Jabalpur) early in January 1932, Congress sympathizers attempted a parade and, when ordered by police to disperse, merely halted, squatted on the roadway, filling it from edge to edge, and refused to move. The police charged and beat them with *lathis*, which are wooden staves, six to eight feet in length, shod at one end with metal. The demonstrators offered no resistance, but submitted to the beating without retaliation, and, still without offering violence, let themselves be bundled off by the hundreds to jail. In 1920–1922 and again in 1930–1932 scenes of this sort were common all over India. Often a demonstration would be preceded by a closing of shops for a one or more days' cessation of business (*hartal*). Arrests were inevitable and so numerous that the government had to set up many special detention camps and confinement quarters to care for the prisoners. It was a form of conflict that left the victorious government embarrassed and shamefaced. Though nonviolent resistance seemed to fail in each single case, in the end it produced an atmosphere in which the government appeared to act illogically, inhumanly, indefensibly.

Gandhi's method differed from any used by his nationalist predecessors. Some of these had proceeded secularly and opportunistically, with no consciously rationalized philosophy of resistance, employing only argument and debate. Most early Congressmen were of this sort. They were for change through constitutional means, by "evolution rather than revolution," and their method was to use persuasion upon the British in the hope that well-reasoned claims would meet with success. This was the method of Gokhale;

it was the method used as recently as 1945 by the Indian Moderates or Liberals such as Sis Tej Bahadur Sapru, Srinivasa Sastri, and Dr. Mukund Ramrao Jayakar. It never got effective response from the British. Such men had the respect of thoughtful Indians for their patriotism, honesty, and political sagacity, but the masses rarely if ever heard of them, acquired no confidence in their method, and never gave them popular support.

Some others of Gandhi's predecessors invoked a religious sanction, but not that of religion in its compassionate, nonviolent mood. Rather, it was that of religion when it uncompromisingly strikes down an opponent with physical force. The most noteworthy of these was B. G. Tilak. The god of Tilak and his school was no more shocked by violence than was Jesus, when he said "I came not to send peace, but a sword." The precise means of attacking the infidel foreigner they borrowed from Russian terrorists, who adopted the pistol and the bomb; the bomb was greeted by Tilak as an "amulet" for India. There followed a long list of political murders in eastern, western, and northern India down to the time of Gandhi's assassination in January 1948. With this violence became associated, especially in Bengal, worship of the Mother Goddess, under the locally popular form of Kali, who is to be appeased by blood, and the victims of assassination were her sacrifices. The Mother Goddess is perhaps the oldest of all existing cults in India, being known to us from the Harappa culture in the third millennium B.C., and in her service young political radicals often showed a marked degree of physical courage and selfless religious devotion.

Political murder added unto itself robbery with the purpose of securing funds for prosecuting nationalist aims. Such terrorism gave the government its chief grounds for refusing to negotiate with the nationalists. Though the Indian National Congress as a whole did not endorse this violence, many of its members were sympathetic and condoned it. Even during Gandhi's period of leadership, after every such murder there was discussion in Congress, and usually a resolution was passed which deplored the use of violence but at the same time lauded the perpetrator for his patriotic motive. These equivocal pronouncements show that even in the years of Gandhi's leadership violence had not been repudiated by most Congressmen on moral grounds but lay just under the surface of the revolutionary movement. On many occasions when

Gandhi's nonviolent campaign seemed futile, Congressmen pressed for the use of violence.

Gandhi's method of nonviolent action to produce change was not the same as passive resistance, which it was often called in the West. He himself repudiated the latter term. Those using his method were not merely to be resisting some evil; they must be striving for some positive constructive end. And they were not just to submit and suffer; this would have been negative. Rather, they were to take positive action against their injurers. The action, however, was to be without the use of violent physical force, and was to employ only force of the spirit. In extreme circumstances they could abandon mere persuasion and employ strike, cessation of business activity, noncooperation, civil disobedience. The method was an outgrowth of Gandhi's own philosophy, and was a fusion of ideas derived from various sources: Tolstoi, Jesus in the Sermon on the Mount, and above all certain tenets of Hinduism. His total philosophy, being meant to accomplish the regeneration of the individual in a state organized to promote spiritual values, advocated an individual and national life of simplicity and self-denial. It included a theory of rulership by rulers who do the minimum of ruling. It demanded abstention from violence toward all human beings, and a corresponding practice toward them of invariable loving kindness. The word which Gandhi used for his method was *satyagraha*, a compound of two Sanskrit words—*satya* "truth" and *agraha* "steadfast grasping"—the two meaning "stubborn adherence to Truth." Gandhi translated it freely as "Soul-Force." He taught that in a "battle of righteousness" it was self-contradictory to employ violence, which was the antithesis of Truth; the only proper, and in the end the only effective, weapon was the power of righteousness inherent in the cause.

The conduct of the struggle was to be fundamentally in the hand of God. The method is one for the weak who are being oppressed by the strong. "Only when he has come to the extreme point of weakness and finds utter darkness all around him, only then God comes to the rescue. God helps, when a man feels humbler than the very dust under his feet. Only to the weak and helpless is the divine succor vouchsafed."

To Gandhi and his followers, the important elements in practicing *satyagraha* were the following: faith in God, a just cause, helplessness, a pure and humble heart. The leaders of such a campaign must begin by purifying themselves. Their intention must be single; they must "adopt poverty, follow truth, cultivate fearlessness"; they "have to observe perfect chastity," and besides denying sex must abstain from all other pleasures of the flesh; they may, perhaps, fast. None of their energy is to be dissipated in ends other than the main one. When the leaders are prepared, the community must observe the same vows and take a solemn oath not to submit to the injustice against which they are protesting; rather they must endure all penalties for refusal. They must, however, bear no hatred against the legislators, the police, and the jailers who oppress them. They must fill their hearts with warm love for these opponents. In the struggle they will suffer; let them be glad to do so. The suffering purifies their own souls, and at the same time becomes a force which mystically operates to their advantage, softening the hearts of their oppressors. With their love, too, they suffuse their opponents until at last a counter love is generated in the once hard hearts. And they must ever be ready to modify their demands when reason is shown for doing so; they must be open to the arguments advanced by the other side. If the community endures unflinchingly, it must eventually triumph. But it triumphs, not by humiliating the opponents, but by bringing to them such a love that they will see that their own happiness as well as that of the community exercising Soul-Force is best served by granting justice. They will be converted. The solution, in theory, will come as a free and joyous gift, dictated by reason and love. Thus Truth shall conquer.

That many of Gandhi's associates never believed in this method with the conviction that was Gandhi's is certain. Some openly opposed it and asked for measures of violence. Some others frankly admitted that they adhered to nonviolence only because they lacked arms. Many political leaders regarded *satyagraha* not as a means of practicing religion but as an opportune way of getting a mass of people to act in disciplined unity for a political end. They had no faith in mystical direction by God and the attainment of victory through the inherent power of Truth. Many, too, among the masses whom Gandhi persuaded to use *satyagraha* did so from opportunism rather than conviction. The bloody wholesale killings at the time of partition showed this and were the great disillusionment of Gandhi's life. To the end he preached *satyagraha*, but in those last months in Delhi, when with hardly intelligible words he spoke his thoughts in his evening prayer meetings, the old fire and confidence seemed to be gone.

The opportunists, however, were not the only ones who marched behind Gandhi. There were close associates who did share his philosophy, and so did, in a simple way, many of the uneducated masses. For his method drew from an ancient and honored metaphysic in India that concerns the very nature of truth. In quite early times truth (*satya*) became invested with magic power. In the *Rig Veda* Truth is identical with the cosmic order, and whatever conforms to it is right and belongs to the created and organized universe, while anything violating it is Untruth and is of the region of chaos where demons dwell. Every creature, man or god, has in Vedic thought his function in the universe, and for him Truth consists in fulfilling that function.

This idea underlies the later Hindu doctrine that the different castes ideally have different specific fixed functions, and their members should fulfill those alone, refraining from others. "Better," says the *Bhagavad Gita*, "to do one's own duty poorly than another's duty well." In this connection there existed in ancient India the concept of a ceremonial Act of Truth (*satyakriya*), which was a solemn asseveration of the complete perfection with which the declarer fulfilled his duty in the cosmic scheme. If in this respect his conduct was flawless, he had attained Truth itself, he had reached his highest goal, achieved his *summum bonum*. He had become one with the universe, and in becoming one had acquired a special power in it, even over it, for it was himself. He could by the formal asseveration of his Truth execute the Truth Act by which he could work what we would call miracles.

Many are the stories in Hindu, Buddhist, and Jain literature illustrating this theme. Righteous kings, pious ascetics, future world saviors, faithful wives, a wide range of other types, accomplish marvelous results. The Truth Act is not confined to persons whose life work conforms to normal social ethics. In the world are persons born to pursue an antisocial calling, which is however needed in the cosmic blend like the drop of bitters in a cocktail, and one of them too may win the power if he follows his calling with 100 percent perfection. In the case of Gandhi's *satyagraha*, the justice of the cause and the completeness of adherence to it were similarly to provide a basis for magical—or mystical—accomplishment. The age-old Hindu confidence that Truth will prevail, so vividly dramatized in Gandhi's *satyagraha* campaigns, is now illustrated in India's national motto adopted since independence, *satyam eva jayate,* which in Sanskrit means "Truth alone is victorious."

Another element in Gandhi's *satyagraha* that had analogues in ancient India was persistence in enduring suffering for the sake of righteousness. This means not merely to undergo asceticism for achieving spiritual perfection. That feature did indeed enter in. But there was also submission to injury from one's opponent or the infliction of self-injury in his name that is a part of *satyagraha* and is also of ancient status in India. There is a custom in India known as "sitting *dharna,*" that is, of sitting in obstruction before the housedoor of one who has injured you. This especially includes fasting, which may be continued unto death if the grievance is not redressed. Frequently, of course, such fasting is only a hunger strike and would not qualify as *satyagraha;* rather it is stubborn or malicious persistence (*duragraha*). The custom of threatening suicide by starvation or some other means to obtain a just demand is a powerful weapon, with a peculiar efficacy lying in the belief that if the faster should die, his death would be a sin, punishable by Heaven, charged to the account of the person against whom the fast was directed.

When Gandhi entered upon his fasts for social and political ends he was utilizing this powerful means of coercion. His opponents must in many cases have feared the consequences upon their own otherworldly future. But whether they did or not, the Hindu public saw in the fast an affirmation of just purpose, certified by Gandhi's willingness to starve to death if necessary, and a corresponding presumptive evil on the part of the opposition. If Gandhi had died in one of his fasts, those against whom the fast was directed would probably have been ruined both politically and socially. In the theory of *satyagraha* there is an added element, also abundantly attested in Indian legend, which translated Gandhi's practice from the level of sitting *dharna* to a higher sphere. This is the idea that disinterested love for an antagonist, persisting in the face of fierce assault, will accomplish conversion.

In *satyagraha* Gandhi adapted these various long-established notions to use by a group. This was a contribution of genius. With the use of *satyagraha* planned by capable leaders and directed in action by trained lieutenants called "volunteers," Gandhi transformed nationalist political protest from a middle class agitation to a mass movement. Though the agricultural and industrial masses had little if any comprehension of the political or moral ends involved, they supported the campaign because of its religious content and the hope of remedying immediately and concretely their present economic distress. They were induced in consequence to make a political alliance with the professional and business bourgeoisie.

There was also a practical point that had nothing to do with religion. Indians could not hope to resist the British by force of arms. Gandhi himself, as we saw above, acknowledged this as a contributory reason for adopting *satyagraha*. Similarly in 1942, when the Japanese had overrun Burma and the British seemed to Indians powerless against them, Gandhi urged the British to quit India and let the Indians face the Japanese with *satyagraha* as their defense. It would be, he maintained, a weapon for the weaponless against which arms could not compete.

After Gandhi introduced *satyagraha* in India, a number of campaigns were conducted successfully with its aid. In 1917 the peasants in the Champaran district in Bihar persisted in refusing to plant three twentieths of their acreage in the, to them, hated and unprofitable indigo for the sake of the landowning planters until finally a commission appointed by the government affirmed the justice of their contention. Another instance was at Khaira (Kaira, Kheda) in Gujarat in 1918, when Gandhi led the peasants in a struggle to have a subnormal crop declared low enough to justify suspension of taxation for the year. Another celebrated case took place in 1928 in the Bardoli *taluq* (small administrative unit) in Gujarat, where reassessment of land for purposes of taxation was undertaken by the government. The new assessments were considered by the peasants to be too high. They refused to pay and were ejected from their homes; their lands were sold for a song at auction; there were fines, beatings, jail sentences. The peasants stubbornly continued their refusal, yet refrained from violence. At last the government had to appoint a new commission, which reported in general in their favor.

Gandhi's method of resistance obviously put mysticism into the nationalist struggle. To him British rule was wrong, as was the rule of any people over another; it was, in his word, "satanic." Whatever may have been the constitutional and economic issues of imperialism, they were in his eyes less than this issue of religion. But further, from the viewpoint of nationalism struggling against imperialism, his method was justified. It won mass support, when no other method had been able to do so, and by doing so contributed materially to final success. It also contributed to the peacefulness with which the transfer of power finally took place in 1947. The relative lack of violence on the nationalist side, joined with the normal British tendency to avoid extremes, let reason operate more generally than could have been foreseen in 1922, 1932, or even in 1942.

In his own major purpose Gandhi may be considered to have failed. His aim was the religious regeneration of India and Indians. As success for nationalism became step by step more likely, the politicians slipped out more and more from his control. They had no faith in the ultimate value of his religious purpose, as he had none in the ultimate worth of any purely secular end. He had said that he made a religious use of politics; many a politician of the time, if frank, would have admitted that he, in his turn, was making a political use of religion. Gandhi's own principle of nonviolence appeared to go finally into political discard at the same time as did India's political subservience to Britain. He is venerated today by word wherever the voice of the politician is heard in the land; the wearing of homespun *khaddar* which he advocated is the mark of the Congressman holding or seeking public office; but his own dearest principle lies rusty and neglected in the political armory.

Even more, though Gandhi abhorred Hindu-Muslim communalism and partition, he nevertheless contributed to them. He could not in his time have become the political leader of the majority group in India, fortified by mass support, without being religious. He could not be religious without being Hindu. He could not be Hindu without being suspect to the Muslim community.

Sometimes, too, nonviolence seemed to have no, or at least little, influence in foreign relations. For with independence came also partition, when bloodshed was the order of the day, and India and Pakistan all but went to war in the months immediately following. Afterwards in the international field India was regularly a peacemaker between East and West, and played an important part in negotiations inside the United Nations and outside, when she herself was not directly involved in the conflict. Even in her quarrels she endeavored to observe nonviolence, most notably in Nehru's policy of the five principles (*panchsheel*) of peaceful coexistence in his treaty with China concerning Tibet in 1954, shattered by the Himalayan conflict when it became an undeclared war in 1962. Whatever other considerations may also have swayed Nehru to formulate that policy, the old doctrines about nonviolence and truth, and their preaching by Gandhi, helped to bring India's policies support among Indians at large.

Gandhi's economic preachings were palliative, not curative. The future building-up of India is not possible merely in his terms of village cottage industry, home spinning and weaving, land gift. Industrial expansion he viewed unsympathetically. Nor did he understand the relation of labor's troubles to national well-being. His message was one from the past, an ancient and great India reasserting itself. Once independence was won, some other leader with a different outlook, a philosophy of modernism, was needed to direct India's life in the middle of the twentieth century, and India had him at hand in Nehru.

6 The Winning of Independence

After the Amritsar Massacre in April 1919 there was no going back for nationalism. Its purpose hardened; the people were in a mood to support it; a leader was at hand with a practical method of revolt. The industrialists had been encouraging a boycott of British manufactures in favor of *swadeshi,* "home-made" goods, especially textiles, which constituted India's greatest industry. This gave Indian industry a stake in nationalism and predisposed it to underwrite the nationwide agitation that was soon to commence under Gandhi and Congress.

At this time India's labor movement was instigating industrial strikes and so helping to create disturbances which handicapped the government in maintaining law and order. Peasant movements were active against landlords and had the sympathetic interest of political personages, among whom was the young Jawaharlal Nehru. Both kinds of movements were ready to hand for the uses of nationalism. Muslims, too, were for the time being available to help because of their discontent over the Khilafat issue.

Nationalists were divided as to the best way to treat the new constitution of 1919. Some favored full cooperation, accepting in good faith Parliament's statement that it was only experimental and after ten years would be superseded by another with terms dependent upon the condition, necessities, and powers of India at that time. Others were in favor of complete boycott. Still others preferred partial noncooperation. Congress after consideration chose first the method of full noncooperation, under the direction of Gandhi, in a movement which started in 1920.

Led by Gandhi, Congress boycotted the first elections under the new constitution, forsook the courts, deserted the government colleges, and refrained from buying European imports, especially cotton goods, which they hoped to replace with handmade Indian cloth that would provide work for many starving Indians. Many prominent Indians, including the poet Rabindranath Tagore, resigned British titles, though Tagore himself thought the noncooperation movement too narrow in its practical program to accomplish results of permanent value. Civil disobedience, as by not paying taxes, was to be the climax if the British did not yield. During 1921 most of the Congress leaders were thrown in jail. The Congress boycott was by no means a complete success since other groups took part in the elections and provincial governments were established. But the campaign, for the first time in the history of nationalism, succeeded in getting outside the cities and reaching the countryside and the villagers. From then on nationalism used the agrarian problem as a major issue.

As the movement spread, many of Gandhi's followers, thinking nonviolence had now served its purpose, wanted to use physical force. The government had fixed gathering points for Europeans in case a revolution broke out; all military precautions had been taken. The nationalists awaited only the word of Gandhi to proclaim full civil disobedience and so inaugurate an uprising. This he was to give unless the volunteers who had been arrested were released from prison and the imperialist repression stopped. Both Indians and British expected that word at any moment.

But it never came. And the reason it did not come was a religious one. Gandhi was in earnest when he said that the first requisite for the individual citizen and the nation was the self-control to observe *ahinsa*, "nonviolence." As his movement came more and more to draw in those whose basic motive was political, not religious, he became disillusioned. There were attacks in rural districts on the licensed liquor shops, and he was glad of the hatred shown for strong drink, but he abhorred the violence. When riots occurred in Bombay at the time of the Prince of Wales' visit in 1921, he deplored the bloodshed. Finally, a notorious affair at Chauri Chaura (February 4, 1922) in the United Provinces (now Uttar Pradesh), where a mob led by noncooperator "volunteers" burned and beat to death twenty-two Indian policemen, convinced him that civil disobedience could not be put into effect without an accompaniment of bloodshed occasioned by his own followers. He would not run the moral risk, no matter what the prospect of political success. He felt that he had been warned from heaven; he withheld his word; the crisis passed. His supporters in their turn were disillusioned and discouraged by losing the opportunity to strike;

the high pitch of revolutionary enthusiasm quickly fell. Gandhi was sent to jail, after a dramatic trial in which he took upon himself the responsibility for all the violence that his followers had perpetrated.

But noncooperation, as directed by Gandhi, had achieved certain striking results for nationalism. It had shown that Indians could unite—much to the surprise of Indians and British alike—that nationalism could get mass support, and that there lay in nonviolent resistance a weapon of tremendous possibilities. It also prompted respect among the British, and induced a greater spirit of conciliation. At the same time it spurred the government to seek allies among the Untouchables by appointing representatives for them in the legislative councils, among the business interests by granting tariffs and other concessions, among the Muslims by observing communal representation in making administrative appointments.

Out of the noncooperation movement was born the Swaraj (or Swarajya) party, aiming at quick attainment of dominion status, which under Chitta Ranjan Das (1870–1925) of Bengal and Motilal Nehru, father of Jawaharlal, held the center of the nationalist stage for several years until Das's death. Das's method was that of partial noncooperation and was aimed at the fundamental weakness of the system of dyarchy established by the new constitution. His party was to capture as many as possible of the elective seats in the legislative bodies, where the elected representatives were to make their demands. If these were met, well and good; but it was self-evident that they would be refused, and then the representatives were to noncooperate by opposing all government measures. The scheme was foolproof, for the legislative bodies were not finally responsible for the government; the responsibility rested with the British-appointed governors, who had the power to enact by certification any legislation they thought necessary that had been refused by the councils.

The Swarajists were successful in some of the provincial legislative councils, thus compelling the government to certify measures repudiated by the people's elected representatives. In the central Legislative Assembly the Swarajists, in combination with members of other parties, in 1924 succeeded in throwing out important parts of the budget, but the upper chamber, the Council of State, where the majority of seats were occupied by government nominees and official members, restored it, saving the government's face. So, too, the Legislative Assembly in 1925, at the challenge of the Secretary of State for India, once adopted by a vote of 72 to 45 a constitutional program moved by Pandit Motilal Nehru, but the upper chamber again saved the government's position by rejecting it. The Swaraj party added to the lesson of the noncooperation movement by teaching India the effectiveness of parliamentary procedure as a weapon for nationalism.

During the years following Gandhi's imprisonment in 1922 other matters of note occurred. In 1923, to balance the budget, the government proposed to double the tax on salt. The nationalists directed a campaign against this measure in the Legislative Assembly and defeated it, but the Governor general restored the proposed tax by his power of certification. Terrorism broke out again in Bengal, and in 1925 a repressive ordinance was promulgated along the lines of the Rowlatt Act. Under it many persons were arrested, some of whom were not released until as late as 1928. In 1930 the nationalists, under Gandhi, used the salt tax as the object of one of their most dramatic demonstrations; and in 1931 the government turned again to ruling by ordinance.

In the Punjab the government in the early 1920s became involved in a struggle between the aggressive puritanical revivalist division of the Sikhs known as Akalis and certain other elements of that community which were in possession of rich Sikh temples. The Akalis demanded that the shrines be turned over to them as the only true Sikhs, and charged the incumbents with licentious living, irreligion, and misuse of temple funds. The mahants (abbots) of the shrines refused, and the Akalis marched, nonviolently, to take possession. At one shrine the mahant in 1921 organized a massacre of Akalis; at others there were lesser but more prolonged disturbances. It was impossible for the government to remain outside the struggle, and in taking part it was automatically committed to support the mahants, who though morally wrong were in legal possession. Then in 1923 one of the Sikh princes, ruler of the state of Nabha, was forced by the government to abdicate for maladministration. The Akalis looked upon the government's action as a blow to the Sikh community, demanded the restoration of the prince, and endeavored to hold religious exercises in a great demonstration at a shrine within the borders of the Nabha state. Five hundred Sikhs in February 1924 marched there and were met at the border by troops; they were dispersed with rifle fire, and many were killed. Successive pilgrimages followed every two weeks, and the pilgrims were arrested, until no less than 14,000 had gone to jail. At last, in 1926, matters were adjusted. The Akalis got most of their demands, though the deposed prince was not restored and in 1928 was even stripped of his title. Since that time, the Akalis have been the effective arm of Sikh nationalism, which from shortly before partition agitated for a separate political entity, whether nation or province, to be known as Sikhistan.

During this period anti-Indian legislation in Kenya, British East Africa, was creating intense indignation in India. In 1927 the government of India protested to the home government in London, and there was much nonofficial agitation in India. This intra-Empire discrimination against Indians fed the nationalist rancor against white rule.

Meanwhile, the temporary alliance between Hindus and Muslims had broken down. In 1921–1922 a backward and fanatical Muslim group known as the Moplahs (Mappila), living along the southwest (Malabar) coast of India, a people periodically notorious since 1836 for violent anti-Hindu activity, undertook to convert Hindus forcibly, with the result that the government had to intervene. This affair ended the Hindu-Muslim alliance except for the association of a handful of political leaders. When Congress organized a boycott against the Prince of Wales in 1921, communal riots occurred in connection with it. From time to time local hostilities broke out between the two communities in other parts of India. Casualties ran into the thousands.

In southern India the non-Brahman elements of the Hindu community were becoming actively hostile toward the Brahmans, and the Justice party representing the non-Brahmans captured power. It, with the somewhat older Liberal party, leaned toward the British hold, and was providing a diversion from Congress nationalists.

In 1927 the fire of nationalism blazed up again. The immediate occasion was the appointment by the British government of an Indian Statutory Commission headed by Sir John Simon to propose the next stages in constitutional reform that had been foreshadowed in the Government of India Act of 1919. When the personnel of the commission, seven in number, was announced, India experienced a great disappointment. For not a single Indian had been included, and India took the omission as an insult.

The British government was unwilling to enlarge the Simon

Commission by appointing any Indian members. The commission itself later invited advice from Indians and asked the various legislative councils to appoint commissions to meet with it, but this did not mollify the nationalists, and two of the eleven legislative bodies refused the invitation. The Simon Commission found its official welcome from the government offset by general popular suspicion, *hartals* (cessation of business activity), strikes, frequent boycott, monster meetings of protest, and other unfavorable demonstrations, including attempted violence.

Violence was, indeed, common, especially in the Punjab. At a demonstration in Lahore the elderly nationalist leader Lajpat Rai was beaten by the police, and a few weeks later died. His physician diagnosed his illness as heart trouble, but many nationalists ascribed it to the beating, and the young English lieutenant of police who had been in charge at the scene of the beating was murdered as an act of reprisal. In April 1929 bombs were thrown into the central Legislative Assembly in Delhi while it was in session.

When the Indian National Congress met during Christmas week, 1928, Gandhi, now back in politics with full vigor, announced that unless the wishes of Congress were met by January 1, 1930, he would call upon India to resist Britain by the use of general civil disobedience, that is, nonpayment of taxes and other forms of resistance. As the year passed, the threat gained evident sympathy among Indians and appeared to disturb the government. The nationalist demand was for two things: first, full home rule, either with complete independence or with dominion status; second, a round table conference to frame a new constitution, at which Indian nationalist interests should have their due representation.

The British response came when Governor General Lord Irwin (later Lord Halifax and British ambassador to the United States) made an official declaration on October 31, 1929, in which he first referred to the celebrated pronouncement by E. S. Montagu in 1917 designating full responsible government as India's constitutional goal, and then went on to say that it was "implicit in the declaration of 1917 that the natural issue of India's constitutional progress as there contemplated is the attainment of Dominion Status." He announced that after publication of the Simon Commission's report, a round table conference of British and Indian leaders of all interested groups, including the Indian states, would be called to make constitutional proposals to Parliament. Later he invited Gan-

111

dhi and some other Indian leaders to confer with him and discuss the membership of the conference. These announcements caused acrimonious debate in Parliament and the British press, and this induced serious apprehension in India and gave ammunition to the Congress extremists.

The meeting of the Governor General with Gandhi and other Indian political leaders, held December 23, 1929, was fruitless, chiefly because Gandhi and Pandit Motilal Nehru, the Congress representatives, demanded that dominion status be granted im mediately, and that the proposed round table conference in London have no duty except to frame a constitution bringing it into effect. This was more than the British would concede. The Indian Liberals and most of the minority groups, however, seemed in favor of entering the round table conference, and working out a scheme in cooperation with the princes and the British.

Among the Congress nationalists there was a sudden crystallization of opinion in favor of complete independence, which became a slogan under the Hindi term "Purna Swaraj." This fact became evident at the meeting of Congress immediately after Gandhi's conversation with the Governor General, and a momentous resolution was adopted declaring it.

This time civil disobedience was begun with an attack on the salt tax. This was an ancient levy coming from long before British times. The amount of money it took from the individual was not great, but it was a burden upon the poor. The fight in 1923 against the doubling of it had shown that it was a good target for popular antipathy. Gandhi organized a march of protesting nationalists from his *ashram* at Sabarmati, near the city of Ahmedabad, to Dandi, a tiny fishing village 165 miles distant on the lower east coast of the Gulf of Cambay, there to manufacture salt from the sea water in defiance of the government monopoly. The party, consisting of Gandhi and seventy companions, started on March 12, 1930. Along the way there were demonstrations, followers grew in numbers, and the publicity throughout the world was enormous. Gandhi reached the sea, went through the motions of dipping up water to evaporate in the sun, and made a crude and unpalatable salt. The intrinsic economic value of the product was nothing; the symbolic political value was incalculable.

The second noncooperation movement, like the first in 1920, was meant to boycott government schools and administrative organs, and sellers of liquor, opium, and foreign cloth, which last was to be displaced by homespun cotton *khaddar* or *khadi*. It was supplemented by local refusal to pay taxes, terrorism (in Bengal), and something close to mutiny in Peshawar.

On May 5, 1930, Gandhi was arrested and interned, to be held without trial indefinitely; his chief followers had already been arrested or soon were; and between that time and the end of January 1931, when he was released, somewhere between 40,000 and 60,-000 Indian political offenders were held for greater or less periods in jails and detention camps. In many parts of the country Congress was declared an illegal body. But the demonstrations did not stop. One of the most striking features was the emergence of women in great numbers to take part in the struggle. Labor, with its red flag, joined the Congress, especially in Bombay. Through it all, Gandhi admonished the resisters to abstain from violence.

The First Round Table Conference met in London in the autumn of 1930, consisting of representatives of British and Indian interests nominated by the government. The King opened it; the Indian princes appeared in great splendor; the Muslims and other minorities were represented; the Indian Liberals were present. Only the Congress members were absent. They were in jail. The conference held its sessions, and recommended a general scheme of government, consisting of a federal India, to be loosely organized at the British-controlled center and to allow for divergent systems of administration in the autocratic Indian states and the partly democratic British India, with most matters of importance being left to the internal control of the provinces and states as constituent members of the federation. But no one considered the proposals final; everybody knew that without the cooperation of Congress no scheme could be successful. As soon as the conference was over, the Indian Liberals hurried back to India to persuade Gandhi.

In due time it became evident that a second conference would be necessary, and Gandhi was released from jail that he might discuss participation with Lord Irwin. On March 4, 1931, the two negotiated the Irwin-Gandhi truce; the civil disobedience campaign was suspended (another frustrating experience for nationalism, as had been the suspension of the first civil disobedience movement in 1922, and a puzzle to leaders like Jawaharlal Nehru); political prisoners were released; and negotiations were undertaken about arrangements.

Gandhi was for long undecided whether or not to go. The chief doubt came from his realization that the various Indian elements would not present a solid front, and he was concerned above all about the attitude of the Muslims. At almost the last minute, after considerable changing of his mind back and forth, he decided to go. He went, however, as Congress' sole representative.

The result was failure. The British wanted military, financial, and political safeguards extending over a nondelimited transition period, and this Congress, represented by Gandhi, considered inadmissable. Aside from that fact, the conference was doomed to wreck on the rock of communal discord. Before it came to a close, the representatives of the various minority communities—Muslims, Europeans, Anglo-Indians, Indian Christians, and Depressed Classes (Untouchables)—made a pact directed against Congress and the residual majority which Congress represented. The minorities wanted separate electorates and separate representation; Congress wished a single general electorate. Gandhi unwillingly conceded that the proposal should apply in principle to the Muslims, but could not agree on the number and proportion of representatives, and he refused to consider it at all for the Untouchables. This widened the already existing gap between Congress and the minorities. In the end the conference was adjourned with unfinished business to be transacted by committees in India.

Just as the Second Round Table Conference was coming to a close with failure certain, the government of India issued the first of a series of repressive ordinances. This was an antiterrorist measure for Bengal, where violent political crime had occurred. It was promulgated on November 30, 1931, and gave the government the power to commandeer property, impound bank accounts, conscript specified classes of the population for maintaining law and order, impose collective fines on areas where certain crimes were committed, make arrests without warrants, hold secret trials by special tribunals, try an accused in his absence, give sentences of death or transportation, and waive right of appeal. Other ordinances of a character more or less like this were afterwards published for other parts of the country.

During December 1931, a "no-rent" campaign moved with great force, and its leader, Jawaharlal Nehru, was arrested on December 26. The agitation on the North-West Frontier increased, and Abdul Ghaffar Khan, leader of the Red-Shirts, a Muslim party sympathetic to Congress, was arrested on December 24. Gandhi, returning from the Second Round Table Conference, landed in Bombay on December 29, and within a week, on January 4, 1932, was again taken into custody. On the same day Vallabhbhai Patel, then president of Congress, was arrested. The arrest of others followed by the hundreds and thousands. On April 24, Congress, already outlawed, was to hold a meeting in Delhi. As the delegates prepared to assemble, the government arrested at different points 369 of them, including the poetess Mrs. Sarojini Naidu, acting president of Congress, afterwards governor of the United Provinces (1948–1949), who was on the point of boarding her train in Bombay. It was officially stated by Sir Samuel Hoare, Secretary of State for India, in the House of Commons, on June 27, 1932, that from December 1931 to June 1, 1932, the number of political convictions under the ordinary law and the ordinances totaled 48,576.

At the time when Sir Samuel gave out these figures, he made two announcements which further exacerbated public opinion in India. The first was that the method of round table discussion for constructing a new constitution would be discontinued. The other was that the ordinances, which would have expired at the beginning of July, would be renewed.

On August 16, Ramsay MacDonald, the Prime Minister, announced the government's proposal for solving the communal question, which was to divide the electorate into twelve separate constituencies, thus extending the political communalism which Congress was opposing. Gandhi had foreseen that the government would separate the Depressed Classes from the general (Hindu) constituency, and on September 20, in protest, began a "fast unto death." Eventually he and Dr. B. R. Ambedkar, chief leader of the Depressed Classes, agreed in the "Poona Pact" (September 24, 1932), which gave the Depressed Classes larger representation than had the government's proposal, but eliminated the principle of separate electorates. To nationalism Gandhi's success was highly important, for he prevented an open fissure in the Hindu body politic, which was the field of nationalist activity.

With the cessation in 1934 of the second civil disobedience campaign, Congress entered upon a period of confusion. The campaign collapsed partly because Gandhi withdrew in August 1934 into private, or at least semiprivate, life; partly because the large contributors of funds to Congress were discouraged by the domination of

Gandhi and his, to them, idealistic and impractical program of nonviolent resistance; partly because there was disagreement inside the ranks of Congress between an economically and socially conservative old guard, with which, on the whole, Gandhi cooperated, and a liberal left element, of which the chief spokesman was Jawaharlal Nehru. The liberals came in time to be flanked by a radical violence-minded wing, led by Subhas Chandra Bose (1897–1945). This was not allied to the Communist party in India, which at that time was outlawed, but was motivated rather by Fascist ideology.

Liberal, or socialist, movements were developing in India during those years. The largest of these was among the peasants, whose various organizations came to center in the All-India Kisan Sabha ("Peasants' Association"). This in 1938 claimed over a half a million members, and both Congress and the Communists endeavored to get control of it. Trade unions also expanded, though not to such numbers; in 1938 the All-India Trade Union Congress claimed 325,000. The left elements in Congress in 1934 had created the Congress Socialist party, which confined its membership to members of Congress, and endeavored to win Congress to a program of organizing Indian society on socialist lines. In 1936 Nehru and his associates succeeded in getting Congress to commit itself to an agrarian program.

In the same year Congress had to decide whether to cooperate with the government of India in working the new constitution of 1935, which by that time had been adopted over the head of Congress, just as in Britain it had met at every point the bitter opposition of Conservatives, especially Winston Churchill, who could not brook any abridgment of Britain's imperialism in India and publicly ridiculed Gandhi as a "half-naked fakir."

The new constitution had two main features. One was the grant of autonomy to the eleven principal provinces known as governor's provinces, through ministries fully responsible to elected legislatures (the remaining parts of British India, known as commissioner's provinces, were to have no legislatures or ministries). The other was a provision for federation of the Indian States and the provinces of British India. The first was put in operation in 1937 after elections. The second was never utilized, since the parties to the proposed federation could not agree on specific terms. The new constitution also contained a series of "safeguards" for

British military, financial, and political interests, which were thoroughly distasteful to the nationalists.

Congress contested the elections and won a sweeping victory, gaining approximately 70 percent of the vote cast, a majority of the legislative seats in seven of the eleven governor's provinces, and a plurality in another. The problem for Congress was then whether to accept ministerial offices, since, by the constitution, the governors of the provinces had powers of vetoing and certifying legislation. Eventually a gentleman's agreement was reached by which the governors were to retain these rights but not to exercise them, and Congress then established ministries. It made the mistake of not forming coalition ministries with the Muslim League. Rather it supported homogeneous Congress ministries, admitting to office no Muslims except such as were Congress members, thus offending the Muslim League. Congress was now supreme; its membership was announced by Jawaharlal Nehru at the beginning of 1938 to be 3,000,000 (it had been only 600,000 in 1936), of whom, however, only 100,000, or about 3.3 percent, were Muslims.

The Congress ministries between 1937 and 1939 moved effectively to improve educational and public health conditions, but were slow to act on agrarian reform and the demands of labor. They offended Muslims by some of the legislation they enacted and so helped set the stage for growth of the Muslim League during the war and the promotion of communalism.

Congress opposed the new constitution's scheme of federation of the provinces of British India, which were developing democratic institutions, with the princely Indian States, which were ruled autocratically and were not obliged by the constitution to liberalize themselves. The States were to have a representation proportionately far greater than would have corresponded to their population. The rulers of the States were lukewarm to federation, fearing the spread within their borders of representative institutions. The federation was never effected, and to the end of the British authority the government of India at the center was conducted under the constitution of 1919.

During World War II, the conflict between Indian nationalism and British imperialism reached a new climax. Indian nationalism was ready to support democracy against totalitarianism, but there was a proviso, sometimes openly expressed, always implicit. This was stated by the Working Committee of Congress on September

14, 1939, to be that the struggle should actually be for the maintenance and promotion of democratic ideals, not for the gratification
of national rivalries. If Britain were really fighting for "freedom,"
then, in the eyes of leaders like Gandhi, Nehru, and many others,
the logical accompaniment would be that India should have freedom. Indians used the slogan "freedom is indivisible" to mean that
freedom should not in logic have geographical or color limitations.
The Working Committee of the Muslim League on September 18
adopted a resolution demanding "justice and fair play" for Muslims
in the provinces if they were to support the war, and an assurance
that no constitutional advance for India would be made without
consulting the League.

Not long before the outbreak of hostilities, the British Parliament adopted an act by which, in time of war, the central government of India, functioning under the Governor General, could suspend many provisions of the constitution of 1935 concerning political autonomy. Congress, in consequence, acting through its "high
command," instructed its representatives in the central Legislative
Assembly not to attend the forthcoming session of that body. When
the declaration of war came on September 3, 1939, the Viceroy,
Lord Linlithgow, without consulting the Legislative Assembly, at
once declared India a belligerent. At the same time he suspended
political reform for the duration of the war. In these steps he was
legally correct but tactically at woeful fault, since India was humiliated and her goodwill toward the British cause was chilled.

From this time on the government of India and Congress engaged in a wearying and profitless exchange. Congress professed
itself willing to support the war if India were given self-rule or
promised it definitely at the end of the war. The government would
not commit itself. In October 1939, the Congress high command
ordered the ministries to resign in the seven of India's eleven provinces where Congress had control. Consequently, in these provinces
the governors assumed administrative and legislative powers under
section 93 of the Government of India Act. Thus Congress entered
the wilderness and diminished its bargaining power with the government of India, since the government now had full control of
those provinces.

The Muslim League, which had been growing stronger during
the time the Congress ministries were in office, was demanding
equality of power and position with Congress. When the Congress

ministries resigned, the League celebrated December 22 as "Deliverance Day." M. A. Jinnah, as leader of the League, took the position that the Muslims in India were not a community but a nation, that India was a "two nation" area. Early in 1940 the Viceroy gave assurance that any new constitution would have to receive the approval of the large minorities. The government wished to retain the Muslim ministries in the three provinces where it had a majority and in a fourth where it had been able to form a new ministry with the aid of other minorities, and it succeeded in doing so. The delicate position of the British in their diplomatic relations with the Islamic Near East was an additional incentive to placate the Indian Muslims. The Congress reply was to elect (for the second time) as president a prominent Muslim scholar and astute politician, Maulana Abul Kalam, called "Azad" (Free), and in so showing its all-Indian rather than communal Hindu character, make a bid for Muslim support.

In March 1940, at a session at Ramgarh, Congress again decided not to support the war effort, declaring that Great Britain was fighting a war for imperialist ends; threatened to launch a civil disobedience campaign in the near future; and demanded an immediate declaration of Indian independence and the summoning of a constituent assembly, based on universal adult suffrage, to frame a new constitution.

When the Muslim League met at Lahore that same month it demanded two things: independence of India and partition of the country into separate Hindu and Muslim states. The latter constituted adoption as a political goal of "Pakistan," a term already in vogue among Muslims, but not used in this declaration. A year later Sir Sikander Hyat Khan, premier of the Punjab and leader of the Unionist party there, which included Muslims, Sikhs, and Hindus, made a speech in the Punjab Legislative Assembly that expressed dissatisfaction with the extreme Pakistan idea and instead advocated division of India into zones, each to be composed of several provincial units, the zones loosely federated at the center. This idea was later partly echoed in the Cripps Mission's proposals of 1942 and the (Labour) Cabinet Mission's proposals of 1946.

In the summer of 1940 Subhash Chandra Bose, who stood at the extreme left in Congress, was arrested for sedition, and was to be tried in February 1941. The day before the trial, however, he disappeared, later to appear in the Axis countries and still later to collaborate in Southeast Asia with the Japanese as *neta* (leader, duce, führer) of the "Indian National Army" and head of a puppet Indian government in exile.

After the fall of France in 1940, and the elevation of Winston Churchill to the prime ministership, Congress, thinking that probably Britain would now be willing to end the deadlock in India, voted in July to cooperate in the prosecution of the war, provided a national government was established at the center, which would be responsible to the legislature. Gandhi at this point ceased cooperating with Congress, because Congress, in intimating that it would support the war, had abrogated his principle of nonviolence.

The British government declined the Congress offer, on the grounds, first, that the Indian political parties were not agreed on political goals, and second, that in time of war it was impracticable to reform the constitution. The Muslim League also opposed the Congress plan. The government, however, made a counterproposal on August 8, the "August Offer," inviting a certain number of Indians to join the viceroy's executive council, and providing for the establishment of a war advisory council with representatives of the Indian states and other national interests. The British government would take up constitutional reform after the war. Neither Congress nor the League would accept the offer, though for different reasons. Some of the other minorities and the Hindu Mahasabha, the orthodox Hindu communal organization, were willing to cooperate, but this was not enough to make the offer a success, and on November 20 Lord Linlithgow announced that for the time being it would not be put into effect.

In September 1940 Congress decided to withdraw its conditional offer to cooperate with the government, called Gandhi to leadership, and on October 13 decided to begin a campaign of limited civil disobedience or *satyagraha* under his direction. This was to be by individuals, not a mass movement, and was to be "symbolic." Prominent congressmen, selected by Gandhi, would court arrest by making antiwar statements in public, previously notifying the police. Vinoba Bhave, later the promoter of the *bhudan* (land-gift) movement, was the first to be selected and was arrested on October 21 and given a sentence of three months. Jawaharlal Nehru was the next and was arrested on October 31 and given a four-year sentence. In this way large numbers of the most prominent leaders were arrested and sentenced. By May 1941, the number held for such offenses was over 14,000.

While relations between the government and Congress were blocked, relations between the government and the Muslim League were also deteriorating. In July 1941, when the German success was at its height, the Viceroy enlarged his executive council by creating five new posts, thus making a total of twelve, of whom seven were Indians; an eighth was to be an Indian when a then imminent replacement was made. The Viceroy also appointed a National Defense Council of thirty members, including the four Muslim premiers of the provinces where representative ministries still functioned. Congress, of course, derived no satisfaction from these developments, and the Muslim League was equally aroused. Jinnah, as leader of the League, compelled the three Muslim premiers of provinces where the League was in control to resign their appointments in the Defense Council, and continued to demand creation of Pakistan.

In August, when the "Atlantic Charter" was framed by President Roosevelt and Prime Minister Churchill, Indians at once asked if the third paragraph applied to India. This paragraph read: "They [Roosevelt and Churchill] respect the right of all people to choose the form of government under which they will live; and they wish to see sovereign rights and self-government restored to those who have been forcibly deprived of them." Churchill replied in September that the paragraph referred only to those nations conquered by the Axis and did "not qualify in any way the various statements of policy which have been made from time to time about the development of constitutional government in India, Burma and other parts of the British Empire." The country burned with anger and disappointment.

On December 3, 1941, the government of India, apparently foreseeing that Japan was on the verge of entering the war, and desiring to conciliate India, announced that it was releasing all those political prisoners who, like Nehru, were guilty of only "symbolic" offenses. Shortly afterwards (December 15), the Viceroy issued a special plea for unity in support of the war. During Christmas week, the Working Committee of Congress agreed to cooperate to the extent of blocking the aggressors, but not to the extent of aiding Britain. This endorsement of violence as a method of resistance again alienated Gandhi, who a second time withdrew his support from Congress.

Throughout this entire period from the outbreak of the war until the end of 1941, and afterwards as well, the moderate Liberal party, a small group led by Sir Tej Bahadur Sapru, M. R. Jayakar, V. S. Srinivasa Sastri, and Sir Jagdish Prasad, made efforts at accommodating the differences of the parties involved, offering valuable and reasonable suggestions. But this group of elder statesmen had no popular support and their wise counsel went unheeded.

In February 1942 Generalissimo Chiang Kai-shek went to India and encouraged the Indians to rally to the war effort; at the same time he urged the British to give India real freedom.

With the political forces of India and Britain thus jammed, and the Japanese, who had taken Malaya and Singapore, rapidly overrunning Burma, Churchill on March 11, 1942, announced that the British war cabinet had decided upon a plan to settle the constitutional problem in India and was sending out Sir Stafford Cripps, long considered sympathetic to Indian nationalism, to secure the acquiescence of leaders of the various parties.

The British war cabinet's proposals provided for dominion status after the war for an Indian Union to be composed of those provinces and princely states which wished to accede to it, and separate dominion status for provinces not acceding to the Union. A constituent assembly was to be called after the war to draw up the terms of a new constitution. Treaties with the Indian States would be revised, and minority rights would be guaranteed by safeguards. During the war the British would retain defense but the Viceroy's council would be indianized at once.

After negotiations and conferences in India during several weeks, Cripps returned to England on April 12, his plan rejected by all the important Indian parties. The failure was partly due to the fact that many of the provisions of the proposal were vague and nothing was being offered to India for the immediate present— Gandhi described the proposals as "a postdated check"—and partly because of specific conditions which were considered inacceptable. First, the scheme opened the way for partition of the country into at least two and possibly many more separate political entities, and Congress viewed such a partition as potentially disastrous. Second, it continued to reserve for the British all control over the army. To Congress no offer could be satisfactory that left the army under complete control of the British instead of a minister responsible to the elected representatives of the Indian people. Congress wanted some kind of civilian minister or secretary of war, even though the actual command in the field during the war would remain with Wavell, then commander-in-chief in India, under the British War Council. In the negotiations Congress found that it could hope for only a very limited kind of control through a ministry which Nehru characterized as one for "Canteens and Stationery." Third, the proposed indianization of the executive council did not in itself provide for an Indian government responsible to the legislature. The council would still have been appointed by the Governor General. The nationalist demand was for a cabinet of the British model, and it was by no means clear that a cabinet of the British model could be established except on the basis of a parliament also of the British model. Fourth, there was no provision that in the proposed constituent assembly the autocratic princely Indian states would be represented by elected representatives of the people. The representatives were instead to be nominated by the princes. This arrangement was in contradiction to the demand which Congress had been making for democratization of the Indian States.

If the war cabinet's proposals had been meant to confuse the Indian political situation, they could hardly have been more skillfully framed. They offered independence on terms liable to shatter India into many parts. Congress considered the offer illusory and refused it. The proffer of something which Churchill—who was well informed on the Indian situation and at the same time a most astute politician and had had advice from the Viceroy—should have known was unrealistic and would be rejected led to frustration of the nationalists. The proposals suddenly transformed the Muslim League program of Pakistan from a bargaining weapon meant to wring concessions from Congress into a realizable goal, and must be considered the most important single step toward the 1947 partition. As V. P. Menon puts it, the proposal gave "the death-blow to Indian unity." The princes were at once warned that they would have to look forward to a change in their position, yet were permitted the hope that they could hold their states as separate dominions within the British Empire. The minorities, such as the Depressed Classes, were provided guarantees in a scheme which Congress had to take the odium of declining. The Communists were encouraged, since they had come to support the war after Germany had attacked Russia. Congress itself was divided three ways among those who in their bitterness would have supported nothing British and were willing to sabotage the war effort, those who like Gandhi would have resisted the Japanese with *satyagraha,* and those who like Nehru wanted to organize scorched earth and guerrilla resistance. The proposal roused contention and magnified the existing internal dissension at a time when Japan was pressing forward in the eastern hemisphere and the Germans were victorious in the western. It seemed to indicate that Churchill believed India had no important contribution to make toward the defeat of Japan.

In the months following, Rajagopalachari, "Rajaji," one of the most prominent and highly respected figures in Congress, later Governor General of India, tried to effect a compromise between Congress and the League, conceding the general proposition that India could be partitioned. He thus greatly encouraged the proponents of the Pakistan idea and offended Congress. Gandhi, for his part, was urging Britain to "Quit India," and his slogan was supported by many for widely varying reasons, though it was unpalatable to the League, the Mahasabha, and some others. On August 8, 1942, Congress passed a resolution on the basis of this slogan, again urging Britain to grant India a government of her own to resist the Japanese, and to recognize India's rights to self-rule, otherwise to face "a mass struggle on non-violent lines" under the direction of Gandhi. Gandhi declared that his first step would be to open negotiations with the Viceroy, but the Churchill government had made preparations well in advance of the Congress meeting, and within a few hours after the "Quit India" resolution was passed, the government of India arrested Gandhi and other leaders. Congress was outlawed, and in rapid steps its chief members were imprisoned to the number of 60,000 and held for periods of varying length. Numerous disorders then occurred, some, such as burning railroad stations and tearing up tracks, harmful to military operations. Congress remained helpless and ineffective until just before the end of the war with Japan. Political activity was restricted to the Communist party, the eight-year ban on which had been removed in the summer of 1942, the Muslim League, and the communal Hindu Mahasabha. Both of the latter rapidly grew in membership; the League continuously promoted its campaign for Pakistan, and the Mahasabha preached violence against Muslims. Some negotiations were conducted between Congress leaders in jail and Jinnah and between Gandhi and the Viceroy, but these came to no successful issue. In February and March 1943 Gandhi engaged in a fast as a protest. In May 1944, he was released for reasons of health, and in the following September he conducted futile conversations with Jinnah. Other Congress leaders were released in the first part of 1945 in anticipation of the victory over Japan.

In spite of all the frustration for nationalism it was evident that independence could not be delayed long after the war. Lord Wavell, Governor General, 1943–1947, took various conciliatory steps in advance of a resolution of the problem, especially by convening a conference in Simla in June 1945, attended by leaders of all parties, to devise an interim plan of national government, but this, too, could not bridge the Hindu-Muslim rift. The fate of the conference was prejudiced in advance, when it was stated that it would proceed on the principle of Caste Hindu–Muslim or Hindu–Muslim parity. Congress was willing to talk in terms of Congress-League parity, but it refused to call itself a "Caste Hindu" or a "Hindu" organization.

On July 1, 1945, the British Labour party swept the Churchill government out of office and in its turn attacked the problem of India, and in August Japan surrendered and the war was over. Churchill had been universally regarded in India as hostile to the country's political aspirations and general best interests, but members of the Labour party had taken an attitude which Indians considered friendly. Most British spokesmen at that time seemed to accept the fact that India must quickly receive independence. One basic reason was Britain's lack of choice. The British power had weakened conspicuously during the war, and it was doubtful if Britain could have afforded the effort to hold India by force. Another was a great public lack of interest in retaining India against her will. Britain was no longer going to receive as much economic profit from India as it had in the nineteenth century and the first decades of the twentieth. Instead India had become a great trouble, if not expense, through its continuous unrest, and among the British public there were many who thought the only answer was to relinquish responsibility at the first possible moment and let India go it alone. With this went a widespread acceptance of the justice in the Indian demand for full self-government, even though the British public at large had little, if any, appreciation of the internal Indian problems involved.

This sentiment was confirmed by events in India during 1945–1946. These included anti-British riots in Calcutta, refusal of the Royal Air Force in India to obey orders in January 1946, and in February of the same year a mutiny of the Royal Indian Navy. Many members of Congress prepared for an armed uprising, which, however, Sardar Vallabhbhai Patel, Deputy Prime Minister, succeeded in restraining. When in that same winter, the government brought to trial for treason the leaders of the "Indian National Army," which the Japanese had organized from prisoners of war and used in Burma, popular feeling in their favor was so intense that the action had to be abandoned. In the circumstances, it was clear in Britain that her problem respecting India was merely to save for herself what she could as she withdrew and in the act of withdrawal to keep to a minimum the dislocation and damage bound to result because of the confused and bitter relations which had developed among Indian groups.

In the winter of 1945–46 new elections were held for the provincial legislatures and in these the Muslim League showed clearly and for the first time in its existence that it had the overwhelming support of the Muslim community. The Mahasabha, however, was repudiated by the electorate. The contesting parties after the elections had been decided were Congress and the League.

In February 1946 the Labour government announced that it would send a three-man cabinet mission to India to draw up a scheme for giving the country self-government. The three cabinet members were Lord Pethick-Lawrence, Secretary of State for India, Sir Stafford Cripps, president of the Board of Trade, and A. V. Alexander, First Lord of the Admiralty. This mission went out in March, and on May 16, 1946, the government published a White Paper offering the plan to Parliament. Its provisions respecting the communal issue and the consequent failure of its proposals will be reported in Chapter 8. It proposed in other respects that the newly elected provincial legislatures should set up a constituent assembly to draft the new constitution, and it indicated that the princely Indian States could not expect Britain to retain paramountcy over them but that they would have to make their own arrangements with the new self-ruling India. Congress and the League quarreled all summer over the plan. No solution seemed yet in sight for the Indian problem and Lord Wavell, who had labored hard to find one, was relieved of his position early in 1947.

The Labour government now sent out Earl Mountbatten of Burma as the new Governor General. In unexpectedly hurried moves it accepted partition and passed the Indian Independence Act in July 1947, by which independence and partition were to be made effective a little more than a month later on August 15, 1947

Thus ended the British Indian Empire. And thus did nationalism win its victory, though only at the great cost of nearly one fourth of India's area and nearly one fifth of its population.

The history of nationalism in India inspires two reflections, one concerning the British, the other concerning Indian nationalism. The first is that, with a moderate degree of political tact, Britain might have prevented the many serious disturbances that accompanied the march of India to independence, and might have succeeded in retaining it undivided as a dominion. If in 1905 Bengal had from the first been divided according to linguistic boundaries rather than on the basis of greatest bureaucratic administrative efficiency; if in 1909 the enactment of the Morley-Minto reforms had not been almost immediately followed by secret planning which led to the surprise removal of the capital from Calcutta to Delhi; if the reforms of 1919 had not had to fight their way through the brutality of the Amritsar massacre and military rule in the Punjab; if in 1927 the Simon Commission had included at least one Indian member; if in 1931 the repressive ordinances had not been issued at all, and especially if they had not come in close conjunction with the (to the nationalists) disappointing issue of the Second Round Table Conference; if in 1935 the new constitution had not been framed with its uncompromising "safeguards" of British power and commerce—if at any of the junctures there had been more of conciliation and less of inflexibility, India might well have developed new political institutions through which unity with Britain could have been preserved.

The other reflection concerns the fact that Indian nationalism rose, grew, and expressed itself in the religio-social group of Hindus. It was not possible for this nationalism to win to itself the Muslims, adherents to another religiocentric manner of life, which in its way was just as intent upon survival as ever was

Hinduism. It is true that the Indian National Congress, the organ of nationalism, never conceded itself to be the voice of Hindu India alone as distinguished from India as a whole. It adopted a secular program meant to produce a secular state; many of its most prominent leaders sincerely and consistently upheld secular aims in politics and eschewed religious and narrow communal aims. Among them were certain Muslims. But the stubborn fact remained that nationalism was a phenomenon of the Hindu community, and this community provided the strength and the direction of Congress, which, when it at last achieved power in 1937–1939, was not wise enough to win Muslim confidence. The rivalries already implicit in the situation were exacerbated by the communal activities of the Hindu Mahasabha, which frankly advocated violence against Muslims and goaded Congress as far as it could to communal action. The masses of each community, and more narrowly the middle classes, which were those fostering political activity, never forgot the contrasts and antipathies of Hinduism and Islam. Hence they could not cross the barrier of communalism and press ahead in common effort to solve the problems posed before their country by the conditions of the mid-twentieth century world.

7 Hindu-Muslim Communalism

When on August 15, 1947, India was simultaneously given self-government and partitioned into two nations, the western world viewed the gain of independence as the more dramatic of the two changes and the more newsworthy. For it ended the epoch of British political rule, thereby diminishing Britain's world power, and at the same time raised India from her unflattering status as the world's greatest colony. But whatever any distant nations in the West thought of developments, the attainment of full self-rule was neither the more sudden nor the more significant for the subcontinent. Rather, those qualities lay with partition. Self-rule had been in sight for years. But partition was a recent thing. It had not been advocated by a political party until 1940, and then it had appeared unrealistic, a mirage, promoted for propaganda and bargaining purposes but never likely to be realized. Very quickly, however, in 1942 when the Cripps offer was made, it acquired a semblance of reality, yet still no certainty. As late as May 1946, at the time of the Cabinet Mission, partition seemed near to death. Not until June 3, 1947, just over ten weeks before the fateful day itself, did it become a certainty, and when it was effected, it was done with such celerity that there was no time to devise adequate plans for a smooth division, to say nothing of creating the necessary machinery for accomplishing it.

Yet the importance of partition was fundamental. It struck the subcontinent where it lived. It disrupted its economy, its communications, its administration. It weakened its defense. It divided it into mutually antipathetic and suspicious nations, with a clashing cultural discord inherited from a long past, which only briefly and temporarily had been muted during the eighteenth century and had been steadily rising during the nineteenth and twentieth. Partition was, in fact, a disaster, the greatest disaster the subcontinent has ever suffered.

Partition was a direct result of communalism. This is the term given in the subcontinent to the sense of insecurity which any community feels and the accompanying action it takes to protect itself and further its own interests. It is applied in different localities to groups differentiated by religion, language, region, historical origin, occupation. That is, it has in different areas marked off Hindus, Muslims, Sikhs, Parsis, Christians; speakers of Hindi, Bengali, Marathi, Gujarati, Punjabi, Tamil, Malayalam, Kanarese, Telugu, and other languages; Mundas, Dravidians, Aryans, Anglo-Indians, agriculturists, jute factory owners, industrial workers. Because a number of these various communities were recognized in British India by separate political constituencies, communalism has had a peculiarly aggravated form. It is above all applied to the ill-feeling existing in Hindu-Muslim relations. The Muslims in prepartition India disliked the beliefs and ways of the Hindus, distrusted them, and as a minority feared for their treatment if they should have to live in a state where the Hindu majority had power. The Hindus in their turn disliked the ways of the Muslims, and, though a majority, feared the rise to power of the Muslims under whom they had experienced centuries of oppression. Before partition the Hindu-Muslim communal hostility was an internal problem of the single undivided India; after partition it became a source of international issues between the two new nations and helped materially to produce a danger of war. It is the subcontinent's most corrosive inheritance from the past. It was destined to produce war, with the ever latent threat of new wars.

The basis of Hindu-Muslim communalism lies in cultural differences. Before partition these appeared to political leaders of the two communities in contrasting ways. The late Mohammad Ali Jinnah, head of the Muslim League, during the latter part of his career consistently said that the differences were not merely those of theology. Hinduism and Islam, he affirmed, were more than two different religions; rather, they were two different civilizations —so numerous and so profound did he consider the antitheses. Therefore, the two communities were more than a majority and a minority within a single India; they were two different nations which were incongruously associated under a single government. That had long been a Muslim position; it became the fundamental dogma in Jinnah's political philosophy. But non-Muslim leaders took a different view. Speaking for the Indian National Congress, Jawaharlal Nehru, himself a Hindu, in viewing the communal problem, said in his *Discovery of India* (1946) that the native Hinduism and the intrusive Islam had become only modifications of a common civilization. The same position was taken by Sir Tej Bahadur Sapru (1875–1950), a distinguished elder statesman of India, and a nonparty conference committee which he headed, called the Conciliation Committee, in its report on *Constitutional Proposals* (published in December 1945). Jinnah emphasized the contradictions between the two communities; Nehru and Sir Tej Bahadur, the correspondences.

In these opposing views is illustrated the most fundamental of the Hindu-Muslim divergences. Muslim civilization is centered around the religion of Islam, and one of the most characteristic features of that religion is the demand for doctrinal and cult uniformity. Only one view of God is acceptable, namely, as Allah; only one series of revelations concerning Him exists, namely, that of the prophets, of whom Muhammad is the last and the "seal"; only one book contains the divine message, the Koran; only one standard of duty lies open to man, submission to this revelation as a Muslim. But the religion of Hinduism, which is the core of native Hindu civilization, does not demand such uniformity, even as an ideal; rather, it is latitudinarian and tolerant. With orthodox sanction and practice, Hinduism permits an unlimited variation in belief concerning the nature of God and a corresponding diversity in cult and standards of behavior.

Hinduism believes that mankind is incapable of achieving uniformity because human beings are inescapably affected by all their actions (*karma*) in previous existences, which give them at the instant of birth unequal endowments of intellect and spirit—as well as unequal physical structure and unequal economic and social position—and therefore impose upon them different duties. Thus it sanctions the institution of caste, with its undemocratic implications. But orthodox Islam democratically views all mankind as born equal; it considers, in fact, that all infants are born Muslims; it is their misguided parents who turn them into Christians, Jews, Hindus, Buddhists, Sikhs, or others. Hinduism logically recognizes different capabilities and prescribes different duties for the different castes. It is, from the Hindu point of view, unrealistic to expect human beings, so unequal in their capacities, to hold the same dogmas. Except in the case of the very few rare souls who comprehend absolute truth, everyone is partly right and partly wrong, though in varying degrees.

What Hinduism demands is that, since difference of position, function, and duty exists as a fundamental feature of the cosmos, people of one persuasion should not interfere with people of another but leave them alone in their relative ignorance or wisdom and in the activities corresponding to their limitations. Proselytism is useless and troublesome; it may even be harmful. If an individual performs adequately the duties of his present state, he may in some future existence repair his present spiritual inadequacy and win nearer to supreme knowledge and truth. But Islam, with equally logical deductions from its premises, believes in missionary enterprise and conversion of the infidel and the erring to the single revealed standard which it recognizes.

These contrasting attitudes are not without exceptions in their own communities. Many Muslims, especially today in the Near East, take a wider view of civilization and even of religion than strict and literal orthodoxy would admit; and there are some such too in India and Pakistan. So also there are in India many illiberal and overly dogmatic Hindus who are intolerant of sectarian belief other than their own and scornful of those outside their own narrow group. Yet the basic contrast remains generally true. Hence Islam makes a bifurcation of civilizations into the Islamic, which fundamentalist Muslims regard as God-inspired, and all other civilizations, which are by nature heterodox and false. But orthodox liberal Hinduism may easily admit all civilizations to be reconcilable as merely variations within a single great civilization. It is a corollary of the Muslim view to regard cultural multiplicity as a temporary evil to be replaced by the solitary existence of the one true culture and extinction of its rivals. Cultural amalgamation is equally a corollary of Hindu theory.

Related to this difference in basic outlook upon life is a difference in the social cohesiveness of Muslims and Hindus. With the high importance which Muslims attach to dogma and their generally democratic social order, they have developed a strong sense of community. This expresses itself to the eye in congregational worship in the mosque. There a great courtyard may be filled with a thousand faithful worshipers, whose voices and bodies rise and fall as one in the unison of prayer. Any similar phenomenon is unknown in Hinduism. When a Hindu goes to a temple, he worships alone and in undertones. Many temples have only recently been thrown open to all castes. Caste has, indeed, split the Hindu's society, and intellectual freedom has individualized his religion. His human utopia is a state of philosophic anarchy; the Muslim's is the well-drilled regiment. The sense of membership in a community, despite sectarian differences, gave Islam the drive that carried it, within 110 years after the Hegira (A.D. 622), across North Africa and into Spain and France in the west and as far as the river Indus in the east. The Muslim consciousness of community has been strong in the Indian subcontinent, where the Muslims have been a minority. There, in spite of sectarian theological and political differences, it gave them a power of aggressive action out of proportion to their numerical strength.

Again closely related to the fundamental contrast between Islam, with its unitary and dogmatic conception of life, and Hinduism, with its multiple and relative conception, is a difference concerning the relationship of the state and religion. It is a general Islamic dogma that Muslims should be governed only by Muslims; Hinduism has no such religious criterion of rulership. The Muslim theory, in its orthodox and extreme form, leads to a view of the state as a theocracy (a term decried by Muslims in Pakistan because Islam has no priesthood), which makes Islam less a state religion than a religious state. Muhammad regarded himself as the "warner" of his people, calling them to "submission" (*islam*); their duty was to become "submissive" (*muslim*) to Allah's will. The function of warner was considered a function of the state, to make conversions to the faith the state's highest purpose. That is why the Islamic religion has been promoted by military and political means as has no other. The law of the state is the Shariah (*shari'ah*), that is, the manifested way, highway, divine law of God, sometimes defined as "that which would not be known had there not been a divine revelation." It is the duty of the divines to ascertain and interpret this and of the Islamic state to enforce it.

The early Muslims viewed the world as composed of two hostile military camps. One was the "abode of Islam" (*dar ul-islam*), where the true faith was established; the other was the "abode of war" (*dar ul-harb*), where Islam was not established and false doctrine prevailed. The ruler of the faithful was under obligation to convert the abode of war into the abode of Islam. This he might endeavor to do by making a demand of conversion upon the unbeliever state. If this were accepted, all was well; but if not, then he must wage a holy war (*jihad*) of compulsory conversion. The con-

133

quered were to be treated in two ways according to their previous religious condition. "People of the Book"—Jews, Christians, Magians, Sabaeans—whose scriptures precede the Koran and are considered by Muslims to be in the correct though incomplete line of revelation, had the choice of becoming Muslims or of accepting "protection" and paying a capitation tax. If they refused conversion, their lives were spared but they could not enjoy citizenship. People who were not of the Book had either to become Muslims or be put to death. Obviously, the harsh and extreme application of Muslim theory was impracticable where the conquered folk was stubborn yet necessary to supply labor for the believing conquerors. For this reason conquered people, including many Hindus, were often allowed to keep their religion and their life, though it might be with impoverishment, humiliation, slavery.

Traditional Hindus have no such theory of the state. They do not regard it as divine will that all people should be Hindu under a single rule. To the traditionally educated Hindu the Muslim theory that state and religion are identical is illogical and untenable. When the Muslims overran India and made forcible conversions, as they often did, the Brahman regarded the conquerors as, in this respect, irrational and mentally immature.

Other important cultural differences separate Hindus and Muslims. The Hindu prestige system, the institution of caste, wherein all men are born to graded places in society, with the Brahman on top as "a god on earth" and the Untouchable at the bottom, deeply offends Muslims, since it relegates them, as it does all non-Hindus, to a low status. Islam is socially democratic. It teaches that all men, at least all Muslims, are equal. Again, Hindus decorate their temples profusely with images of gods, human beings, and animals, and use idols in worship as symbols to call a deity to mind. But the Koran strictly forbids the representation of any animate objects, and conquering Muslims destroy the Hindus' temples and images, thus in Hindu eyes committing sacrilege. The Hindu attaches a peculiar sanctity to the cow and considers cow-killing only less heinous a sin than Brahman-killing; the Muslim regards the cow as legitimate food or sacrificial victim and when he can do so with impunity will not hesitate to slaughter the sacred animal. Hinduism uses the native Indian Sanskrit as its classical and sacred language and writes its books in native Indian scripts; Islam uses the imported Arabic and Persian languages and writes in the Perso-

Arabic script. Hence the two, with only rare exceptions, have not read and cannot read each other's books. Muslims have generally felt it useless to understand the beliefs and social practices of the Hindus, and in past centuries the Hindus have as a rule been prevented by traditional caste rules from marrying outside their endogamous groups or even interdining and so have been denied much social intercourse that would have helped to bring understanding and toleration.

Bitter and historic enmity divides the two faiths. The Hindus cannot forget the thousand years from the Arab invasion in 711 to the end of the emperor Aurangzeb's reign in 1707, when Muslims periodically plundered their homes, looted their cities, burned their books, demolished their temples, slew their priests, abducted their women. And they fear a recurrence of these horrors if they should have to live again under Muslim power. With the Muslims it rankles that, under the pax Britannica, they came to take second place to the Hindus whom they had once vanquished and ruled.

Before the agitation that led to partition, in trade unions and peasant groups members of the two communities had often learned to work in cooperation. Among the ruling princes, the antipathy might be suppressed or ignored. It was the middle classes, economically ambitious, that were the chief field of hostility. They attached the most value to strict religious dogma; at the same time the system of communal legislative representation and political appointment produced in them heated rivalry and permanent tension, which they communicated on opportunity to the masses. Thereupon on some minor provocation Muslim mullahs, Hindu priests, or fanatic laymen of either community might by raising the Muslim cry of *Din* ("the Religion") or the Hindu charge of sacrilege precipitate a riot.

Several aspects of Hindu-Muslim relations that showed some degree of cultural assimilation used to give proponents of the one-nation theory some ground for hope that at a future time, however remote, the hostility might disappear. The one that leaders of the Indian National Congress most often used to stress is the fact that Hindus and Muslims in each locality belong to the same racial and ethnic stock. Islam spread in India by conversion more than by immigration. And conversions were made not so much by force, though force was often used and the memory is bitter among Hindus, as by missionary enterprise among the lowest in the Hindu social and economic scale, who found relief from many disabilities in accepting Islam. In every part of the subcontinent Hindus and Muslims are alike physically; they can be distinguished only by externals, such as dress, treatment of facial and head hair, sectarian markings, customs of eating and drinking. Moreover, in every locality both parts of the population use a common speech.

Socially, too, there has been occasional assimilation of the two groups, for example, in using similar wedding ceremonies and in sharing each other's religious festivals. Muslim dress affected, though seldom completely supplanted, native Hindu middle class costume. The Muslim habit of secluding women became a local practice of those Hindus who could afford it. Caste, though contrary to Muslim doctrine, nevertheless exists in a number of Muslim groups, which did not rid themselves of caste distinctions when accepting conversion.

On the intellectual level there exists a body of common learning, as in the traditional mathematics, astrology, medicine. For several centuries, particularly during the sixteenth and seventeenth, Muslims translated Sanskrit works into Persian, which probably were not read much, yet showed a tendency toward community interrelationship. During that same period both communities had a certain amount of common vernacular literature. In architecture native Indian and imported Persian have blended to produce forms frequently employed in both Hindu and Muslim secular buildings, while in temple and mosque construction there has been exchange of many individual structural and decorative elements. Painting as practiced by both communities during the past three centuries has also been a fusion, in varying degrees in different localities, of native Indian and imported Persian.

Even in religion there have been approaches to each other. Muslim mysticism, that is, Sufiism, though unpalatable to Islamic orthodoxy, renders its adherents and Hindu mystics mutually intelligible. Compromise religions have been preached by persuasive teachers who drew ideas from both Hinduism and Islam. Kabir (1440–1518) was one; there are still sects bearing his name. Another was Nanak (1469–1538), the founder of Sikhism. The great Mughal emperor Akbar, who ruled from 1556 to 1605, tried unsuccessfully to bring Hindus and Muslims to a common type of worship, which he called *Din-i-Ilahi,* "Divine Faith," but he probably doomed it by naming himself God's vice-regent; it had only the merest handful of adherents and perished with him. Generally the reconcilers of the two faiths have done less in bringing them together than in creating new sects to complicate still further the varied array of India's religions.

Finally, the two communities have much common history. Rulers of one faith have frequently made alliances with rulers of the other against rulers of their own faith. Muslim rulers have often used Hindus as civil administrators and generals, and Hindus have done the same with Muslims. During the British period the hereditary rulers of each group were deprived of their political power by the intruding Europeans, and the masses of both suffered economically as their agrarian system was revolutionized and their handicrafts put in competition with western machine industry. The two communities, on high and low levels alike, had a measure of joint interest in gaining self-rule.

The various religious and other cultural differences defined the two communities and produced their primary misunderstandings. But these might have been overlaid and become negligible in their effect upon national life if they had not been supplemented by economic disparities and political rivalries. It happened that in several large areas there was a religious dichotomy of landlords or moneylenders and peasantry. The one would be Muslim, the other Hindu. Thus, in the United Provinces (now Uttar Pradesh), where the peasantry was Hindu, there was a large class of Muslim landholders, called *taluqdars*. The reverse situation existed in parts of Bengal and the Punjab, where the Muslim peasantry paid rent to Hindu landlords or interest to Hindu moneylenders. In such situations, the clash between economic classes was sure to become identified with religious difference.

There was also rivalry between the Hindu and Muslim middle classes created in part by an accident of geography. Because the Muslims had entered India from the northwest and were chiefly concentrated in the north and away from the seaports where the British had entered and conducted most of their activities, it was the Hindus, living in and near those ports, who first profited economically from British commerce and first took advantage of the new western education. They became the agents to spread this education, and this fact, too, operated to the Muslim disadvantage and discontent. In Bengal Muslims avoided the learning which was brought by western unbelievers and propagated by Hindu idolators.

Further, when the British reorganized the system of land tenure, the new landlords under the British were Hindus, who had previously been only tax farmers under the Muslim regime. The old Muslim upper classes remained as landowners in their own areas, but the newly appointed Hindus became their upstart rivals as a prestige group and partly displaced them and reduced their numbers.

It was also the Hindus who developed the new bourgeoisie. By the time of the Indian (Sepoy) Mutiny in 1857 the Muslim community had only a small middle class against the relatively large Hindu professional, clerical, and commercial groups. This condition persisted down to the time of partition. It was said that in East Bengal, now Bangladesh, 80 percent of trade and commerce was in Hindu hands. Moneylenders were almost all Hindus, and the jute business, which is the major industry of East Bengal, was also Hindu. Similarly, about 90 percent of the professional classes were Hindu. This situation altered under Pakistan. It was also the Hindus (and Parsis) who became the new industrialists, not the Muslims, most of whose leaders continued to be of the old landholder class.

There was another situation in the nineteenth century operating to Muslim disadvantage. When the Indian Mutiny occurred it was considered by the British to be a responsibility of the Muslims. Most of the Indian princes involved were Muslim, and the head of a freed India, as the Mutiny would have made it, was to be the titular Moghul emperor in Delhi, around whose shadowy figure the mutineers had assembled their forces. Because of this fact, the British, after quelling the Mutiny, laid the heavier part of the penalty upon the Muslims. It was approximately a decade before they lifted this discrimination.

During the second half of the nineteenth century the Muslim community contained the larger part of India's dispossessed and unhappy great. It no longer had the political supremacy enjoyed under the Mughals, whose might had been destroyed by the Hindu Marathas and the Christian British, both of them infidels. The greater number of government posts open to Indians fell to Hindus, and the profits of business were theirs as well. By the time the century was three-quarters past, the old Muslim landlords, who held their position under government title, were still in possession of large sections of Bengal, Bihar, Orissa, and the United Provinces, but in other respects Hindus had the better status. It was inevitable that this situation should produce intercommunity middle class jealousy.

The Muslim reaction in the nineteenth century to the community's inferior position was twofold. On the one hand it was religious, puritanical, revivalist, fundamentalist; on the other, it was secular and modernist.

The religious and fundamentalist reaction was the older, and consisted of Wahhabiism. This movement originated in Arabia in the late eighteenth century, and its ideas, though not its name, came to India early in the nineteenth century. They gave rise to such organizations as the Ahl-i-Hadith (People of the Traditions) and Ahl-i-Qur'an (People of the Koran), which the Indian census returned as sectarian groups. Wahhabiism had as its essence the slogan "Back to the Koran!" It strove to eliminate from Islam everything which it considered an innovation since the time of the Prophet, such as paintings, musical instruments, domes and cupolas on mosques. It tried to restore the holy war. In India during the first half of the nineteenth century the movement was widespread. It attacked all elements which Indian Islam had adopted from Hinduism and all the features of modern life which Muslims were inclining to accept. Western learning and culture were, of course, included. The result was to retard progress of the Muslim community and foster strife between it and the Hindus. But, since the Wahhabis were mostly poor, the movement assumed also something of the aspect of proletarian unrest, and as early as the 1830s was alarming the Muslim middle classes, among whom arose later the secular and modernist effort to restore Muslim prestige.

The chief prophet of this second movement was Sir Syed Ahmad Khan (1817–1898). He was one of the most influential Indian Muslims during the nineteenth century. His philosophy was aligned with that of Islamic modernists in the Near East, as in Egypt, who passed beyond the old dogmatism and felt that the holy Koran applied to all peoples at all times. The two camps of Islam and war, they taught, were not so much political conditions as states of the human heart. Muslims should spread Islam by precept and example rather than by violence; the true teaching of Islam was love for all fellow human beings. The political consequence of this teaching was that Islam was not to be an international state under the Muslim banner of religion, but a state of mind and soul among the faithful, who might be rendering temporal fealty to many national governments, including those that were non-Muslim.

Sir Syed was faithful to the British rule in India and did not favor political nationalism. He had been loyal during the Mutiny; he did not share the Muslim resentment of the British discrimination in repressing it. He wished that rule perpetuated, since under it both Hindus and Muslims had the privilege of living according to their own religious law. He pleaded publicly for freedom and independence of thought, and the application of historical criticism to Muslim tradition. He preached a liberal philosophy to the Muslim community, and he had a keen intelligence and a persuasive personality to enhance the effect of his message.

As a part of his program he tried to separate Muslim education from the traditional religious instruction so as to give it a secular character, utilizing modern scientific methods and historical data. In 1875 he founded an institution known as the Muhammadan Anglo-Oriental College at Aligarh, which was immediately successful and in 1920 was chartered as the Aligarh University. It was until partition the leading force in shaping Indian Muslim opinion. Sir Syed had early diagnosed Indian nationalism as predominantly Hindu and therefore potentially prejudicial to the interests of the Muslim community. When the Indian National Congress was founded in 1885, he urged his fellow religionists to avoid it. As liberalization of India's political system gave Indians increased opportunity in public life, intercommunity rivalry increased. At the Aligarh University anti-Hinduism was expressed in modern terms and applied to modern issues; though religion was not emphasized, sectarianism was promoted in the economic, social, and political spheres. Both the religious and leading secular cultural reactions of the Muslim community in the nineteenth and twentieth centuries, therefore, tended to promote communalism.

Muslim communalism was also in part a reaction against Hindu communal political activity. Particularly irritating to Muslims was the activity of the Arya Samaj, which, differing from usual Hindu practice, promoted reconversion of Muslim groups to Hinduism under the guise of "purification." This practice led in the 1920s and 1930s to considerable intercommunal violence and bloodshed. The Indian National Congress was for long periods under the control of religiously motivated leaders, such as Tilak, who, by means of his aggressive propaganda for "cow protection," alienated Muslims. Gandhi, though deploring communalism and preaching Hindu-Muslim unity, preached unity on what always seemed to Muslims to be Hindu terms, that is, acceptance of nonviolence, *ahinsa,* which meant that the cow was to be inviolable; he put it, "The central fact of Hinduism is cow protection." The rank and file of Congress membership was indifferent, if not actually hostile, to Muslim interests. The worst offender of all was the ultra-Hindu political party called the Hindu Mahasabha.

Communal tension between Hindus and Muslims in the latter half of the nineteenth century produced numerous riots in British India. The precipitating cause might be a quarrel over ownership of a parcel of land and the right to erect a religious building on it, or the playing of music by a Hindu wedding procession as it passed a mosque where such noise constituted sacrilege, or exaction of exorbitant rent or interest by a landlord or moneylender of one religious persuasion from a tenant or debtor of the other, or sacrifice of a cow by Muslims, or the clash of crowds when a Hindu and a Muslim festival coincided. Urban riots were especially common in areas where the disparity of population between the two groups was not great; where one group had a clear numerical or political superiority they were rare.

The growth of Indian nationalism during the twentieth century brought an accompanying increase in the number and intensity of intercommunal riots and took the clash between Muslims and Hindus out of religion and economics into politics. Intercommunity relations grew critical in 1905 over the partition of Bengal, which became a polemical issue of Hindu versus Muslim. The Muslims correctly foresaw that the Hindus might get the partition reversed —as it was in 1911—and to prevent the reversal as well as generally to advance Muslim interests, some of their leaders in 1906, with the blessing of the Viceroy, Lord Minto, organized the Muslim League. Among its specific aims one was to secure for Muslims a due share of government posts. Another was to give the Muslim community a political organization; for it was apparent that India would soon be granted the right to elect some of the members of the provincial councils. Indeed, that right was later defined in the Indian Councils Act (Morley-Minto reforms) of 1909.

It was the Morley-Minto reforms that inaugurated modern Indian political communalism. In giving the country a limited form of representation in provincial legislative councils these reforms introduced the principle of communal representation through separate electorates and weighting of representation for minorities. By that system legislative seats and political appointments were apportioned among the general constituency and a number of special constituencies, most of which were defined along communal lines. One of these consisted of Muslims, who had their own representatives, for whom only Muslims voted. The general constituency was the non-Muslim population and corresponded closely with the Hindu community.

When the system of separate representation and separate electorates was introduced, its sponsors stated that it was meant to solve the communal problem; instead it intensified it. From time to time every minority increased its demands for weighting in representation and appointments. The general constituency, speaking through Congress, resisted these demands, but was compelled to concede more and more. The chief dispute was always with the Muslims. In the two successive constitutions granted India after the Morley-Minto reforms, namely those of 1919 and 1935, the principle of communal representation was extended instead of curtailed, and it thus became the most poisonous single feature of Indian politics in this century.

During the 1920s the tension between the two communities increased. In part this was due to the prominence of Gandhi in Congress, which made Muslims as a group fear that in a self-governing India the Hindu majority would control parliament and use the strongly centralized government to discriminate against them. Their alarm seemed to them all too well justified in 1928 at the time of the Simon Commission's activities, when the distinguished lawyer Motilal Nehru and a Congress committee under his chairmanship drafted a constitution for India as a dominion. This frightened the Muslims because it provided for a strong central, nonfederal, government, and at the same time took no account of special Muslim claims. The Muslims replied by calling a conference in 1929, presided over by the Agha Khan, head of a small but wealthy Muslim sect, which drew up demands for a separate Muslim electorate; a loose federation of provinces, so that Muslim provinces would be practically self-governing; Muslim membership in all cabinets, central and provincial; and provisions that communal issues brought before legislatures should be decided on terms that would preclude discrimination against Muslims. The

Muslim demands and the Motilal Nehru draft constitution illustrate the contrast that from then on existed in the political philosophy of the League and Congress.

During the 1930s most of the numerous minor political parties were crowded out of the field and their adherents joined Congress or the League. Congress gained most. Temporarily it received the moral support of several non-League Muslim organizations. The League was reorganized when Congress led by Jawaharlal Nehru in the late 1930s instituted a program of agrarian reform, which alarmed Muslim landowners, intellectuals, and other community leaders.

The political issues between the League and Congress became intensely critical in 1937–1939 during the years of the Congress ministries under the 1935 constitution. When the ministries resigned, the League celebrated December 22 as a "Day of Deliverance" and continued to commemorate the day each year thereafter until partition. It thanked God in the name of Muslims for "freeing them from the oppression of the Congress ministries" and recited a list of "atrocities" committed by the ministries under the direction of the Congress high command. The chief charge was that the ministries excluded Muslims except those belonging to Congress, whom the League considered renegade and unrepresentative. Other atrocities included the use as a national language of the Hindi literary variety of Hindustani rather than the Urdu, employment of the Congress flag as the Indian national emblem, and adoption as the national anthem of the Hindu Sanskrit hymn "Bande Mataram," which had an anti-Muslim origin. The League opposed the Wardha scheme of education, fostered by Gandhi and supported by Congress, as parochial, communally Hindu, and neglectful of Muslim interests. It also alleged discrimination against Muslims in public office and deplored the promotion of Congress propaganda among the Muslim masses.

In Bengal during the time of the Congress ministries, the Muslims, who controlled the legislature, endeavored to reverse the advantages enjoyed there by the Hindu community by enacting economic legislation to favor Muslims. In the Punjab, where a similar imbalance existed, they made a similar attempt.

During this period Hindu-Muslim communal riots became increasingly frequent and bloody. Riots between Muslims and Sikhs were also frequent. The tension was enhanced by the activities of the Hindu Mahasabha, which attacked the Congress for being too conciliatory of the Muslims.

The Muslims had a genuine alarm that their community might not be able to maintain itself against the Hindu community, which during the millennia of history has quietly absorbed other rivals. They feared that their faith might perish in the land, and they and their descendants be reduced economically and socially. Their attention was kept focused on the communal quarrel; their leaders were slow in evolving a social or economic program for the community; they offered little more hope than vague benefits to be derived from establishing a religiously motivated state. This was the meaning Muslims gave to nationalism, and generally they preferred an India under Britain to a free India which might be dominated by the Hindus. Political activity they saw as their rivals' most potent weapon for their oppression; they made it, therefore, their own chief weapon for community protection.

8 The Creation of Pakistan

In the 1940s the Indian Muslim community acquired the goal of a national Muslim state to be created by the partition of India into two separate nations, one Muslim, the other Hindu. The proposed Muslim state was popularly called Pakistan. The Muslim League at a meeting in Lahore, on March 23, 1940, formally adopted the goal but did not then give the proposed state a name.

"Pakistan" was not originally a political term; it was coined to describe a spiritual or religious ideal, which the poet Muhammad Iqbal advanced in 1930, though he soon came to feel that this could be realized only in a separate Muslim state. The name was urged as a political slogan by C. Rahmat Ali and some associates at Cambridge, England, in 1933. The word is derived from Persian *pak*, "the Pure or Sacred," and *stan*, "land, country," and in the religious sense means "Land of the Pure." When it acquired a political sense it was given a second, alternative interpretation as an acrostic referring to the component areas which the proposed nation was to include: *P* for the Punjab; *A* for the Afghan (North-West Frontier) Province; *K* for Kashmir; *S* for Sind; (*S*)*TAN* for the last syllable of Baluchistan; the acrostic rather unflatteringly made no reference to what became East Pakistan. The other part of India, in contrast to Pakistan, Land of the Pure, was referred to by Pakistan advocates as Hindustan, Land of Hindus. Following partition, and after the adoption of the Indian constitution, Pakistanis in the government as well as out of it, taking their cue from the wording of the Indian constitution (1950), "India, that is, Bharat," made a practice of using the term "Bharat" with a derisive or pejorative implication, thereby irritating the Indians. The name Bhārat is an ancient one meaning the land of the legendary king Bharata. The Pakistani government relinquished the practice late in 1959. Though the name Pakistan was not employed in the

Muslim League's Lahore resolution (1940), it soon afterwards won wide currency among Muslim nationalists.

What part of India was at first claimed for Pakistan? For a long time the League did not define it. In its 1940 resolution it merely stated that "the North Western and Eastern Zones of India" should constitute " 'Independent States' in which the constituent elements shall be autonomous and sovereign." The wording implies that two separate sovereign states were contemplated, and in February of the following year reports circulated in the press that a subcommittee of the Muslim League whose duty was to study the various proposals for Pakistan was making this assumption. Jinnah later denied that the subcommittee had made a formal proposal to this effect. Various other specific delimitations were offered unofficially by supporters of Pakistan. Many proposals went outside the boundaries of India to include Afghanistan. Hindus frequently suspected that the real motive behind Pakistan was to establish Muslim rule over all India by force, and Muslims often made statements which gave some basis for that fear. For example, in April of 1947, H. S. Suhrawardy of the Muslim League, then premier-designate of the Bengal province, was reported in the New York *Times* to have said to the convention of Muslim legislators of Bengal, "The Muslims want to be the ruling race in this subcontinent." Less sweeping claims than Suhrawardy's were made officially by the League and its president, M. A. Jinnah. They demanded six provinces of British India. Four of these were in northwest India, namely, the three governor's provinces of the Punjab, the North-West Frontier Province, and Sind, and the commissioner's province of Baluchistan, all of which were predominantly Muslim in population. The other two were governor's provinces in northeastern India: Bengal, which was about 54 percent Muslim, and Assam, which was only about one third Muslim, but was included on the ground that it would be too weak to stand alone if separated from Hindustan by Bengal. These six provinces contained about 62 percent of India's Muslims and about 16 percent of the non-Muslims. Indian States, such as Kashmir, that were predominantly Muslim and by reason of geographical position seemed to Muslims designated for Pakistan were not officially claimed, since constitutionally the states would have the right to dispose of their own future.

There were from the beginning obvious and weighty objections to dividing India into two nations. First, the Hindu-Muslim communal problem, which the creation of Pakistan was to solve, clearly would still exist. In Hindustan there would be a Muslim minority and in Pakistan there would be non-Muslim minorities, which were already protesting. The Sikhs, for example, who lived chiefly in the eastern Punjab, were uncompromisingly opposed to Pakistan or anything that looked like it. Again, western Bengal, containing India's premier city, Calcutta, was predominantly Hindu. Jinnah indicated at various times that provincial boundary lines might be redrawn, but he and the League were never reconciled to any redrawing that would entail, as was nevertheless inevitable, the loss of Calcutta.

Second, there were administrative and economic disadvantages sure to result from Pakistan. A newly formed Pakistan would come into existence in chaos, without a well-ordered government organization, and would have severe handicaps threatening its very existence—as indeed became the case. Operation of the railroads, postal and telegraph services, and probably some other departments of national life, which were organized on an all-India basis, would be inefficient in a divided subcontinent. Economically, the proposed Pakistan would contain some weak members: Baluchistan and the North-West Frontier regularly required financial assistance from the rest of India. Division could not fail to hinder seriously the exchange of agricultural products and impair industrial development. It was sure to produce tariffs and customs barriers.

Third, the two parts of the proposed Pakistan would be separated from each other by a gap of 700 miles, across which they could communicate only by courtesy of the proposed Hindustan. When partition was effected, the area of Pakistan was lessened and the gap became over 900 miles. Finally, the princely Indian States would have to adjust themselves to two independent nations, instead of one. These disadvantages were so certain, so clearly pointed out, so much calculated to affect Muslims as well as Hindus, that they seemed to most foreign observers to forbid creation of Pakistan.

More ominous yet was another consideration. Partition now would produce an ancient, recurring, and sinister incompatibility between the Northwest and the rest of the subcontinent, which, but for a few brief periods of uneasy cohabitation, had kept them politically apart or hostile and had rendered the subcontinent defensively weak. When an intrusive people came through the northwestern passes and established itself, it was spiritually closer to the relatives it had left behind than to any group already in India. Not until it had been separated from those relatives for a fairly long period and had succeeded in pushing eastward would it loosen the external ties. In period after period this seems to have been true. In the third millennium B.C. the Harappa culture in the Indus valley was partly similar to contemporary western Asian civilizations and partly to later historic Indian culture of the Ganges valley. In the latter part of the next millennium the earliest Aryans, living in the Punjab and composing the hymns of the *Rig Veda,* were apparently more like their linguistic and religious kinsmen, the Iranians, than like their eastern Indian contemporaries. In the middle of the next millennium the Persian Achaemenians for two centuries held the Northwest as satrapies. After Alexander had invaded India (327/6–325 B.C), the Northwest was Hellenized, and once more was partly Indian and partly western. And after Islam entered India, the Northwest again was associated with Persia, Bokhara, Samarkand, Central Asia, rather than with India, and considered itself Islamic first and Indian second.

The periods during which the Punjab has been culturally assimilated to the rest of northern India are few if any at all. Periods of political assimilation are almost as few; perhaps a part of the fourth and third centuries B.C. under the Mauryas; possibly a brief period under the Indo-Greek king Menander in the second century B.C.; another brief period under the Kushanas in the first and second century of this era; an even briefer period under the Muslim kingdom of Delhi in the last quarter of the twelfth century; a long one under the great Mughals in the sixteenth and seventeenth centuries; a century under the British, 1849–1947.

This ambivalence has made the Northwest a menace to the rest of the subcontinent. It has always had a typical frontier characte., being turbulent, full of adventurers, proud to call itself "the sword arm of India," dissatisfied with its skimpy economy, constantly tempted to use that arm to move eastward and better itself. The Pakistan proposal, in advocating separation of the Northwest from India, was a twentieth century illustration of the ancient uncongeniality and contained an implied threat of renewed aggression. The rest of India could not fail to be uneasy about its security.

There was yet another ground for apprehension in having the

Northwest separated; that was its frequently demonstrated inability to resist a strong invading force from beyond the passes. Its own resources are small; its subdivisions as then drawn (the Punjab, the Frontier areas, Sind, Baluchistan) have had little coherence; it has needed the full support of what is now India to make a defense. The British understood that fact and shaped their military policy in India in the nineteenth century accordingly. They feared a Russian advance through Central Asia into Afghanistan and thence by the classic route through the passes into India. To defend the frontier they took Sind (1842–1844), destroyed the Sikh kingdom and annexed the Punjab (1845–1849), and fought two wars with Afghanistan (1838–1842, 1878–1880). They considered that only a united India could be defended.

The advocates of Pakistan might also have had some uneasiness about the defense of what became East Pakistan. It was to contain the subcontinent's vulnerable eastern frontier with Burma, though this was less likely to be penetrated than the even more vulnerable northwest frontier. East Pakistan, however, would be practically at the mercy of India. It had no natural defenses; it was remote from the dynamic western part of the proposed Pakistan; its people were not warlike. It was less vigorous in promoting the Pakistan proposal. Pakistan would need East Bengal's jute crop as its principal asset in foreign trade, but the area was a strategic liability.

But all the disadvantages inherent in the Pakistan proposal were insufficient to deter the Muslims. The sense of Islamic community need and the urge to attain power were more important than all other considerations. Muslims were willing to accept all the disadvantages and risks involved in order to set up their new state.

Much of the strength behind the Pakistan movement came from the personality of Muhammad (or Mahomed) Ali Jinnah (1876–1948). He was born in Karachi on December 25, 1876, in a small and unorthodox Muslim sect, and during the first forty-five years of his life had no reputation for Muslim piety or special interest in his community. He chose the law as his career, where he was brilliantly successful, and entered politics early in this century. In 1906 he was secretary to Dadabhai Naoroji (1825–1917), a Parsi, who is known as "the grand old man of Indian politics" and at that time was serving his third term as president of Congress. In 1910 Jinnah, then prominent in Congress, became a member of the Imperial Legislative Council, and was already on record as a progressive anti-communal Muslim. He condemned the principle of communal representation, which had been accepted in the Morley-Minto reforms of 1909, urged general Indian unity, and was considered by Muslim religious fundamentalists to be anti-Muslim. He remained faithful to Congress until 1920, when Gandhi, with his strong religious motivation, won an overwhelming ascendancy over that body. At that time the liberalizing reforms of the 1919 constitution offered greater political opportunities to Indians than before and consequently brought the ever latent and potent communal rivalry of Hindus and Muslims into heightened activity. During the years 1920–1922 Jinnah and many other prominent Muslims who had held membership in both the League and Congress resigned from Congress, because they thought that its policies were jeopardizing Muslim interests, and that therefore the Muslim community must organize an effective defense.

In 1934 Jinnah was elected permanent president of the Muslim League. The enlarged political opportunities given Indians by the 1935 constitution further increased the friction between the Hindu and Muslim communities. Under the conditions so created Jinnah converted his position as president into a dictatorship. His followers gave him the title of *Qa'id-i 'Azam*, which means Great Leader, and regularly used it in addressing him or speaking of him. His domination was indicated by numerous items, of which we may cite as typical a resolution adopted on March 23, 1942, at a Pakistan celebration in Calcutta, stating, "This meeting emphatically declares the Quaid-i-Azam Muhammad Ali Jinnah, President of the All-India Muslim League, alone represents and is entitled to speak on behalf of the Muslim nation." Jinnah exercised this function without equivocation; anyone opposing him, even the premier of Bengal in 1941, was forced out of the League. Jinnah was a man of quick and biting repartee, egotistic and sensitive to insult. He had the keenest sort of legal mind, and conducted his arguments with intricate and baffling reasoning. He was noted for his personal honesty, which he carried into his public life, having shown himself unsusceptible to political bribery; on several occasions he refused government offers of high office. In his devotion to Pakistan he attacked ferociously and without prejudice anyone—Hindu, British, or Muslim—who opposed the demand. With his leadership the Indian Muslim community acquired some of that quality of a well-drilled regiment which the Islamic religion had inculcated in the seventh century Arabs.

During the first three or four years after the Muslim League formally adopted Pakistan as its goal (1940), the vogue of the idea in the Muslim community as a whole was restricted. A number of Muslim parties were relatively indifferent to it; some others were directly opposed. The latter were not only the anti-communalist Muslim members of the Indian National Congress, who were organized as a subparty called the Nationalist Muslim party, but also other Muslim groups. Among these were the All-India Momin Conference, a rather loosely organized party drawn from the economically depressed Muslim classes; the Majlis-i-Ahrar, a belligerently left-wing and religiously fundamentalist group which originated in the Punjab to relieve the Muslim majority of Kashmir from the discrimination it suffered under the rule of the Hindu maharaja; the Azad party of Sind; the Jam'iat-al-'Ulama, a convocation of Muslim divines; many Shiah, or sectarian, Muslim groups (the Shiahs comprised about 8 percent of undivided India's Muslim community); the Ahmadiyas, a small sect motivated by a Messiah theory. Most of these bodies either never were effective in politics or by 1946 had lost the effectiveness they once had. The Nationalist Muslims, for example, won only 11 seats against the League's total of 426 in the 1946 provincial elections; the Jam'iat-al-'Ulama won only 5; the Momins, 5; the Ahrars, 1.

One group that was always opposed to Pakistan, and was the only really strong Muslim organization combating it, was that of the Khuda-i-Khidmatgar ("Servants of God"), the so-called "Red Shirts" of the North-West Frontier Province. This was a group closely affiliated to Congress; its leader, Abdul Ghaffar Khan, was deeply influenced by Gandhi's teaching and practice of nonviolence and introduced similar doctrine and methods among his Pathan followers in resisting the government of India. In the 1946 elections this group won 19 of the 34 seats reserved for Muslims in the North-West Frontier Province; the League won the other 15. The Red Shirts' seats together with the nine general seats and two of the three Sikh seats gave them control of the province, and Abdul Ghaffar Khan's brother, Doctor Khan Sahib, became premier of the province.

For several years after the League adopted Pakistan as its goal, the chief support for it came, not from the Muslim provinces that were expected to constitute the Muslim state, but from Muslims in provinces that were not to be included. It was opposed in Assam as well as in the North-West Frontier Province. In the Punjab, Bengal, and Sind the support was lukewarm and the opposition too strong for the League and Jinnah to overcome until after the Churchill government in 1942–1945 had confined the leaders of Congress and so crippled it. The premiers of those three provinces were at first all outside the League. It was the United Provinces (now Uttar Pradesh) and other regions where the Muslims were numerically inferior to the Hindus and therefore apprehensive that gave Pakistan its early strength.

After the Churchill government in 1942 sent Sir Stafford Cripps to India with constitutional proposals that would have made Pakistan possible, the impression got around among Muslims that the British, who after all had the power, felt that the proposal for Pakistan was reasonable and should be granted—or, at least, that the Churchill government was supporting it. The Cripps offer went a long way toward making the League inflexible on Pakistan.

Whenever it was proposed to Jinnah that a general plebiscite on the Pakistan issue should be held in the provinces which would constitute it, he refused. It was clear in 1946, however, that the Muslims as a whole supported it; for the League's brilliant success in the 1946 elections was based on a campaign in which Pakistan was almost the only issue.

The League and Jinnah often tried to attract moral support for Pakistan from Muslim countries outside India, especially those in the Near East. They got little answer except silence. They specifically inveighed against the further admission of Jews into Palestine, thus aligning themselves with the Arabs, but the Near Eastern Muslim states gave no encouraging response. These states had for many decades been fighting a nationalist battle against Britain and France. In India it was the Indian National Congress which they saw conducting a similar struggle; hence their sympathy was with it, rather than with the Muslim League, whose program seemed likely, by dividing India, to perpetuate the very imperialism which they were resisting.

Outside the Muslim community the chief popular support of Pakistan came from the Depressed Castes or Classes (Untouchables, Fifths, Harijans, Scheduled Castes). Under the 1935 constitution these received special representation through reservation of

151 of the 1585 seats in the various provincial legislatures. They nominated their own candidates, but the electing was by the general constituency, not by a separate electorate, as had been proposed by Ramsay MacDonald in 1932 when the constitution was being drafted but defeated by Gandhi through his "fast unto death." Politically conscious members of the Depressed Classes were dissatisfied with their gains under the Congress ministries (1937–1939) and developed their own parties. Their chief leader was Dr. B. R. Ambedkar, educated in the United States, who headed the Scheduled Castes Federation. He gave the League a measure of support, though he never let his party become its satellite. From the Depressed Classes' point of view Muslims or British or almost anyone would have been better as rulers than upper-caste Hindus.

Other support of the Pakistan proposal came from the Communist Party of India, which at its first Congress (May 1943) adopted a resolution concerning the solution of India's constitutional problem. The party affirmed that by its plan "Every section of the Indian people which had a contiguous territory as its homeland, common historical tradition, common language, culture, psychological make-up and common economic life would be recognized as a distinct nationality with the right to exist as an autonomous state within the free Indian union or federation and will have the right to secede from it if it so desires." The resolution enumerated a number of such potential nationalities: "Pathans, Western Punjabis (dominantly Muslims), Sikhs, Sindhis, Hindustanis, Rajasthanis, Gujeratis, Bengalis, Assamese, Beharis, Oriyas, Andhras, Tamils, Karnatakis, Maharashtrians, Keralas, etc." By these terms, the resolution stated, the Muslims, if they should wish, would be able to form a separate state, and it defended its stand concerning Pakistan by maintaining that it "concedes the just essence of the Pakistan demand and has nothing in common with the separatist theory of dividing India into two nations on the basis of religion." The recommendation was to lead to "a greater and grander unity of India than our country has ever seen."

The Communist Party of India from time to time reaffirmed or redefined or modified its position respecting Pakistan, trying to be at once both for the unity of India and for multinational separatism into "autonomous" or "sovereign" states, and in consequence was bitterly attacked by Congress. At the end of 1945, because of the Pakistan issue and other matters, there was a complete rupture between it and Congress, though some years before they had worked together against British rule. Later, when the Muslim League, during the quarrel over the Cabinet Mission's plan, observed "Direct Action Day" on August 16, 1946, the Communist Party joined in the demonstrations. It and the Muslim League, however, were never more than strange and temporary political bedfellows, and the Pakistan government had been no friend of Communists.

Various compromise solutions of the Pakistan issue were proposed during the years 1940–1946. The common element in all was decentralization of government. Some proposals would have retained the existing general structure of provinces and states united at the center in a common government exercising limited powers; others would have redrawn provincial boundaries on linguistic or economic lines; still others suggested an even looser arrangement, that is, the granting of Pakistan, but with the condition that Pakistan and Hindustan should form a federation for defense and promotion of common economic interests.

In promoting Pakistan, however, the Muslim League was inflexible and would accept no compromise. From the time of the war cabinet's offer in 1942, the prestige of the Muslim League as promoter of Pakistan steadily increased. At the same time the strength of the Indian National Congress was declining under the attack of Churchill's government, which outlawed both the all-India and the provincial Congress organizations, confined the leaders, and seemed bent on destroying Congress as a political force. The 1945–1946 elections in India, which the League fought on the sole issue of Pakistan, showed the growth of its power. Though in the last previous elections (1937) for the provincial assemblies the Muslim League had been able to win but 104 seats out of the 482 constitutionally reserved for and elected only by the Muslim community, in 1946 it won 412. The League also won 14 other seats, including 9 of the 10 reserved for Muslim women; in 1937 it had won only 5 other seats. Again, in the elections to the general Legislative Assembly, the League won all the 30 seats reserved for the Muslim constituency.

Confirmed then by this solid support, the League and Jinnah demanded Pakistan as an unalterable condition precedent to any further steps leading to solution of the constitutional problem. The Indian National Congress refused to accept this, though it was willing to move from its stand in favor of a strong closely knit central government to one with very limited powers.

The climax was now not far distant. In March 1946 the British Labour government sent out a three-man Cabinet Mission (including Cripps) to try to solve the constitutional problem. The mission held interviews with representatives of the various political, regional, religious, and social groups involved. On May 16, 1946, its plan was read in the House of Commons by Prime Minister Attlee as a White Paper. The Cabinet Mission, though rejecting the Pakistan demand in its full and complete form, made extensive concessions to it. Two of these we may note here. The first and more basic was a narrow limitation put upon the powers of the proposed Indian union's central government. It was to deal only with foreign affairs, defense, communications, and the financing of these subjects. All other subjects were to rest in the provincial governments. In this way the mission thought to reduce to a minimum, if not entirely eliminate, the danger that Hindu provinces might practice discrimination against Muslim provinces.

Second, the eleven governor's provinces of British India were to be free to form themselves into "groups." Each group could have its own executive and legislature functioning over the provinces in it and could determine the provincial subjects of government to be taken in common. Since the government of a group was not to be limited to the narrow range of subjects prescribed for the central union government, it was potentially able to become a very compact, highly centralized, and efficient political body, in contrast to the central Union. Further the Cabinet Mission's plan proposed to put something like grouping into operation at once, in advance of the drafting of a constitution. It divided the eleven provinces into three "sections," which if they wished could later become "groups." Representatives of the three sections were to deliberate separately in the constituent assembly which the Cabinet Mission was providing for. Two of the sections were to be predominantly Muslim in population and corresponded closely to current geographical demands for Pakistan (one was to include the Punjab, Sind, the North-West Frontier; the second, Bengal and Assam); the other, non-Muslim. A province might opt out of the section to which it was assigned in the plan when the new constitution should come into effect, provided the province's legislature should take such a decision after the first general election under the new constitution. The result at the beginning of the plan's operation was to be a kind of Near-Pakistan.

The mission further laid down as a principle that whenever in the executive and the legislature there should arise a question touching a major communal issue, decision should require the assent not merely of the majority of representatives present and voting, but also a majority of the representatives of each of the two major communities. This provision seemed to the Cabinet Mission a sufficient safeguard to prevent the Hindu community from forcing its will upon the Muslims.

The princely Indian States would regain all the rights which they had had to surrender in recognizing British paramountcy and the terms on which they would accede to the Indian union would have to be the subject of negotiation.

To carry on government until a constituent assembly could be elected, the mission's plan provided for the appointment of an interim cabinet, which was to be a coalition and have "the support of the major political parties."

At first both Congress and the League seemed to be favorably impressed by the plan, but in the end it failed, and as it was failing the tense relations between the two communities snapped strand by strand. The League demanded parity with Congress in the interim government (five portfolios each out of a total of twelve) and the sole right to nominate any Muslim. Congress would allow only five portfolios to the League against six to itself, feeling that in view of its greater strength parity would be unfair—it held 56 seats in the central Legislative Assembly against the League's 30, and in the provincial legislatures held more than twice as many. Nor would it relinquish the right to nominate a Muslim; it was not a communal body, as was the League, and was not going to be jockeyed into appearing as one. The League at first boycotted the interim government, but afterwards, when such a government took office (September 2) with its membership nominated by Congress, it finally entered (October 26), not having won its points. This government, however, operated without teamwork, the members apparently never meeting in full session but transacting most of their cabinet business by correspondence.

In respect to the constituent assembly which was to frame India's new constitution, the League refused to cooperate. Jawaharlal

Nehru, president of Congress, had made an indiscreet statement on July 10, 1946: "The probability is, from any approach to the question, there will be no grouping." He had indicated that the arrangement of provinces in sections for the constituent assembly, as provided in the Cabinet Mission's plan, was unacceptable to two provinces (Assam and the North-West Province), then controlled by Congress but included in the Muslim sections, and would therefore be abrogated by them as soon as the sections should meet, instead of at the later time indicated in the plan. The League said that such statements showed that Congress had been insincere in accepting the plan, and continued to affirm later that Congress had not actually accepted it.

When the announcement was made that a government would be formed even without the League's cooperation, the League endeavored to rouse the Muslim community. Jinnah said, "This day we bid goodbye to constitutional methods," and the League adopted a resolution directing "the Working Committee to prepare forthwith a programme of direct action . . . and to organize the Muslims for the coming struggle to be launched as and when necessary." It named August 16 as "Direct Action Day," calling for demonstrations, which it said should be nonviolent. But Bengal and Bihar had had almost continuous riots throughout 1946, and that day and several following were marked by the bloodiest communal rioting in Calcutta which India had yet known. Bengal had a Muslim government and the premier, H. S. Suhrawardy, was afterwards accused of complicity. In the weeks following there were communal riots in Bombay and many other cities, and the disturbances in Bihar against Muslims and in Eastern Bengal against Hindus broke out again in the most extreme form. The district of Noakhali in Bengal, where Muslims outnumbered Hindus four or five to one, was pacified only when Gandhi made a tour through it. These various disturbances seemed like possible opening moves in the civil war which Jinnah had prophesied would be inevitable if India were given self-government without the accompanying award of Pakistan.

The dispute between Congress and the League over the grouping of provinces in the constituent assembly continued uninterruptedly and inconclusively through the summer and autumn. The British government, evidently trying to stimulate agreement, reaffirmed its position on December 6, just three days before the constituent assembly met, and in reply the All-India Congress Committee on January 7, 1947, adopted a resolution over considerable opposition in which it expressed hope for successful working of the assembly and then said that there must be no "compulsion of a province." Matters were not advanced by these two statements.

Hindu-Muslim violence meanwhile remained continuous in Bengal, Bihar, the United Provinces, the Punjab, Assam, and elsewhere. In the Punjab it brought about the downfall of the government which had been set up by the Unionist party, a coalition of Hindus, Sikhs, and non-League Muslims led by Khizr Hyat Tiwana and working closely with Congress. His government, already shaky from Muslim League attacks, had tried at the end of January to curb the disorders. It had arrested a number of Muslim leaders, including sixteen members of the Punjab legislature, some former high officials of the government of India, and the president of the Punjab Muslim League; had outlawed the Muslim national guard, which since being organized in 1937 had acquired a semimilitary character; and had declared illegal the Rashtriya Swayamsevak Sangh, a militant Hindu action body which later (like the Sikh organization called Seva Dal) at the time of partition was held responsible for organizing and executing much of the violence against Muslims in Delhi. The Punjab disorders, however, did not cease. The Muslim League launched a campaign that drove Khizr Hyat Khan out of office early in March. Riots of extreme violence followed all over the Punjab, so severe as to be like battles, and the governor, Sir Evan Jenkins, assumed control under section 93 of the constitution. Congress' power in the Punjab had by this time been destroyed.

In the constantly deteriorating situation the Labour government now made a desperate—but not yet its most desperate—effort to stop the bloody dispute. Prime Minister Attlee announced on February 20, 1947, that if an agreed constitution were not worked out by June 1948 at the latest the British government would grant full self-government to British India in one of three ways: either to British India as a unit, or in some areas to the existing provincial governments, or in some other way that would be "in the best interests of the Indian people." At the same time Admiral the Viscount Mountbatten (of Burma) was being appointed Viceroy in place of Lord Wavell.

When Lord Mountbatten got to India on March 22, he made a

quick examination of the situation, ascertaining that the Cabinet Mission's plan would not be accepted, noted statements of Congress leaders (Nehru, Rajendra Prasad) showing them receptive to partition as a means of ending the bloodshed, found Jinnah aware that he would have to accept a smaller Pakistan than he had been demanding, and discovered the Sikhs ready to concede division of the Punjab. He then returned to London on May 18, where he recommended a drastic course of action which was promptly accepted. He then returned to India and got acquiescence in a general way from most of the leaders. On June 3 in the House of Commons Attlee outlined the plan, which called for partitioning India, and the next day Lord Mountbatten said that the appointed day for independence and partition would be August 15. On July 15 the House of Commons passed the Indian Independence Act by which India was divided into two independent nations, each with full dominion status, while the Indian States were left free to accede to whichever they wished.

At the conferences between British officials and Indian party leaders held in India and leading to acceptance of the terms of independence and partition it had been tacitly assumed that the Dominion of Pakistan and the Dominion of India would both ask Lord Mountbatten to be the first Governor General. India did ask him and he became Governor General, but Jinnah took the position of Governor General of Pakistan for himself, and held it until his death in September 1948. Mountbatten had the support alike of Indian leaders and in Britain of leaders of the Labour and Conservative parties. This was a tribute to his skill in effecting an agreement and a peaceful solution of what had seemed to be a hopeless problem bound to lead to civil war. The very speed of his decisions, however, laid him open to charges of excessive haste, lack of adequate planning and groundwork, and neglect of the interests of the Sikhs, whose area was sliced through by the line of partition.

Provision had been made in the case of questionable areas to ascertain preference in joining India or Parkistan by reference to the electorate or its representatives. Two boundary commissions were appointed to demarcate the division in Bengal and the Punjab respectively, headed by a British lawyer, Sir Cyril (later Lord) Radcliffe. When both commissions became deadlocked, he made a decision (Radcliffe Award), odious now in each nation. Some boundary questions remained unsettled until 1960. In respect to national assets the general basis was 82.5 percent to India, 17.5 percent to Pakistan; but in some matters the percentages were altered by partition committees. Everything had to be done with the greatest haste. As Lord Mountbatten put it: it had taken three years to separate Burma from India, two years to separate Sind from Bombay, and two years to separate Orissa from Bihar, but only two and a half months were taken to divide all India in two. The result was action without adequate administrative preparation.

The two new nations started off badly. In the capitals great crowds celebrated the independence—in Karachi with the slogan "long live Pakistan" (*pakistan zindabad*); in Delhi with "victory to India" (*jay hind*). But this was only a minute fraction of the total response, which was opposite, savage, and appalling. For the violence that now occurred was colossal, beyond all that Indian, Pakistani, or British officials had feared. It had begun before August 15. In West Punjab and the North-West Frontier, Muslims murdered Sikhs and Hindus; in East Punjab and the Sikh states, Sikhs and Hindus murdered Muslims. In parts of the United Provinces Hindus and Muslims murdered each other. In the border regions of Jammu and Kashmir Sikhs crossed as refugees from West Pakistan to spread violence. Peaceful villages suddenly became two hostile camps, one portion of the population trying to exterminate the other. In the cities, especially in Lahore and Delhi, terrorism was in control. Houses were fired, looting went unchallenged, women were kidnapped, massacre took place on the main highways. The leaders of neither side could control the situation. Pakistanis charged that the Sikhs and the armed and drilled Rashtriya Swayamsevak Sangh operated by plan in well-directed organization, as apparently they did; the further charges that high Indian officials abetted them have not been substantiated. Indians charged that Pakistani troops detailed to guard Sikhs and Hindus instead took part in the slaughter. The number of deaths by direct violence is unknown; claims run up to a million. Various Americans and British working at relief in the affected areas at the time have guessed —and they have claimed to do no more than guess—that it was over 100,000, possibly at the outside 200,000. Besides the deaths by violence there were others from disease, hunger, and exposure, for floods came at this time, too. The total may have been close to half a million. For weeks there were wide areas where the situation was little short of anarchic. In Bengal, killings were fewer, partly because Gandhi exercised a check there.

A corollary of the violence was mass migration. Fearful Hindus and Sikhs left West Punjab and Muslims left East Punjab and nearby regions of the United Provinces. There was probably not a Sikh (except for members of some quietistic sects in Sind) left in West Pakistan, and few Hindus. Many Muslims left India. The migration extended over months, even years. The total number of migrants both ways in all parts of the subcontinent is set at 12 million; if the two governments' claims are added it comes to about 17 million. This was the greatest movement of population known to history.

The immediate responsibility for the tragedies occurring at the time of partition must be laid to Hindu-Muslim communal antipathy, fomented by the Muslim League, the Hindu Mahasabha, and many individuals not belonging to either organization but animated by the communal spirit. But Indian National Congress shortsightedness and Muslim League intransigence had set the stage, while the British, by their political policies for fifty years, had augmented the communal mistrust. At the last moment the British were also unequal to the double demand of abrogating power and at the same time protecting those who had been subject to it.

9 Sequel to Partition

When independence and partition were jointly proclaimed, the less sophisticated Hindu nationalists thought that India had at last started on the road to prosperity and the less sophisticated Muslim communalists expected something like the millennium in the new nation they had acquired. Both were quickly disillusioned. The violence accompanying partition produced internal problems for each nation, and at the same time, quarrels developed between the two.

The first problem was that of caring for refugees. Pakistan had experienced the greater violence, and its difficulties, too, were greater. It had a less well organized—one might say, a still scarcely organized—administration to preserve law and order and protect evacuees leaving its territory, and fewer available resources to help arriving refugees. In each country evacuee railroad trains proceeded slowly to the border, almost invariably suffering long halts with little or no food, often attacked and plundered, frequently violated by murder. Peasants loaded their movable possessions on their carts, yoked up their bullocks, took any additional stock on lead, and set out in convoy on a laborious trek to the other nation. They might lose animals on the way, perhaps from starvation, perhaps from hostile raids. The economically less fortunate, the poorest landholders or tenants and landless laborers, who owned no carts, would travel by foot, old people, children, and ailing, as well as the able-bodied. Protection was often inadequate; food was scarce for human beings and might be entirely lacking for animals; medical attention hardly existed.

The refugees would reach their new homeland in desperate straits, and there too might find food and medical services meager. When, for example, a Muslim convoy from India came to the Pakistan end of the bridge across the Sutlej at Sulaimanki, it was not enough, even for those who could read, to see the signboard at the camp entrance congratulating them on reaching an Islamic land. The new arrivals needed a more substantial welcome. They wanted more food for themselves than the new state could make available; they required grain or grass for their bullocks and there was none. They wanted medicine, hospitals, mere resting places, which Pakistan was furnishing as well as it could but as yet inadequately. Most of all they demanded new land holdings on which to settle and reestablish their lives, and of these too there were not enough to go around.

For similar refugees coming to India, there were several camps, of which the largest, located at Kurukshetra, about 100 miles north of Delhi, was a model in organization, sanitation, feeding, and housing. But most of the others were desperately inadequate. In these unhealthy, poorly organized, demoralizing quarters refugees were held for relocation.

Besides peasantry there were large numbers of the less prosperous villagers and urban dwellers—artisans, coolies, and others of the lower economic levels who were generally attracted to cities. Camps were established in the suburbs to accommodate them, but these could not hold all. Eight years after partition, in 1955, many streets in the capitals, Delhi and Karachi, were lined with flimsy shelters, where families were living, totaling hundreds of thousands of persons, some under only a piece of matting or gunny sack supported on bamboo poles, others, better off, with walls of the same material or of cut and flattened oil cans, while inside were a few cooking utensils and a blanket or two. In front might be some trifling objects displayed for sale. Still other refugees, without families and with no shelter at all, slept in the open on the sidewalks. Over all swarmed countless flies. Such people had little or no employment and obtained relief on a bare subsistence basis. They presented critical health and police problems, were a constant drain on public morale, took an important slice of the national resources for their support, and by their very presence inflamed the public of each country against the other.

The refugee problem had been partly relieved by 1962 in both India and Pakistan by the construction of residence colonies, as at Karachi and Delhi, and by rehabilitation, but by no means all had been cared for. Many regugees were still living in substandard quarters in Karachi and Calcutta, apparently sunk in permanent poverty. In 1962 the Indian registrar-general's office reported an abnormal influx of Muslims into Assam from Pakistan. The number of illegal immigrants was unofficially estimated at one million. Even as late as 1971 there were still refugees living in vaguely defined areas of or near Bombay and Calcutta and some other cities and towns. Some of these were with children or grandchildren, according to report. Similar reports came from Karachi. This was before the revolt in East Pakistan and the suppression of that revolt with its unimaginable harshness that sent about 10 million Pakistani citizens seeking refuge in India, many of whom went to live in the Calcutta area in the same squalor.

Promptly, too, after partition in 1947 there arose a dispute between the nations concerning possessions abandoned by evacuees, whose rural or urban immovable property was liable to forfeiture, while there were severe restrictions concerning the export of jewelry and other valuables, bank deposits, and securities. The evacuees, some of whom were prominent and influential, indignantly demanded that the nation to which they had fled should recoup their losses from property left behind by evacuees emigrating to the other nation. Some managed to effect property exchanges across the borders with refugees of the other persuasion. Some others through the press, friends, or any other available means agitated for the government of their new nation to employ economic sanctions or military force in recovering their claims— which would have meant war.

In each country restrictions on sale and ownership were quickly placed upon evacuees' rural or urban holdings; this often amounted to confiscation. There were many persons who at some personal risk remained behind to care for their property, hoping when they had disposed of it to migrate to the other country for permanent residence. It became a lawyer's problem to determine who was an evacuee. Was the so-far-unmigrated relative of someone who had migrated an "intending evacuee" and if so how was the law to deal with him? The legal definition of an evacuee came to be extended, and more and more persons were included in the category. Title to an evacuee's property came by ordinance to vest in the government of the nation he had left. The question inevitably had to be handled at the government level and chronically inflamed the articulate public.

With respect to evacuee property the two governments had a wearying succession of discussions, conferences, disagreements, agreements, and then charges of nonimplementation and bad faith, and complaints by each government that the other had been making harsher and more repressive laws concerning evacuee property. In 1955 the problem of movable property and bank accounts seemed to have been settled. The problem of immovable property, however, was stated by Pakistan to be incapable of settlement until the Indus valley canal-waters dispute (to be discussed below) was settled, since much of the agricultural land involved was watered by canals from the Sutlej and Ravi rivers and its value would depend upon the terms of whatever settlement should be made. With the signing of an agreement on September 19, 1960, that obstacle seemed to be removed.

Another dispute which promptly arose concerned Pakistan's assets. The successor government of India had been left in possession of the cash balances of undivided India, and by agreement was to transfer 55 crores of rupees (Rs. 550,000,000, then about $170,000,000) to Pakistan. After the Kashmir quarrel developed, many Indians, including some high officials, opposed paying the sum on the ground that Pakistan would use the money for war against India. This was one of the issues said to have been espoused by Gandhi in January 1948, when he fasted to obtain generally better treatment of Muslims in India. A payment was arranged at that time. Pakistan maintained that India unjustly withheld other sums due her and did not hand over her full share of military stores. India, on its side, made counterclaims. These issues were well cleared up in 1960.

A third subject of caustic dispute was the distribution of the Indus valley canal waters, a matter of long-term national economic importance to both nations. The situation was briefly as follows. In West Pakistan, where rainfall is scanty, agriculture depends largely upon irrigaton from the river Indus and its five tributaries, the Jhelum, Chenab, Ravi, Beas, and Sutlej. During the British period the old system of irrigation was enlarged by the building of huge dams or barrages, and the Punjab became one of the most prosperous provinces of British India.

The problem that developed under partition arose from the fact that Pakistan makes greater use of the water, while India controls the upper courses of rivers supplying much of that water. The Ravi, Beas, and Sutlej, which were used to irrigate 11 million acres in West Punjab, 5 million in Sind, and 3 million in the Bahawalpur and Khairpur states, flow through Indian territory before reaching Pakistan. India, therefore, could divert their water from Pakistan's canals, and thus seriously injure the country's basic economy. If India should retain Kashmir, whose ownership was disputed, she could exercise some of the same sort of control over the Indus, Jhelum, and Chenab, which flow from it into Pakistan. The entire Indus system would then be involved, and the total situation would give India a mortal grip on West Pakistan's agriculture.

In 1947 the Punjab Boundary Commission and the Partition Committee dealing with canals took the position that the distribution of water would remain the same as in the undivided Punjab, and that it would not be very difficult to execute such an arrangement. But there was no time to devise a permanent scheme for administering those works which serve both parts of the Punjab. The Arbitral Tribunal, a temporary body created under the Indian Independence Act, set up a temporary scheme which expired at the end of March 1948, when the Tribunal came to an end. A dispute thereupon started, in which neither side was for long willing to make any concessions, though a working arrangement existed.

Connected with the Punjab canal-waters problem was a dispute about the construction of a large dam by the government of India at Bhakra on the upper Sutlej, to provide additional water for Punjab (India) irrigation, and a weir eight miles lower downstream at Nangal to furnish power. Pakistan affirmed that this scheme would divert from her territory some of the water which she was then receiving, and would also deprive her of the share of power to which she was entitled by international precedent. India pointed out that the Bhakra scheme was not something she had thought up since partition but that it "has been under consideration or preparation for the last thirty years." Pakistan also claimed that India was building a headworks below the junction of the Sutlej and Beas to divert water from those streams out of the Indus valley area and convey them across the divide to the Jumna basin to irrigate land there. This would injure agriculture in large parts of Punjab (Pakistan) and the state of Bahawalpur.

In correspondence between Prime Ministers Liaquat Ali Khan and Jawaharlal Nehru, as well as in other documents, Pakistan asked that the canal-waters dispute be referred for adjudication to the International Court of Justice. India replied, however, that negotiation should be continued between the two countries or that a judicial tribunal should be appointed representing both India and Pakistan to deal with the problem. This left matters in a deadlock, with no resulting injury to India, but with Pakistan's situation urgent. In May 1952, the matter came to the attention of the International Bank for Reconstruction and Development, which was trying to devise a plan for comprehensive utilization of the Indus basin waters. The Bank, through long and difficult negotiation, at last succeeded in getting the two nations to sign an agreement on September 19, 1960, involving distribution of the water and providing for extensive engineering projects financed by loans covered by the United States, Great Britain, Canada, Australia, New Zealand, and West Germany, and by contributions by India and Pakistan.

An economic war between the two nations began shortly' after partition. In undivided India the areas of the two new nations had had a complementary economic relationship which was vital to both. What became West Pakistan produced more wheat than it consumed and sent the surplus to deficit areas in what is now India. Sind and the Punjab (Pakistan) grew cotton, but lacked enough mills to manufacture it, and so used to ship about a million bales yearly to regions now in India, whence the present Pakistan areas received back most of the 500 million yards or more of cloth required for their needs above their own production. In what became East Pakistan three fourths or more of the world's jute crop was raised, including almost all of the best quality. But the raw jute was manufactured in and near Calcutta (in India), where were located about 57 percent of the world's jute looms. Coal in the subcontinent is almost exclusively an Indian product and the Pakistan areas needed to import about three million tons of it annually. Pakistan had an annual deficit of about 370 million pounds of sugar, which could be supplied from India's surplus. Iron is mined in Bihar and made into steel in Bihar and Bengal in India. This and other miscellaneous products needed in Pakistan, which before partition was virtually without factories, were most readily supplied from the products of industry situated in the present India. Foreign trade of the subcontinent flowed chiefly through four main ports—Calcutta, Bombay, Karachi, Madras—on which the railway systems converge. Karachi served West Pakistan, but East Pakistan had no good port, and after partition endeavored to make one of Chittagong in East Bengal not far from the eastern frontier. But Chittagong was never more than a second-class port. A decade before partition the economic interdependence of India's parts seemed natural, necessary, and bound to continue. But with partition the system was rudely shattered.

Just before partition, India and Pakistan made a standstill agreement to run until the end of February 1948 (six and a half months), which provided for free trade and precluded any interruption as by customs barriers. Existing import and export policies were to be continued, and there was to be free movement of goods, persons, capital, and money remittances, without transit duties. The arrangements quickly broke down. In November 1947, Pakistan imposed an export levy of Pakistan Rs. 15 (about $4.60) on each bale (400 lbs.) of jute. This was a blow to the jute mills of Calcutta, which could not keep busy on the meager and inferior Indian-grown jute. To meet the increased cost of raw jute, India increased the price of the manufactured product, and the government imposed an export duty on it which was far in excess of Pakistan's export duty on raw jute. Later, Pakistan levied an export duty of Rs. 60 a bale on raw cotton, again striking at Indian industry, and a 10 percent ad valorem export duty on raw hides, skins, and cottonseeds. The ostensible purpose of these duties was to produce revenue, but in the existing atmosphere of animosity, they were regarded by the public in both countries as acts of hostility. India retaliated with export duties on machine-made cloth and cotton yarns, oilseeds, vegetable oils, and manganese, and also raised the price of coal. Pakistan spokesmen accused India of trying to break Pakistan economically, and especially to destroy the economy of East Bengal, where the burden of the jute war fell. This region was already dissatisfied with its unfavorable tax position in relation to West Pakistan, and Pakistanis claimed that India hoped to produce discontent and in consequence a movement for reunion.

The crisis came in September 1949, when most sterling bloc countries including India devalued their currency but Pakistan did not. The refusal to devalue was regarded in India as hostile. India had an adverse trade balance with Pakistan estimated at Rs. 350,000,000 (about $73,500,000) and nondevaluation would make her pay 44 percent more than before for imports of raw materials from Pakistan. Pakistan also was considered by India on the basis of "a very rough guess" to owe her a debt of 3 billion rupees, payable in Indian rupees, now worth only two thirds as many Pakistan rupees. India immediately severed trade relations, thus depriving her mills of needed supplies and causing shutdown, but also denying Pakistan her necessary coal imports and the profit from disposing of her exportable products.

The advantage seemed at first to lie with India, which had a basically stronger economy, but Pakistan's position was saved by the Korean War and the western nations' rush to stockpile cotton, jute, and wool. Meanwhile, India's diminution of industry further weakened her economy, which was already crippled by the urgent need to use all available resources for the purchase of food. India, therefore, came to see that she had to end the trade war, and on February 25, 1951, the two nations signed an agreement to run until the end of June 1953, but it was less comprehensive than the earlier agreement. It excluded jute, cotton, rice, and coal, which were the main commodities in India-Pakistan trade. Trade and commercial questions were not finally settled until 1960.

A long-running quarrel developed over the treatment of the Hindu minority in Pakistan and the Muslim minority in India. The critical area was the two Bengals (Indian and Pakistani); to a much less extent Kashmir, (the then) Hyderabad, the Punjab, and Uttar Pradesh were involved, and some others to a still less extent. The intercommunal violence accompanying partition never completely subsided and there was a constant movement of population each way between India and Pakistan. In the process Pakistan was assuming a more homogeneous character; non-Muslims were all but purged out of West Pakistan; and the Hindus of East Pakistan, who were esimated at about 12 million at the time of partition and 9.3 million in 1951 were emigrating in the 1951–1961 decade at a rate sufficient virtually to cancel out their natural increase. Thus, while their total number was reported in the census of 1961 as just over 10 million, they constituted only 10.67 percent of the total population as against 22.1 percent in 1951. By late in 1971 the percentage must have shrunk a great deal, how much, of course, it is impossible to say, but it seems likely that most of the East Pakistan Hindus had gone to India or been slaughtered. The Muslim portion of the population of Pakistan, which was 76.7 percent for those regions in 1941, was estimated to be 83.3 percent in 1949 and 85.9 percent in 1951; the 1961 census put the total at 88.1 percent. The state was rapidly moving toward Muslim control of its government, and of its economic life. Hindus were dropping out of business, factory work, and agriculture. In India, however, where the Muslims were a minority, the shift in their percentage was slight—from 11.9 percent of the population in 1941 in the areas later concluded in the Indian Union to 11.1 percent in 1949, 9.9 percent in 1951, and about 10.5 percent in 1961. In India there has been no appreciable change toward establishing a religious structure of the administration except for a diminution of Muslim elements in the police and military, nor has there been evidence of religious reconstitution of the national economy.

By the latter part of 1949 the tempo of violence between Hindus and Muslims in Bengal in consequence of the economic war had accelerated rapidly. Hindus forced out of business in cities of East Bengal and migrating to Calcutta were bitter against the Pakistan government, which they charged had encouraged the dispossession and had withheld their property as they left. Hindu peasants, fearful of attack, on arriving in India found no place to go and were equally bitter. Retaliation was inevitable, and many imperiled Muslim peasants of West Bengal and inhabitants of Calcutta emigrated to East Bengal, where they too found themselves destitute.

The press in each of the two Bengals published inflammatory accounts of atrocities, exaggerated and poorly authenticated, often based upon events long since passed but freshly reprinted as though current news. Active communal organizations in West Bengal—the Hindu Mahasabha, the Rashtriya Swayamsevak Sangh, and the Council for Protection of the Rights of the Minorities—demanded that partition be repudiated and East Bengal be forcibly made a part of India, or that it be constrained by economic pressure. Anti-Muslim riots broke out in Calcutta in January 1950, and in February anti-Hindu riots followed in Dacca, capital of East Bengal, and then in other parts of the state. The Prime Ministers of the two nations each charged that the other nation was carrying on hostile propaganda and arousing the public against the minority within its borders. Hindus again fled from East Bengal in great numbers, bringing their suffering and anger to Calcutta. When the Holi festival of the Hindus came in the first week of March 1950, tension was high not only in Bengal but in other parts of India and disturbances were numerous.

By this time Hindus were speaking of a "deep-laid plot" in East Pakistan to expel all Hindus, and the excution of it was ascribed to the *ansars* ("helpers," originally of the Prophet), a kind of militia said at the time to be about 40,000 strong; the *ansars* came into prominence again in 1971, being reported to share with the military and the police in crushing the East Pakistan revolt. At the time of the 1950 anti-Hindu activities in East Pakistan responsible Pakistani officials—the Prime Minister of the country and the Prime Minister of East Bengal—spoke of a "master plan" directed by India's Deputy Prime Minister Patel to spread hatred of Muslims. Suspicion grew on each side, and it was reported that India was mobilizing troops for war. Both Jawaharlal Nehru and Liaquat Ali Khan, however, had no desire for war, and each by endeavors in his country's part of Bengal calmed the population until they could meet and effect negotiations. On April 8 they signed the Delhi Pact affirming the rights of minorities in their respective states in explicit terms.

The agreement assured minorities of "complete equality of citizenship irrespective of religion, a full sense of security in respect of life, culture, property, and personal honour, freedom of movement within each country, and freedom of occupation, speech, and worship, subject to law and morality." Minorities were to have equal right to participate in the public life of the country, and their allegiance and loyalty were stated to be due to the state of which they were citizens—"it is to the Government of their own State that they must look for redress of their grievances," not to the government of the other state. Other provisions dealt with property rights of migrants and the right to return to their homes, and were to affect the 1,500,000 Hindus who had left East Bengal and the many Muslims who had fled from Bihar and West Bengal. Antagonistic propaganda was to be curbed. The pact allayed public fear, and the war scare was dissipated.

Communal antipathy, however, was not dispelled. Eleven days after the pact was signed (that is, on April 19, 1950), two members of the Indian cabinet, Shyama Prasad Mookerjee and K.C. Neogy, resigned. Mookerjee, a prominent member of the Hindu Mahasabha, made a long statement in which he condemned the agreement as a product of "drift and indecision," offering no solution of the basic ill, which he described as "Pakistan's concept of an Islamic state and the ultra-communal administration based on it." He complained that blame had not been fixed squarely on Pakistan as the aggressor, nor were Hindu refugees receiving compensation. He asserted that the agreement would not stop the exodus of Hindus from Pakistan.

In the other nation six months after the pact was signed, on October 8, 1950, Jogendra Nath Mandal, Minister for Law and Labour and the only Hindu in the Pakistan cabinet, himself a Panchama (Untouchable) from Bengal, resigned his position as a mark of protest against the treatment of Hindus in Pakistan, especially in Bengal. He accused Pakistan of "squeezing out Hindus from Pakistan," a process which he said "has succeeded completely in West Pakistan and is nearing completion in East Bengal." He regretted his own former collaboration with Pakistan, which had seemed to him a way of safeguarding the interests of the Depressed Classes in Pakistan. The resignation was a sharp denial of Pakistan's claim to be treating Hindus fairly, and Liaquat Ali Khan denounced him as a warmonger, who had been traitorously intriguing with communal Hindu elements in Calcutta against Pakistan.

Minority commissions were set up in the two Bengals, and government officials in both India and Pakistan and prominent nonofficial citizens from time to time issued reassuring statements. But from each side came continued tales of mistreatment of minorities, and as the refugees came with their stories they kept the public agitated. Fully verifiable cases of mistreatment actually occurred, as at Jabalpur (Jubbulpore) in February 1961, when large-scale attacks were made upon the Muslim community lasting for more than a week. There was retaliatory violence against Hindus in Pakistan. In May 1962 stories appeared in Indian and Pakistani newspapers of new communal disturbances in the two Bengals.

In the spring of 1952 Pakistan and then India decided to impose passport and visa regulations upon travel between the two nations. The first result was an alarmed increase in migration between the two Bengals and an accompanying increase of ill feeling between the two nations.

Very quickly after partition political issues arose between India and Pakistan concerning the accession of certain princely states. Strictly speaking, the Indian Independence Act of 1947 applied directly only to former British India and not to the Indian States, which were, in theory, independent. But it had a provision opening the way for the Indian States to accede to one or the other of the two dominions. It was evident that the States could not exist except as parts of the new dominions, while it would also be dangerous to the dominions for the States to remain independent political entities. Lord Mountbatten, as Governor General, used his good offices before partition to induce them to accede and in so doing to recognize in the new dominions the paramountcy previously recognized in Britain.

Three States, however, held out, not wishing to accede to the dominion to which by reason of geographical contiguity and their system of communications they would naturally have allied themselves. These were the two largest, namely, Kashmir in the extreme northwest and Hyderabad in the south, and the small state of Junagadh in the west (and a petty holding called Manavadar). Junagadh (and Manavadar) endeavored to accede to Pakistan; Kashmir formally acceded to India; and Hyderabad strove to maintain its independence, with implications that, if accession could not be avoided, its ruler would prefer to accede to Pakistan rather than to India. All three cases became subjects of controversy between India and Pakistan and were carried to the United Nations. The status of Junagadh and Hyderabad as belonging to India seems to be finally settled; that of Kashmir still remains in dispute.

Junagadh, named after its capital city, was a small coastal state of 3337 square miles and a population of 671,000 in 1941, situated in the peninsula of Kathiawar, connected by all land routes with areas that came to be included in the Indian union. Its population was about four-fifths non-Muslim, but the ruler was Muslim. He entered into a standstill agreement with Pakistan on August 15, 1947, and signed an instrument of accession on September 15, 1947. India promptly objected in August and proposed that the matter be referred to a plebiscite, but Pakistan ignored the suggestion for many weeks. Early in September India sent troops to points nearby. Many of the state's subjects had protested the accession and organized resistance had developed. As disorder broke out, a provisional government was formed, and the government of India took over the city of Junagadh on November 9, 1947, to save it from "administrative breakdown." In February 1948 a plebiscite was held and the result was overwhelmingly in favor of accession to India. Junagadh was integrated in the then state of Saurashtra (the United States of Kathiawar) and now is a part of Gujarat. It could not be doubted that the Junagadh question was quickly dead, as Nehru often said, and Pakistan could not realistically hope ever to receive the territory. But the Pakistan government tried to keep the issue alive, perhaps only to use it as an argument in the Kashmir dispute, and has never admitted the legitimacy of Junagadh's accession to India.

The case of Hyderabad was much more complicated than that of Junagadh. The Hyderabad State, now no longer in existence as a political entity, was named after its capital city, and was the second largest among the Indian States in prepartition India, covering 82,313 square miles (about the size of Kansas). It had the largest population, which in 1941 was a little under 16.5 million. It lay completely landlocked in southern India, where it occupied much of the plateau known as the Deccan. The inhabitants were 87 percent non-Muslim, of whom most (81 percent of the total) were Hindu. In non-Muslim hands lay most of the trade. The ruling dynasty, however, was Muslim and the ruling class was drawn mostly from the elite of the Muslim community. The head of the state was the Nizam, very wealthy, hard-working for an Indian prince, but inelastic in his official attitudes. The public economy was exploited for the benefit of him, some 1100 feudal landholders, and a few commercial and industrial middlemen, chiefly Muslim.

Economically and educationally the masses were below the general Indian average. The system of forced labor for the state was declared abolished only in 1947. The great body of Muslims aside from the landholders were urbanites, among whom were many sunk in the bleakest poverty and hence predisposed to profit, if opportunity offered, at the expense of non-Muslims. The state was, in broad terms, retarded politically, economically, socially, and culturally, in character conservative if not actually medieval, its institutions outmoded, while such modern developments as it owned were directed toward the satisfaction of narrowly communal Muslim interests.

Hyderabad was regarded by Indian nationalists during the struggle for independence as a natural opponent of liberal political institutions and an ally of imperialism. In 1938 a Hyderabad State Congress was formed and became a member of the Indian States People's Conference, through which it had a spiritual association with the Indian National Congress. The purpose of the State Congress was to establish responsible government in the state, and it quickly inaugurated a campaign of *satyagraha,* which the Nizam's government repressed.

If the Nizam had been willing to negotiate with this group in 1938 and 1939, he might have avoided the humiliation he suffered in 1948. For by banning the State Congress until 1946 and keeping its leaders in jail, he left the field open to communal organizations, both Hindu and Muslim, and to the Communists. On the Hindu side the active bodies were the aggressive Arya Samaj and the Hindu Mahasabha. The latter was particularly strong in the northwestern part of the state where the population was Maratha and cherished an anti-Muslim tradition inherited from its great leader Sivaji of the early eighteenth century. On the Muslim side the active group was the Majlis-i-Ittihad-ul-Muslimin ("Assembly of the Association of Muslims"), commonly called the Ittihad, which was founded in 1927 as a cultural body, but through the years had become increasingly political. In 1947, under a president named Qasim Razavi, the Ittihad developed a fighting corps known as Razakar Volunteers, who pledged themselves to "fight to the last to maintain the supremacy of Muslim power in the Deccan." As independence for India drew near, this body practiced ever greater violence against Hindus.

The Communists, working through an organization known as the Andhra Mahasabha or Andhra Sangham (both of which mean "Andhra Association"), were active in the eastern part of the state. This and the adjacent part of the Madras province constituted the region known as Andhra, where there existed a regional nationalism of Telugu-speakers; the area is now the Indian state of Andhra. The Communists had led a peasant revolt there, and in 1943–1944 the peasants refused to pay taxes or to supply forced labor and successfully resisted police action. Its success in Hyderabad State led to its spread in neighboring Andhra territory in British India.

A further element to confuse the total picture was the Hyderabad State's official claim that it had substantially equal status with the Paramount Power (Britain). The theory, however, was never more than a fiction. Hyderabad had been subordinated to Britain in fact since 1798. From time to time circumstances had developed which had prompted the currently reigning Nizam to claim equality, which was always denied. The Nizam who headed the state in 1947 had been rebuked for this in 1919 and again, in the plainest of terms, in 1926, when the Viceroy Lord Reading in an official document told him that the British crown was supreme in India and "no Ruler of an Indian State can justifiably claim to negotiate with the British Government on an equal footing."

As self-rule drew near for British India, the Nizam asserted his intention of remaining independent. In February 1947, when independence was assured though partition was still in issue, his government released a note to the press in which it indicated that Hyderabad would not join the proposed Indian union. The Hyderabad State Congress responded three weeks later that the people of the state would tolerate no attempt to keep Hyderabad out of the union, and initiated a *satyagraha* campaign. Later the chief promoter, Ramanand Tirth, and other leaders were arrested. On June 26, 1947, after the June 3 plan of independence and partition was announced in the House of Commons by Prime Minister Attlee, the Nizam issued a *firman* (order) declaring that he would not join the proposed Indian union. When the Indian Independence Act (July 15, 1947) formerly provided for partition, the Nizam announced that he would join neither dominion until he could see developments. Just after partition, on August 21, 1947, in a public decree he proclaimed the "resumption" of independence. To this India at once objected in a statement which declared that "an issue like this involving the defense of India, the integrity of her territory, the peace and security of the country, and above all the common interests of the State of Hyderabad could not be allowed to be solved by mere legalistic claims of doubtful validity."

It was obvious that the Nizam, if he should feel it necessary to relinquish his hope of sovereign status for Hyderabad, would only with the greatest reluctance accede to India. Accession to Pakistan would have been preferable in his view but was impracticable; further, many sympathizers with the Ittihad were opposed to any status except full sovereignty. He therefore wished to conclude a treaty with India as between equal sovereign states. India, however, pressed for accession, and, failing that immediately, a standstill agreement. Such an agreement was signed at the end of November 1947, after serious Muslim demonstrations in the state against it. Negotiations for a final settlement continued, but with each party promoting its original objective.

Shortly afterwards sharp quarrels broke out between India and Hyderabad. India in January 1948 charged Hyderabad with violating the agreement by lending 20 crores of rupees (at that time

worth about $62 million) to Pakistan—Hyderabad replied that
the loan had been arranged before the agreement was negotiated.
The Razakars, whom the government of India estimated, probably
with exaggeration, at 100,000, were now engaging in serious mob
violence against Hindu villages in Hyderabad and others across
the border in India, and India demanded that they be suppressed.
Hyderabad replied that the Razakars were needed to supplement
the police force, and maintained that raids on Hyderabad were being organized in Indian territory. India insisted that the Nizam
liberalize his government, and, as he temporized, India applied an
economic blockade.

During these developments the Communists are accused of having helped first the Hyderabad State Congress, then the Razakars.
Their own power increased until they had "liberated" over 2000
villages (according to their own claims) and had acquired actual
control of the government in a large part of the state. In May, when
it looked as though India might employ force, the Nizam's government removed its ban on the Communist party, which then instructed the "liberated" villages to resist Indian troops if they should
attempt to pass through.

In these disturbed circumstances negotiators produced an agreement on June 15, 1948, but the Nizam would not sign it. India then
began to prepare for invasion, and Hyderabad appealed to the
Security Council. But before the appeal was considered, India, on
September 13, entered Hyderabad from five different points in a
"police action" to restore law and order, and in a "hundred-hour
war" had taken over (September 18). Hyderabad was kept as a
state, and the Nizam left as ruler, but an Indian military administrator was put in charge. The Razakars were disbanded, the Communist revolt quelled, and steps taken to institute liberalized government. In the aftermath large numbers of Muslims appear to
have been killed, some in private revenge, while others, according
to claims made in Pakistan, were slaughtered by troops. The Nizam,
when a new government was formed, withdrew his complaint at
the United Nations. In later reorganization in India Hyderabad
was extinguished as a political entity, and its territory is now divided
among the states of Andhra, Mysore, and Maharashtra.

In British and American newspapers there was considerable
criticism of India's conduct toward Hyderabad and the Nizam, and
this was resented in India, on the ground that the case was imper-

fectly understood. Whatever the legal rights and wrongs of specific acts in the Hyderabad controversy, India could not have tolerated the state's existence as a sovereign political entity. To do so would have jeopardized the economy, political structure, and security of India itself.

Pakistan had no legal claim at issue in the Hyderabad dispute, but its sympathies were strongly involved. It gave the Nizam support before the Security Council, while its press and public reaction were unanimously anti-Indian on the subject, and it still does not acknowledge the legitimacy of Hyderabad's accession. The dispute, like that concerning Junagadh, had features which Pakistan has claimed are analogous to features of the Kashmir dispute, though with India's position reversed. Pakistan has, therefore, used both cases repeatedly in arguments to support its side of that great and continuing controversy.

10 The Quarrel over Kashmir

The quarrel over Kashmir has been the most critical of all between India and Pakistan. It led to undeclared war, which three times— in December 1947, May 1948, and August 1951—threatened to become overt and in 1965 actually did become so. The stakes are of major economic, political, and strategic significance to Pakistan, while to India Kashmir has become a symbol of national prestige and international justice. The seriousness of the dispute brought it before the Security Council on the last day of the year 1947, where it still lies unsettled in spite of the efforts of a United Nations Commission for India and Pakistan and three distinguished mediators.

Kashmir, properly referred to as the Jammu and Kashmir State, was the largest of the Indian States before August 15, 1947. It had an area of 84,471 square miles (about the size of Minnesota), and in 1941 had a population of about 4,002,000, of whom 3,101,000, or about 77 percent, were Muslims. The rest were Hindus (20.12 percent), Sikhs (1.64 percent), Buddhists (about 1 percent), and a few Christians. The ruling family was Hindu. Almost all the state is mountainous or high plateau country, but it has two small cultivable plains, one of which is the renowned Vale of Kashmir, about 85 miles long and 20 to 25 miles wide, and the other the Jammu flatlands at the foothills of the Himalayas, a part of the Punjab plain. It contains Mount Godwin Austen in the Karakoram range, the world's second highest peak, and has throughout a spread of scenic splendor possibly unequaled anywhere else in the world. The beauty, too, of the women in the Vale of Kashmir has long been proverbial in both Asia and Europe.

The state consisted of a number of separate parts, which possessed no geographic, linguistic, cultural, or historic unity, but were first united politically in the second quarter of the nineteenth century. It was administered in three divisions. The first of these was Jammu, situated in the south. Its capital, the city of Jammu, was the state's winter capital and the seat of the ruling dynasty. This was a family of so-called Dogra Rajputs, which rose from obscurity in the 1830s under an adventurer named Gulab Singh (1792–1858). By associating himself with the Sikhs he built a kingdom piece by piece through conquest, intrigue, and finally the blessing of the British. In 1846, because he had been friendly to them in their dark hours of the first Afghan War and had abstained from helping the Sikhs, his masters, in the Sikh War, the British gratefully let him pay them £750,000 and then confirmed him and the heirs male of his body to hold "forever in independent possession" a territory approximately that of the state in 1947. Jammu province contained one seventh of the state's total area and nearly one half (1,981,400) of its population. In 1941 its population was about 53 percent Muslim but after partition some Muslims left and Hindus and Sikhs entered.

North of Jammu province beyond the first Himalayan range known as the Pir Panjal was the division of Kashmir, accessible from Jammu city by a single road that was regularly snowbound in winter until snowplows were introduced in 1948. Otherwise it was reached by a road from Rawalpindi, now in Pakistan, connecting with another road, from Abbottabad, which also is now in Pakistan. This division contains the Vale of Kashmir, celebrated in over two thousand years of history, through which flows the river Jhelum. In this land of mountains and lakes, glaciers, rivers and canals, rice fields and flower-covered alps, plane trees and deodars, ancient civilization and modern handicrafts, live most of the rest of the state's population. Here is situated the city of Srinagar, the summer capital. The Muslims did not enter the Vale of Kashmir until the fourteenth century, but once in, they rapidly converted the population. In 1941, of its 1,729,000 inhabitants all but about 113,000 were Muslims. The minority consisted mostly of the elite Kashmiri Brahmans or pandits. The Muslim peasantry there was notoriously poor and timid in dealings with authority.

The third division of the state was called the Frontier Districts, a miscellaneous group of diverse areas lying east, north, and northwest of the Vale of Kashmir, covering three fourths of the state's area, but having a population of only 311,500. Its eastern part, called Ladakh, is linguistically and culturally affiliated to western Tibet.

The state has considerable strategic significance. It marches with Tibet and Sinkiang on the east and north and with Afghanistan on its northwest corner. The long narrow Wakhan strip of Afghanistan separates Kashmir from the Soviet Union. Communications, however, are difficult with all these regions. The state commands the northern flank of Pakistan, and the upper reaches of four of the rivers (Indus, Jhelum, Chenab, Ravi) on which Pakistan's agriculture depends are in or border it. In 1947 all the state's communications by road, rail, and river led into West Pakistan, including the only road from Jammu, the winter capital, which went by way of Sialkot in Pakistani Punjab. But in 1947–1948 India built a road to Jammu from Pathankot, which is east of Jammu in Indian Punjab.

Though the British gave Gulab Singh the state to hold "in independent possession," they did not mean in sovereignty. Alarmed by Russian advance in Central Asia, in1885 they compelled the maharaja Partab (or Partap or Pratap) Singh to accept a resident. This he did with such bad grace that he was temporarily deprived of the throne. Neither before nor after Partab Singh's time did Kashmir's ruler relish having a resident. Hari Singh, maharaja at the time of partition, had an additional grievance against the British, who had let him figure as "Mr. A" in a notorious divorce suit in England in 1952 shortly before he became ruler. As maharaja, Hari Singh was a playboy, extravagant, devoted to polo and horse-racing, uninterested in his subjects' economic improvement, incompetent in politics.

The uncongenial elements composing the state never acquired a common national consciousness. The two elite Hindu groups, the Dogras in Jammu and the Brahmans in Kashmir, were favored in state affairs and held almost all the political posts; the Muslim majority got only a small fraction of them. The state army was recruited almost wholly from the Dogras. The rule was backward, oppressive, and unpopular among the masses. Dogmatic Hindu law, such as that against cow-killing, was sternly enforced upon all subjects, including Muslims and Buddhists, who had none of the Hindu feeling for the sanctity of the cow. Forced labor for the state existed until the 1920s, when it was legally abolished as one of several reforms instituted after a minor popular revolt. During the next decade uncorrected economic, administrative, and social ills produced an accelerating popular discontent, which led to another set of political reforms including creation of a legislative assembly in 1934, with election of forty members (twenty-one of them Muslim) by a very limited electorate (8 percent of the population) and nomination of thirty-five others by the maharaja.

The principal reform organization was the Jammu and Kashmir National Conference, formed during 1938–1939, when it took over the Muslim Conference, which had been organized in 1932. The new conference (like the Hyderabad State Congress) was affiliated with the States People's Conference in India, and had an ideological association with the Indian National Congress, especially the latter's left wing. The chief mover in the States People's Conference was Jawaharlal Nehru (himself a member of a Kashmiri pandit family which emigrated to India about 1716); the founder and president of the Jammu and Kashmir National Conference (as of the previous Muslim Conference) was Sheikh Mohammad Abdullah, a former schoolteacher, a Muslim but not a communalist and not sympathetic to the Muslim League. In 1939 the Conference wrung administrative and juridical concessions from the maharaja. In 1943 it prepared a program of far-reaching social, economic, administrative, and political reforms in a draft constitution and an economic plan, which were entirely secular in motivation and provisions. In 1946, when the Cabinet Mission came to India, Sheikh Abdullah fomented a movement which demanded "absolute freedom" from Dogra rule and called upon the maharaja to "quit Kashmir!" The Cabinet Mission ignored this, Sheikh Abdullah's popularity declined, and the Conference leaders, chief of whom was Sheikh Abdullah, were arrested. At the time of partition Abdullah was serving a nine-year sentence which had been imposed in September 1946.

In the meantime a new (or "revived" in its own terminology) Muslim Conference had been formed in 1941 which supported the Muslim League and opposed the Jammu and Kashmir National Conference. At this time, too, the Muslims in Poonch, an infeudated state in the western part of Jammu province, were complaining against discriminatory treatment by the maharaja. The protest was led by Ibrahim Khan, and out of it later evolved the Azad ("Free") Kashmir movement under his leadership.

If on partition the Indian States had been assigned to the two dominions on the principles which applied to the provinces of British India, that is, religious predominance and geographical contiguity, the state of Jammu and Kashmir would presumably have gone to Pakistan, though it might have been divided, and the eastern parts of Jammu province, which were predominantly Hindu, or possibly the whole province, given to India. But since choice lay with each separate state, the maharaja Hari Singh, as autocratic ruler, had the right and duty of making the decision. He was not equal to this task. He disliked the idea of becoming a part of India, which was being democratized, or of Pakistan, which was Muslim. He did not yield to Mountbatten's urging to make a decision, not having much trust in the British. For some time he seemed to think he could remain independent, as was implicit later in his letter accompanying the instrument of accession (October 26, 1947), but the realities of the situation made such a status absolutely impossible.

Apparently with the motive of avoiding any final decision he inquired of both dominions about making a standstill agreement. India held back. But Pakistan, on August 15, after a telegraphic request from Hari Singh's government on August 12, made such an agreement, involving the continuation of railway, post and telegraph, and commercial communications. Pakistan understood the agreement to imply control over defense and foreign affairs, in short, to convey to Pakistan all the rights which the government of undivided India had had respecting Kashmir. She also interpreted it to point toward eventual accession. It seems doubtful that this had been Hari Singh's intention, since he had approached both governments at the same time. When later in the general confusion that prevailed in the Punjab after August 15, Kashmir failed to get the supplies of petrol, sugar, cloth, and other items due it and badly needed, its government was apprehensive. And on the other hand, when Kashmir failed to follow the standstill agreement with accession, the Pakistan government, already apprehensive because of maneuvers and rumored actions involving India, suspected that the maharaja was secretly planning not to accede to it but rather eventually to accede to India when this could be done with assurance of effective defense.

During the communal strife in the Punjab, Sikh and Hindu refugees crossed the border into Jammu province and in their anger clashed with the Muslims they met there. From Jammu there were raids into western Punjab, and from the Punjab raids into Jammu. The situation got out of hand for the local police.

At the end of September, the maharaja unexpectedly released Sheikh Abdullah, who promptly made an address to a large public gathering in which he asked for "a complete transfer of power to the people in Kashmir . . . Of course, we will naturally opt to go to that Dominion where our own demand for freedom receives recognition and support." Possibly the maharaja hoped to make use of Abdullah's support. He continued to hold in detention the leader of the Kashmir Muslim Conference, which Jinnah had endorsed and which openly favored accession to Pakistan.

At about this same time India started to build the road from Pathankot to Jammu. Pakistan took this to indicate that India was preparing to receive the state's accession. Also in September a Muslim revolt against the state government broke out in the already disaffected area of Poonch.

Everything was now prepared for the dramatic catastrophe which came in the latter part of October. It consisted of an invasion of Kashmir by armed Muslim tribesmen, some from nearby Hazara, others from around Peshawar, over a hundred miles distant. Their route was through Pakistan, and they came with the knowledge and assistance of Pakistan officials, who possibly felt a sense of relief that the tribesmen were not raiding Pakistan territory. They were permitted to have their base of operations in Pakistan, and Pakistan allowed additional tribesmen to go to the fighting front and often helped with motor trucks.

Tribesmen began to cross the state's border on October 20; on October 22 they had reached Domel and Muzaffarabad, and moved up the Vale of Kashmir toward Srinagar. They were then possibly only about 2000 strong, though the number was put at 5000 by some reporters. On the fourth day a provisional Azad ("Free") Kashmir was proclaimed with its own government. The maharaja fled across the mountains to Jammu on October 25. On October 26, when the invaders were not far from Srinagar, looting industriously and murdering Muslims as well as Hindus and a few Europeans, and the state forces were completely unable to halt them, the maharaja with the advice of V. P. Menon, secretary to the States Ministry of India, and the support of Sheikh Abdullah, executed an instrument of accession to India, as apparently seemed legally necessary to Lord Mountbatten, the Governor General of India, before assistance could be given. The next day (October 27) Lord Mountbatten accepted the accession provisionally. Legally

184

this seemed to satisfy the procedure prescribed in the Indian Independence Act and India was then free to dispatch troops, and did so. Immediately they began to arrive in Srinagar by air, barely saving it from the undisciplined tribesmen who were loitering on the way to loot. These troops pushed the tribesmen back by stages and gradually cleared the valley.

Pakistan refused to recognize the accession, considering it a violation of the standstill agreement and an act based on "fraud and violence" plotted long in advance; instead it assisted the Azad Kashmir government. In the maharaja's part of the state, control now lay with the Jammu and Kashmir National Conference and on October 31, at the "request" of the maharaja, Sheikh Mohammad Abdullah was sworn in as Head of the Emergency Administration. Later (March 1948) under a government reorganization he became prime minister. From then on the maharaja was the forgotten man of Kashmir, and in due time he was virtually retired from his position and his son Karan Singh performed the royal functions, while Abdullah and his associates ruled the state.

Pakistan now openly gave the Azad Kashmir government weapons, vehicles, and regular troops, who went to Kashmir as "volunteers," commanded by General Akbar Khan under the pseudonym "General Tariq," and permitted and assisted ordinary volunteers recruited in its territory to go to the front. Pakistan had an open road into Kashmir from the headquarters at Rawalpindi in the Punjab just across the border; India could at first enter only by air to Jammu, and from there could reach Kashmir either by further air flight or by the mountain road through the 9300-foot-high Banihal Pass over the Pir Panjal. The Azad Kashmir and Pakistan forces had a clear advantage in communications; the Indian and Kashmir state forces held the large centers, especially Sringar and Jammu.

Lord Mountbatten in accepting Kashmir's accession had said that when the invaders had been expelled and law and order reestablished, "the question of accession should be settled by a reference to the people." A few days later (November 8) Nehru confirmed the principle of decision by the people in a telegram to Liaquat Ali Khan, Pakistan's premier, but reiterated that the invaders must be driven from Kashmir and peace restored before a reference would be possible.

Liaquat Ali at once announced his agreement with the idea of a plebiscite, but stipulated certain conditions on which his government would urge the Azad Kashmiris to cease fire and disband. These were withdrawal of Indian troops and immobilization of the state forces, substitution for Sheikh Abdullah's government of a coalition government (including the Azad Kashmir elements), and following these two steps the holding of a plebiscite under international auspices. These accessory conditions Nehru declared unacceptable. Here was born an issue which ever since has been debated continuously.

Several small states in the far northwest which were feudatory to Kashmir, namely, Gilgit, Hunza, and Nagir (Nagar), at about this time repudiated their connection and acceded to Pakistan. Meanwhile the warfare continued indecisively, though India regained some of the territory held by the Azad Kashmir forces. Pakistan was not yet formally in the fighting.

In West Pakistan enthusiasm for the Kashmir action was intense. It was a symbol of secession from Hindu India, which Muslims viewed as a sinister intriguer against their rights. In the gunfire of war they could convert their resentment and hatred from words to deeds. In India the feeling against Pakistan was strong, but tempered by consideration of other problems. In certain regions, such as south India, the Kashmir fighting seemed rather distant in comparison with current local matters. Some persons there spoke of it as a relatively unimportant issue which was being contested by north Indians at a cost far beyond its worth to India as a whole—better to withdraw and let Pakistan have Kashmir; such surrender, though morally questionable, would be politically sound.

Each nation confidently professed to believe that it would win in a plebiscite, if it were conducted fairly. Pakistanis relied on the communal issue, that is, the bond of Islam, and the Kashmir Muslim majority's dislike for the Hindu rule of the past hundred years. Indians and members of the Jammu and Kashmir National Conference, often conceding that on the date of partition the popular will might have favored Pakistan, argued that revulsion against the atrocities committed by the invading tribesmen and the increasing popularity of Sheikh Abdullah's liberal reform movement now outweighed Muslim unity.

Now began the stage of official public debate. On December 31, 1947, when discussions between the two nations had produced no solution and the military operations were proving indecisive as well as costly, India laid the matter before the Security Council, charging Pakistan under article 35 of the United Nations Charter with "an act of aggression against India," and giving specifications. Pakistan met the charge with vigor, dispatching one of its ablest public servants, Chaudhry (also Sir) Mohammed Zafrullah Khan, to Lake Success to conduct its side of the case. India appointed as chief of its delegation Sir N. Gopalaswami Ayyangar, an elderly and distinguished member of the Madras Civil Service and prime minister of Kashmir, 1937–1943, who in 1951 became India's cabinet minister for states and in 1952 minister of defense.

At Lake Success Pakistan obtained the first advantage. India's case was that the invasion of Kashmir by tribesmen and the support given them by Pakistan were illegal. But Sir Zafrullah, instead of merely defending the charge, took the offensive and attacked India. He described the deaths of Muslims during the postpartition violence in East Punjab (Indian territory) as genocide; he characterized the enforced accession to India of the state of Junagadh, after its Muslim ruler had tried to accede to Pakistan, as aggression and an act of hostility against Pakistan; and he branded as nonimplementation of an international obligation India's reluctance to give Pakistan its agreed portion of prepartition India's assets in money, military munitions, and other items. Along with all these allegations, he charged India with "fraudulent procurement of the accession of Jammu and Kashmir State," and in a larger sense yet of being insincere in its attitude toward partition and the accompanying creation of the new state of Pakistan, which it hoped to strangle. In the Security Council the debate came to concern not so much India's complaint against Pakistan as Pakistan's demand that the future of the Jammu and Kashmir State be considered.

On January 20 the Security Council adopted a resolution to appoint a three-member commission to investigate and mediate, but this was never implemented.

After three months' further consideration, the Security Council on April 21, 1948, adopted a second resolution advising that both Indian troops and the tribesmen should be withdrawn, that an interim government should be established representing "the major political groups" (meaning both the National Conference and the Azad Kashmir elements), and that a five-man United Nations Commission on India and Pakistan (UNCIP) should go to Kashmir to exercise its good offices in helping the two nations restore peace and arrange a fair plebiscite.

This resolution pleased neither India nor Pakistan. In regard to troop withdrawal and the conduct of the plebiscite it agreed essentially with Pakistan's terms of November 1947, which India had already rejected. Pakistan did not like the resolution, for, though it provided for widening the Kashmir government by adding to it representatives of the Azad Kashmir government, it still left Sheikh Abdullah at the head. In such circumstances, Pakistan contended, an impartial plebiscite would be impossible. Both nations, therefore, rejected certain terms of the resolution.

When the commission got to Pakistan on July 7, 1948, it at once got a frank acknowledgment from Zafrullah Khan that Pakistan troops had been fighting in Kashmir since May 8. This fact was widely known but had not previously been admitted by the Pakistan government. In the eyes of the commission it constituted "a material change in the situation," and it so stated in correspondence with the Pakistan government. Pakistan also admitted in August 1948 that the Azad Kashmir forces were under the operational control of the Pakistan army.

After a month's inquiry, the commission on August 13 presented to the two governments a resolution which provided for a cease-fire and the subsequent negotiation of a truce agreement. The government of Pakistan was to use its best endeavor to secure the withdrawal of the tribesmen and Pakistani nationals ("volunteers") not normally resident in the state who had entered for the purpose of fighting, and administration would lie with "local authorities" under United Nations surveillance. After the departure of the tribesmen and "volunteers," and as the Pakistan regular forces were being withdrawn, the bulk of the Indian troops, too, were to be withdrawn in stages agreed upon with the commission. Only those needed to maintain law and order would be left.

This proposal India found acceptable and assented to on August 20, with certain "clarifications"; Pakistan, on September 6 also agreed to accept the proposal, but only on condition that India would also accept the Security Council's proposals of April 21, which at the time had not been agreeable to either nation. Since those earlier proposals of the Security Council partly contradicted the commission's own later proposals, the commission in a reply

(September 6, 1948) released to the public observed that Pakistan's "Government have found themselves unable to accept without reservation the proposals of the Commission," and treated Pakistan's reply as a refusal. A truce did not seem possible at that time, and the blame was placed at Pakistan's door. Pakistan then continued the discussions.

During this period Sheikh Abdullah's government ruled in Indian-occupied Kashmir, endeavoring to initiate the type of reform to which the Jammu and Kashmir National Conference had long been committed. In the part of the state controlled by Pakistan the Azad government was at least nominally in charge. India resumed her military offensive in September, and Pakistan then complained to the Security Council, which instructed the commission to continue its efforts.

After further negotiations the commission, on December 11, 1948, enlarging a suggestion it had made in the August 13 resolution, offered a program for a free and impartial plebiscite, to be inaugurated after the cease-fire and truce arrangements had been fulfilled and peace had been restored to the state. This program departed from the Security Council's plebiscite proposals of April 21 by making concessions on some of the points to which India had objected. The government of the state, headed by Abdullah as prime minister, was to be left unaltered. The plebiscite administrator, who was to be named by the Secretary General of the United Nations in agreement with the commission, was to be appointed to office by the government of the State of Jammu and Kashmir, and was to derive from the state the powers he should consider necessary for organizing and conducting the plebiscite and ensuring its freedom and impartiality. Final disposal of Indian and state armed forces was to be determined by the commission and plebiscite administrator in consultation with the government of India, after the cease-fire and truce proposals of the August 13 resolution were implemented. In the part of the state held by Pakistan and in Azad Kashmir, it said, "final disposition of the armed forces in that territory will be determined by the Commission and the Plebiscite Administrator in consultation with the local authorities."

India agreed to the proposals on December 23 and Pakistan on December 25, and a resolution embodying them was formally adopted by the commission on January 5, 1949. The cease-fire line, essentially along the then stabilized military front, was made effective as of January 1, 1949 (later, on July 27, 1949, the line was agreed upon and in due time was demarcated). The tribesmen withdrew in the early part of 1949.

Unfortunately difficulties in executing the resolution of January 5, 1949, arose almost at once. India understood that the "local authorities" who were to administer the territory in Azad Kashmir hands meant the state government headed by Sheikh Abdullah, and that the Azad Kashmir government was finished. Pakistan, on the contrary, held that in that area "local authorities" meant just the Azad Kashmir government, which was therefore not eliminated. Disagreement also arose about the method by which the withdrawal of the Pakistani and Indian troops would be synchronized.

At this point the situation became deadlocked, and the cease-fire line has remained the dividing line between Azad Kashmir, under the protection of Pakistan, and the rest of the Jammu and Kashmir state, which constitutes a part of India. Azad Kashmir consisted of the western and northwestern parts of the original state, with a population of about 700,000, and is of much less economic importance than the rest of the state, which includes the Vale of Kashmir, eastern Jammu, and Ladakh. The latter has a population of 4,615,176 (1971) and controls the upper courses of the Jhelum and Chenab rivers.

The commission recommended that the two nations submit their disagreements over the implementation of the resolutions of August 13, 1948, and January 5, 1949, to Fleet Admiral Chester W. Nimitz, who had been accepted by them as plebiscite administrator. Pakistan was willing, but India refused, and the whole question again went back to the Security Council in December 1949. The then president of the Security Council, General A. G. L. McNaughton of Canada, on instructions of the Council, endeavored to mediate, but unsuccessfully. The Security Council, on March 14, 1950, asked the governments of the two nations to prepare and execute within five months a program of demilitarization precedent to the making of arrangements for the plebiscite, and provided for appointing a mediator to help in framing and implementing this program. The two nations accepted the resolution.

The mediator was Sir Owen Dixon, a distinguished Australian jurist. He reached Delhi May 27, 1950, and worked in India, Pakistan, and Kashmir until August 22, when he issued a public statement of failure. In the negotiations the first breakdown had concerned the terms of demilitarization, the next the terms of a plebiscite. The differences concerning demilitarization were the old ones. In respect to the plebiscite, Sir Owen brought before the two governments the question of a limited or partial plebiscite. But Pakistan would agree to nothing less than one that was overall and would settle the fate of the entire state, while India would not accept partial plebiscite in the Vale of Kashmir if the local government were to be superseded by a United Nations administrative body and troops were to be introduced drawn from Pakistan sources as well as Indian. These features, Nehru said afterwards, were contrary to the commission's previous resolutions. Sir Owen in closing his report made a strong plea for partition as a solution with a plebiscite in a limited area.

A spark to touch off the explosive situation appeared in the autumn, a couple of months after Sir Owen Dixon had reported. On October 27, 1950, the general council of the Jammu and Kashmir National Conference adopted a resolution recommending that the state government convene a constituent assembly, under the provisions of the constitution of India, to determine the "future shape and affiliations of the State of Jammu and Kashmir." The Conference, as we saw above, had been working toward a liberal constitution for the state since at least 1943, and after attaining power had gone ahead with its economic program. The proposed assembly, to be elected by the people, would on the one hand build a new order in the state, and on the other would attempt to settle the question of the state's accession. It was clear that the elections for it could be held only in the part of the state held by India, which, however, contained by far the greater part of the population. It was also clear that the elections would be arranged and supervised by Sheikh Abdullah's government. Pakistan felt that in such circumstances the result was prejudiced: the assembly was bound to be just a creature of the Conference; it would do the will of Sheikh Abdullah, which was also the will of Nehru and India. Though the legality of its deliberations and actions might be doubtful, it would nevertheless present the world with an accomplished action, which would make Pakistan's position even more difficult than it already was. Pakistan, therefore, protested at once and strongly.

In the Security Council, on February 21, 1951, the United Kingdom and the United States introduced a joint resolution, which disapproved the plan for convening a constituent assembly as contrary to the Council's resolutions previously accepted by both India and Pakistan and endorsed Sir Owen Dixon's proposals for demilitarization.

The resolution contained various other provisions which the two nations had previously found offensive and both promptly objected. Thereupon the United Kingdom and the United States lowered their sights and submitted a new resolution, still condemning the constituent assembly and providing for a new mediator but assigning him no duty except that of expediting demilitarization. The Security Council adopted the revised resolution on March 30; Pakistan accepted it; India rejected it. The Security Council appointed Dr. Frank P. Graham as the new mediator. He went out in early June. India refused to help him implement the resolution, though it treated him with full courtesy. In the inauspicious circumstances it was not surprising that his preliminary report in October was inconclusive, scarcely even encouraging.

The circumstances had been worse, in fact, than inauspicious; they had become warlike and menacing. In July India had charged Pakistan before the Security Council with violations of the cease-fire line and complained of anti-Indian and pro-*jihad* (holy war) propaganda. Pakistan's Premier in rebuttal declared that 90 percent of India's army was at Pakistan's border. Communalists on both sides urged action. Both nations massed troops, but the crisis passed. When Graham made his third report on April 22, 1952, he felt that progress had been made toward an agreement on demilitarization though several vital points were still unsettled.
In May the United Kingdom and the United States suggested that Graham return to India and Pakistan to try again to settle the dispute.

Graham made two other reports (September 19, 1952, and March 27, 1953) without achieving agreement between the two nations. Their principal point of difference concerned the quantity of forces each should maintain after demilitarization and the time when the plebiscite administrator should assume his duties. In the circumstances Graham left the problem to direct negotiation between the two disputants.

In Azad Kashmir the course of events has been relatively smooth since the stabilization of the cease-fire line. The percentage of non-Muslims in the population has decreased notably; its government is dominated by the Muslim Conference; there has been some economic and land tenure reform; administration has had some problems of corruption; a system of government based upon general democratic elections was promised (June 1954), but has never been inaugurated. Most of the area on the Pakistan side of the cease-fire line is part of the mountainous north, where the population is sparse, communications poor, and political power rests for all practical purposes in local chiefs.

The course of events has been far from smooth on the Indian side of the cease-fire line. A Constituent Assembly was elected while Graham was conducting his negotiations (September and October 1951). In some districts no candidates offered themselves against those of the Conference; in others a few candidates offered and later withdrew. Abdullah's party won an overwhelming, all but unanimous, victory. Pakistan claimed intimidation. The Assembly convened on October 31. On November 6 Sheikh Abdullah called upon it to decide "the state's future political affiliation." Hence on November 20 the Assembly in the Jammu and Kashmir Constitution Act stripped the maharaja of all important powers, permitting him to act only on advice of the government, which was made responsible to the Assembly, and again affirmed the state's autonomy in all matters except defense, foreign affairs, and communications. A few months later (April 10, 1952) Sheikh Abdullah in a speech denied that the Indian constitution could be made applicable to Jammu and Kashmir. He specifically expressed fear that communalism, which he said was rife in India, might be extended to the state, especially if something should happen to Nehru. Subsequently, after negotiations with Abdullah, Nehru announced (July 24, 1952) in the Lok Sabha that Kashmir was to have status unlike that of any other Indian state. Its citizens were to have special rights while in their state; the state could pursue its social and economic reforms in spite of certain sections of the constitution of India; and it was to elect its own chief of state (Sadar-i-Riyasat). This pact and other developments following it were bitterly criticized in Pakistan. The Kashmir Assembly abolished hereditary rule in the state; Hari Singh, the unpopular maharaja, agreed to abdicate; and the Assembly then elected his son, the popular heir apparent Karan Singh, as a commoner, to be the first chief of state for a period of five years. Thus ended the hated Dogra rule. Under Abdullah, many reforms, especially economic, including some drastic changes in land tenure, were instituted; education was stepped up; an effort was made to expand the area's meager industry; cooperatives were encouraged; nationalization of commerce was promoted. To carry on, the state received financial aid from India.

Sheikh Abdullah was never warm toward merging the state with India, and this attitude was responsible for his downfall. He maintained that by the instrument of accession "Kashmir is completely free and autonomous in all but three subjects—communications, defense, and external affairs." It was on this basis that he negotiated the pact with India in July 1952, which gave the state its special status. But his rule was unpopular with sections of the population in east Jammu, who wanted close ties with India and at the same time disliked much of Abdullah's economic program. They expressed themselves through a party called the Praja Parishad (People's Party). Also, there was dissatisfaction in Ladakh, which might have welcomed close association with India or even with Tibet, to which it is culturally allied, but in no case relished being part of an independent state presumably to be dominated by elements that had in the past been inattentive to Ladakh's interests. Rightist parties in India, such as the Hindu Mahasabha, the Jan Sangh, and the Ram Rajya Parishad, came to the Praja Parishad's aid and sent representatives there, one of whom, the well-known Dr. Shyama Prasad Mookerjee, was arrested in May 1953 and died of a heart attack in jail a month later. There were *satyagraha* demonstrations for complete integration with India. Abdullah's own party finally split, and his chief lieutenant Bakshi Ghulam Mohammed, deputy prime minister and home minister, turned against him. The situation was complicated by the rumors, never confirmed, that in May Adlai Stevenson, when in Kashmir, had encouraged Abdullah to seek either independence for Kashmir or affiliation to Pakistan. Early in July Bakshi went to Delhi, where it is said that he set the stage for displacing Abdullah. On August 9 Karan Singh dismissed Abdullah as prime minister and nominated Bakshi to the post, and then had Abdullah arrested.

Sheikh Abdullah was held in jail without charges until January 8, 1958, when he was freed, but he immediately began to charge Bakshi's government with mistreating Muslims, and to excoriate India for refusing to let a plebiscite be held. Fifteen weeks after his release he was rearrested (April 29, 1958) and in October of the same year charges of treason were preferred against him and fourteen others. The trial was long delayed, and formal charges of plotting to overthrow the government were preferred only on December 29, 1961. On June 28, 1961, speaking at the close of his defense, he had reiterated his old positions, attacking India, demanding a plebiscite, and not retreating from his stand that the state had a right to independence. At the time of the formal charge Abdullah again denounced the whole proceedings as a "fraud" and reiterated the right of Kashmir to "self-determination."

After Sheikh Abdullah's arrest in August 1953, Bakshi's government led the state step by step toward integration with India. On February 6, 1954, the Constituent Assembly ratified the state's accession to India. On April 13 the customs barrier between the state and India, an institution of long standing, was removed, and on May 14, India's President Rajendra Prasad, invoking article 370 of the Indian constitution, issued an order to endorse the relationship between the Republic of India and the Jammu and Kashmir State as formulated in the Delhi Pact of July 1952 and the Constituent Assembly's action of February 1954. A constitution for the state was drawn up and adopted on November 19, 1956, by which the state was made an integral part of India, and on the following Indian Independence Day, January 26, 1957, India formalized the accession of the state and made it "irrevocable." Three years later (January 20, 1960) India's Supreme Court assumed jurisdiction over the Jammu and Kashmir State, thus apparently sealing the integration.

These developments naturally stimulated Pakistanis to resentment, indignation, demonstrations, and demands for the use of force, that is, war. The government of Pakistan made use of such means as it could to block the developments and instead to get the long discussed and promised plebiscite implemented. All were futile. Graham recommended in March 1953 that direct negotiation be tried, and on a number of occasions the then current incumbent of the Pakistan premiership, as also later President Ayub Khan, met with Prime Minister Nehru (1953, 1955, 1956, 1959, 1960). On the first such occasion Pakistan's Prime Minister Mohammed Ali went to Delhi and conferred with Nehru and the two issued a press communique (August 20, 1953) to the effect that "the Kashmir dispute . . . should be settled in accordance with the wishes of the people of the State . . . The most feasible method of ascertaining the wishes of the people would be by fair and impartial plebiscite . . . The plebiscite administrator should be appointed by the end of April 1954." But before that date arrived the agreement of the United States to give military aid to Pakistan had been announced (February 25, 1954), and India took the view, which was expressed on various occasions afterwards by Nehru and other responsible government officers, that this put the whole question of relations between India and Pakistan, including the question of the Jammu and Kashmir State, in a different light. It was and still is a general view in India that, however much the United States might try to prohibit Pakistan from using American arms against India, such potential use was Pakistan's real motive in asking for aid and accepting it (and this view seemed to be confirmed in the India-Pakistan War of December 1971). Hence President Rajendra Prasad's order of May 14, 1954, was not to be considered a violation of the India-Pakistan agreement of August 20, 1953, but rather a natural consequence of the newly arisen situation.

Pakistan made several attempts to get the United Nations to influence the situation but again without succeeding in affecting India's stand. The question of Jammu and Kashmir was considered by the Security Council in March 1957, and a representative, Gunnar V. Jarring of Sweden, was sent to Pakistan and India, but in May he returned, his mission a failure. Later that year the Security Council adopted a proposal to send out Graham again, and he proposed a plan which Pakistan accepted but India rejected (April 3, 1958).

The question of the plebiscite has been raised in the United Nations frequently by Pakistan and was even asked for by the Security Council (January 24, 1957), but India has taken the position that, though the plebiscite might be discussed, it was essentially unrealistic to expect that it could be conducted under conditions leading to any definite results (April 2, 1956), or that it could be conducted at all after India had ratified the state's accession and the state had come under the constitution of India (January 1957), a statement that amounted to a rejection of the Security Council's direct request for a general plebiscite (January 24, 1957). On April 27, 1962, the Kashmir issue was again brought before the Security Council by Pakistan with Sir Zafrullah Khan again as its spokesman, and India, in the person of Krishna Menon, on May 3 again affirmed that Kashmir's accession was "full, complete, and final." The motion in the Security Council was for India and Pakistan to resume conversations concerning Kashmir and was supported by various other countries including the United States and Great Britain. The Security Council voted on June 22 for the motion, but it was defeated by a Soviet Union veto. In consequence India voiced strong resentment against the United States and Great Britain, and Pakistan against the Soviet Union. Among many delegates to the United Nations—for example, Professor G. P. Malalasekera, head of the Ceylonese delegation—the American support of the Pakistan position was attributed to the Pentagon rather than the White House; this was stated in a secret official dispatch of Malalasekera which got into the news on August 22, 1962.

Throughout the long and always acrimonious dispute about the status of Kashmir the most conspicuous figure has been Sheikh Mohammad Abdullah, who was leader of the state at the time of independence and partition in 1947 and became Head of the Emergency Administration and later Prime Minister, until deposed in August 1953. After five years in prison he was released in January 1958, but for only four months, being rearrested in April 1958. In 1962 he was charged with "seditious conspiracy," but was released again in 1964 when his friend and old political comrade Muhammad Sadiq became Prime Minister. Sadiq declared Abdullah to be "unfettered," with all charges against him unconditionally withdrawn. On May 8, 1965, when Abdullah returned to India from a pilgrimage to Mecca, the government of India arrested him at the Palam airport in Delhi. It was assumed by many persons that this was because Abdullah had met briefly with Chou En-lai in Algiers. The government of India, being suspicious of Abdullah because of various contacts with Chinese, took him into detention, holding him in south India for almost three years.

In March 1968, on being released, Abdullah made a triumphal entry into Srinagar, summer capital of the Jammu and Kashmir State, and has been involved in politics there ever since. A new party led by him and known as the Plebiscite Front exists now in Kashmir, vigorously supporting the demand for a plebiscite. In August 1969, in the first elections in nine years, this party swept the Village Council returns. In the campaign the Plebiscite Front symbolized the issues as a battle between the Koran and the Bhagavad Gita, in plain words a contest between Muslims and Hindus.

Sheikh Abdullah's stated position on the future of Kashmir is always that it should be decided by the people of Kashmir themselves and by no outside authority. Whether he anticipates that the people will decide for adherence to India or adherence to Pakistan or existence as an independent state Abdullah does not say. The best guess concerning his expectations, in the light of the fact that the Muslims are in an overwhelming majority in Kashmir, is that the people would vote for adherence to Pakistan, thus showing their preference for the Koran rather than the Bhagavad Gita. Abdullah himself has the reputation of being a devout Muslim. A *New York Times* correspondent (December 9, 1967) quotes a Muslim in Srinagar as saying, "To hear Sheikh Sahib read from the Koran is the greatest joy on earth!"

After the Indo-Chinese war of 1962 the quarrel between India and Pakistan over Kashmir continued to be critical. The first crisis was relatively mild. Late in December 1963 a hair of the Prophet Muhammad which was kept in the Hazratbal mosque in Srinagar disappeared. There was mass rioting in Srinagar and attacks on Hindus in East Pakistan so that many fled to India. The hair was recovered in two weeks' time, but Muslim passions remained inflamed, while stories of violations of the cease-fire line were plentiful.

India and Pakistan were chronically charging each other with violations of the cease-fire line in Kashmir and the Punjab border and in the sparsely inhabited area of the Rann ("Wilderness") of Cutch. The Rann of Cutch was once a gulf of the sea, into which one arm of the Indus flowed; it is now a region of desolate salt flats between Gujarat in India and Sind in Pakistan. Hostilities between the two nations broke out there in April 1965; the conflict was terminated under a cease-fire agreement signed two months later on June 30, under pressure from the United States and Great Britain. From early in the year India had been pressing its program of assimilating Kashmir. This prompted Pakistan to counteraction, and in August it sent a force of approximately 3000 across the line into India. This move, of course, led to renewed hostilities, this time of a severe nature. India got the better of the fighting and even threatened Lahore. The war was brought to an end by a cease-fire agreement signed on September 23 at the strong insistence of the United States and the Soviet Union acting through the Security

Council, where they pursued parallel courses on this issue. In the following year at a meeting arranged by the Soviet Union in Tashkent President Ayub Khan of Pakistan and Prime Minister Shastri of India, on January 10, 1966, signed an accord by which each nation would withdraw its forces to the position it had occupied before August 5, 1965. Secretary General U Thant of the United Nations reported on February 26, 1966, that the withdrawal had been fulfilled. (Lamentably Prime Minister Shastri died of a heart attack the day after the accord was signed.)

Today, as throughout the entire period of the controversy from its inception in 1947, the position of India and Pakistan respecting the Jammu and Kashmir State seems fairly clear. Each nation is convinced that it should have the state, Pakistan for economic, defensive, and prestige reasons, India for defensive and prestige reasons. Pakistan believes than an overall plebiscite, if conducted on unprejudiced terms, would result in a decision in its favor. Certain districts in Jammu might vote in favor of India, but the total would cancel these out. Therefore, Pakistan wants a simple, universal, and prompt plebiscite, with no provision for partition, and wants it under the best terms obtainable, which means, viewed practically, under United Nations auspices. It vigorously opposes any consideration of the legality of its own presence in Kashmir, and, whenever that issue rises, counters by questioning the legality of Hari Singh's accession to India in 1947, charging conspiracy, and the legality of the subsequent accession by the Jammu and Kashmir Constituent Assembly, which it denounces as an improperly elected body, while the acceptance of the accession by India it describes as "fraudulent."

India, on the other hand, stresses the illegality of Pakistan's support of the raiders in 1947 and its presence and actions in the state, and demands that that question be settled before any other is considered, being convinced that a juridical decision would affirm the charge. Such a decision would lead to an order for Pakistan to evacuate the portion of the state it holds. Out of this development would flow abolition of the Azad Kashmir government and confirmation of the government established first with Sheikh Abdullah as prime minister and later with Bakshi Ghulam Mohammed in that position.

There is no certainty that the plebiscite will ever be held. If the wishes of the people could have been ascertained at the time of independence and partition in 1947, they might have been found to favor independence, and there is some opinion that this would even now be the vote in both parts of the state. Otherwise, many observers think the vote would be for accession to Pakistan. But whatever the decision it would bring new disturbances. There would be migration out of the state, an increase of the refugee problem, and possibly a renewal of killings and lootings, such as took place at the time of the partition of India and afterwards. India has seemed resolved not to permit a plebiscite and Pakistan has not been in a position to force it. After being decisively defeated in the India-Pakistan war of December 1971, it is less able than ever to demand accession. Whether or not India's stand on this issue is morally or legally justifiable, Pakistan's own condonement of the invasion by the tribesmen, if not connivance, and later assumption of hostilities itself are seriously questionable. Each nation has pursued a policy in its own interest and has had a less than perfect case. The most potent consideration might possibly be that of need; Pakistan's was the greater in 1947, but having reached an agreement with India on the Indus basin waters in 1960, the extent of Pakistan's needs seems to be diminished.

India has not had the same stimulus to press for a decision as has Pakistan. It is in possession of the better and more valuable part of the state, with much of the greater part of the population, and time operates to its advantage. But Pakistan cannot afford to wait. It gets no profit from the part of the state it holds, only expense, and in being kept on the edges and away from the best parts Pakistan loses prestige, while the reform program in the Indian part has been abolishing landlordism and has had an opportunity to win growing support. If a plebiscite were delayed long enough, Pakistan seems to fear, India might have a chance even in a fair election. Pakistani spokesmen have accused India of practicing delay and obstruction for this reason. The question of Jammu and Kashmir has been Pakistan's most important foreign problem; failure to reach a solution of it has been a national depressant and frustration.

What would be better for the state itself? No one can answer this convincingly. The administrations of both Sheikh Abdullah and of Bakshi Ghulam Mohammed have been criticized severely as being dictatorial and repressive, not observing even the externals of democratic institutions. Some economic advance, however, seems to have accompanied them. In Azad Kashmir not even economic improvement seems really demonstrable, while the general instability of government in Pakistan since 1947 is a deterrent to extending its borders. Many people, especially in India, seem to think that the people of Jammu and Kashmir are not really competent to judge the question for themselves; they would be swayed by communal considerations rather than those of economic, social, and political welfare. The state remains, as A. M. Rosenthal put it in speaking of the Vale of Kashmir, "a land of loveliness dressed in rags." There are few, if any, areas in the subcontinent so poverty-stricken and wretched as Jammu and Kashmir.

Partition with limited plebiscite, as proposed by Sir Owen Dixon in 1950, or with no plebiscite at all, seems to offer better possibilities for solving the problem than anything else so far proposed. Certain areas might be assigned to India and Pakistan respectively on the basis of known preference. The northwestern frontier districts now held by Azad Kashmir and Pakistan would thus go to Pakistan; the eastern district of Jammu would go to India. The people of the western part of Jammu would presumably prefer to go to Pakistan; this might be decided by a plebiscite. In Kashmir province, containing the Vale of Kashmir, a plebiscite could be conducted after complete demilitarization and under United Nations auspices, according to the resolutions of August 13, 1948, and January 5, 1949. The eastern and northern frontier districts of Ladakh and Astor (Baltistan) might vote with Kashmir province, since all their communications are with it, and go with it as a unit, though a case could be defended for assigning them to India without plebiscite. Nehru proposed partition along the cease-fire line in April 1956, but Pakistan vociferously repudiated the proposal. At one time in 1960 it was rumored that President Ayub Khan would agree to such a solution but he himself explicitly said (September 24, 1960) that there was no possibility of a settlement on such terms.

The issue of the Jammu and Kashmir State not only concerns India and Pakistan separately, but is vital to them jointly as a common defense problem. Afghanistan and the Pakhtunistan movement (see pp. 255–256) threaten the integrity of Pakistan's border with that country and thus the safety of the whole sub-

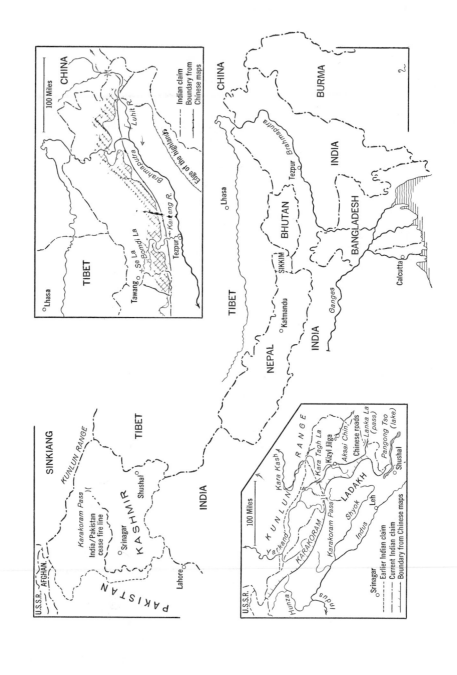

Inset (top):

CHINA

TIBET

Lhasa

Tawang Se La Bomdi La

Tezpur

Brahmaputra

Kameng R.

Luhit R.

Edge of the highlands

100 Miles

Indian claim
Boundary from
Chinese maps

Main map:

CHINA

TIBET

Lhasa

NEPAL

Katmandu

SIKKIM

BHUTAN

Tezpur

Brahmaputra

BURMA

INDIA

BANGLADESH

Ganges

Calcutta

INDIA

Inset (left):

U.S.S.R.

AFGHAN.

SINKIANG

KUNLUN RANGE

Karakoram Pass

TIBET

Shushal

Srinagar

KASHMIR

India/Pakistan
cease fire line

PAKISTAN

Lahore

INDIA

Inset (bottom right):

U.S.S.R.

KUNLUN RANGE

Kara Kash

Yarkand

Kara Tagh La

Kizyl Jilga

Aksai Chin

Lanka La (pass)

Pangong Tso (lake)

Shushal

Chinese roads

KARAKORAM

LADAKH

Karakoram Pass

Shyok

Leh

Indus

Hunza

Srinagar

100 Miles

Earlier Indian claim
Current Indian claim
Boundary from Chinese maps

continent, which throughout history has been penetrated from that region. Of more immediate and concrete concern has been the forward policy of China in Ladakh.

China, since taking Tibet, has been pressing on India's Himalayan border. In 1956–1957 it made a road across the Aksai Chin ("White Stone") desert in western Ladakh, leading into western Tibet, through territory which India regards as its own, though there is no demarcated border between India and Tibet in this region. In September and October of 1962, China advanced steadily, driving the Indians back, and in November occupied an extensive area. In late November and December China drew back its forces from their advanced posts in the eastern end of the Himalayan front, but held the positions it had gained in Ladakh, possibly wanting to guarantee its access to Tibet from the west.

China also appeared to be threatening Pakistan, but the two nations had talks in 1962 before the Chinese advance into Ladakh, and in this way China seemed to have neutralized Pakistan in order to prevent concerted action by it and India. Rather, Pakistan became a potential positive menace to India as the Chinese pressed forward: if India were to transfer forces from its Pakistan border, Pakistan might make a hostile move in Kashmir.

Ever since the middle fifties there have been reports of Communist activity in Kashmir, especially in the Indian portion of it, thus producing a situation that both India and Pakistan regard as hazardous. With the 1962 developments there was an increasing possibility that not only western Ladakh but all of Kashmir might be affected in a way satisfactory to neither India nor Pakistan. Even if China were not to try to occupy the whole state, the Kashmir part of it might gain a new status, perhaps that independence which Gulab Singh, Partab Singh, Hari Singh, and Sheikh Abdullah as well had desired. This would be an independence that could hardly be maintained, and the area might easily become no more than a satellite or component unit of a larger Communist power—as has happened to Tibet and to other areas not far distant, such as Uzbekistan and Tajikistan in the Soviet Union.

The possibilities of the situation in Kashmir, as part of the total situation created by China's forward policy, were clearly disturbing to India and were also a concern to the United States and Great Britain, which renewed their efforts to bring the Kashmir issue to a settlement, and employed their diplomatic resources to that end. At the end of November 1962 it was announced that India and Pakistan would enter into negotiations over Kashmir, and the prospects of terminating the costly and embittering quarrel seemed brighter than at any time previously during the fifteen years that the quarrel had lasted. But the prospect was never realized, and the situation still remains unresolved.

Late in November 1949, when the disputes between India and Pakistan and the communal violence in Bengal and elsewhere had raised public feelings in both countries to a point where the likelihood of open hostilities had become a real fear, Prime Minister Nehru tentatively proposed that the two nations should issue a joint declaration to abstain from war with each other. On December 22, 1949, he submitted a draft of his proposal to Prime Minister Liaquat Ali Khan. The latter expressed agreement with the basic motive of Nehru's proposal, but evidently also felt that acceptance of the simple declaration as proposed by Nehru would tie Pakistan's hands in cases where India had a present advantage and would not proceed to a final solution. Nehru had not included in the draft any procedure that would compel a settlement in case first negotiations failed.

Liaquat Ali, therefore, presented a counterdraft, which corresponded fairly well in its first part with Nehru's draft, but then added specific provisions concerning procedure and the subjects then under dispute to be so settled. The steps were to be, first, negotiation, which, if it failed, was to be followed by mediation, which, if it failed, was to be followed by arbitration. A time schedule was to be set for the successive stages. From then until the end of November 1950 the two Prime Ministers engaged in a long and repetitious and fruitless correspondence, since published, on the subject of the No-War Declaration, in which they reviewed the various disputes and went over the old ground but in neither case budged an inch from an original position. India would not agree to Liaquat Ali's proposed procedure; Pakistan affirmed that without an agreed procedure settlement of disputes could be blocked indefinitely. During the period of the correspondence the crisis of March and April 1950 over the minorities came and went and the Delhi Pact was signed. Though the two nations could not agree upon a formula for settling their dispute, they were able in that moment of extreme tension to avoid war.

Nineteen years later, in late August 1968, Mrs. Gandhi brought up the same No-War proposal, but without any success. President Ayub Khan, speaking on September 1, replied that "to talk of no-war pacts without settling the Kashmir dispute is meaningless and an attempt to mislead and hoodwink the world." So deep and tense is the feeling about the Kashmir issue in the two nations.

It is possible that a new element was injected in the dispute over Kashmir at the United States–Chinese conference in Peking in February 1972. In the official communiqué published in the American newspapers on February 27, 1972, the problem was mentioned. Referring to a resolution of the United Nations Security Council on December 21, 1971, votd by the majority but defeated by a Soviet Union veto, it was stated that "the United States favors the continuation of the cease-fire between India and Pakistan and the withdrawal of all military forces to within their own territories and to their own sides of the cease-fire line in Jammu and Kashmir; the United States supports the right of the peoples of South Asia to shape their own future in peace, free of military threat, and without having the area become the subject of big-power rivalry." The Chinese position was expressed as follows: "It [China] firmly maintains that India and Pakistan should, in accordance with United Nations resolutions on the India-Pakistan question, immediately withdraw all their forces to their respective territories and to their own sides of the cease-fire line in Jammu and Kashmir and firmly supports the Pakistan Government and people in their struggle to preserve their independence and sovereignty and the people of Jammu and Kashmir in their struggle for the right of self-determination." Thus the United States and China, which had both supported Pakistan in the India-Pakistan War of 1971–1972, appear also to stand with Pakistan on the Kashmir situation.

11 The Birth of Bangladesh

The greatest disaster that has befallen the subcontinent since partition in 1947 was the brutality connected with the revolt of East Pakistan which broke out in March 1971 and resulted in the birth of Bangladesh. It was a direct result of partition and the inability of the two parts of Pakistan to live together. From the time of the creation of Pakistan the two wings had been in recurring rivalry with each other for political dominance of the nation, with the West consistently the winner. There had been serious disturbance in 1969, and then in 1971 revolt broke out in uncontrollable form, accompanied by the worst horrors of civil war and relentless military suppression of dissidents. The revolt had its roots in cultural antipathies and economic discontent, which as East Pakistan's grievances became more galling and were being increasingly expressed in vocal complaints led to inevitable political agitation. When it became clear that the people of East Pakistan were deeply disturbed by the issues involved and were giving their discontent overwhelming expression at the polls, the government of Pakistan, which was located in West Pakistan and had the Pakistani army under its control, set out to crush the dissidence peremptorily and forcefully, with resort to maximum brutality and terrorism. The method failed. East Pakistan succeeded in becoming an independent state, Bangladesh, "Bengal Land."

At the time of the discussion in the 1930s and 1940s leading to partition there were those in Bengal who felt that partition of India was not a desirable way of satisfying Muslim aspirations and was liable to produce trouble. First, there was the obvious difficulty of establishing and maintaining understanding and co-operation between the two parts of the proposed Muslim state, which were vastly different from each other in cultural background and temperament and separated by a distance of over 900 miles across a none too friendly neighboring nation. The two parts of the proposed Pakistan spoke different languages, not mutually intelligible except with special study. Consequently, much of official communication in Pakistan has always been in English. Besides the basic difficulty of conversation and written or printed communication, the two regions had quite different literary traditions and contemporary activity. Bengali, the language of East Pakistan, has an extensive and distinguished literature, of considerable age, drawing much of its inspiration and style from traditional Hindu literature, including that in Sanskrit, though in recent centuries it has also produced some Muslim literature. The chief spoken languages of West Pakistan are Punjabi, Sindhi, and Urdu; some of the area's belles lettres and philosophical writings are in Persian, but Persian is not easily intelligible to the general public. Punjabi and Sindhi have only a slender literature. Urdu has a fairly extensive literature, composed not only in West Pakistan but also in greater amount in the parts of India to the east of West Pakistan. Urdu literature borrows greatly from the Persian and Arabic languages and literary traditions. The principal newspapers of West Pakistan are published in English, Urdu, Sindhi, and Punjabi. In what became East Pakistan the principal newspapers and periodicals are published in Bengali. The scripts used are different in the two regions. In East Bengal the script is Bengali, which is allied to the native scripts of India, and is written from left to right, like the roman script in which English is written. West Pakistan's Urdu always, and Sindhi generally, are written in a variety of the Perso-Arabic script, which is written from right to left. Another script called Gurmukhi is also used in some parts of West Pakistan but nowadays only slightly (it is more widely used in East Punjab in India, being employed by the Sikhs). These differences of literary, as well as popular, vocabulary and script complicate the problem of mutual understanding.

The two regions had had very different histories. West Pakistan consists of the area watered by the Indus River and its tributaries. This region has been constantly invaded throughout all its known history by peoples or armies coming from the barren regions north and west of it, who have made their way through the mountain passes, especially through the Khyber Pass. These invaders have all been seeking the cultivable plain of northern India, either to settle there or to loot. War has been a constantly recurring experience, and between invasions there has always been turmoil along the western and northern borders.

Bengal has had much less invasion. Peace there, though often broken, has been common enough for Bengal not to feel that warfare is an unavoidable way of life; peace is perhaps looked upon as normal. This is one of the circumstances of history that has contributed to greater intellectual activity in Bengal than in West Pakistan. And because literature and the arts generally have been more intensively cultivated in Bengal than in the Punjab and Sind, the Bengalis have had a stronger feeling about their cultural heritage than have the Punjabis and Sindhis. The Bengalis have a stronger feeling of regional loyalty, we might call it patriotism, and pride in their heritage than the western Pakistanis. They have a pronounced feeling about the unity of Bengal, East and West, and the desirability of keeping it intact. This feeling has shown itself in many ways; for example, in 1905 when, for administrative purposes, Lord Curzon, then Governor General, and his government had the area then known as Bengal—a much larger area than the combined present West and East Bengal—divided into two provinces. By some inadvertence or obtuseness the dividing line was so drawn that it cut right through the Bengali language area. The adverse reaction of the Bengalis apparently took the government of India and the India Office in London by surprise, for the reaction was so stubborn that the partition of Bengal had to be reversed in 1911 (see Chapter 4).

The Bengalis are physically smaller than the Punjabis and less "martial," just as the Punjabis are less well developed intellectually than the Bengalis, have less appreciation of literature and the arts and are less productive in them. Each has a stereotype about the other, which may be summarized by saying that the Bengalis tend to regard the Punjabis as stupid bullies, while the Punjabis think of the Bengalis as timid, with the spirit and capacities of office clerks (*babus*), volatile and unreliable.

Though West Pakistan was about 5.7 times the size of East Pakistan, the population of East Pakistan was much the larger. In the 1961 census the figures were approximately 51 million for East Pakistan and 43 million for West Pakistan. Estimates for 1970 give figures of about 60.8 million for the East and 53.5 for the West. The population superiority meant that East Pakistan had an advantage in the polls. With that population advantage, nature had given East Pakistan an advantage over West Pakistan in economic resources. East Bengal produces most of the world's jute, which was one of Pakistan's few exportable commodities and the principal source of its foreign exchange. East Pakistan also produced tea, another exportable product. The profits of foreign exchange from these exports, however, were not used to the advantage of East Pakistan. Rather, they were used for the benefit of industrial growth in West Pakistan and presumably also for the purchase of arms. East Pakistan, therefore, had a grievance in that it earned the foreign exchange but got none of the profits from it. West Pakistan dominated the nation's government from the inception of Pakistan, and East Pakistan came to speak of itself as a colony being exploited by West Pakistan. At the same time it regarded itself as being used as a market for the products of West Pakistan's industry, which it was being compelled to finance.

Besides this economic grievance, East Pakistan made a minor issue of the fact that in the brief Indo-Pakistan war of 1965 all the nation's defense forces were used to protect West Pakistan and none were assigned to care for East Pakistan. India made no attack upon East Pakistan, and hence no defense force was needed there, but East Pakistan felt that it was being treated as of less importance than West Pakistan. Similar was the view about relief from the ravages of the cyclone and tidal wave of November 1970 which swept the head of the Bay of Bengal. The East Pakistanis felt that the government of Pakistan, being under the dominance of West Pakistan, was inexcusably lax in aiding the stricken area.

The major grievance of East Pakistan, however, was that it did not have as strong a voice in the counsels of the nation as it deserved, that it had been kept out of national decision-making and its interests had therefore been neglected. This conviction led to the formation and growth of the Awami (People's) League, which stood in opposition to the Muslim League and to West Pakistan. Rectification of the injustices East Pakistan was suffering was the substance of the Awami League's political aims.

East Pakistan had never been fully satisfied with its position in relation to West Pakistan. The Pakistan resolution voted at the Lahore meeting of the Muslim League on March 23, 1940, stated that the northwestern and eastern zones of India should constitute "independent states [plural] in which the constituent elements shall be autonomous and sovereign." The East Bengalis had not expected to be dominated by the West Punjabis. Federation, of a rather loose sort, seems to have been the maximum kind of bond they expected, but as time passed the control by the center increased.

Almost from the start of the national existence concessions had to be made to claims rising from differences of language and culture. In November 1947, barely three months after the partition of India and creation of the state of Pakistan, a Pakistan Educational Conference—which did most of its business in English —meeting in Karachi, then the capital of Pakistan, adopted a resolution which avoided the use of the term "official language" but recommended that "Urdu should be recognized as the lingua franca of Pakistan." The constitution of1956 named both Urdu and Bengali as the state languages of Pakistan (corroborated in the 1962 constitution) but this did not seem to still the mistrust. Whenever regional difficulties arose some sentiment was always expressed in East Pakistan for existence as a separate state, though it never was strong enough to command much support. Sometimes it was suspected that there was sentiment for reunion with West Bengal (in India). As time passed East Pakistan's dissatisfaction continued to be expressed. In 1954 the politically prominent Fazl-ul-Huq, venerable, highly respected, and the most influential leader in Bengal over a long period of time, stated that the partition of India had been a mistake and that his own objective had been an independent East Pakistan.

Among the early proponents of the idea of Pakistan who had expected that East and West Pakistan should be two separate political bodies rather than a single nation was H. Shaheed Suhrawardy, chief minister of Bengal at the time of partition, who opted to Pakistan, became head of the Awami League, and in 1956–1957 was prime minister. In the East Pakistan provincial elections in 1954, the Awami League under his leadership thoroughly defeated the Muslim League government, winning 233 seats against the Muslim League's 10. The result was that the Governor General of Pakistan shortly afterwards dismissed the East Pakistan administration and sent General Iskander Mirza there to rule without a legislature. Suhrawardy was one of a number of veteran politicians who, under the findings of tribunals appointed by General Ayub Khan, then military dictator and president, were disqualified from holding any office until 1966. On January 30, 1962, Suhrawardy was taken into detention. The Home Ministry of Pakistan said that his "activities in the recent past have been fraught with such danger to the security and safety of Pakistan that one could fairly describe them as treasonable." Many members of the Awami League were arrested in February, whereupon student demonstrations followed. Suhrawardy was released on August 19, 1962; the official announcement said, "The Government is now satisfied that Mr. Suhrawardy will not henceforth participate in any disruptive activities." A month later he was the leader in uniting various outlawed parties in common action to protest against the new constitution adopted not long before.

There continued to be relatively minor protests in East Pakistan against domination and exploitation by West Pakistan. A serious situation developed in the fall of 1968 as a protest movement against the unpopular regime of General Ayub Khan, who had seized power in 1958 and in 1962 had promulgated a military dictatorship throughout Pakistan and a new system of government for the country. Opposition parties had been agitating against Ayub Khan and several leaders had been arrested in 1966 for being involved in a protest movement. This movement became stronger in East Pakistan in 1969 and serious disorders occurred, which led Ayub Khan's government to make a large number of arrests there. Similar disturbances in protest against other features of Ayub Khan's administration were occurring at the same time in West Pakistan. The most prominent of the protesters in West Pakistan at that time was Air Marshal Asghar Khan, who was quoted in a news dispatch from Karachi as saying, "In his person, President Ayub Khan rightly or wrongly symbolizes in the eyes of the people all that is evil in our society." At that time (January 6, 1969) five opposition parties, one of which was the Awami League, uniting as the Pakistani Democratic Movement, threatened to boycott the general elections, which were due in 1970, unless the following conditions were satisfied: direct election on the basis of adult franchise; full powers to the directly elected Parliament and provincial legislatures; immediate removal of the state of emergency; immediate restoration of civil rights and freedoms; immediate release of all political prisoners. On March 25, 1969, Ayub Khan resigned his office and made immediate transfer of power to the armed forces under General Yahya Khan as military dictator. The nature of the political administration, however, did not change, except perhaps that at first Yahya Khan stepped more carefully than Ayub Khan had been stepping and tried to avoid some of Ayub Khan's mistakes. But by the end of 1970 he had discarded any gestures he had made toward democratic procedures in government and was prepared to exercise military rule of the most uncompromising sort.

The real heart of the situation that in 1971 burst into the great Pakistani tragedy was the rivalry between West Pakistan and East Pakistan for domination of the nation. West Pakistan had the wealth, the industry, the commerce, the ruling elite, and the army. East Pakistan had the larger population. West Pakistan was dominating the nation, but if the new constitution, which was due to be drafted now that Ayub Khan's constitution of 1962 had been repudiated, should provide that power should lie with the majority of the electorate, East Pakistan seemed sure to become dominant and West Pakistan then would lose its dominance. This would be intolerable to West Pakistan, but any other result would be intolerable to East Pakistan, which knew it had a majority and by any democratic process would be bound, potentially at least, to win control of the nation.

It had been determined by the then government of Pakistan that elections should take place on December 7, 1970, for the National Assembly, which when convened should have as its first order of business the drafting of a new constitution. The freely elected National Assembly would be convened in Dacca, the eastern capital of Pakistan. It was evident that there would be bitter quarreling between the aggrieved East Pakistan wing, which was obviously anxious to have provincial autonomy, and West Pakistan, which wished to retain its advantages, but no one, at least no one in West Pakistan and possibly in East Pakistan as well, really foresaw the full extent of what would happen in the election. Apparently Yahya Khan did not. Thus the stage was set for the tragedy to begin.

At this juncture nature provided a curtain-raiser for the great political drama which was to come. On November 12 a cyclone struck at the head of the Bay of Bengal, followed on November 13 by a devastating tidal wave, the two phenomena causing enormous loss of life, property, crops, and housing in the lower Ganges-Brahmaputra delta. Such calamities occur there from time to time, as, for example, about a quarter of a century before, in 1946. Then, as in 1970, the loss of life and property was enormous. In the 1970 cyclone and tidal wave disaster the number of persons drowned, dead from starvation, and killed by cholera and typhoid was appalling. The governor of East Pakistan, Vice Admiral S. M. Ahsan, on November 20 gave the number as 150,000. On November 25 the official death toll was given as 175,103 with another 23,927 missing. Unofficial estimates indicated that the final tally might be as much as three times the official figure, that is, over half a million. Relief measures by the government, augmented by large contributions from outside sources, were balked in reaching the stricken areas, chiefly because of transportation difficulties. But great as was this disaster created by Nature, it was only fractional of the human-made long-developing catastrophe that was poised to overwhelm East Pakistan.

The scheduled elections took place on December 7. For twelve years and especially in 1969 the Awami League and its leader Mujib-ur-Rahman had been promoting a program of political reorganization, which had started out as a demand for equalization of the status of the two wings of the country but was now promoted as a program to equalize the status of all the component subordinate states that constitute West Pakistan—there were no such subordinate constituent states in East Pakistan. This program was expressed by the Awami League in the 1970 election campaign in a kind of manifesto as "Six Points," presented as a framework for drafting the new constitution. These were the following.

1) The character of the government shall be federal and parliamentary, in which election to the federal legislature and to the legislatures of the federating units shall be direct and on the basis of universal adult franchise. Representation in the federal legislature shall be on the basis of population.

2) The federal government shall be responsible only for defense and foreign affairs and, subject to the conditions provided in 3 below, currency.

3) There shall be two separate, freely convertible currencies for the two wings of the country, or alternatively a single currency, subject to the establishment of a federal reserve system in which there will be regional federal reserve banks which shall devise measures to prevent the transfer of resources and flight of capital from one region to another.

4) Fiscal policy shall be the responsibility of, and the power of

taxation shall vest in, the federating units. The federal government shall be provided with requisite revenue resources for meeting the requirements of defense and foreign affairs, which revenue resources would be automatically appropriable by the federal government in the manner provided and on the basis of the ratio to be determined by the procedure laid down in the constitution. Such constitutional provisions would ensure that the federal government's revenue requirements are met consistently with the objective of ensuring control over fiscal policy by the governments of the federating units.

5) Constitutional provisions shall be made to enable separate accounts to be maintained of the foreign exchange earnings of each of the federating units, under the control of the respective governments of the federating units. The foreign exchange requirements of the federal government shall be met by the governments of the federating units on the basis of a ratio to be determined in accordance with the procedure laid down in the constitution. The regional governments shall have power under the constitution to negotiate foreign trade and aid within the framework of the foreign policy of the country, which shall be the responsibility of the federal government.

6) The government of the federating units shall be empowered to maintain a militia or paramilitary force in order to contribute effectively toward national security.

In West Pakistan none of the twenty other parties presenting candidates offered a program of constitution-making. By far the strongest party there was the Pakistan People's Party (PPP). Its leader was Zulfikar Ali Bhutto. The PPP had no program for the election campaign, and did not discuss the Awami League's Six Points. All the small parties, though without programs, nevertheless attacked the Awami League, with the exception of the section of the National Awami party of the North-West Frontier province and Baluchistan headed by Abdul Wali Khan, which won six seats in the election. Not until the election was over did Bhutto give any indication of his views on constitutional issues.

Whatever Yahya Khan may have expected or wished from the election, the result was obviously a blow to him. The total number of seats in the National Assembly was to be 313. Of these the Awami League won 167, and was thus assured of a majority.

The election had taken place on December 7 and the Assembly

was scheduled to meet on March 3, 1971. It was never convened. On December 15 Bhutto, whose party was second in number of seats won, having got 87, indicated that he had reservations about the drafting of a constitution that might impair the country's unity, and offered to meet with Sheikh Mujib-ur-Rahman, leader of the Awami League, for discussions which would presumably result in some kind of compromise. Mujib repudiated the idea of a compromise. On December 21 Bhutto then proposed that he, Mujib, and Yahya Khan should come to an agreement and that the Awami League and the PPP should share the power in the nation. Mujib refused. Late in January Mujib and Bhutto met, but no compromise resulted.

About this time two Kashmiris, who were later identified as double agents for India and Pakistan, hijacked an Indian airliner, flew it to Lahore in Pakistan, and there blew it up. Bhutto praised the hijackers; Mujib deplored their action. The government of India and the government of Pakistan could not come to an agreement about reparations, and India put a stop to the permission it had been giving Pakistan to overfly India, thus complicating communication between the two wings of Pakistan.

Mujib had wanted the National Assembly to convene on February 15, Bhutto wanted the convening to take place soon, and the date March 3 was agreed to. On February 15 Bhutto announced that if the Assembly were to be convened without a compromise being reached, the PPP would boycott it. The Awami League leaders then gave Mujib full authority to take whatever steps he considered appropriate "in the face of difficulty in constitution-making." Bhutto threatened to start a demonstration movement from Khyber to Karachi, that is, to arouse all West Pakistan. Then on March 1 Yahya Khan issued an order of postponement of the Assembly—this was two days before the date of convening that had been set only two weeks before. Yahya Khan did not then appoint another date for convening the Assembly.

The postponement of the date for convening the National Assembly aroused strong protest in East Pakistan, including a general strike and civil disobedience. The military rule that had been set over East Pakistan by Ayub Khan in 1969 now endeavored to stem the disorders but without success. Rather, the Awami League gained popular confidence and assumed a sort of de facto rule headed by Sheikh Mujib. President Yahya Khan then assured the East Pakistanis that the National Assembly would be convened and set a date of March 25.

Mujib had announced on March 7 that he would attend the Assembly, provided four conditions were satisfied. These were (1) withdrawal of the troops to barracks, (2) the holding of a judicial inquiry into killings by the military, (3) retraction of martial law, (4) immediate transfer of power to the people's representatives. He had already on March 4 authorized some relaxation of the strike. Yahya Khan had appointed a new military governor, General Tikka Khan, but on March 8, when Tikka Khan arrived in Dacca to be sworn into office, the chief justice of East Pakistan, B. A. Siddiqui, complying with a call by Sheikh Mujib on March 7 for a weeklong strike in government offices and the courts against the military administration of East Pakistan, would not swear him in.

At this time East Pakistan appeared to have two rulers simultaneously, one of them an appointee of the national government, the other a de facto ruler in the person of Sheikh Mujib as recognized by popular will.

Sheikh Mujib, born in Faridpur, East Bengal, March 22, 1922, comes from modest circumstances, is a man of strong principles, courage, and charm, and has a reputation for honesty and kindness. He had the adoration of the people as their leader. On March 15 there was a mass demonstration in Dacca, with processions and crowds shouting *joy bangla desh,* "Hail to Bengal land!" By March 23 a Bangla Desh flag had appeared.

On March 16 General Yahya Khan, having flown to Dacca, had a conference with Sheikh Mujib, and the conference continued for several days without any results. On March 23, thirty-one years to the day after the Muslim League at a meeting in Lahore had adopted its resolution for the goal of creating a separate Muslim state—or states—by partition of India, the Bangla Desh flag was hoisted at Sheikh Mujib's home, constituting a declaration of autonomy and, if that were not granted, for secession and the splitting of Pakistan. Demonstrators marching past Mujib's home were tearing up the flag of Pakistan. Sheikh Mujib at that time declared a general strike for March 27, but before that day arrived Yahya Khan struck.

On March 25, the day the National Assembly had been scheduled to meet, the armed forces, without giving any warning, moved into Dacca after dark with mortars, machine guns, and tanks. They fired the houses of Awami League members, killing occupants, and attacked the Hindu areas of the city as well. Not long after midnight they took Mujib into custody and, it was said, promptly flew him to Attock in West Pakistan. Either there or elsewhere in West Pakistan he was put on trial on charges "carrying the death penalty." It was announced months later that he had been found guilty, but the sentence was never executed. Later, when Mujib was released (by Bhutto, who had by then come to power), and was in London on the way to East Pakistan on January 8, 1972, he said that the sentence had been death by hanging.

On the night of March 25–26, 1971, the terror in East Pakistan started. Newspapers in the United States, Great Britain, India— and other countries—carried accounts of wanton murder of civilians in indiscriminate slaying of East Pakistanis by West Pakistani troops, most of them being Punjabis, who comprise the bulk of the Pakistani army. With this went rape, often followed by murder of the raped women, burning of houses, looting, all continuing for months not only in Dacca and nearby but in all parts of East Pakistan. Armed troops were flown in from West Pakistan until, it was estimated, the number amounted to 70,000, a number said to be one third that of all the Pakistani forces. The number of slain was reported by Mujib, on the basis of inquiry after his return, to be three million. Promptly after the terror started East Pakistanis began to migrate to India, to a total of approximately 10 million, according to Indian claims. There they lived in poverty, being cared for by India, a poor country at best with slender economic resources, and by contributions from abroad. Not until Pakistan was defeated in the war that developed between it and India, and the Pakistani army in East Pakistan, harried by guerrillas and rendered helpless by the Indian forces, had surrendered, did the refugees commence returning to what was left of those homes, and the places where their villages had once stood. It was an evidence of the East Pakistanis' power of endurance that they could make the difficult trek to West Bengal in India and a tribute to India's compassion for the poor and destitute that it supplied from its own scanty resources the needs of the refugees—food, poor though it was, yet sufficient to sustain life; shelter, of the crudest sort; medical care in places where physicians, nurses, and medical supplies are few; clothing, such as could be got together; blankets, badly needed in the winter in north India. The refugees and the victims who died in East Pakistan were both Hindus and Muslims. The slaughter by the Pakistan soldiers was indiscriminately perpetrated upon Muslims and Hindus, and upon men, women, and children. It was unmitigated terrorism, evidently authorized by military command. In view of the atrocities in East Pakistan, the hope expressed by Bhutto, after he became Pakistan's new president, that Pakistan would some day again become a united nation seems unrealistic.

On March 29 the Pakistani government had announced that the revolt in East Pakistan had been quelled, the independence movement defeated, and that the military forces were in control there. Yahya Khan invited the refugees to return, but none seemed ever to have done so. Instead the migration continued until the final defeat of the Pakistani armed forces.

The victory of the forces for independence was achieved through the aid India rendered the East Pakistanis. This turned out to be of two kinds: one was the arming and training of the guerrilla force, known as the Mukti-Vahini, "Liberation Army"; the other was the invasion of East Pakistan by the Indian army.

On the outbreak of the revolt on March 25 the Awami League was outlawed and the 167 seats it had won in the December 7 election therefore became vacant. In due time Yahya Khan indicated that the National Assembly would be convened on December 27, 1971. But first it was necessary for him to say what disposition would be made of the 167 seats won by the Awami League. On November 2 he announced his decision. Of the 167 seats won by the Awami League 78 of the winners were ousted on the ground that they had committed crimes against the state and their seats were therefore vacant. The seat won by Sheikh Mujib was to be held in escrow pending the outcome of his trial on charges of treason. With respect to the 78 seats which were declared vacant 53 would be filled without contest, that is, it seemed, by government appointments. The remaining 25 seats would be contested in special by-elections in December. The candidates for these by-elections had been "carefully screened by the Government." All politicians subscribing to the views of the Awami League were barred from the by-elections, and other potential opposition candidates were prohibited from access to the press, which was controlled by the government. The government was backing certain minor right-wing groups which were strongly religious and had pro-government leanings. The most favored party was to be the Jama'at-i-Islami, which in the December 7 elections had won only 8 seats, none of them in East Pakistan, though it had put up 70 candidates there. This party was being allotted 14 seats, being more favored by the government than any other party. The government had asked the 88 members-elect from East Pakistan who were not barred from their Assembly seats to take them, but it was reported in the press that most of the 88 had migrated to India or had joined the Bengali underground guerrilla force, the Mukti-Vahini.

The headquarters of the Mukti-Vahini was in Calcutta, as was also the headquarters of the Bangla Desh "government." The name "Bangla Desh," which the revolutionists used, was a name which dissidents had been using for at least two years, perhaps longer, as a proposed substitute for "East Pakistan." When the revolt later proved successful and the name was adopted for the newly created nation, it was written as one word, Bangladesh.

Civil war was waged intensively in East Pakistan. Yahya Khan's troops were well equipped and apparently instructed not to spare any measures that would terrify the rebellious populace. His troops were aided by the Biharis in East Pakistan, Muslims who had emigrated from Bihar in India after partition in 1947 and from time to time afterwards to escape Hindu hostility. In East Pakistan they were not liked, having become shopkeepers with a reputation, perhaps not deserved, of hard dealing. Many of these Biharis became *razakars,* a kind of irregular volunteers, who were especially hostile to Hindus and virulent toward Indians. They were accused by the revolutionists of brutality equalling in character that of the Pakistani troops who came in from West Pakistan. After the defeat of the West Pakistani troops and accompanying the triumph of the Awami League the razakars were the objects of popular vengeance for the brutality the East Pakistanis had suffered.

India had observed with horror the sufferings of the East Pakistanis, and vigorous speeches had been made in the Indian Parliament. As the Pakistani troops poured into East Pakistan and were deployed throughout the region, India took measures to guard her borders, evidently fearful that they might be violated. Indian forces were kept ready for use both in the east and the west. The apprehension was obviously based in part upon the fact that India was training and arming guerrillas. During the month of November there were charges passing back and forth between India and Pakistan of Pakistani firing across the border and Indian firing in return. Each side accused the other of armed aggression across the East Pakistan border. In the west India claimed that Pakistani forces had made incursions into the Indian-held part of Kashmir. Popular sentiment in West Bengal was strong against the treatment their cultural relatives in East Pakistan were receiving from the government of Pakistan. With the two nations of India and Pakistan for a quarter of a century in a constant state of irritation with each other—one might call it hostility, sometimes only latent but at other times vigorously expressed in words and even with shots across the cease-fire line in Kashmir and the Punjab border— the East Bengal revolt with its accompanying brutality was dangerously inflammatory. The situation exploded in the first week of December. India claimed that Pakistan had been shelling her installations along the border between East Pakistan and India. Each side charged that the other had bombed airfields or military installations in the west as well as in the east. A full-scale war, though a brief one, had started.

The Indian forces easily defeated the Pakistani forces on both fronts. On December 16 India, after 14 days of fighting, took Dacca and accepted the surrender of the Pakistani forces in East Pakistan. India then ordered a cease-fire on both fronts. Yahya Khan had claimed that Pakistan was winning in the west, and stated that it would continue the war, but the next day he accepted the cease-fire. India reported that Pakistan had taken about 50 square miles of Indian territory in Poonch in the Jammu part of the Jammu and Kashmir state, while she herself had taken about 1500 square miles of territory which Pakistan had been occupying.

There were two matters requiring Pakistan's immediate attention. These were the reconstruction of its government and the return of Sheikh Mujib to what had been East Pakistan, which had set up a temporary system of government pending Mujib's return and had changed its name to Bangladesh. India and Bhutan, which accepts Indian control in its foreign relations, had already recognized Bangladesh; it would be the new state's urgent business to get further recognition by other states and to seek admission to the United Nations.

The rehabilitation of Pakistan after its defeat fell to Zulfikar Ali Bhutto, leader of the Pakistan People's Party, which had won the second largest number of votes and seats (87) in the December 7 elections. On December 18 President Yahya Khan asked him as Deputy Prime Minister to form a new government. This Bhutto did. On December 20 he was sworn in as President and Martial-Law Administrator, Yahya Khan having resigned the day before. Bhutto appointed a Bengali, 78-year-old Nurul Amin, as Vice President. Bhutto reestablished civilian rule of the country, announced that Sheikh Mujib would be released, stated that he would work toward friendly relations with India and East Pakistan (which he did not yet recognize as Bangladesh but as still a wing of Pakistan).

Sheikh Mujib was freed on January 8 and promptly flown in a British airplane to London, where he met and talked with Prime Minister Heath. On the way to Dacca he stopped in New Delhi, met Prime Minister Mrs. Indira Gandhi, received a warm reception from Indian officials and the Indian people, and then proceeded to Dacca. His entry into Dacca on January 10 was triumphal, for his welcome was that of Bangladesh's liberator. He had been named President of Bangladesh, the preceding April, while he was in prison. He set to work at once on the great problems facing the new nation. First was the organization of a government. On January 12 as President he declared a temporary constitution in effect and appointed a new Chief Justice of the High Court. He then resigned, and a new President who had been chosen by the cabinet, Abu Sayeed Choudhury, was sworn in. Mujib had already been chosen Prime Minister and the new Chief Justice then swore him into office. Besides being Prime Minister he retained for himself the ministries of Defense, Home Affairs, Information, and Cabinet Affairs. Abd-us-Samad was continued as Minister of Foreign Affairs, a post to which he had been appointed under the caretaker government that had been set up after the occupation of Dacca and surrender of the Pakistan forces on December 16. At that time a twelve-member cabinet had been appointed, and the incumbents to other ministries appointed then were continued in office under the new government.

When Mujib addressed the welcoming citizens on his arrival in Dacca, he stressed Bangladesh's need to be a united country with no thought of revenge upon those members of the new nation who had participated in the terror, presumably meaning the Biharis and the razakars. He seemed clearly to believe that unity would be essential to the success of a rehabilitation program.

The world's three superpowers—the United States, the Soviet

Union, and China—were all much concerned about the revolt of East Pakistan and the Indo-Pakistan tension growing out of it that burst into war. All three apparently feared that the impending and finally realized war might spread and involve one or all of them. Though no one of the three actually engaged in any of the hostilities, they all showed their partisanship, the Soviet Union toward India, China and the United States toward Pakistan. The Soviet Union had long sought close relations with India and had maintained an extensive program of cultural activities there. The People's Republic of China for a number of years after World War II had had a warm friendship with India, which had tried, but unsuccessfully, to get China admitted to the United Nations. Just what soured that friendship is not clear, but by 1962 it had dissolved, and a brief war developed between the two countries concerning boundaries in the Himalayan areas, a war which China won with very little effort. After that the two nations viewed each other with obvious distaste and evident suspicion, and China and Pakistan grew friendly in joint dislike of India. At the end of World War II the United States had the friendliest sort of relation with India, giving much financial assistance and economic advice and help. During the long period of the Cold War the United States, like the Soviet Union, wanted India's support, but India under Jawaharlal Nehru adopted a policy of "nonalignment," which was looked upon by the United States as illogical, ungrateful, and in the terms in which India expressed it as "sanctimonious." The United States also had a policy of friendship for Pakistan, including financial assistance and development aid, though on a less generous scale than the aid given India. Throughout these years the United States conscientiously, and in general successfully, observed a posture of neutrality toward the two nations.

When the East Pakistan revolt broke out it seemed possible that India might get involved. When the refugees were streaming to India in great numbers, and especially when it became known that India was arming and training the Mukti-Vahini in guerrilla warfare, it seemed inevitable that India would be drawn into hostilities with Pakistan. In that case China and the Soviet Union might easily be drawn in also. The unfriendliness that had grown up between those two would have conduced to that result. The chief preventive to the development of such a catastrophic issue may have been the fact that the Soviet Union provided a convincing documentation of its friendship with India.

On August 8, 1971, Soviet Foreign Minister Andrei A. Gromyko flew to New Delhi and on August 9 he and India's Minister of External Affairs, Swaran Singh, signed a twenty-year Pact of Friendship between their two countries. The important clause in the pact says: "Each high contracting party undertakes to abstain from providing any assistance to any third party that engages in armed conflict with the other party. In the event of either party's being subjected to an attack or a threat thereof, the high contracting parties shall immediately enter into mutual consultations to remove such threats and to take appropriate effective measures to insure peace and the security of their countries."

Though this was not a security pact in the normal diplomatic sense, since neither party was put under obligation to give the other military support in case of conflict, the pact seemed strong enough to deter any country from hastily declaring war on either of the contracting parties. With China apparently rendered immobile by reason of the Indo-Russian Pact, India could feel more secure in any policy she might feel it necessary to adopt. The United States found this pact of interest because it seemed to indicate that the Indian policy of nonalignment in the Cold War was terminated.

Early in November 1971 Prime Minister Indira Gandhi traveled to Washington to seek aid in supporting the needs of the refugees who had come to India from East Pakistan and to ask President Nixon to press West Pakistan to reach a settlement with East Pakistan. She pointed out that India was trying in every possible way not to become involved in a war with Pakistan, but that Pakistan was at her border with its army poised for aggression. At the same time the burden of caring for 9.6 million refugees was more than India could bear by herself. Mrs. Gandhi also made the point in at least two television interviews that India had no quarrel with Pakistan. The quarrel was between the Pakistan government and its citizens in East Pakistan. It was an internal situation in Pakistan that had brought unearned trouble upon India. Mrs. Gandhi's reception from the United States was correct but at the same time chilly. As far as the published reports indicated, she got nothing.

The Chinese sympathies were clearly expressed at the United Nations on November 18. The Chinese representative Fu Haq, speaking before the General Assembly's Social Committee, vigorously attacked India for interfering with Pakistan's internal affairs, for blocking Pakistan's efforts to restore peace in the subcontinent, and for making capital of the refugee situation. He did not mention India by name but referred to it as "a certain country."

The attitude of the United States press, with some exceptions, and apparently of the United States people as well, seemed to be one of shock and horror at the brutalities to which the East Pakistanis were being subjected. This was also the attitude of many members of Congress. But it did not turn out to be the attitude of the administration, which had an ambivalent stance. On the one hand the administration sent aid for the refugees, but on the other hand it shipped arms to Pakistan. Many American newspaper editorials criticized this policy of aiding Pakistan in murdering its own citizens; the administration's defense was that it was permitting the shipment only of arms which it had contracted to supply before the East Pakistan revolt broke out. In the circumstances and in view of the use to which the arms would be put it seemed to many Americans that it would have been possible and humane to stop the shipments. The Department of State, seeming after some hesitation to be inclined to get in step with public opinion, announced on November 7, 1971, more than eight months after the East Pakistan revolt started, that it had decided to cancel licenses for the export of something more than $3 million worth of military equipment covered by agreement with Pakistan but not yet dispatched. On December 3 the United States government announced that it had cancelled remaining export licenses amounting to $11.3 million for India for military and other "sensitive equipment" (apparently meaning electronic and other materials that could be used in warfare) because of "continuing Indian incursions into Pakistan"; two days earlier it had cancelled licenses of $3 million for India.

On December 3 India and Pakistan each declared that the other had started warfare by attacking. India claimed that Pakistani airplanes had bombed eight Indian airfields in Kashmir, the Punjab, and Rajasthan; Pakistan announced that India had attacked air bases in West Pakistan. On the next day each side announced that the other's ground forces were endeavoring to invade its territory. It will perhaps never be possible to say which side struck first, but it is clear that both sides had built up forces on both fronts, eastern and western, and the movements of the two sides against each other must have started so close together in time that an effort to establish priority is meaningless. By the next day each side was announcing that a full-scale war was in progress, having been begun by the other.

On December 4 "a senior State Department official," speaking at a special news briefing at the State Department, said "the beginning of the crisis can fairly be said to be the use of force by Pakistan. We believe that since the beginning of the crisis Indian policy, in a systematic way, has led to the perpetuation of the crisis, a deepening of the crisis, and that India bears the major responsibility for the broader hostilities that have ensued." The briefing, reported in the *New York Times* the next day, was called as the United States announced that it had joined in requesting an emergency session of the United Nations Security Council to discuss the India-Pakistani fighting. The United States decision, announced by Secretary of State William P. Rogers, followed virtual round-the-clock deliberations in Washington. Rogers said the decision had been made because the "deteriorating situation posed a threat to international peace and security." The State Department spokesman who read the announcement added that the United States hoped the Security Council could take prompt action on steps to bring about a cease-fire and withdrawal of forces.

The Security Council considered a resolution incorporating the views of the United States but without being able to adopt it because of Russian opposition, which, because the Soviet Union has a permanent right of veto, negated the majority view. The matter was then transferred to the General Assembly. There the sentiment was in favor of the resolution, the vote being 104 in favor and 11 opposed, with 10 abstentions. But a vote of the General Assembly is not binding, and India would not accede to the majority vote. The United States firmly supported the resolution; the Soviet Union just as firmly opposed it. In India the position of the United States in affirming that "India bears the major responsibility for the broader hostilities" was deeply resented, while the position of the Soviet Union was warmly appreciated. The Indian resentment was accentuated by the fact that on December 6 the State Department announced that it was cutting off $87.6 million in development loans to India, aid which was entirely economic in character and not military. The State Department spokesman defending this action said that "The United States is not making a short-term contribution to the Indian economy to make it easier for the Indian government to maintain its military efforts."

On December 10 the American nuclear-powered aircraft carrier *Enterprise* with a task force of several amphibious ships and destroyers left Saigon for the Straits of Malacca and the Bay of Bengal. The purpose of this move was not made clear. It was said that the *Enterprise* was to be at hand if Americans had to be evacuated from Pakistan as the Indian forces closed in on Dacca; it was also said that the Soviet Union was increasing its naval strength in the Indian Ocean. By January 11, 1972, the *Enterprise* and accompanying vessels had left the Bay of Bengal for the Philippines, its mission in the Bay of Bengal still not explained to the public. In India the general belief is that the American purpose in dispatching the *Enterprise* to the Bay of Bengal was intimidation of India.

The three nations involved in the creation of Bangladesh promptly began to react after the cessation of hostilities, but in different ways. In Bangladesh an immediately pressing problem was to disarm the guerrillas lest widespread disorder should develop, and on January 17 Sheikh Mujib ordered them to surrender their arms to government agents within ten days. In (formerly West) Pakistan President Bhutto launched into activity to restore national self-confidence, proceed with framing the new constitution, build up the economy, prevent disaffection in the northwest frontier area and Baluchistan, and shore up foreign relations. In India Mrs. Gandhi began to capitalize on the popular victory over Pakistan as campaign material for the forthcoming elections for the state assemblies.

The rehabilitation of Bangladesh after the rapine, destruction, torture, and slaughter its people have suffered is now one of the world's problems and obligations. The country's own resources will not be adequate to repair all the damage that has been inflicted upon it. The wealthier nations of the world will have to come to her aid.

12 Internal Political Developments

At the time of partition and independence in 1947 the most urgent problems of India and Pakistan differed and their resources for meeting them differed as well. Hence there has been a great contrast in their political and economic progress.

India inherited from British India the capital, the administrative machinery, much the greater part of the administrative personnel, the bulk of the transportation system, and all but one of the great seaports. In addition the new nation had most of undivided India's industrial resources at its command, enabling it in fair measure to cope with the unexpected problems arising from partition. To attack the problem of political reorganization, India had an advantage in that the Constituent Assembly was already in session in New Delhi and had made some progress toward drafting a constitution. Further, India had an asset in the fact that the Indian National Congress, which had directed the march toward independence, had since its inception in 1885 concerned itself with political, social, and economic problems of the country and hence had acquired a philosophy of national growth and development.

Pakistan, however, had to devote all its energies to the problems of its own housekeeping. It had no national capital. It had inherited the capital of the Punjab, Lahore, when that province was divided, but Bengal was ruled in Calcutta, and Pakistan had therefore to create a provincial capital for East Bengal at Dacca, an ancient center of culture, education, and political distinction, but lacking administrative equipment. For a national capital Pakistan chose its then second largest city, Karachi, a seaport without a historic tradition, but having an advantage over its first city, Lahore, the cultural center of West Pakistan, which was militarily exposed to India. (Later Pakistan was to create a new capital called Islamabad near Rawalpindi in the north.) The national government moved into the buildings in Karachi built for the Sind provincial government. The Sind government had then to find makeshift quarters and was relegated to Hyderabad, a hundred miles to the northeast.

The new governments were allotted office equipment from the old Indian government, the pertinent portions of the files, and other necessities, but the division had to be made hastily and Pakistan had the disadvantage of being on the receiving end, not the dispensing. Further, rail communication was precarious because of disturbances in the Punjab. Pakistan felt that it received less than its share, whether by intent in New Delhi or by arson or other sabotage on the railway.

Another handicap was that the trained office personnel of the government of undivided India was more Hindu than Muslim and elected to remain with India rather than transfer to Pakistan. On the higher administrative levels similar situations existed; the Muslims had less than a proportionate amount of trained executives and administrators. This was a consequence of the Muslim failure to patronize modern education.

Added to this was the fact that Karachi was quite unprepared to accommodate the administrative machinery of a nation then numbering somewhere around 70 million persons. Sudden expansion was the consequence. In the census of 1941 Karachi's population had been only 360,000; in the 1951 census estimate it was given as 1,118,000. There were few available houses for officials, quarters for the new workers, shelter for the great number of refugees who poured in. Nor were the materials at hand for building new accommodations. Old residents lucky enough to have good houses but unlucky enough not to be in government service were firmly dispossessed. Houses of less value, especially those of non-Muslims, located in something less than the best parts of the city, if left vacant for a day or two, or perhaps only a few hours, were liable to be occupied by refugee squatters, whom the government either could not or would not evict. One result was a steady exodus of non-Muslims, among whom were many Parsis prominent in the city's commercial life. As they left they took their capital, as far as they were able, with them, depriving the city and nation of means that might have helped it adapt to the critical conditions. Conciliatory words from the government, which recognized the disadvantage in letting these people leave, did not assuage their fear as they heard what was happening in the Punjab or as close as in Hyderabad (Sind), only a few hours away by train or motor road.

Another severe handicap lay in the fact that East Pakistan was almost a thousand miles distant from West. There was no rail connection; communication by water, which required a voyage all the way down the Arabian Sea, around Ceylon, and up to the extreme end of the Bay of Bengal, 2700 miles or more, was slow at best. With crowded port conditions at Karachi and only a second-class port, Chittagong, available to receive ships in East Pakistan, little could be sent by sea. Because of the economic war with India, what facilities Chittagong had were soon preempted for shipping raw jute, Pakistan's chief source of foreign exchange. Mail service and personal travel could use air, and Pakistan quickly established its own airline, but this needed supplementing by ground and water to be adequate.

In the circumstances government was a difficult matter, particularly since the Bengalis and the West Pakistanis as groups had no very high degree of congeniality. For from before the birth of the nation the two wings had had troublesome cultural and economic contrasts leading to political maladjustment. Linguistically, the West Pakistanis vigorously promoted Urdu, while the East Pakistanis tenaciously defended the status of Bengali. Economically, East Pakistan was less advanced in industry, in trade, and in urban development than West Pakistan. It was a rice and jute area, and through the export of unprocessed jute gained the nation most of its needed foreign exchange. It also had the larger population, though the smaller territory. West Pakistan was a wheat- and cotton-growing region, produced little foreign exchange, and, though the smaller in population, had the greater weight in the nation's councils. East Pakistan therefore from the beginning of the nation's existence felt itself the victim of discrimination.

Nor had the Muslim League, as the driving machine in the making of Pakistan, been accustomed to think in terms of economic and social creativity. Ever since its birth in 1906 it had devoted itself almost solely to consideration of the Muslim community's grievances and satisfaction of its minority interests. It had never developed a constructive national political, social, and economic viewpoint. At the time of partition it was boycotting the Indian Constituent Assembly, which was meeting in New Delhi; its energies were given only to separatism.

The chief asset of the state of Pakistan in getting a start lay in the spirit of the personnel in its service. In the autumn of 1947 Karachi had an air of creative enthusiasm and crusading zeal something like that among the hastily assembled staffs of the newly established war agencies in Washington in 1941–1942. Most of the executives in Karachi were filling posts several echelons above any they had held in government service before; many were in government service for the first time, and the average age was low for the degree of responsibility. But they had a sense of purpose; they had drive; they were working for God and their new country, which they had struggled to create and at whose birth many of them had lost jobs, property, kin. Just across the border was Hindustan, Land of the Hindus, which they called "the enemy," and from whose malignancy they felt they had freed themselves. They were convinced that they could outmatch this enemy again. His mere presence was a stimulus to build their nation. The ramshackle offices in the old secretariat held the amateur's ardor and a democratic camaraderie different from the routine and often jaded calm of the professional bureaucrats in New Delhi. By 1950 some of this first fine freshness had already gone, as had the Great Leader, but the Pakistanis still saw the plotting Hindu foe to the eastward, denying them Kashmir, checking the flow of their rivers, fighting an economic war. Though fissures existed in their body politic, when they thought of India their anger mounted and they united in action.

Both nations, during the critical first years after partition, lost great national heroes and leaders. India lost Gandhi in 1948 and Patel in 1950; Pakistan lost Jinnah in 1948 and Liaquat Ali Khan in 1951.

In the first five years after partition each nation had serious economic situations complicating the political problem. Pakistan's condition was more critical than India's and each aspect of the situation put an even heavier drain upon Pakistan's resources than upon India's. Each had to handle a tremendous refugee problem, which especially in East Bengal and West Punjab, both lying in Pakistan, might have brought anarchy.

Each nation was also on a war footing, Pakistan more fully so than India. Pakistan was supporting a front at the extreme north, some 800 miles by rail from Karachi, which was the only port of ingress for equipment, fuel, and other supplies. When coal from

India failed to arrive, Pakistan converted as many locomotives as possible to oil burners, for which the oil had to be imported, and curtailed drastically the passenger and normal freight service. In consequence during 1947–1948 the railway stations throughout Sind and the Punjab held large quantities of unmoved wheat and cotton, which being unmarketed became an economic liability, and hence a political issue.

The refugee situation that followed partition contained a second economic problem besides that of relief and rehabilitation. The farms vacated in the Punjab by Sikhs were left without care at a critical time. They could not be saved by incoming refugees, who came too late and in confusion and could not be moved in rapidly enough to take over. During the season of 1947–1948, therefore, much was lost. In the spring of 1948, when it was time to sow for the next crop, the withholding of water by India in the canal waters dispute caused further damage. This was the situation in West Pakistan. In East Pakistan the refugee movement and the economic war with India involving the disposal of jute brought additional serious loss. Pakistan's position was temporarily aided when the Korean War in 1950 produced a greatly enhanced demand for jute, of which Pakistan then had virtually a world monopoly. When that demand ceased, economic gloom again descended on the country.

India was able to institute economic planning, inaugurating its First Five-Year Plan in 1951. Pakistan drafted its First Five-Year Plan to go in operation in 1955, but the plan did not get the government's formal approval until 1957 and, according to a statement in the Second Five-Year Plan, never received full support until Ayub Khan's government came into power in October 1958. The targets reached were very few.

India was able to get through that first quinquennium with some slight economic progress and consolidation of the political aspects of government. In the ten years following it had to meet many internal crises. So far it has survived without impairment of the democratic political institutions with which its leaders started in 1947 and, in fact, it has extended them. Pakistan was not able to preserve the kind of political democracy it received from the days of British rule over unpartitioned India, and in October 1958 it accepted peacefully a military dictatorship. Less than a year later in June 1959 it accepted the idea of a different kind of democracy, which General Ayub Khan, forsaking the despotism traditional in a military dictatorship, proposed in its place, and this was formally written into the constitution of 1962.

Because of these differences in political and economic resources and national outlook it was possible for India to proceed at once to political reorganization, while Pakistan had to attend to other matters first. Hence there has been a notable difference in their political progress.

On becoming dominions at the time of independence in 1947, India and Pakistan acquired status like that of the other dominions in the Commonwealth. In each the ceremonial head of state was a governor general appointed by the British Crown on the advice of the dominion cabinet. The Indian cabinet had asked that Earl Mountbatten, the last governor general and viceroy under the old order, should be governor general under the new, and he was so appointed. He remained in this position until June 1948, when Chakravarti Rajagopalachari, who was then governor of West Bengal, succeeded him, to continue until the new constitution went into effect in 1950, whereupon, as India became a sovereign republic, the position lapsed. At that time Babu Rajendra Prasad, a Congress party stalwart of long standing, became head of state as president of the Republic and continued in this position until May 1962, when Dr. Sarvepalli Radhakrishnan, philosopher and scholar, succeeded him. The cabinet was headed from the beginning by Pandit Jawaharlal Nehru, who had headed India's interim government (1946–1947) up to partition.

Pakistan would not have Lord Mountbatten as governor general and Jinnah took the position, holding it until his death in September 1948. He was much more than a ceremonial head of state, functioning instead as the autocratic, though honored and trusted, Great Leader (Qaid-i-Azam), the active ruler of the nation exercising what was in effect a kind of dictatorship. His successor was al-Haj Khwaja Nazimuddin, who had been premier of East Bengal. In October 1951, when Prime Minister Liaquat Ali Khan was assassinated, Nazimuddin himself took the premiership. He was succeeded by Ghulam Mohammed, till then finance minister of the Pakistan cabinet, who held the office until he retired ill in September 1955. Ghulam Mohammed was succeeded in October by Major General Iskander Mirza (1899–1969), who after the adoption and promulgation of a constitution in March 1956 became the first

President of the "Islamic Republic of Pakistan." Mirza abrogated the constitution on October 7, 1958, and invited the army to take over power, which it did. Then promptly on October 27 the army overthrew him; General Mohammad Ayub Khan, commander of the army, took the presidency, which he held until 1969.

In each dominion its portion of the Constituent Assembly that had been created in undivided India after the 1946 elections acted as an interim parliament. In the provinces the legislative assemblies which had been elected in 1945–1946 continued to function; in the case of the divided provinces of Bengal and the Punjab, the legislature was split also.

When partition took place, India was able to start at once to solve its problems of integrating the Indian states and framing a constitution. The Constituent Assembly adopted a constitution on November 26, 1949, which went into effect on January 26, 1950, when India became a republic. The first general elections under the constitution were held in 1951–52, when a central legislature or parliament and state legislatures were elected. A second general election was held in 1957, a third in 1962, a fourth in 1967, and a fifth in 1971.

Pakistan's Constituent Assembly produced no definite result until March 12, 1949, when it adopted an objectives resolution. By September 1954 it had all but completed a constitution, but on October 24 Governor General Ghulam Mohammed dissolved it to prevent enforcement of bills which would have restricted the Governor General's powers. In 1955, however, the Pakistan Federal Court ruled that a new Constituent Assembly must be created. A second Constitutent Assembly was therefore convened in July. A new constitution was enacted and put in force on March 26, 1956, by which Pakistan became an "Islamic Republic." This constitution, however, was abrogated in October 1958 by President Iskander Mirza, an avowed secularist, who also declared that the nation's name was henceforth to be simply "Pakistan." General Ayub Khan, who dispossessed Major General Mirza as president that same month, continued using the nonreligious name for the nation. Under General Ayub Khan political parties were outlawed and a new constitution was promulgated on March 1, 1962.

The provincial legislatures of Pakistan have fared much like the federal assembly. Their life, by a bit of legalistic juggling, was extended from the five-year period for which they had been elected in 1946, before partition, to 1953 and then to 1954, whereupon in March fresh elections were held. In East Pakistan (East Bengal) the United Front, which was hostile to the Muslim League and the federal government, swept the elections, but the legislature so elected was not allowed to meet until the Federal Court ruled in 1955 that a new Constituent Assembly had to be convened and this could be done only through elections by the provincial assemblies. By that time the United Front had cracked apart, and the government reestablished cabinet government in East Bengal. In the western wing of Pakistan the various provinces were in 1954 fused into a single united province called West Pakistan thereby putting it and East Pakistan on a parity, and in January 1956 the members of the former provincial assemblies elected an interim legislature for the new province. When the constitution of 1956 was abrogated in 1958, the central and provincial legislative assemblies were dissolved and dismissed in both West and East Pakistan. On June 12, 1959, Ayub Khan's government ("the Revolutionary Government") announced that rule would be by a system of representative government, known generally as "Basic Democracies," which will be described below. Under the new constitution of 1962, using the method prescribed in it, Pakistan elected a national assembly at the end of April 1962 and provincial assemblies on May 6, 1962.

Pakistan's political instability affected not only the governor generalship and the legislature but also the premiership, which had seven incumbents from 1947 to 1958, when it was discontinued. The seven premiers were: Liaquat Ali Khan (1947–October 16, 1951); Khwaja Nazimuddin (October 1951–April 1953); Mohammed Ali (April 1953–August 1955); Chaudhri Mohamad Ali (August 1955–September 1956); H. S. Suhrawardy (September 1956–October 1957); I. I. Chundrigar (October 1957–December 1957); Firoz Khan Noon (December 1957–October 7, 1958). In October 1958 Iskander Mirza suspended parliamentary government. General Ayub Khan, on sending Mirza into exile and himself taking the government on October 27, became his own prime minister.

Reorganization of the political structure of the two nations had proceeded on the basis of the structure existing in preindependence India. This was administered at the center by a governor general (viceroy), who was appointed by the British Crown on the advice of the British cabinet. It contained two kinds of political entities.

The first was British India, consisting of eleven governor's provinces and six chief commissioner's provinces. The governor's provinces were administered by governors who were appointed by the British Crown and functioned under the governor general; in these provinces there were elective legislative bodies and ministries responsible to them; the provinces were Assam, Bengal, Bihar, Bombay, Central Provinces and Berar, Madras, the North-West Frontier Province, Orissa, the Punjab, Sind, the United Provinces. The chief commissioner's provinces were administered directly under the governor general and possessed no legislatures; they were Ajmer-Merwara, British Baluchistan, Coorg, Delhi, Panth Piploda, and the Andaman and Nicobar Islands.

The second political element was princely India, known as the Indian (formerly Native) States, 565 in number, autocratically ruled with varying degrees of autonomy. Some of them had acquired legislatures, usually of very much limited powers, whose members were partly elected by a small electorate, partly appointed by the ruler. The constitution of 1935 had provided for federation of British India and the Indian States, but his had never been effected and the central government was still operating under the 1919 constitution. At the center and in the provinces of British India legislatures had been freshly elected during the winter of 1945–1946, and in 1946 the provincial legislative assemblies so composed had acted under the provisions of the British Cabinet Mission's plan of that year to elect a constituent assembly which was to frame a new constitution. The Indian States, having remained unfederated, were not in a legal position to participate in the constituent assembly.

One of the first tasks which the government of the new India set itself was to eliminate the contradiction in form and spirit between the autocratic rule of the Indian States and the liberalizing rule of the provinces. This had been an avowed Congress policy since 1938. Until it was done the country could not have a constitution uniformly applicable throughout all its parts. The procedure was first to get the accession of the Indian States and secondly to assimilate them to the new national political structure. The means lay at hand in the authority which the new dominions had received under the Indian Independence Act to call into effect by an Order in Council the unused provision of the 1935 constitution for federation. The task of bringing the States into line fell to

Sardar Vallabhbhai Patel, Deputy Prime Minister and Minister for States and Home Affairs. He was another party stalwart, noted for his mental brilliance, sharp repartee, inflexible will, "the iron man" of Congress. He had an able assistant in V. P. Menon, secretary of state affairs.

The Indian government knew what it wanted, and the princes were in a defenseless position. Most rulers hastened to conform to the obvious necessities when the government told them its will. The first step was to have the States sign standstill agreements at the time of independence or shortly thereafter. Lord Mountbatten took a large part in urging them to do so. Then came the process of accession and "integration" (Patel's term) of the approximately 550 States that were in India's orbit.

There were three kinds of integration. A number of small States not separately viable, were merged with those former governor's provinces that had fallen to India and were later known under the first schedule of the constitution of 1950 as Part A states. Of the medium-sized and the other small States 275 were integrated into five large political unions, in each of which a council of the rulers in the union elected one of their number to be *rajpramukh* (chief of state). Such a union had to develop an elected legislature and government by a cabinet responsible to it. Three of the largest States—Kashmir, Hyderabad, Mysore—were allowed to retain separate existence, and the rulers of Hyderabad and Mysore automatically became *rajpramukhs*. Kashmir elected as its chief of state (*sadar-i-riyasat*) the heir apparent to the throne. These unions and separate states had identical status under the constitution of 1950, which called them Part B states. Finally 61 medium-sized States, some maintaining their preintegration identity and some being made into new units, and three of the former chief commissioner's provinces (Ajmer, Coorg, Delhi) were placed under the direct administration of the central government and were classified by the constitution of 1950 as Part C states. They were later given democratic institutions.

By various moves the whole former array of provinces in British India and the partly autonomous Indian States were reorganized, until in 1962 the states of all India numbered fifteen, while legislative provision had been made for a sixteenth (Nagaland), and with them were eight territories (including the former French and Portuguese possessions under the designations Pondicherry, Goa, and Daman and Diu) and one protected state (Sikkim).

In this way India ended the princes' autocratic rule, and the princes were reduced in income and prerogatives until most of them became a kind of landed gentry. The transition proved far simpler and more successful than many observers, even some who were sympathetic to Indian nationalism, had foreseen. In the 1951–1952, 1957, 1962, and 1967 elections a number of former princes ran for legislative office and many won.

Pakistan also effected the accession of those former Indian States that lay within its orbit, always remembering that the status of Jammu and Kashmir was in dispute. In the case of Kalat in Baluchistan it had to suppress a revolt.

Work on the new constitution of India was begun before partition by the Constituent Assembly, which, however, was being boycotted by the Muslim League. The Assembly convened in New Delhi on December 9, 1946, and on January 22, 1947, adopted a resolution that India should become an "independent sovereign republic," thus to fulfill the Congress aim of "full self-rule." Late in 1948 after partition, the drafting committee presented a draft, on which debate began in November. The revised document was finally approved by the Assembly about a year later, on November 26, 1949, and the constitution was made effective on January 26, 1950, the official Indian Independence Day, observed annually in commemoration of the day in 1930 when Congress first formally celebrated the adoption of full self-rule as its goal.

The Indian constitution as printed in 1950 is a book of 251 pages, comprising 395 sections and eight schedules, one of the largest, perhaps the largest, such document known. It was drafted by a committee of distinguished Indians, under the chairmanship of Dr. B. R. Ambedkar (1891–1956), an Untouchable, who was law minister of the Indian cabinet. It embodies many principles for which the Indian National Congress had been an advocate before independence. For one, it is secular, meaning to discriminate neither for nor against any religious group. For another it denies, by simply ignoring, the "two-nation" theory, on which the Muslim League succeeded in getting India split into two nations. It makes no provision for separate electorates or administrative appointments to Muslims, Sikhs, or any other community, with the exception of some temporary ten-year concessions to Anglo-Indians, the Scheduled Castes (Untouchables), and the backward Scheduled Tribes. Thus it repudiates political communalism.

The positive purposes of the constitution are indicated in its preamble, which declares that India is to be "a Sovereign Democratic Republic," which has as its purpose "to secure to all its citizens: Justice, social, economic, political; Liberty of thought, expression, belief, faith, and worship; Equality of status and opportunity; and to promote among them all Fraternity assuring the dignity of the individual and the unity of the Nation."

A bill of rights is contained in part III, which specifically declares invalid any laws of the state (meaning the Union, the separate states, and local authorities) infringing them. It provides for equality before the law and forbids titles. It prescribes that "no citizen shall, on grounds only of religion, race, caste, sex, place of birth, or any of them, be subject to any disability, liability, restriction, or conditions with regard to—(a) access to shops, public restaurants, hotels and places of public entertainment; or (b) the use of wells, tanks, bathing ghats, roads, and places of public resort maintained wholly or partly out of State funds or dedicated to the use of the general public." It says specifically " 'Untouchability' is abolished and its practice in any form is forbidden."

Citizens are to receive equality of opportunity for public employment through a clause providing that "No citizen may, on grounds only of religion, race, caste, sex, descent, place of birth, residence, or any of them, be ineligible for, or discriminated against in respect of, any employment or office under the State."

With respect to the guaranteed rights of freedom of speech, assembly, and others, there is a modifying provision for "reasonable restrictions." Freedom of conscience and the right to profess, practice, and propagate religion are guaranteed subject to public order, morality, and health. But the state reserves the right to regulate or restrict economic, financial, political, or other secular activity, to provide for social welfare and reform, and to throw open "Hindu" (including Sikh, Jain, and Buddhist) religious institutions of a public character, meaning chiefly temples, to all classes and sections of "Hindus."

In institutions supported wholly by state funds no religious instruction may be offered, and in no other institution recognized by the state or receiving any financial assistance from the state may any student be required to attend religious instruction or religious worship except with his own or his guardian's consent.

The constitution contains a list of directive principles of state policy, which are "fundamental in the governance of the country and it shall be the duty of the State to apply these principles in making laws," though they "shall not be enforceable by any court." They include the fostering of an "economic system which does not result in the concentration of wealth and means of production to the common detriment; development of decent working conditions for workers; equal pay for equal work of men and women; old-age, unemployment, and disability benefits; protection of children; the fostering of village panchayats (councils)." The state is required by the constitution, within ten years after the date of its enforcement, to provide free compulsory education for all children under fourteen, a provision it has not yet been possible to implement, though progress has been made. The government also is to bring about prohibition and is to prevent "slaughter of cows and calves, and other milch and draught cattle"—two provisions that echo Hindu religious dogma, though some apologists maintain that they were entirely economic in motivation. In its foreign affairs India is to promote international peace and security, maintain just and honorable relations between nations, foster respect for international law and treaty obligations, and encourage the settlement of international disputes by arbitration. Many of the various provisions, prohibitions, and principles, such as the abolition of untouchability, are still not fully achieved, though some legislation has been enacted and some change is discernible, especially with respect to untouchability. Those statements concerning international relations Pakistani spokesmen repeatedly declare India ignores in relations with Pakistan.

The government structure is federal, but its prevailing tone is centralization of power. The head of state is a president, who is also supreme commander of the defense forces. He is elected for a five-year term by an electoral college consisting of the elected members of both legislative chambers of the central government and the elected members of the legislatures of the states, whose separate votes are weighted to correspond to the population of their constituencies. The president is "aided and advised" by a Council of Ministers headed by a prime minister, whom he chooses and with whose advice he chooses the other ministers. The president is intended to function as a ceremonial head of state, acting on the advice of the prime minister; his position, therefore, is analogous to that of a constitutional monarch. There is a vice president, elected in a joint session of both houses of the central legislature, who presides over the upper house.

The central legislature is bicameral. The upper chamber is called the Council of States (*Rajya Sabha*) and consists of 250 members, of whom 12 are appointed by the president for distinction in literature, art, science, or other fields. The rest are elected by the members of the lower houses of the state legislatures. The members of the Council of States serve for six years; one third of the total number complete their terms each biennium.

The lower chamber is called House of the People (*Lok Sabha*). It consists of 500 members, elected for a term of five years, by universal adult (21 years or over) suffrage so that each member represents not more than 750,000 persons or less than 500,000. The Council of Ministers is responsible as a whole to this body as the British cabinet is to the House of Commons, and must command its confidence to function. No one not a member of the Parliament may remain a minister longer than six months.

To become a law a bill other than a money bill must be passed by both chambers. As with the British Parliament, the upper chamber cannot initiate a money bill and cannot prevent enactment of one passed by the lower chamber, but may, if it acts within fourteen days, make recommendations concerning it. The president may assent to a bill, withhold his assent, or refer it back with recommendations, which, however, the Parliament need not accept, whereupon the president may no longer withhold assent.

The judiciary belongs to the central government, which appoints it, and has ample safeguards; there are no separate state judiciaries. At the top is a Supreme Court, which decides constitutional issues.

The administrative machinery of the states is modeled in many respects on that of the central government. The states have governors appointed by the president (that is, the national cabinet) to hold office during his pleasure, normally for a term of five years. Each governor, like the president, is aided and advised by a council of ministers, which is responsible to the state's legislature—if the legislature is bicameral, to the lower house. The governor is closely dependent upon the central government and is more than a ceremonial head; there are certain functions which he exercises "in his discretion" and not on the advice of his ministers.

The states have bicameral or unicameral legislatures. An upper house is called a Legislative Council; the lower house, Legislative Assembly. An upper house in any state may be created or abolished by a majority of the central parliament if the lower house of that state passes a resolution for such action. The legislative assemblies have a representative for each constituency of approximately 75,000 persons. A governor, besides having the power to assent to a bill, refuse his assent, or refer it for reconsideration, may reserve it for the assent of the president of the union.

The division of powers between the union and the states is clearly defined. All powers not specified, that is residual power, vest in the union. The constitution gives the union and the states concurrently broad power over economic and social planning; commercial and industrial monopolies, companies, and trusts; social security and social insurance; employment and unemployment. The way is thus laid open for economic and social development under whatever degree and variety of government control conditions may make advisable.

In the case of an emergency "whereby the security of India or any part of the territory thereof is threatened, whether by war or external aggression or internal disturbance" (actual or potential), the president may issue a proclamation of emergency which remains in force for two months and longer if approved by both houses of parliament. During that period the guarantees to individuals under the bill of rights may be suspended, the president may issue administrative orders for any state, and the union parliament may legislate on subjects normally restricted to state action. There is a similar emergency provision for the government of any state to be assumed by the president.

The Indian constitution has operated with but little change since it was put in force in 1950. A number of amendments have been enacted under the terms laid down by the constitution. Two of them established the principles for redrawing state boundaries and safeguarding linguistic minorities within states. The other amendments increased the power of the central government in respect to social reform, limitation of freedom of speech, reapportionment of seats on the basis of census returns, reservation of seats for certain constituencies, transfer of territory to Pakistan, creation of legislatures and councils of ministers in union territories, nationalization of the banks. There have been some alterations in the list of legislative subjects handled concurrently by the central and state governments, and procedure has been devised for settling disputes over compensation of landlords in effecting agrarian reform.

The first elections to the House of the People and to the state legislatures under the new Indian constitution took place in the winter of 1951–52, and the number of eligible voters was estimated at about 176 million. Of these about 106 million (60 percent) valid votes were polled for the House of the People and about 102.5 million (58 percent) for the state legislative assemblies. There were eight principal national parties and over forty other local parties in the various contests. For balloting purposes the boxes were designated by party symbols. Congress was overwhelmingly victorious in the central and most state elections. In May 1952 Dr. Rajendra Prasad was elected president and Professor Sarvepalli Radhakrishnan, who had been India's ambassador to the Soviet Union, was elected vice president. Nehru was named prime minister. The same three persons received the same offices after the 1957 elections. After the 1962 elections, Radhakrishnan was elected president, Dr. Zakir Hussain, distinguished educator and governor of the state of Bihar, was elected vice president, and Nehru remained prime minister. In 1962 Zakir Hussain was elected president to succeed Radhakrishnan, who had retired. Hussain died in office May 3, 1969, and was succeeded by V. V. Giri. Nehru was prime minister until 1964; Lal Bahadur Shastri served in that post from 1964 to 1966, when he was succeeded by Mrs. Indira Gandhi.

Constitutional development in Pakistan has been quite a different story. Pakistan's first Constituent Assembly adopted a resolution of aims and objectives in March 1949, but never got a constitution accepted before it was dissolved on October 24, 1954. The second Constituent Assembly produced a constitution of 234 articles, with five schedules, which was put in force March 26, 1956. Two and a half years later (October 1958) it was abrogated by President Mirza. President Ayub Khan, after assuming the rule of Pakistan and being confirmed by the people of Pakistan on February 14, 1960, set up a commission to draft a new constitution, which he promulgated on March 1, 1962.

By the terms of the 1956 constitution the Islamic Republic of Pakistan was a federal structure. The constitution contained a bill of rights and a section of directive principles of state policy. The president of the republic was elected by the members of the national and provincial assemblies. He governed through a prime minister and cabinet appointed by him and enjoying the confidence of the National Assembly. The National Assembly was unicameral, half in each province, that is, half in East Pakistan, and half in West Pakistan, and consisted of 300 members, though for ten years additional seats were to be provided for women. It was normally to have a life of five years. The president had the power to summon, prorogue, or dissolve the National Assembly, and fix the time and place of its meeting, except that at least one session a year had to be held in Dacca. To become law a bill required the assent of the president; if he withheld it and it was revoted by a two-thirds majority he was required to give his assent. A proposal for expenditure could originate only with the government. The government in the two provinces was patterned in large part on that of the federal government. Each province had a governor appointed by the president and he had a cabinet. Each provincial assembly had 300 members. There were federal, provincial, and concurrent lists of legislative subjects. The judiciary was federal. The president had emergency rights to assume the powers of a provincial government and legislative assembly and to legislate for the province. During the period of an emergency the president could suspend fundamental rights. A proclamation of emergency was valid for two months but could be extended by the National Assembly for another four months.

There was a Muslim flavor to the constitution. The preamble opened with the words "In the name of Allah, the Beneficent, the Merciful"—translation of a familiar Muslim invocation in Arabic— and proceeded directly to say, "Whereas sovereignty over the entire Universe belongs to Allah Almighty alone, and the authority to be exercised by the people of Pakistan within the limits prescribed by Him is a sacred trust; Whereas the Founder of Pakistan, Quaid-i-Azam Mohammad Ali Jinnah, declared that Pakistan would be a democratic state based on Islamic principles of social justice; And whereas the Constituent Assembly representing the people of Pakistan have resolved to frame for the sovereign independent State of Pakistan a constitution . . . wherein the Muslims of Pakistan should be enabled individually and collectively to order their lives in accordance with the teachings and requirements of Islam, as set out in the Holy Quran and Sunna (tradition) . . ." (the preamble then indicated that "provision should be made for the minorities freely to profess and practice their religion and develop their culture"). The president had to be a Muslim (article 32 [2]). In part XII, chapter I, entitled "Islamic Provisions," articles 197–198 provided that "the President should set up an organization for Islamic research and instruction in advanced studies to assist in the reconstruction of Muslim society on a truly Islamic basis . . . No law shall be enacted which is repugnant to the injuctions of Islam as laid down in the Holy Quran and Sunna."

No general election was held in Pakistan until 1959, though one had frequently been promised. Some Pakistani critics have said that this is the reason government fell into chaos in Pakistan; others have maintained that it was the inefficient and self-interested activity of irresponsible politicians that prevented a general election and good government alike. Whichever, if either, view is correct, the political instability at last led to a break with the existing administrative structure and system of administration.

After the constitution of 1956 was abrogated by Mirza in 1958 and a military dictatorship was accepted by the nation, General Ayub Khan as military dictator promulgated a system of government by "Basic Democracies," announced by "the Revolutionary Government" on June 12, 1959, enlarged by the Basic Democracies Order of October 26, 1959, and then fixed in the constitution of 1962. This proceeds from the premise that a type of democratic government based on the British system, such as was established by the Pakistan constitution of 1956, is not feasible in Pakistan. Ayub Khan frequently developed this thesis. In his words, in an underdeveloped and poor country, where the "rate of literacy is appallingly low" and the "means of communication are poor, even primitive," among the rural population, "which constitutes over 80 percent of the total," some other system is required to ascertain the will of the people, bring them good government, and prevent the kind of abuses, corruption, and misgovernment that were flourishing in 1958, and to satisfy the pressing national need for reconstruction. His system recalls some features of the Soviet government structure and the system inaugurated in Egypt under Nasser, and also, at its local level, of the village Panchayat system traditional in India and now being promoted there.

The scheme of Basic Democracies aimed to achieve reconstruction at five levels: (1) union councils or town committees, (2) subdivision (thana) or tehsil councils, (3) district councils, (4) division councils, (5) provincial advisory development councils, one for East and one for West Pakistan. At every level membership was partly by election and partly by central government appointment, but the lowest level was the only one at which general direct election by the enfranchised population actually took place.

For the first or grass-roots operation of the system each wing of Pakistan was divided into 40,000 constituencies with an average population of around 1,000. Each constituency elected one representative by universal adult franchise, who was designated an elector. Ten such elected representatives, representing ten constituencies or approximately 10,000 people, plus five members appointed by the central government to represent special interests that might otherwise be unrepresented, formed a union council in a rural area or a town or union committee in an urban area. It elected its own chairman from among the elected members. Such rural union councils were considered to be the most important part of the whole system and chairmen of them were included in the higher tiers. They had extensive executive, judicial, and social functions in respect to local matters, and had their own funds and budget. In urban areas the town and union committees had only limited social and petty judicial functions, since their areas already had well operating municipal and cantonment boards.

The chairmen of the various union councils and town committees within the entire area that comes under the jurisdiction of a police station, plus nominated members, official and nonofficial, the latter being not more in number than half of the representative members, constituted the next, the subdivisional, tier of administration, called a tehsil council in West Pakistan and a thana council in East Pakistan. It was chaired in the West by the tehsil officer and in the East by the subdivision officer. Its function was conceived as being largely coordinative.

Above this was the district council, consisting of nominated official and nonofficial members, the latter never to be fewer than the former, while at least half of these nonofficial members had to be chosen from chairmen of union councils and town and union committees. The chairman of a district council was the administrative officer of the district, who was called a deputy commissioner. The nominated official members were chairmen of the tehsil or thana councils and municipal bodies, vice presidents of cantonment boards, and senior officers representing such departments as might be specified by the government. The district councils were expected to play an important part in the system, just as the district administration during the British period was the pivotal unit of government and deputy commissioner (or collector) who headed it was the key figure in administrative personnel. These councils had compulsory functions respecting primary education, community social activities, agricultural production, health, and highways, along with the right to extend their functions further, if they wished, in the fields of education, social and economic welfare, public works, and health.

The next tier above was that of the division council, which again functioned for an administrative unit corresponding to a unit (commissionership or division) which existed under the British rule. Its chairman was the division commissioner and its duties were largely coordinative of the activities of the local councils, municipal bodies, and cantonment boards. It consisted of representatives of government departments, municipalities, cantonment boards, and an equal number of nominated nonofficials. At least a quarter of the membership of a division council had to be composed of chairmen of union councils and town and union committees.

Finally above the division councils were the provincial development advisory councils, one for East Pakistan, and one for West Pakistan, each headed by the governor of the province and composed of equal numbers of nominated members, some of whom were official (including heads of appropriate government departments) and some nonofficial (at least one third had to be chairmen of union councils and committees). These councils advised the government on plans for reconstruction and the allocation of grants for execution of the plans.

The first elections at the grass-roots level, on which all the rest rose as a pyramid, were held in December 1959. President Ayub Khan has stated that 67 percent of eligible men voted and 42 percent of eligible women. On February 14, 1960, a single simple question of confidence in President Ayub Khan was referred to the

80,000 persons elected, being presented in English, Urdu, and Bengali, and phrased in the English version as follows (*Pakistan News Digest*, February 1, 1960): "Have you confidence in the President Field-Marshal Mohammad Ayub Khan, H.P., H.J.?" In front of it were two squares, one marked "Yes," the other "No," with symbols in the squares for illiterate voters. The results were announced as follows: "Over 95.6 percent of the elected members of the Basic Democracies who took part in the Presidential Ballot held on February 14 throughout Pakistan voted for President Mohammed Ayub Khan. The total number of votes was 79,850 (150 less than the aggregate strength of the elected members of the Basic Democracies, the vacancies being due to the pending by-elections). Of these 78,720 members cast their votes and 1,130 abstained from the vote. Of the total number of votes cast 75,283 were in favour of the President giving him a percentage of slightly over 95.6. The number of votes cast against the President was 2,829, slightly less than 3.6 percent of the total number of votes cast. The number of invalid votes was 608 or .8 percent of the total number of votes cast. Only such votes that did not give any indication of the intention of the voter were declared invalid."

After the returns were in, Ayub Khan was sworn in as President in Rawalpindi, the capital, on February 17, 1960. On the same day, in line with his previous statements, he announced the appointment of an eleven-man commission to draft a constitution. The commission completed its report April 29, 1961, and shortly thereafter submitted it to the President. The new constitution was promulgated by the President on March 1, 1962, to go into force June 8, 1962. Under its provisions the 80,000 electors elected the National Assembly of 156 members on April 28, 1962, and the two provincial assemblies of 155 members each on May 6. Martial law, under which the country had been ruled since 1958, was to cease when the new constitution should go into effect on the day of the first meeting of the National Assembly.

The Pakistan constitution of 1962 as printed is a volume of 134 pages. It has 250 articles, a preamble, and three schedules. The sturcture is federal, with a president who is not responsible to the legislature, and who is empowered to appoint ministers to assist him. The legislature is unicameral both nationally and in the two provinces of East and West Pakistan. The country bears the name "Republic of Pakistan," eliminating the word "Islamic" that appeared in the 1956 constitution, but the president still must be a Muslim. Both he and the legislative bodies have a five-year term of office, though the first president and legislatures under the constitution were to serve only three years. Political parties remained prohibited. No law might be enacted which was repugnant to Islam. Dacca in East Pakistan was to be the principal seat of the National Assembly, the new capital at Islamabad was to be the principal seat of the central government. This separation of location was an obvious device to avert jealousy between the state's two wings, even at the expense of government convenience and efficiency. Both Bengali and Urdu were national languages but English was to be continued for official use for ten years, when a commission would be appointed to consider its replacement.

The National Assembly was to have a strength of 156, exactly half of which would come from each wing of Pakistan; 6 of the seats were reserved for women (women might also stand for election to the other seats). The provincial assemblies were to have a strength of 150 plus 5 seats reserved for women. The president had to assent to a bill for it to become law. If he withheld assent and so vetoed it, the veto might be overridden by a two-thirds majority vote of the Assembly. He might dissolve the Assembly, in which case a new election had to be held within 90 days, while he himself had to stand for reelection within 120 days. There were provisions for removing him from office. He might serve no more than two terms, unless specially permitted by a joint session of the National and provincial assemblies. He appointed the governors of the provinces, which operated under ministries. There was no vice president; the speaker of the National Assembly was to function in case the president was absent from the country or ill. There was a list of "fundamental rights" and other safeguards of individual civil rights. The judiciary was to be independent. There was a list of subjects over which the central legislature had control. All other subjects were left to the provinces, though the central legislature might legislate in respect to provincial subjects when national security, or coordination of economic development, or coordination between the two provinces was concerned. An advisory council of Islamic ideology was to be appointed by the president in order that Muslims might order their lives in accordance with the teachings of Islam. It was to be supported by an Islamic Research Centre to be established by the president. The constitution had a special provision applying to the State of Jammu and Kashmir and the Republic of Pakistan "when the people of the state decide to accede to Pakistan." The relationship was to be determined in accordance with the wishes of the people of that state.

By no means all the best brains and honorable citizens in Pakistan had confidence in Ayub Khan's Basic Democracies, though all seemed to concede that his government was more efficient and more honest than any other which Pakistan had had. The first issue to rise when the new parliament was convened was that of the prohibition of political parties. The discontent over this was so great that the leaders of the prohibited parties united against President Ayub Khan on the issue to form an opposition. Thereupon the government introduced a bill to authorize the formation of parties under license. The leaders of political parties opposed this bill, but the President succeeded in July in getting it passed. Discontent with Ayub Khan's dictatorship steadily increased, especially in East Pakistan, and in spite of stern measures to control it Ayub announced on February 21, 1969, that he would not stand for reelection in the impending election. In March he agreed to opposition demands for adult franchise and a parliamentary form of government. On March 25 he announced that he was resigning his office and transferring power immediately, but not to an elected parliament, instead to the armed forces under General Agha Mohammed Yahya Khan.

Bangladesh immediately on establishing a government started work on setting up a Constituent Assembly, which Sheikh Mujib expects to draft a constitution providing a parliamentary system like that of Great Britain.

Both India and Pakistan have had serious political problems arising from regionalism, and in consequence have made changes in the country's political structure by redrawing state lines in India and provincial lines in Pakistan. Such subnationalism may have a historical background of ancient glory, now diminished, and profess economic and political goals, but it is generally expressed in terms of culture, specifically of language, which is usually both the organ and the symbol of cultural integrity. Properly manipulated subnationalism can of course become the tool of a political leader or a political party to gain power.

The desire of linguistic groups to constitute separate states is deep seated and of long standing in the subcontinent. It was first manifested in recent times when Lord Curzon partitioned Bengal in 1905. The line cut right through the Bengali language area and was regarded by speakers of Bengali as designed to destroy their ethnic solidarity and cripple political progressivism, which was much better developed in Bengal than elsewhere in India. Bengal succeeded in having the dividing line abolished and a new solution to the administrative problem adopted.

In 1920 the Indian National Congress used the concept of provincial linguistic integrity as a weapon against British imperialism. As part of its complaint, it deprecated the existing political division, calling it illogical because the lines sliced through cultural groups and so frustrated their natural aspirations. Congress, therefore, in its party constitution, adopted in that year, divided itself in the area of British India where it operated (and excluding the Indian States where it did not exist) into "Congress provinces," which were mostly delimited by language boundaries. Congress then demanded reconstruction of the political provinces according to this division. The demand was reaffirmed frequently after 1920. At the time of independence Congress had twenty so-called provinces in the eleven provinces of British India. It was widely expected that one of the first steps to be taken in independent India would be a provincial reorganization, and the Constituent Assembly set up a linguistic provinces commission chaired by Justice S. K. Dar, and hence called the Dar Commission, to advise it. But by that time there was no longer use for the idea as a club to beat imperialism and the Dar Commission looked upon the idea as calculated, if put into execution, to impair the unity so necessary to the new nation and to start a process of disintegration that might shatter the country into bits. Such provinces would all have lesser languages as well as the dominant languages, and the minorities speaking them would be liable to suffer from discrimination. In any case they were sure to make charges of discrimination. Creation of these provinces would encourage local patriotism at the expense of national interest and would generate ill feeling between neighboring provinces over the areas to be transferred when the boundaries were redrawn. Further, a number of the new provinces being advocated would be deficit provinces, not economically viable. The commission's report, therefore, disappointed the numerous and politically powerful linguistic provincialists. The Congress party therefore appointed its own linguistic provinces committee, consisting of Jawaharlal Nehru, Vallabhbhai Patel, and Pattabhi Sitaramayya—called after the members' initials the JVS Committee–which in its report conceded the justice of linguistic distribution as a basis for provincial reorganization, but felt the time inopportune to apply it.

The JVS Committee, however, made an exception of Andhra, the region where Telugu is spoken, then lying chiefly in Madras, with extension into Hyderabad and Orissa. There had once been a great Andhra empire (second century B.C. to about the end of the third century of this era), and the Andhra area has had a well-developed self-consciousness throughout history since then. The first draft of the constitution conceded the future creation of an Andhra state, but this was omitted from the final version. The proponents of an Andhra state were not quieted and engaged in agitation, demonstrations–including a fast by a Gandhi follower named Potti Sriramalu ending in death on the fifty-eighth day (December 15, 1952) –and political activity. At last on October 1, 1953, though Nehru did not relish creating a new state where Communism was stronger than anywhere else in India, an Andhra state came into existence, consisting of the northern part of Madras; in 1956 the Telugu-speaking section of Hyderabad, called Telingana, was added to it.

The desire of other linguistic regions for separate statehood was whetted by the establishment of Andhra. One area was that of the Marathi speakers, living in Bombay, Hyderabad, and Madhya Pradesh, who agitated for a state to be called Maharashtra. The area had had a period of historic greatness, starting with Shivaji (1630–1680) in the late seventeenth century and continuing into the eighteenth and early nineteenth century. Another was the Kannada-(Kanara, Kanarese) speaking area, consisting chiefly of Mysore but extending into Hyderabad and Madras. Still another was the Malayalam-speaking region, consisting of most of Travancore, Cochin, and a part of Madras along India's west coast. The Tamil speakers living in Madras and the lower end of Travancore constituted another linguistic area; the speakers of Oriya another, but much less vocal, such area. In the east the Bengali speakers, whose region had been split by partition, wanted some areas of Bihar, and in the extreme northeast speakers of various local dialects were already moving for a Naga state. In the northwest of India the Sikhs, speaking Punjabi, were loudly demanding a separate political unit.

So general was the demand that at the end of 1953 the government of India appointed a states reorganization commission to report by June 30, 1955, later given an extension of time to September 30, 1955. In 1956, to clear the way for a scheme or reorganization, the seventh amendment of the constitution was enacted. The classification of states into three categories adopted when the constitution was put into force in 1950 was now abolished and only one kind of state was recognized, with provision also for "union territories." When the constitution was adopted provision had been made for nine Part A states, eight Part B states, and ten part C states. The new Part A state of Andhra had afterwards been established and the Part C state of Bilaspur had been merged with the Part C state of Himachal Pradesh. The total therefore remained 27. The reorganization scheme put into effect September 1, 1956, reduced the total number of states to fourteen with six territories. Four Part B states were eliminated: Hyderabad, Madhya Bharat, the Patiala and East Punjab States Union, and Saurashtra. The name of one of the four remaining Part B states, Travancore-Cochin, was changed to Kerala, and the area of the state was increased by nearly 60 percent. Five of the nine Part C states were eliminated: Ajmer, Bhopal, Coorg, Kutch, and Vindhya Pradesh. Four of the Part C states were made into territories: Delhi, Himachal Pradesh, Manipur, and Tripura. Thus with the Andaman and Nicobar Islands and the Laccadive, Minicoy, and Amindivi Islands there were six centrally administered territories. Since then two other territories have been added. One was Pondicherry, composed of the French possessions in India which were formally made over to India by France in 1956; the other was Goa which was taken by India in 1961, and soon afterwards became a centrally administered area.

Bombay provided the thorniest problem. It could be made a single province, combining all the Gujarati- and Marathi-speaking areas (except some in the eastern part of the Marathi area); this proposal led to demonstrations in 1955. Or it could be divided into three units, Gujarat, Maharashtra, and a separate unit for Bombay City to be administered by the central government; this proposal led to serious rioting and bloodshed in 1955 and 1956, and the resignation on July 24, 1956, of Finance Minister C. D. Deshmukh, a Maharashtrian. In the end, the reorganization scheme of 1956 provided for a single bilingual state retaining the name Bombay. But on May 1, 1960, the state was divided into two states, Gujarat and Maharashtra, with Bombay City included in Maharashtra. The number of states then became fifteen.

There remained two dissatisfied groups, the Nagas in the extreme northeast of the subcontinent and the Sikhs in the northwest of India. The Nagas, largely led by the Naga National Council, had been resisting Indian rule and agitating for autonomy for years, claiming that their linguistic and cultural differentiation from the rest of India justified their existence as a separate nation. The demand had been firmly denied. They continued to resist, disorder developed, and Indian troops were sent to quell this in 1955 and 1956 but without succes. In 1957 the area was put under central government administration (it was previously under the Assam government). At last in July 1960 Nehru agreed that it should be a separate state. Thus India's sixteenth state was to come into being. The Nagaland (Transitional Provisions) Regulation was promulgated in January 1961 to make ready the way for the creation of the new state. In August 1962 a bill was introduced in the Lok Sabha to establish the state, which for the first ten years was to be ruled by a governor appointed in New Delhi. And Nagaland came into being on December 1, 1963.

The Sikhs' discontent has been based less on language as the decisive issue than on religion. Its roots lie deep in history, from the days of Mughal persecution, and it expressed itself in preindependence India, causing the British considerable trouble in the 1920s. In the new India the demand for separate statehood began right after independence. The Sikhs comprise over a third of the population of the Punjab. They sometimes speak of their demand as being for a Gurmukhi area, rather loosely applying to it the term for the script in which they write the Punjabi language. The Sikh area centers in Amritsar, where is located the Golden Temple, the central shrine of the Sikh religion. Their demand was promoted by an aggressive revivalist party called the Shiromani (or Shromani) Akali Dal, led by Master Tara Singh, a venerable former school master, who looked like a benevolent grandfather but was jailed numerous times by the government of India for subversive actions of various sorts, and was held by Muslims to have incited the Sikhs to much of the violence at the time of partition. A Sikh political center had existed in the Patiala and Eastern Punjab States Union (PEPSU), but political conditions became so disturbed there that in March 1953 the government of India suspended the regime. The Akalis cultivated a technique of nonviolent resistance, with bearded, blue-turbaned, slogan-shouting demonstrators good-naturedly letting themselves be taken to jail by the hundreds and even thousands, as in 1955, when the states' reorganization plan was announced and their hopes for a Sikhistan (land of the Sikhs) or Sikh *subah* (province) were denied in favor of the Greater Punjab (Mahapunjab), which the rest of the residents in the area wished.

The Sikhs have had a quarrel with the government of India over the control of their *gurudwaras* (shrines) in the Punjab, an issue inherited from the first quarter of the century during the period of British rule. In January 1960 the Akali Dal decided to abrogate the pact it had made with Nehru before the 1957 elections to enter Congress, and it instructed its members to withdraw. In June there was so much agitation in Delhi that on October 1, as a concession to the Sikhs, Punjabi was made the official language of the western part of the Punjab.

In 1961 demonstrations were renewed, and the government of India by a resolution dated October 31, 1961, appointed a three-man commission to inquire into Sikh charges of discrimination against them in the Punjab. The commission was boycotted by the Akali Dal. In its report on January 31, 1962, the commission denied the charges of discrimination, and opposed the division of the Punjab on grounds of language, discounted the status claimed for Punjabi, rejected the demand that it be written only in the Gurmukhi script, and took a hostile position to any sort of attempt to create a Sikh subah.

Finally in 1966 there was created Haryana, which was essentially a Sikh state. The capital, which had been the capital of Greater Punjab, is Chandigarh, an internationally celebrated example of city planning and architecture, largely planned by Le Corbusier.

Most of the Sikh demands now seem to have been satisfied. The Sikhs are a forceful and courageous people, and obstinate as well, disliked by Muslims but respected by other Indians.

Elsewhere in India disturbances often occur in which difference of language or of language plus religion is an element, sometimes possibly the principal element, as in Cachar in Assam in June 1961. Sometimes religion alone seems the basic cause as at Jabalpur in Madhya Pradesh in January and February 1961, when there were Hindu riots against Muslims. In south India, where the Dravidian languages are dominant, there is a movement toward establishing a Dravidastan; the chief source of contention is the promotion of Hindi as the national language and the effort stemming from north India to make it the official language of the Dravidian areas. Feeling in the south is strong, but the actual sentiment for secession seems weak.

India now consists of eighteen states and eleven union territories and other areas (see Appendix 1).

Now that Pakistan has lost the eastern half of itself, there may be some reason to wonder if the surviving half may at some time also suffer an amputation. At the extreme west of Pakistan there has been a problem for the government, stubborn and potentially ominous. This is the movement for Pakhtunistan, that is, for a political entity composed of the wild mountainous area where the Pashtu (Pashto, Pakhtu, Pushtu) language is spoken and where the inhabitants are loosely called Pathans. The proposal includes large parts of the former North-West Frontier Province of India, now in Pakistan, and the adjacent Pashtu-speaking part of Afghanistan. The turbulent Pashtu region has never been successfully assimilated within any state since it first appeared in history at the time of the Emperor Ashoka in the third century B.C., whose capital was in Bihar in eastern India. The Pathans have looked upon the lowland Punjabis as a good deal less than themselves and fit victims for cattle lifting and other forms of marauding. The British never succeeded in establishing firm rule in that region but had a sphere of influence on both sides of the "Durand Line" (1893). The tribes living there came to accept a life of relative quiet in return for subsidies to maintain a Frontier Rifle Corps. Thus they could meet their economic necessities. The Afghan government, on its side, could not impose its authority upon the parts of the area which it claimed; instead it tolerated the British arrangement. When the British withdrew and Pakistan became the power in the northwest part of the Indian subcontinent, Afghanistan saw a possibility of advancing its own interests. The Pakhtunistan movement, therefore, had Afghan support.

The principal leaders of the Pakhtunistan movement were the brothers Khan Abdul Ghaffar Khan—leader of the Khudai Khidmatgar, "Servants of God," the so-called "Red Shirts," who was known as the "Frontier Gandhi"—and Dr. Khan Sahib. It is possible that if the government of Pakistan had been willing to allow the formation of a separate Pakhtunistan province, an accommodation might have been effected, but the government, under pressure to equalize the eastern and western wings of the nation, instituted the unit policy of consolidating all the parts of West Pakistan into a single province. This has not satisfied the Pathans, who have had moral, and doubtless material, support from Afghanistan. Neither Ayub Khan's government nor Yahya Khan's was able to establish itself firmly over all the forces tending to divide Pakistan, including the Pakhtunistan movement, which remains a danger to the state.

It is not to be thought that the forces of division have been over-come in either India or Pakistan. Wise and delicate handling of the problem is needed in both countries. What the subcontinent needed after World War II and the achievement of independence was steady progress toward consolidation under a single government. What it got was partition, partition into two nations, hostile toward each other, each of which in its turn has had to cope with tenden-cies toward subdivision. India had the leadership of Nehru to ward this off, has possibly risen above it, and so may preserve the unifi-cation so necessary to its advancement. Pakistan at the very time of its formation had a built-in divisive polarity between its two wings, which the country's leaders have been incapable of recon-ciling. Further disintegration is a clear and present danger. Ban-gladesh has not yet had to face problems of disintegration: Mujib may possess the spirit of nonviolence and conciliation that will bring his country internal peace.

13 Political Parties

In India the political party structure since independence has been almost monopolistic. In Pakistan it was almost monopolistic until 1954; after then it rapidly became chaotic. In 1958 political parties were banned in Pakistan, to remain so until July 1962, when the Legislative Assembly meeting under the new constitution granted them status under license. In India the Indian National Congress was dominant from having fought and won the battle of independence and from having constructed while doing so the country's most powerful party machine; it has retained its dominance by promoting, even though not always successfully, a program of national development. In Pakistan the Muslim League at first had a corresponding supremacy. It had split the old India and so brought the new nation into existence, and it possessed the only well-built party apparatus, but lacking a philosophy of national reconstruction it lost its position of supremacy.

The Indian National Congress at the elections held in 1946 still campaigned on the issue of nationalism versus imperialism, and the Hindu-Muslim communal issue of partition. By means of the first issue it had for some decades succeeded in transcending the conflicts between mutually antipathetic ideologies, those of violent revolution and constitutional evolution, or religious conservatism and social modernism, or a controlled economy and laissez faire, and so had fairly well kept together the secularly motivated part of the small electorate (about 11 percent of the population could vote in the provincial elections). Because of the partition issue Congress had been guaranteed almost the total vote of the Hindus. Both issues became dead letters in August 1947. The subsurface fissures of Congress were already showing before that date; after it they widened. Gandhi's death at the end of January 1948 was a blow to Congress unity, for all elements in Congress respected him, though some disagreed with him and some were actually opposed. A few of the cracks became cleavages, and various new parties split from Congress, though none of them ever seriously rivaled it.

Congress is still the dominant political party in the new India. In the 1951–1952 elections for the House of the People it got 45 percent of the total vote cast and won 74 percent of the total seats elected (362 of 489). Its nearest rival, the Communist party with its allies, won 27 seats and got 5.5 percent of the vote. For the state legislative assemblies Congress got 42.5 percent of the votes cast and won 68.6 percent of the total seats, gaining a majority (2248 out of 3283) in all the then Part A and Part B states except Madras, Orissa, Hyderabad, PEPSU (Patiala and East Punjab States Union), and Travancore-Cochin. The nearest rival in number of votes was the Socialist party with 9.7 percent of the votes but only 3.8 percent of the seats (126). The Communist Party of India and allies got the second largest number of seats (180 or 5.5 percent), and 6 percent of the total votes.

In the second general elections, held in 1957, Congress again swept the country. It got 45 percent of the votes cast (about 51.3 million out of 113.5 million) and won 371 out of 494 seats open to contest in the House of the People. In the state legislative assemblies it won 1,893 out of 2,906 seats, and had control of eleven out of fourteen states; of the three others one, Jammu and Kashmir, was dominated (68 seats out of 75) by the National Conference, which functioned essentially as a Congress affiliate. The Praja-Socialist Party got about 10 percent of the votes cast (about 11.4 million), winning 19 seats in the House of the People (shortly afterwards becoming 20) and 195 in the state assemblies (shortly afterwards becoming 205). The Communist Party of India and its allies got 8 percent of the vote cast (about 8.73 million), winning 27 seats in the House of the People and 161 in the state legislative assemblies (shortly afterwards increased to 171). The right-wing party Jan Sangh got about 4 percent of the total vote, winning 4 seats in the House of the People and 46 in the state legislative assemblies. Other parties and independents got about 37 percent of the votes (37.7 million), winning 73 seats in the House of the People (later 79) and 611 in the state legislative assemblies (later 711). (The percentages here add up to more than 100 perhaps because votes for both the Lok Sabha and the state assemblies are involved. The inconsistency is not great enough to constitute a significant error.)

In Orissa Congress had a plurality of 56 seats out of 140, the Ganatantra Parishad having 51 seats. There a coalition government was established by those two parties headed by Harekrushna Mehtab, a prominent Congress leader. The coalition collapsed in February 1961, disorder followed, and President Rajendra Prasad, acting under the constitution, dissolved the legislature and put the state under central government rule. In June 1961 new elections were held and Congress got a sweeping victory winning 60 percent of the seats, the Ganatantra about 2 percent, the Praja-Socialists about 7 percent, the Communists only 3 seats, and the rest being won by independents.

In Kerala the Communist Party had a plurality of 60 out of 126 seats, Congress winning 43 seats. There a situation developed which will be discussed below in the treatment of the Communist parties of India and Pakistan. We may note here only that in July 1959 the central government suspended the Communist-controlled administration and in 1960 ordered elections, in which the Congress party won exactly one half of the seats in the Legislative Assembly (63 out of 126). It proceeded to set up a government with the aid of the Socialists. During the summer of 1961, therefore, Congress controlled fourteen of India's then fifteen states, and had a working arrangement for controlling the fifteenth.

In the 1962 elections Congress retained its dominating position. It won 356 seats out of 494 in the Lok Sabha (and later added 5 others) while its nearest competitor, the Communist Party, won 29. The left-wing DMK (Dravida Munnetra Kazhagam) won 7. The right-wing Jan Sangh won 14, the Swatantra party 18. The Praja-Socialist Party won 12 seats, and other parties and independents 53. In the elections for the state assemblies 2,855 seats were in contest, no elections being held in Kerala and Orissa, where there had been midterm elections. Congress won 1,772 seats, the Communist Party 151, DMK 50 (all in Madras State), Praja-Socialist Party 149, Swatantra 166, Jan Sangh 116, Socialists 58, other parties and independents 393. The Congress Party won a clear majority in all states except Madhya Pradesh (142 out of 288) and Rajasthan (88 out of 176). The nearest rivals in those states were: in Madhya Pradesh, Jan Sangh with 41; in Rajasthan, Swatantra with 36. Significant new developments were a general loss of strength by the Communist and Praja-Socialist parties, and the increase of strength of the right wing, represented by the Swatantra and Jan

Sangh parties. Curiously, the leaders of all the opposition groups in the Lok Sabha lost their seats. Even Dr. Katju, chief minister of Madhya Pradesh, belonging to Congress, lost his seat though running in his home constituency. This development was the result of party factionalism.

In the 1967 elections Congress won only 283 seats out of 520 in the Lok Sabha, or 54.4 percent—a notable reduction from its previous majorities. Its nearest rivals were the radical left-wing Communist Party (Marxist), with 19 seats, and the Communist Party of India with 23 seats; then came the moderate left-wing Samyukta Socialist Party, with 23 seats; the Praja Socialist Party, with 13 seats; the right-wing Jan Sangh with 35 seats; the right-wing Swatantra Party with 44 seats; the South Indian locally oriented Dravida Munnetra Kazhagam with 25 seats. In spite of the reduction which Congress suffered, it seems that a substantial plurality of the people retained their confidence in that party. The midterm election of 1971, which will be discussed below, confirmed that Congress (R), the part of Congress headed by Prime Minister Indira Gandhi, still had unchallenged, though weakened domination of the parliament, with the support of the people.

In its manifesto for the 1951 election, the first after independence, Congress led by Nehru declared its program, which has not altered basically since then. This was unequivocal progress toward a secular socialist state. It announced as its aim "freedom of the masses from want" and stated that "economic progress must therefore be given first priority," to be achieved by "cooperation and the avoidance, as far as possible, of competition and conflict." The manifesto called for "a planned approach to development, in which the first and vital step in the effort "to live the good life" was to free the land from the burden of the old and out-of-date agrarian system of tenure. "Increased agricultural production," it said, was "absolutely essential" and the conditions of agricultural labor had to be improved. Improvement of cattle breeding it called another need; so, too, the encouragement of small and cottage industries. "Basic industries," it said, "should be owned or controlled by the State." This would lead to a mixed economy with a "public sector as well as private sector," all fitted into the "national plan." It advocated controlled distribution of commodities with a well determined price policy. It included the development of scientific research. It proposed to encourage corporate savings for development purposes.

Economic equality and social justice were strongly supported. The rights of labor were recognized. Railway services were to be rehabilitated and improved. Transport services should be nationalized. The public services should be supported by a training program. Corruption must be ended. Education, public health, the control of epidemic disease, and provision of sanitation, were to be furthered. The Depressed Classes and Tribes were to be helped in their self-development. Displaced persons from Pakistan should be rehabilitated. Every citizen should have "full freedom to profess and practice his religion." Women must be relieved of "social and other disabilities." Redistribution of provinces on a linguistic basis "ultimately should depend upon the wishes of the people concerned." Foreign policy was to continue as "an independent line in her [India's] own national interest and in the interest of peace." This was Congress' definition of the good life for India. The voters gave it their overwhelming approval.

It is significant that the Congress program then, as since, repudiated all religious conservatism and communalism. Such forces had tried to assert themselves. In September 1950, at the party's annual convention, conservatism, headed by Purushottamadas Tandon (1882–1962), an old-timer who opposed many innovations, including smallpox vaccination and modern medical practices, won the contest for the presidency over Nehru's candidate. Nehru, threatening to resign if not supported, got Congress at the same meeting to endorse his domestic and foreign policies. But he did not then have full control over Congress and found himself frustrated over a number of points including the membership of the central election committee, which was to select the candidates for the 1951–52 general elections. Tandon had won control over this body in May. In August 1951, therefore, Nehru submitted his resignation from both the Congress governing body (the all-India Congress committee) and the Central Election Committee. Since he was Congress' best vote-getter and could possibly carry the country for any existing party he might join or any new one he might create, other Congress leaders got Tandon to step down. Nehru then took the presidency and with it domination of the Central Election Committee. After that his leadership was never seriously challenged.

Most of the conservative industrialists have uneasily remained with Congress, having no place else to go, though in 1962 many seemed to support the Swatantra Party. Most of the religious conservatives of a modern dye have stayed too, presumably not convinced that they should bolt Congress for any existing extremist religious organization like the Jan Sangh or the Hindu Mahasabha.

Congress has consistently reaffirmed its program of a "socialist (or socialistic) pattern of society." This included economic planning, and India began its Third Five-Year Plan in 1961. The Fourth Five-Year Plan, however, though discussed was not implemented, and was not succeeded by a fifth plan. After 1951 Congress pressed less vigorously for state ownership, giving more freedom to the private sector.

Congress won two important victories over left-wing alliances in elections in Andhra in 1959 and in Bombay City in 1957 and 1962, when Krishna Menon as the Congress candidate in one district was an object of intensive attack. Congress' status was also enhanced by the ever increasing prestige in international affairs that India was winning after independence. It suffered loss of prestige, however, when the facts about China's forward move along India's northern border came to public knowledge in 1959, and severe embarrassment when India met defeat in the Indo-China War in 1962. By the time of the 1971 general elections Congress had recovered its position.

A continuing problem for Congress—and indeed for all India—was Nehru's successor. Since he was born in 1889, by the time of the 1961 elections he was not expected to guide the country much longer. Some people said that without Nehru the Congress party would disintegrate, its existing factional cleavages becoming wide chasms. Others relied upon the party's effective political machine to save its position. The Congress party was, as it still is, better organized than any other in India except the Communist Party, and covered much more of India than did the latter. Further, no other party has produced a program of national development that is even distantly comparable in appeal to the Indian people with that promulgated by Congress. The Communist party has been the most vigorous and in several provinces has achieved the greatest measure of success. The 1967 elections were indeed a setback for Congress and contributed to the opposition that developed against Mrs. Gandhi when she became Prime Minister. Those elections were, in fact, a kind of revolt against her. However, she conducted a skillful campaign in the 1971 elections, won an overwhelming victory, and restored the prestige of the Congress party, that is, of that part of the party—Congress (R)—that she headed.

Several political parties were created by bolters from Congress. Some left Congress because it was not radical enough, some because it was not conservative enough. One such group of long standing is the Socialist Party that had its origin in 1934 when the Congress Socialist Party was organized by Jayaprakash Narayan (b. 1902) and other liberals, including Jawaharlal Nehru, to work for agrarian and labor reform. It constituted at that time a left wing of Congress and, though Jayaprakash had a Marxist philosophy, he and the party were opposed to the Communist Party of India. Instead he became a devoted follower of Gandhi, though often disagreeing with him. By 1947 most of the Congress Socialists were discontented with Congress for its failure to take an aggressive position for social reform. They were also unrelenting opponents of communalism, and when Gandhi was assassinated they all but publicly accused Vallabhbhai Patel of having been responsible through letting Hindu communalism run loose in the land. Shortly afterwards they entered candidates against Congress in an election in Bombay, and in March 1948 voted to become an independent party known as the Socialist Party of India. Jayaprakash Narayan's chief associates were Acharya Narendra Deva; Ashok Mehta, prominent in labor movements but a loser in the 1962 elections; Ram Manohar Lohia, former close disciple of Gandhi and associate of Nehru; Kamala Devi Chattopadhyaya, a woman long active in promoting advanced socialist principles; and Achyut Patwardhan. The party protested against the Congress-controlled government's failure to provide the masses with food and housing and to check black marketing. In August 1951, when Nehru offered his resignation from the all-India Congress committee, various commentators thought he might align himself with Jayaprakash Narayan, who was an old personal friend, coworker, and congenial political theorist. In 1952–53 it appeared possible that Jayaprakash Narayan might lead the party back to Congress, but his position was too far to the left of Congress for this to succeed. In 1954 he announced that he was retiring from politics (later he was again involved in political activities). By that time, that is, in 1953, the Socialist Party had united with the Praja (Kisan Mazdoor Praja) Party as the Praja-Socialist Party (PSP), with the objective of creating a non-Communist leftist opposition to Congress, but Congress itself, by coming out early in 1955 for a "socialistic pattern of society," cut a good deal of ground out from under it. One faction of the PSP split off under the leadership of Ram Manohar Lohia to form the Socialist party. In 1957 Jayaprakash Narayan announced that he had "finally renounced" politics to join Vinoba Bhave's *bhoodan* "land gift" movement. In 1958 he advocated a "partyless" government of India, with all parties that speak for socialism cooperating to frame a minimum socialist program. There should be no party action, he urged, in local politics. The voters should select their candidates themselves for state and national legislatures and then the parties should enter the picture. In 1960 Kripalani, the original leader of the other half of the party, also resigned because of differences with other leaders, but in 1962 he was back and was defeated by Krishna Menon.

In the 1951–1952 elections the Socialist party got 10.5 percent of the vote, won 12 seats in the Lok Sabha and 126 seats in the state legislative assemblies. The Praja party got 5.8 percent of the votes and won 9 seats in the Lok Sabha and 77 seats in the state legislative assemblies. In 1957 the combined Praja-Socialist Party got about 10 percent of the vote and won 19 seats in the Lok Sabha, 195 seats in the state legislative assemblies (afterwards becoming 205). Thus the new combined party held its own in relation to the successes of the two separate parties in 1951–1952. In 1962 its position deteriorated, and it won only 12 seats in the Lok Sabha and 149 in the state assemblies.

The Praja (Kisan Mazdoor Praja—Peasants', Workers', and People's) party had been formed in June 1951 by another dissident group of bolters from Congress led by Acharya J. B. Kripalani, a Gandhian stalwart. His candidates had been defeated for the central election committee in May 1951, and shortly afterwards he left Congress. This party expressed itself as dissatisfied with Congress' measures for the peasantry and labor, advocated redistribution of land and cooperative farming, but opposed nationalization of industry. In foreign affairs it agreed with Nehru's policy of "strict neutrality." It was merged with the Socialist party at about the beginning of 1954.

Another defection from Congress in anticipation of the 1951–1952 election was that of Dr. B. R. Ambedkar (1893–1956), leader of the All-India Scheduled Castes Federation, the strongest organization among the Untouchables. He was dissatisfied with Congress' failure to put through Parliament enforcing legislation for the anti-untouchability provision of the constitution, and he therefore resigned from the cabinet in October 1951. "What is the position of the scheduled castes today?" he is reported to have asked. "So far as I see, it is the same as before—the same old tyranny, the same old oppression. The same old discrimination which existed before exists now and perhaps in worse form." He condemned the Nehru government's policy in dealing with Pakistan—he had favored the creation of Pakistan when it was an issue—deploring the military expenditures and urging settlement of the Kashmir question by partition and limited plebiscite. He also criticized the Congress party for its neutrality in the Cold War, which he said had left India friendless, and for championing the cause of Communist China and so forfeiting "financial and technical aid from America on a large scale." In 1951–1952 the Scheduled Castes Federation won only 2 seats in the Lok Sabha and 12 in the state legislative assemblies. It had ceased to have national importance by 1971.

An extreme party known as the Forward Bloc split from Congress in 1940. It was led by Subhas Chandra Bose (1897–1945), who fled India in 1940 and went to Germany, later headed the "Indian National Army" in Malaya and Burma, which was a Japanese auxiliary force. After his death Subhas Bose became a national hero of India. The Forward Bloc had a fascist ideology at that time; later it had two wings, both of them radical and violent, one of them Marxist, the other Socialist (Subhasist) led by R. S. Ruikar. Without Bose as leader the party had internal quarrels. In March 1955 it decided to dissolve and give its support to Congress, which in the January preceding had declared its objective to be a "socialistic pattern of society." At that time the Forward Bloc held 2 seats in the Lok Sabha and claimed 21 in state legislative assemblies. In 1962 it had revived sufficiently to win 2 seats in the Lok Sabha, 13 seats in the West Bengal legislative Assembly, and 3 seats in the Madras assembly. By 1971 it had lost any national importance.

In 1959 the highly respected and venerable, but exceedingly active, Chakravarti Rajagopalachari (b. 1879) led the organization of a new party called Swatantra ("Independence, Self-Rule, Freedom"). Rajagopalachari, generally known as "Rajaji" or "C.R.," has held important posts in the Congress party, including the presidency, and in government, including the governor generalship of India from 1948 until the office ceased to exist in 1950. His daughter married a son of Gandhi, Devdas Gandhi (1900–1957), a prominent journalist and long-time managing editor of an influential newspaper, *The Hindustan Times* (New Delhi). Rajagopalachari had been chief minister of the state of Madras from 1952 to 1954, when he "retired from politics," ostensibly to devote himself to writing books on religious themes and in other ways to promote religion, in which he has a deep interest. He considered the government of Nehru, a close personal friend of his, to be "pure autocracy or dictatorship," though "a mild form without bloodshed." His Swatantra Party is rightist, stands for free enterprise, addresses an appeal to business and other conservative interests, advocates peace and defensive collaboration with Pakistan, the formation of which Rajagopalachari had urged Congress to accept during World War II. Nehru called the Swatantra Party reactionary. One of the most influential supporters of the Swatantra party was the late K. M. Munshi of Bombay, novelist, Gujarati literary historian, and founder of the Bharatiya Vidya Bhavan, a distinguished literary and general cultural institution in Bombay, as well as former prominent Congressman and political leader in Gujarat. In the 1962 elections the party made a good showing, but not in the home state of its chief leader, Madras. There it elected no member of the Lok Sabha and only 6 (out of 206) in the state assembly. Its strength lay in Gujarat (the cultural home of K. M. Munshi), Rajasthan, Andhra, Bihar, and Uttar Pradesh. In Rajasthan its most popular candidate was a princess (by title only now) of the family formerly ruling the state of Jaipur. She was reelected to the Lok Sabha in 1967. The Swatantra Party won 8 seats in the Lok Sabha in 1971.

A party of local strength and interest is the Ganatantra Parishad of Orissa, centered around former rulers of princely states in Orissa, which were many. It elected 7 members of the Lok Sabha in 1956 and 51 members of the Orissa state legislative assembly. In 1962, having merged with the Swatantra Party, it won 4 (out of 20) seats from Orissa in the Lok Sabha.

In recent decades Santalis and other speakers of Munda languages have become politically conscious and have felt that Congress has not been sufficiently attentive to their interests. They call themselves Adivasis or Adibasis (Original Settlers). Some members of Congress have also been leaders of political parties representing the Adivasis, especially the late Jaipal Singh, a member of Parliament. He headed the Jharkhand party, which advocates an Adivasi state to be called Jharkhand. In the 1951–1952 elections this party won 3 seats in the Lok Sabha and 32 seats out of 330 in the Bihar legislative assembly. In 1957 it won 6 seats in the Lok Sabha and again 32 seats in the Bihar legislative assembly. In 1962 it won 3 seats from Bihar in the Lok Sabha and 20 seats in the assembly. In 1952 and 1957 another Adivasi party was in the field in Bihar called the Chota Nagpur Santhal Parganas Janata Party, or just the Janata (People's) Party which in 1952 won 1 seat in the Lok Sabha and 11 seats in the assembly and in 1957 won 3 seats in the Lok Sabha and 23 seats in the Bihar legislative assembly.

The leading communal party in India has been the Hindu Mahasabha (Hindu General Association), whose vague beginnings go back to the first part of the century when the Muslim League was being founded (1906). For many years the Mahasabha was headed by Pandit Madan Mohan Malaviya, long vice chancellor of the Benares (Banaras) Hindu University, a traditional orthodox Hindu, who had a ceremony of rejuvenation by rebirth in his eighties, but to little effect since he died soon afterwards. The Mahasabha became prominent about 1934 under V. D. Savarkar, who had served a jail sentence for terrorism. Its platform has always been to preserve India for the Hindus. It actively attacked the Muslims in the decade before partition and consistently fought Congress for trying to reconcile Hindus and Muslims in an India which they would jointly occupy without discrimination. It never had much of a following, but during the war years, when the British war cabinet kept Congress leaders in jail (1942–1945), the Mahasabha became powerful beyond its intrinsic importance, and contributed notably to Hindu-Muslim terrorism. Gandhi's assassin (Vinayak Godse) had earlier been a member of the Mahasabha, and this fact led the public to express intense hostility against the party and contributed to its decline. Savarkar was tried for complicity but was acquitted. Another leader of the party was Dr. Shyama Prasad Mookerjee, who was minister of industry and supply in Nehru's cabinet but resigned April 19, 1950, in protest against the government's pusillanimous attitude, as he regarded it, toward Pakistan on the treatment of Hindu minorities. He was succeeded by Dr. N. B. Khare, formerly a member of Congress. In the 1951–52 elections the Mahasabha won 4 seats in the Lok Sabha and 20 seats in state legislative assemblies. In 1957 it won only 2 seats in the Lok Sabha and 8 seats in state legislative assemblies, of which 7 were in Madhya Pradesh and 1 in Bombay. In 1962 it won one seat from Uttar Pradesh in the Lok Sabha, 2 seats in the Uttar Pradesh assembly, and 6 seats in the Madhya Pradesh assembly.

Spiritually associated with the Mahasabha was the RSS, the Rashtriya Swayamsevak Sangh (National Volunteer Association), also sometimes called the Sangh, a fascist-type action organization, hierarchically structured, with all communication proceeding from above downwards. It was founded in 1925 by Dr. Keshav B. Hedgewar (1889–1940) to bring about Hindu unity against Muslim encroachment. On his death he was succeeded by Madhav Rao Sadashiv Gowalkar (b. 1906). All its chief leaders (these two included) have been Maharashtrian Brahmans. The RSS was held responsible for a large part of the violence in the Punjab at the time of partition. On February 4, 1948, after Gandhi's assassination, when communal feeling was running high, the Indian government outlawed the Sangh and put its leaders under arrest. At the same time the Mahasabha went into seclusion. Both the Mahasabha and the Sangh emerged in December 1948, and the Sangh launched a civil disobedience campaign to gain reinstatement, which continued until January 24, 1949, by which time 40,000 of its members had been arrested. Like the Mahasabha the RSS stood for pro-Hindu communal activity directed toward reconstituting Indian unity (*Akhand Hindustan*), that is, abolition of Pakistan, and the establishment of a Hindu *rashtra* ("realm"), and fed upon and nourished Hindu hostility toward Pakistan. The two organizations had no formal connection, and differed in that the Mahasabha is a political party and the RSS a cultural body, but in the words of Asutosh Lahiri (like Savarkar a former terrorist) in 1949, when he was general secretary of the Mahasabha, "ideologically there . . . is . . . no difference between the Mahasabha and the RSS." The ban on the RSS was lifted July 12, 1949, by which time it had submitted to the government and adopted a constitution limiting its activities to the cultural field and eschewing politics. Since then it has sunk out of sight.

Dr. Shyam Prasad Mookerjee, dissatisfied with the Mahasabha as well as with Congress, in 1952 led the organization of a new party called the Bharatiya Jan Sangh (Indian People's Party), commonly known as the Jan Sangh, which contested the elections that year on the issue that Congress had failed to take a strong enough line on the plight of the Hindu refugees from East Bengal, the issue on which he had resigned from Congress in 1950. The Jan Sangh attacked Nehru savagely and incontinently in speeches and in its official news publication *The Organizer*. It is anti-Muslim and anti-Christian. In the 1951–1952 elections it won 3 seats in the Lok Sabha and 32 in state legislative assemblies, chiefly in West Bengal and Rajasthan. In 1957 it won 4 seats in the Lok Sabha and 46 in state legislative assemblies, chiefly in Madhya Pradesh and Uttar Pradesh. It gained considerable ground in 1962 winning 14 seats in the Lok Sabha and 116 seats in state assemblies. In 1967 it won 35 seats in the Lok Sabha and in 1971 it won 22. Its chief strength lies in Madhya Pradesh, Rajasthan, and Uttar Pradesh.

Another Hindu orthodox communal party is the Akhil Bharat (All India) Ram Rajya Parishad (Society for the Rule of Rama, that is, return of the epic Ramayana's Utopian Age). In 1951–1952 it won 3 seats in the Lok Sabha and 32 in state legislative assemblies, mostly in Rajasthan. In 1957 it won no seats in the Lok Sabha and only 22 in state legislative assemblies, all in Madhya Pradesh and Rajasthan. In 1962 it won 2 seats in the Lok Sabha (one each from Madhya Pradesh and Rajasthan), 10 seats in the Madhya Pradesh Assembly, and 3 in the Rajasthan Assembly.

It can be seen that Hindu communal parties have had only thin support in the elections.

The Dravida Munnetra Kazhagam (DMK), which advocates separate sovereign statehood for the Dravidian language area, to be known as Dravidastan, showed great strength in the 1962 elections, winning 7 seats in the Lok Sabha and 50 seats in the Madras legislative assembly, a warning to Congress and northern India. In 1967 it won 25 seats in the Lok Sabha and in 1971 it won 23. In the 1969 Tamil Nadu assembly election it won 138 seats out of 234, and in 1971 it won 184. It clearly dominates Tamil Nadu politics.

There are other small or local parties, for example, the aggressive revivalist Sikh party known as the (Shiromani) Akali Dal, the leading political group of the Sikhs. In the 1951–1952 elections it won 4 seats in the Lok Sabha and 33 in state legislative assemblies, all in the Punjab and PEPSU. In the 1957 elections it had reached an agreement with Congress and did not contest. In 1962 it won 3 seats in the Lok Sabha from the Punjab and 10 seats (out of 154) in the Punjab assembly. Both in 1962 and 1967 it won 3 seats in the Lok Sabha; in 1971 only 1 seat.

Since partition the Muslim League has had no national existence in India. It had achieved its great purpose, and Muslims generally could not risk the general opprobrium that would have been attached to renewed support of a communal Muslim party. The one place where the Muslim League could maintain itself with impunity was in the Malabar district of Madras, now a part of Kerala, among the Moplahs (Mappila). This is a Muslim community descended from Arabs and local low-caste people, with low standards of living and education, frequently engaging in anti-Hindu violence, as in 1921–1922. The Muslim League championed their rights and was left-wing in its advocacy. In the 1951–52 elections it won 1 seat in the Lok Sabha and 5 in the Madras state legislative assembly. In the 1957 elections it won no seats. In 1962 it won 2 seats in the Lok Sabha from Kerala.

The lack of a Muslim party in India is not due to a lack of feeling among Muslims that they suffer from discrimination at the hand of the government with respect to government jobs, political position, and education, and that they are handicapped in business life as well. Abortive efforts have been made to organize Muslim parties, as in the "Fourth party" inaugurated by Muslim women after partition, but these cannot gain public support and either fade away or dissolve, as the Fourth party did in September 1955. Muslims usually give their votes to Congress or the Praja-Socialists, or some other noncommunal party.

Throughout India party membership is low. Though the total eligible voting population is about 216 million, it was estimated in July 1961 that only about 3 million belonged to political parties, of whom more than 2.5 million were members of Congress, while the Praja-Socialists had 200,000 and the Communists nearly 180,000.

The 1971 elections in India were the most dramatic ever held there. They had been preceded by a split in the Congress party, which had put Mrs. Gandhi in a defensive situation against the party bosses, popularly known as the Syndicate, who seemed confident that they could destroy her. Their hostility to her was very personal, but at the same time it was due to a difference in political ideology. She was on the side of legislative and administrative measures in line with the socialistic aims of Congress as expressed in its annual sessions and election manifestoes since the first elections in 1951. The Syndicate's position was that of big business, which felt trammeled by socialist public policy and was certain that what was good for business was good for India.

The 1967 general election had shaken the position of Congress, as we have seen above. Two years later, in February 1969, there were midterm elections for the assemblies of four states and one union territory, and they had shown a further weakening of the Congress position. After these elections with their bad news for Congress Mrs. Gandhi reorganized her cabinet, making appointments that seemed to indicate distrust, or at least disregard, of the Syndicate. When President Zakir Husain died on May 3, Vice President V. V. Giri became Acting President, and since he had Mrs. Gandhi's support it was assumed that he would be made President. But the Congress parliamentary board, which was controlled by the Syndicate, proposed N. Sanjiva Reddy, speaker of the Lok Sabha. Nevertheless, at the presidential election, held in August, Mrs. Gandhi continued to back Giri, and he won, though by only a small majority.

Mrs. Gandhi had also antagonized the Syndicate by announcing that she was taking steps to nationalize the banks, and at about that same time she dismissed her finance minister, Morarji Desai. He had for a long time been a controversial figure in national politics on one ground or another. On being dismissed he had resigned as deputy prime minister.

The situation which had been created alarmed the working committee of the Congress party, which handles party affairs between the annual meetings, and it issued an appeal for "unity." S. Nijalingappa, president of the Congress party, then dropped two of Mrs. Gandhi's supporters from the working committee. Mrs. Gandhi responded by refusing to attend a meeting of the working committee set for November 1 and instead herself called a meeting of the committee. The regular meeting drew eleven members; Mrs. Gandhi's meeting drew ten. The working committee, as thus reduced, then read her out of the party for "acts of indiscipline." She rejected the action as illegal and invalid, and laid the matter before the Congress parliamentary board, which by a decisive vote of three fourths of its members gave her a vote of confidence.

When the winter session of Parliament opened in November the supporters of the syndicate all took seats in the opposition benches as a Congress Opposition party, in contrast with the rest of the Congress party members, who remained as the Congress Ruling party. Hence the two divisions of the Congress members of Parliament came to be referred to as Congress (O) and Congress (R). Congress (O), evidently expecting enough support against Mrs. Gandhi to force her resignation, introduced an adjournment motion, but the motion was defeated 306 to 140, and thus Mrs. Gandhi was confirmed as leader of the Congress party and ratified as Prime Minister.

In the 1971 election campaign Congress (O) ran its own candidates. The contest was an acrimonious one, in which Congress (O) spoke relatively little to issues, but attacked Mrs. Gandhi personally, using such slogans as "Indira must go!" and "Drive out Indira!" Mrs. Gandhi, on the other hand, campaigned on issues: nationalization of the banks (the courts had struck down a parliamentary act nationalizing them and she wanted a stronger act, which when Parliament reassembled she got); abolition of the former princes' privy purses; measures to counteract the deteriorating economic situation; action to cope with the rise of prices and with unemployment. Besides such issues she referred, apparently successfully, to the alliance of Congress (O) with the conservative Jan Sangh, Swatantra, and Samyukta Socialist parties. Her overwhelming victory seemed to show that the electorate was more moved by issues than by personalities. Congress (R) won 350 seats in the Lok Sabha; Congress (O) won 16. The extent of her victory was a surprise and shock to Congress (O) and its allies, a reaffirmation of the traditional policies of Congress, and an assurance that she remains the most astute political diagnostician in India. Throughout the campaign she never seemed to have any doubt that she would win. She knew that her "moderately left-of-center" (as it was called) program was what the voters wanted.

To a non-Indian it looked as though she had what every political leader needs—personality, charisma, the power to charm the people, for which her father was unexcelled. When he wrote his history of India for her as a girl he must also have taught her something about how to acquire and use the art of political persuasion in a democracy.

The election was accompanied by violence, particularly in Bengal, where political violence had been common for years. Much of it seemed to be the work of hooligans belonging to or hired by

political parties—both charges were made. Most of the violence
was attributed to splinter groups of the two Communist parties and
to the Naxalites (see below in this chapter). Whatever the facts
are about its instigation, it is true that almost every day the newspapers reported political slayings, sometimes as many as six or
even more. It all gave one the feeling that what was going on
was what someone called "election by murder."

For Mrs. Gandhi the election showed that she had received an
assignment of economic and social progress. It is a hard assignment.

In Pakistan the history of political parties after independence
was one of progressive deterioration and chaos until 1958, at which
time the institution of political parties was killed. This was the
result of lack of social and economic philosophy in party thinking.
Keith Callard (*Pakistan, A Political Study,* p. 5) characterized the
situation thus: "The period from 1947 to 1957 has been one of
change and uncertainty. There have been few fixed ideas and few institutions whose validity has not been open to question. In Pakistan
political parties have waxed, waned and suffered eclipse. Political
leaders have argued, intrigued and reduced each other to im-
potence. Men of religion have laid claim to complete authority and
have achieved almost none. In the meanwhile the state has been
run largely by the Civil Service, backed by the Army, which has
carried on much as it [the Indian Civil Service] did before independence."

Since there never were any general elections in Pakistan under
the parliamentary system of government that existed until October
1958, there was no arena for political parties to meet.

The Muslim League, after partition, was for a brief time allowed
to decline but it became evident by the spring of 1948 that the
leaders of the government were going to revive it. The feeling in
Pakistan was at first that a political party should not be permitted
to have a large influence in government. The government, however,
came under considerable criticism from communally minded Muslims for various reasons and the League was an instrument at
hand that could be used to maintain the government's prestige.
The provincial League organizations, therefore, were encouraged
and began to regain their importance. By mid-September 1950 the
government of Pakistan was not only strongly supporting the

League but was demanding that it have a monopoly of the political situation. At that time, on the second anniversary of Jinnah's death, in a speech on government policies, Prime Minister Liaquat Ali Khan referred to Jinnah's insistence on the "three golden principles of unity, faith, and discipline." He quoted a speech Jinnah made in March 1948, wherein he warned against internal "enemies of Pakistan . . . [who promote] sedition and treachery" and seek to create "new political parties," and affirmed that "the Muslim League is a sacred trust in your hands." Liaquat Ali inveighed, therefore, against political division in a period when Pakistan had great problems to solve such as the quarrels with India and Afghanistan. Though admitting shortcomings in the League, he said, "It is our duty to make the Muslim League a strong organization and a living force." He assailed in the most vigorous terms those who would found other parties, calling them "traitors, liars, and hypocrites," and singled out for specific attack Huseyn Shaheed Suhrawardy and the Awami Muslim League. "Those who are founding different political parties," he said, "are aiming at weakening this national organization [the Muslim League] and thus to cause disruption. It is the duty of us Leaguers to strengthen the League. The existence of Pakistan depends on this."

The Awami (People's) Muslim League headed by Suhrawardy was the leading opposition to Muslim League government and for a time was the most powerful party in Pakistan. Suhrawardy, member of a wealthy and aristocratic family, was a prominent Bengali politician before partition, and was premier of Bengal at the time of the Muslim League's "Direct Action Day," August 16, 1946. After partition he seemed undecided where his future career lay. Should he seek a place in Pakistan or should he stay in India and try to lead the Muslims to participate noncommunally in the new nation's public life? He seemed inclined at first toward the latter, but evidently was discouraged by the poor prospect for any organized Muslim effort. When he turned toward Pakistan he was met with coolness and suspicion in various high quarters and seemed to have no bright future with the Muslim-League-dominated government. He then endeavored to build up the Awami Muslim League as his organ, appealing to the masses and the forlorn refugees inhabiting the disheartening camps around Karachi. He criticized the government for rashness and precipitance in supporting the United Nations on the Korean issue, and at the same time for being dilatory and weak in not demanding that the Security Council adopt and enforce a decision against India on the Kashmir issue—positions in basic contradiction to each other, as Liaquat Ali Khan pointed out with relish.

The difficulties for the Muslim League started in the competition between the East and West wings of Pakistan and were increased by the rivalry among factions within separate provinces. In the Punjab, Sind, and the North-West Frontier Province the rivalry led to such severe discord, rioting, violence, and deaths that the central government suspended government by provincial ministries and legislatures and ruled through appointed governors. Elections were held in the Punjab and the North-West Frontier Province in 1951 and in Sind in 1953, in all three of which the Muslim League was victorious with a large majority. In Bengal, however, matters went differently. There the Muslim League was the symbol of the central government, operating in Karachi and viewed in East Pakistan as an instrument of the West Pakistanis for favoring themselves and discriminating against East Pakistan. A United Front of four opposition parties led by Suhrawardy, intent on ousting the existing League-controlled government, defeated the League in provincial elections in 1954 so thoroughly that the United Front won 233 seats and the League only 10 out of 309 in the East Bengal (that is, East Pakistan) legislature. One member party of the United Front was the Krishak Sramik (Peasants' and Workers') Party led by the elderly, popular Fazlal Huq (1873–1962), whose political career, with its alliances and about-faces, was a frequent subject of shifting applause and opprobrium. He became chief minister and inaugurated some hasty reforms. Shortly after the election he was reported to have made a statement (May 4, 1954) that the partition of India was a mistake and another one (May 22, 1954) that his objective was an independent East Pakistan. A few days later, on May 30, the governor general dismissed the administration of East Bengal and sent General Iskander Mirza to rule without legislature. Afterwards, when it became necessary to reactivate the legislature and the administration so that it could do its part in helping to set up the second Constituent Assembly in place of the first assembly which the Federal Court ruled had been illegally dismissed, the United Front coalition was seen to have collapsed. The opposition, however, had succeeded in undermining the monopoly of the Muslim League in the central government, and the central cabinet was reorganized in 1954 to include members of parties other than the Muslim League and also some members without party affiliation.

No one party could set up a ministry when the second Constituent Assembly convened in July 1955, and a coalition was formed consisting of the Muslim League and the Awami League. Chaudhri Mahomad Ali, newly elected head of the Muslim League, became prime minister. But a little over a year later, in September 1956, that government fell when the Muslim League was rent by factional strife. Suhrawardy then (September 10) became prime minister, again in a coalition government, this time of the Awami League with the Republican party, a factional group split from the League and led by Dr. Khan Sahib. This coalition fell apart in October 1957. A new coalition was formed of the Republican party, the Muslim League, an orthodox Muslim party called the Nizam-i-Islam, and the Krishak Sramik ("Peasants and Workers") Party with Ismail Ibrahim Chundrigar as prime minister. However, he could not get together a cabinet and after seven weeks resigned. Firoz Khan Noon then became prime minister in December supported by a coalition of Republicans, Awami League, the National Congress (an East Bengal Hindu party), the Scheduled Castes Federation, and the National Awami Party. This lasted until the revolution in October 1958 brought about the barring of all political parties. Suhrawardy, the most prominent figure in the various moves against the Muslim League, was taken into detention on January 30, 1962, for conduct characterized as "treasonable"; shortly afterwards other persons prominent in the Awami League were also taken into custody. In December 1970 the Awami League, standing for East Pakistan autonomy, swept the elections for a National Assembly and thus became the object of a West Pakistan military campaign of suppression, which failed. The Awami League, after the defeat of Ayub Khan's government, reorganized East Pakistan in 1972 as the new nation Bangladesh.

While Jogendra Nath Mandal was a member of the Pakistan government the Scheduled Castes Federation, which he led, seemed to have status in the country. But when he resigned in protest in 1950 that group lost most of its effectiveness.

Minor opposition parties have included a Socialist Party and an Azad (Free) Pakistan Party, which seems close to Communism in its ideology. Active in the Azad Pakistan party was Iftikhar ud-Din, publisher of two newspapers in Lahore, which for some time seemed to support Communist ideology.

In the North-West Frontier Province there existed before partition the Khuda-i-Khidmatgar (Servants of God) party, commonly called the Red Shirts, affiliated with the Indian National Congress. They had opposed partition and when it became unavoidable had unsuccessfully campaigned for secession of the province or part of it from Pakistan to become an independent area known as Pakhtunistan (Land of the Pakhtus, that is, the Pathans). The party was liquidated shortly after independence. Its principal leader was Khan Abdul Ghaffar Khan, a close friend of Gandhi's, user of Gandhian tactics, and himself often known as "the Frontier Gandhi." He had been jailed before independence by the government of India for his nationalistic activities. Shortly after partition was effected he was jailed by the Pakistan government, even though a member of the Constituent Assembly, and held for six years (1948–1954). He has campaigned vigorously for Pakhtunistan and was arrested for doing so, as in Baluchistan in September 1955, and in April 1961.

His older brother, Dr. Khan Sahib (1882–1958), was a Congress leader in the North-West Frontier Province in the 1930s and headed the provincial cabinet in 1937. In 1946 he headed a non-Muslim League coalition government of Red Shirts, Sikhs, and independents. After Pakistan was created he headed the provincial government, making his first act the release of his brother, then in jail. Shortly afterwards he resigned, and was soon thrown in jail again for political offenses, but he was released in 1953 and served in two Pakistani cabinets. In October 1955, when the then separate provinces of West Pakistan were unified as a single province as West Pakistan, paralleling East Pakistan, he became chief minister and remained so until parliamentary government was suspended there in 1956. He was reinstated in July 1957, but resigned the next day. Khan Sahib was the leading figure in the Republican party when it was formed in April 1956. A disgruntled job seeker assassinated him on May 9, 1958. He had supported the move for a Pakhtunistan province, but when the unification of the then four separate provinces of West Pakistan was being discussed, he stated that in the changed political organization the proposal for Pakhtunistan was no longer pertinent, thus taking a position at variance with that of his brother.

Religio-political groups, of no great importance in point of view of numbers, have succeeded in creating serious political disturbances in Pakistan. One such disturbance was the anti-Ahmadiya movement of 1953. The Ahmadis are a messianic sect centered in in the Punjab, followers of Mirza Ghulam Ahmad (1839–1908). Their most prominent member in recent decades has been Sir (or Chaudhri) Muhammad Zafrullah Khan, foreign minister from December 1947 to October 1954, and president of the United Nations General Assembly in 1962; he was the personal focus of the attack. The attack was started by the Ahrars (Majlis-i-Ahrar), a religiously fundamentalist group opposed to partition, who claimed that the Ahmadis were heretics and should be exterminated. The movement snowballed and got support in all West Pakistan, even among some government officials. Violent demonstrations took place, blood flowed, the government was lax in suppressing the violence, civil government in the Lahore area was brought to a halt, and the army had to be called upon early in March 1953 to establish military rule and restore order. In consequence, the governor of the Punjab, Mian Mumtaz Mohammad Daultana, resigned. In April Prime Minister Nazimuddin was dismissed by Governor General Ghulam Mohammad. A commission headed by the greatly respected Chief Justice Muhammad Munir, and hence called the Munir Commission, was appointed to investigate the disturbances. It published a thorough report in Lahore in 1954 (*Report of the Court of Inquiry into the Punjab Disturbances of 1953*, commonly known as the "Munir Report").

Of quite a different stamp is the Jama'at-i-Islami headed by Maulana Abdul 'Ala Maududi, a learned, conservative, and devout Islamic scholar. He considers that none of the efforts made in forming a government of Pakistan or in producing a constitution were truly calculated to produce an Islamic state, only a secular state. He is against nationalism as such, and looks upon the true Islamic state as one governed according to the *shari'ah* (sacred law.) This would be a single unitary Muslim state throughout the world uniting all the separate substates. A state might have its own legislature, but it should be limited by God's law. The members of the legislature should be elected by the people, according to his scheme. Instead of the *ulema* (learned divines) interpreting the law, the people, through voting for their representatives, would determine whether or not the state was following the law of Islam. The

Jam'at-i-Islami has an organization to promote its ideas by lecturing and publication. As a political party the Jama'at-i-Islami got 4.4 percent of the vote in the Punjab provincial election of 1951, winning 1 seat in the legislature. The organization for a time ceased to function as a political party, having been banned after the October 1958 revolution, but became active again in 1970–71.

With one exception the political parties in India and Pakistan have their origin within the subcontinent and may be considered indigenous. The exception is the Communist Party, which owes its origin to outside stimulus. Communism came to India from Russia shortly after World War I. All Asia at that time became a field for the new Russia's activities, and especially India, as the most important part of the British Empire, which Lenin and others had openly named as an antagonist. A number of Indians, among whom the most prominent came to be M. N. Roy, a Bengali Brahman, received training in those years in the Russian Communist training schools. Because of agitation in India in 1924 a group of four Communists (the "Cawnpore Conspirators") were sentenced to imprisonment for conspiracy against the King-Emperor. One of them was Shripad Amrit Dange (party leader in 1952 and party chairman in 1962). That year the Communist Party of India was organized but it had little strength because the chief Communists had been jailed.

In 1926–1927 several British Communists, including S. Saklatvala, an Indian who had been elected to the British Parliament, came to India to establish cells of workers' and peasants' parties in Bombay, Bengal, the Punjab, and the United Provinces. The party held a conference in 1928 in Calcutta and decided to act in accordance with the program of the Comintern and the policy adopted from time to time by the party with the agreement of the Comintern. It organized a militant left-wing labor movement, which participated in many strikes. In March 1929 the government of India arrested thirty-one leaders, all but two of whom were Communists, in the Meerut Conspiracy case. Most of these were released in 1933, but the four most prominent were held longer. When another wave of strikes broke out in 1934, the government of India banned the Communist Party and it went underground, where it stayed until 1942. It seems to have had a membership in 1934 of 150; by 1942 the number was perhaps between 2500 and

2700 (its own varying claims ran up to 5000), recruited from various outlawed groups or individuals and from Congress Socialists who were dissatisfied with the meagerness of gains under Congress. Congress and the Communists contended during this period for domination of the labor movement and the peasant organizations, and in 1942–1944 when the government held Congress leaders in detention but lifted its ban on the Communists, the Communists gained control of the principal organizations.

Before the Communist Party was banned in India in 1934, the Communists there had opposed Congress and its leaders, including Gandhi, as tools, conscious or unconscious, of imperialism and bourgeois feudalism and capitalism, deceiving the people and betraying the nationalist struggle, a menace to the proletarian revolution. When the left wing of Congress—that is, the group including Jawaharlal Nehru, Jayaprakash Narayan, and other socialistically inclined leaders—emerged in 1931, they condemned it unequivocally. Later they denounced as a bourgeois blind the Congress Socialist Party, which was being formed when the Communist Party of India was coming under government ban. When the ban was imposed and Communism in Europe was entering upon its struggle with Fascism and Nazism and generally promoting a united front, the Communist Party of India too changed its policies. It urged a united front in India against imperialism and gave Congress its support, though recommending some changes in Congress tactics, for example, abandonment of nonviolence. It usually supported Congress in the 1936–1937 elections but was not satisfied with the work of the Congress ministries (1937–1939).

When World War II broke out in 1939, the Communist Party of India, following the general Communist line, stigmatized it as an imperialist war and admonished India not to support it. In March 1940 the government of India took Communist leaders into custody under the Defense of India Rules. When Hitler invaded the Soviet Union, the Indian Communists called the Russian part of the conflict a "people's war," but still did not support the British part. They did not cease their hindrance to the Indian war effort until the Japanese were advancing in Southeast Asia and threatening India, whereupon they accepted the British war as also a people's war and urged India to support it. By this time the Indian political parties had shown that they were at best only lukewarm about the war, and after the Cripps Mission (March 1942) had failed, the government of India removed the ban from the Communist Party, and released the leaders whom it had confined over two years before. At this time the party published a lively organ called the *People's Age*. During the period from August 1942 to March 1945, when the government was holding Congress leaders in confinement, the Communist party strengthened both its position and its membership. By the end of the war it had grown to at least 25,000 (party spokesmen claimed more).

During the war years 1942–1945 the Communist Party, with P. C. Joshi as its general secretary, maintained a wary cooperation, first, with the government of India, which, though using the party's support in prosecuting the war, continued to arrest its leaders; second, with the Indian National Congress, which welcomed its support in advocating release of Congress leaders but deplored its compromise on the Pakistan idea, and regarded its support of the war as traitorous to nationalism; third, with the Muslim League, which being a group dominated by landlords found the Communists uncongenial but appreciated the Communist Party's support of the Pakistan proposal; and finally, with the Untouchables, whose social aims the party approved but whose failure to support the war effort it criticized. At the end of 1945 the association of Congress and the Communist Party, as brittle during the war years as that of the United States and the Soviet Union, was shattered and has never been repaired. In the 1945–1946 elections the Communist Party took a relatively moderate position, not resorting much to extreme proposals of reform or violent language. In this period the Communist Party of India received much advice from R. Palme Dutt, British Communist author on India. While the final struggle between Congress and the League over Pakistan was in progress (1946–1947), the Communist party sided with the Muslim League rather than the Congress, which by that time was operating the interim government under Nehru's leadership.

After partition the activities of the Communist Party increased further. It made capital of the Indian government's removal of economic controls late in 1947, which sent food prices up, and in 1948 it staged a large-scale operation among the peasantry in the eastern part of the then Hyderabad state and the adjacent parts of Madras. Various leading figures in the national and state governments, especially Vallabhbhai Patel, who was home minister as well as deputy prime minister, accused the Communist Party of fomenting strikes and sabotage and other types of violence and took action against them through arrests and raids on their offices. In late 1947 the party began a long series of attacks on Nehru, practically declaring war on him.

In February 1948 the Communists called an Asian Youth Conference in Calcutta, which is generally considered to have planned a Communist campaign for all South and Southeast Asia. Immediately afterwards in the same place the Communist Party of India held its second congress (February 28–March 6, 1948), where it removed from the secretary generalship P. C. Joshi, who had held the position during the days of the united front, and installed B. T. Ranadive, a Communist labor leader, and adopted a new and violent program, published (July 1948, May 1949), and defended at length in a *Political Thesis*. The program amounted to abandonment of constitutional Communism and instead employment of the techniques of revolution.

The basic motives of the party as stated in its 1948 program included severance of India from the Commonwealth; no "collaboration with Anglo-American imperialism"; adult suffrage and proportional representation; self-determination of nationalities, with "a voluntary Indian Union; autonomous linguistic provinces"; accession of the former Indian states to either nation not on the basis of the ruler's choice, as had been the procedure adopted, but by reference to the people; extension of full democratic rights to the tribal and backward peoples; cooperation between India and Pakistan; abolition of landlordism; liquidation of rural indebtedness and abolition of usury; confiscation by the state of foreign capital in banks, industrial and transport concerns, plantations, mines, and so forth, and nationalization of those concerns; nationalization of big industry, banks, and insurance companies, and guarantee of workers' control; minimum living wage; eight-hour day; economic planning; repeal of repressive legislation; elimination of bureaucratic administration; arming of the people; right to free education; equal democratic rights for women.

These demands were to be promoted by *shanti senas* ("peace armies") and common "Left cooperation" in a "Democratic Front." The fight was to be waged by a united working class with the aid of strikes and the support of the All-India Trade Union Congress. The party called for warfare against the non-Communist labor organizations, Congress, the Muslim League, and the Socialist

Party; the rousing of the peasantry under the All-India Kisan Sabha; organization of students, youth, women, and Untouchables; organization of mass political action. The movement was to support the Soviet Union and the Chinese People's government. This program, with modifications in its use and a good deal of alteration, was ostensibly the party manual until the Third Congress of the Communist Party of India in Madura, December 23, 1953 to January 4, 1954.

Before that time serious ideological differences had developed in the Communist Party, which led to public repudiation by Ranadive in 1949 of some of his opponents' views, a statement of adherence to Russian principles respecting Indian Communism, as had been enunciated by E. Zhukov and A. Dyakov, and even an attack on Mao Tse-tung (*Communist,* June-July issue, 1949). Shortly afterwards, however, a Russian endorsement of Chinese doctrine and tactics was published and Ranadive had to recant, at least in part (1950). Ranadive was then removed from the secretary generalship.

The Indian government had set out in March 1948 on a policy of repression in Bengal, where the Communist Party was then strongest, and in Bombay, Madras, and other centers, and had outlawed it in several states. In February 1949 the government reported discovery of a plot to wreck railways and bridges, and that same month there were raids on arms depots near Calcutta by groups which the government said belonged to a Revolutionary Communist Party of India (distinct from the Indian Communist Party). The government arrested large numbers of persons in an anti-Communist drive (a report shows 3000 in one week in February 1949, and there were many others).

At the end of 1949 the government issued a booklet describing "Communist Violence in India," and citing instructions found in captured documents for armed assaults on authority through guerrilla bands preparatory to a general revolution, for methods of silent killing, raids on police stations, and many other similar activities. Communists were also held responsible by the government for much other miscellaneous disturbance, such as inciting the head-hunting Naga tribes in Assam to raid their neighbors. (Later the Nagas were reported to have yielded to pressure to refrain and adopt a less anti-social attitude; by March 1952, certain Naga tribes were seeking independence.) In Assam over 300

Communists were said to have been arrested in October 1950, and over 1000 others in March 1951. In February 1950, at the request of Patel and for the purpose of checking subversive persons, the Indian Parliament had passed a repressive act (Preventive Detention Act), valid for one year, giving the government wide and unusual powers of arrest and detention without trial. In 1952 the government had the act extended for two years. The government had been in part provoked by Communist disturbances in the Telingana area of the Hyderabad state, which Nehru described as civil war.

By 1950 the party was already returning to constitutional Communism, and in preparation for the elections of 1951–1952, it took several steps to get back on an operating footing in the country. In February 1951 it made a "peace offer" to act as a regular political party in the open if the government would withdraw its preventive measures. This the government rejected. In July the Communists in the Hyderabad state made a similar offer to the state government. At the end of April, the Communist Party's headquarters in Bombay issued a "fundamental program" of political and economic emancipation for the Indian people's democracy under the leadership of the working classes and the Communist Party, including confiscation of feudal estates without compensation, nationalization of industry and other large enterprise, support of the Soviet Union and the Chinese People's Republic, withdrawal from the Commonwealth, and alliance and friendship with Pakistan and Ceylon. It called for a united democratic front of all left organizations. At the beginning of August it established its right to enter candidates for the elections in areas where it was not banned; meanwhile the number of areas where it was banned had been notably reduced by court decisions ordering various states to lift their bans. The party aimed at that time to function through local leftist groups.

In late October the party announced that it had failed in its fight to overthrow the government by violence and would cease its hostilities in Hyderabad. On November 8 one of the party's local officers in Delhi announced that a third national congress of the party had been "held somewhere in India late in October" and Ranadive had been removed from the position of general secretary. (This actually seems to refer to Ranadive's removal by the central committee in May 1950.) The announcement was understood to mean that the party was for the time being relinquishing terrorism, evidently meaning to contest in the elections wherever it could. Its election manifesto contained many of the usual demands of the Communist Party and also a clause demanding that India withdraw from the British Commonwealth and join "the peace camp led by the Soviet Union and the People's Republic of China." At the end of November 1951, S. A. Dange, having come out from underground and acting as the party's head or chief spokesman, announced that the party would compete for 500 seats for the state legislatures but would not enter the contests for the central Lok Sahba, though later it did and won some seats. He outlined plans for a mass peasant revolution but rejected violence as a method to overthrow the government. He also stated that under government persecution and intraparty purging the party's membership, which had stood at 80,000 in 1946, had declined to 30,000.

In the 1951–1952 elections the Communist Party of India and its allies won 27 seats in the Lok Sabha, thus being the strongest opposition party. In the state legislative assemblies it won 180 seats (out of 587 contested), and there too it ran second to Congress. After the elections the Communists actively made alliances with other parties in an effort to capture control of state legislative assemblies in Madras, where it had won 62 seats (out of 375) against Congress' 152; in Travancore-Cochin (now part of Kerala), where it had won 32 seats (out of 108) against Congress' 44; and in PEPSU, where it had won 2 seats (out of 60) against Congress' 26.

In Madras Rajagopalachari was able to hold the leadership for Congress by gaining support of the independents.

The Communist strength in Madras had been in the Telugu area in the north. This was made into the Andhra state in October 1953. In an Andhra state election in 1955 the United Congress Front won 146 seats in the legislative assembly, the Communists 15, and the Praja-Socialists 13. After Andhra was enlarged in the states reorganization of 1956, the 1957 election gave Congress 213 seats (out of 301), the Communists 12, the Praja-Socialists 11.

In PEPSU the quarrels had been so severe that the government of India suspended the regime in March 1953. Elections were held in February 1954, in which Congress won 37 out of 60 seats. In the reorganization of states in 1956 the state of PEPSU was abolished and its territory was absorbed in the Punjab.

The greatest successes of constitutional Communism were in

Travancore-Cochin, afterwards Kerala. There after the 1951–1952 elections Congress had led a coalition government, but in September 1953 the Praja-Socialists united with the Communists and some others to defeat the Congress government on a vote of confidence. The Socialists, however, would not follow this up by forming a coalition government with the Communists, and a state-wide election was necessary. In this (February 1954), Congress won 45 seats, a Communist-dominated united front won 40 seats, and the Praja-Socialists won 19, the Praja-Socialists thus holding the balance of power. With the support of Congress the Socialists formed a ministry (March 1954), which did not, however, last long, and until the 1957 elections no stable government existed in the state.

The States Reorganization Scheme of 1956 established the state of Kerala, consisting of most of Travancore-Cochin and the west coastal districts of Madras, which like Travancore-Cochin had a strong Communist element. The area seemed ideally suited for Communist penetration because of the low economic status of the population. In the 1957 assembly elections in Kerala the Communists won 60 seats (out of 126), Congress 43, the Socialists 9, and independent candidates 14. The Communists had supported 5 of the 14 independents; with these they now made an alliance to secure for themselves a majority in the legislative assembly and so set up a government. The Communist leader Elankulam Manakal Sankaran (E.M.S.) Namboodiripad, a Brahman by birth, became chief minister. Strong opposition developed against his rule. This came to a head in 1959 on the issue of private schools, which, by an act passed in September 1958, were to be taken over by the state with authority to regulate salaries and service conditions of teachers, award scholarships, and prescribe the curriculum. Most of the schools involved were Roman Catholic and Hindu. Kerala has the greatest concentration of Christians in India and also has a recalcitrant Muslim group known as Moplahs (Mappila). The issue was seized by the Congress party, the Praja-Socialists, and the Muslim League, who comprised the opposition in the legislative assembly. In June violence developed. On Nehru's advice Namboodiripad suspended some provisions of the act late in June, but the demonstrations and violence continued into July. On August 1 the President of India, Rajendra Prasad, turned the Communist government out of office and put the state under governor's rule. Elections were held February 1, 1960, in which an alliance of Congress, the Praja-Socialist Party, and the Muslim League won 94 seats (out of 126), though the Communist Party got a higher percentage of the total vote than in 1952 (43 percent against 39 percent). The chief minister was Pattom Thanu Pillai (b. 1886), head of the Praja-Socialist Party.

In the 1962 elections the Communist Party won 29 seats in the Lok Sabha and 166 in the state assemblies, though no elections were held for the Kerala and Orissa assemblies.

There is a Communist group in India which does not believe in elections, viewing them as a blind of the bourgeoisie. This is the Naxalite movement, which originated among farmers in the Naxalbari district, which is located in the narrow strip of Indian territory, only twenty miles wide, which separates Nepal from Pakistan. The Naxalites do not vote, but believe in instant revolution. They frankly say that they use violence and terrorism, and that their guerrillas have been directed to "finish" all vote-seekers. This seems to be a kind of participation in elections without resort to the ballot. Their ideological affiliation is with the Communist Party of India (Marxist) and with Maoism.

Between the 1962 and 1967 national elections in India the Communist Party split into the Communist Party of India, regarded as the right wing of Indian Communism and supporting the Soviet Union, and the Communist Party of India (Marxist), regarded as the left wing and supporting China. In the 1962 elections the as yet undivided Communist Party of India won 29 seats in the Lok Sabha. In the 1967 elections, after the split, the Communist Party won 23 seats in the Lok Sabha and the Communist Party (Marxist) won 19. In the 1971 elections the Communist Party won 23 seats and the Communist Party (Marxist) won 25.

The Communists in India sell large numbers of well-printed books at cheap prices, and speak much in public and in private. They make an important point of showing that Communists concern themselves with national cultural aspirations and support the claim by stimulating small amateur and semiprofessional theatrical groups. In this way they appeal to some of the same sort of sentiment that gave nationalism its strength. They get a great deal of their material into the newspapers in editorials and news items. Their workers industriously circulate among the masses. The Communist achievements in Russia and China are exploited to a maximum as examples of what India might expect if it became a Communist country. Early in 1952 an exhibition was staged in Bombay, the headquarters of the Communist Party of India, to show the agrarian, industrial, and cultural advance of Russia and China. Many Indian literary, artistic, and motion picture figures are invited for visits by the governments of those countries. The total effect of this program has been large, and has, of course, been pointed to show a contrast with the United States.

The Communist Party of India was seriously embarrassed by the Chinese advance along India's northern frontiers in 1962, and will doubtless long be further embarrassed by the Chinese support of Pakistan in the Indo-Pakistan War of 1971. The Chinese advance in 1962 split the party between those who were censorious of China, including Ajoy Kumar Ghosh, secretary of the party from 1951 until his death in January 1962, and those who favored China. Because of the general Indian resentment of the Chinese move, support of it by the Communist Party was politically damaging, however much suggested by theoretical considerations. Similarly the ideological dispute between the Soviet Union and China has divided the sympathies of the Indian Communists. So, too, the Indian Communists are said to have had conflicting opinions on Khrushchev's de-Stalinization policy. Within the Indian party, the West Bengal Communists are considered to favor the Chinese.

When the party's national council met in New Delhi in April and May 1962, the issues became critical in the search for a successor to A. K. Ghosh as party secretary. The post finally went to E. M. S. Namboodiripad of Kerala, who supported the Chinese. The other wing of the party was given the post of party chairman (in the person of the veteran S. A. Dange) in an effort to keep the factions within the party from sundering it. In a communiqué issued by the national council the statement was made that "The ideological-political activities of the party are unsatisfactory and there is need for remolding in certain vital respects the way in which party units at various levels have to function." The new secretariat, consisting of six left-wing (pro-Chinese) members and three right-wing (pro-Russian) members, was entrusted with drafting recommendations concerning the ideological and organizational matters at issue. After the Chinese-Indian undeclared war became critical, the Indian government put a number of the "China lobby" Communists under arrest, and the party's secretariat came out with a statement condemning the Chinese for their attack on India.

The Communist movement has had much more weight in national affairs in India than in Pakistan where as an organization it has had none at all. The government of India's success in confining significant Communist activity to a few areas is a consequence of improved living conditions, stability of the government, and the effective organization of Congress as a political party. The success of the five-year plans for economic development remains critical in the contest between the democratic socialist advance under Congress leadership and the Communist effort to capitalize on India's economic backwardness and social misery.

Although the Communist movement has been much less active in Pakistan than in India, it has a number of open members and sympathizers, and, as in India, has been vigorously opposed by the government. It has been supported by various newspapers, among them the *Pakistan Times* (Lahore), one of the nation's two largest English-language newspapers, its Urdu counterpart called *Imroz*. The most prominent members or supporters for some years were Iftikhar ud-Din, publisher of the *Pakistan Times*, and a member of the first Constituent Assembly; Faiz Ahmed Faiz, editor of the same newspaper, president of the Pakistan Trade Union Congress, member of the World Peace Council; Syed Sajad Zaheer, general secretary of the Communist Party of Pakistan; Syed Sibtey Hassan, formerly a correspondent in the United States for the *People's Age,* a Communist organ in India during the war.

From time to time reports have been published of Communist activity in Pakistan and government retaliation. The chief government charge against the Communists was of a conspiracy to assassinate its leading figures and establish a military dictatorship, discovery of which was announced on March 9, 1951. The government arrested sixteen prominent military and civilian persons. The leading ones were Major General Akbar Khan, chief of staff of the Pakistan army, who in 1947 had borne the pseudonym "General Tariq" as commander of the Pakistan forces operating with the Azad Kashmir forces in Kashmir; Faiz Ahmed Faiz; Syed Sajjad Zaheer. The Constituent Assembly (functioning as the Pakistan Parliament) passed a Special Tribunal Act in April, authorizing abrogation of usual judicial procedure, and in June fifteen (or fourteen) of those arrested were brought to trial. The Communists claimed that the conspiracy trial was a blind, and that the real motive for the arrest was that the accused were opposing secret negotiations of the Pakistan government with the United States. The Pakistan government also considered Communists largely responsible for riots in East Bengal in February 1952, which agitated various issues including that of language. In 1954 the government banned the Communist Party. Ever since then public statements have been made by officials concerning Communist efforts to infiltrate labor organizations or to influence students or to disrupt government activity, but these efforts have not been regarded as important.

In Pakistan since its dismemberment the leading political party has been the Pakistan People's Party (PPP), headed by Zulfikar Ali Bhutto, who became President when Yahya Khan's rule collapsed. The second most influential party is the Awami League of Pakistan, which is headed by Wali Khan, son of Abdul Ghaffar Khan, who had been head of the "Red Shirts" and was called the "Frontier Gandhi."

In Bangladesh the only political party of any strength is the Awami League. In the 1970 election for the National Assembly it won 162 seats in what was then East Pakistan. In special elections in constituencies that had been devastated by the November cyclone it won 5 more. Some other parties had nominated candidates but with no success in the election. Bangladesh started its existence as a single-party state, but with the declared intention of operating on strictly democratic principles.

14 Social Progress and Problems

When India and Pakistan attained independence they had scope to promote social reform and progress beyond that which had been possible for the British. Touchy questions involving tradition, especially in the area of religion, had had to be handled gingerly by the British. There had been unpleasant and sometimes violent response to such well-intentioned and beneficial innovations as smallpox vaccination, including the murder of a highly esteemed British civil servant and Indic scholar, A. M. T. Jackson, in 1909. The improvement of women's status could not be effected without countering customs of great age sanctioned by religion. Such a drastic practice as *sati* (suttee), prevalent among the ruling classes and often imitated by others, was made illegal by Governor General Lord William Bentinck in a proclamation of 1830 without serious opposition, but there were not many institutions that could safely be abolished so peremptorily. Indians, however, did not suffer the same restraints as did foreigners in dealing with traditional prejudices.

Nor could the British expend the country's public financial resources, however wisely, without being subject to attacks of a peculiar virulence, which has not been present when the expenditures have been authorized by the elected representatives of the population. Hence, problems of education, public health, community development, social discrimination, women's rights, the inheritance rights of minors, and other social matters could be handled by the government with better public support in the new nations than under British rule. During the British period progress in these areas had been initiated and in some of them much had been done. The way was open at independence for an indicated further development.

The most useful modernizing social tool which Britain bequeathed to India and Pakistan was a system of public education.

It is true that it was below western standards; that by 1941 it had made literate only 15.1 percent of the population aged ten and above; that many pupils attended for only a year or two and then lapsed into illiteracy; that it presented modern social and natural science incompletely; that it ignored the traditional Indic material in the humanities side of its program and instead presented western and British materials; that it gave college instruction a disproportionate place in the system; that it included little of technical and applied science. Nevertheless, it brought new and stimulating ideas to India, introduced the country to a secular view of life, gave it English as a common language, and so put it into direct contact with the learning, thought, history, and politics of the outside world.

At the close of World War II the subcontinent had eighteen universities, some of which were examining bodies of affiliated colleges, while some others gave "postgraduate" (a term equivalent in India, as in Britain, to the American "graduate") instruction, and the rest gave both postgraduate and undergraduate instruction. There were around 450 arts and science colleges, including four-year and intermediate colleges and second-grade colleges; and about 115 professional schools, dealing with law, medicine, teaching, agriculture, commerce, engineering, technology, art. There were in British India in those years approximately 4200 high schools, with about 1,350,000 students, among whom were 171,000 girls; less than 1000 secondary schools teaching professional subjects; about 10,300 middle schools (more or less equivalent to American junior high schools), with 1,420,000 pupils; 187,000 primary and special schools, having about 12,000,000 pupils out of possibly 40,000,000 children of primary-school age. In British India about 5.2 percent of the entire population was receiving instruction—the percentage was probably not much different in the Indian states as a whole, though both the lowest and the highest rates of literacy and school attendance were found in them. The schools were chiefly in the cities; most of the more than 650,000 villages in the subcontinent had nothing at all.

Various important studies of India's educational system were made during the British period, of which the latest was begun in 1938 and published in 1944. This was an elaborate Report by the Central Advisory Board of Education, entitled *Post-War Educational Development in India,* commonly known from the name of its chairman, Sir John Sargent, as the "Sargent Scheme." This was aimed to provide basic mass education, which it was hoped would become universal in a period of forty years, as well as secondary, higher, and professional education adapted to the social, economic, and political needs of India as a modern state. The scheme was criticized on the grounds that it would take too long to achieve, and on the ground that it was too expensive to be realized and therefore overoptimistic. To many observers at the time who were not involved in Indian politics it seemed to be a realizabale combination of restrained idealism and fiscal courage.

Since independence India and Pakistan have added many new universities, colleges, professional and technical schools, high schools, and lower schools. Bangladesh is now the heir to the educational developments that were made in East Pakistan. The latest figures available (see *Statistical Abstract India 1969*, pp. 633–668) show that by 1965–66 India had 80 universities, 1940 arts and science colleges including research institutions, 93 agricultural and forestry colleges, 73 commerce colleges, 64 law colleges, 386 medicine and veterinary science colleges, 1523 teachers' training colleges, 638 engineering, technical, and architecture colleges, 1550 other professional and technical colleges, with a total of 6,267 colleges. With these there were schools for general education, nursery schools, schools for vocational and professional education, and schools for other education.

Pakistan by 1956 had in West Pakistan 6 universities and 300 colleges. In East Pakistan, now Bangladesh, there were 4 universities and 180 colleges. Later figures are not available.

The subcontinent, whether in the Indian or Pakistani areas (including the new nation of Bangladesh), has lacked the facilities to meet educational demands. Applicants have had to be rejected for higher education, while the demands from villages, towns, and cities for more secondary and primary schools have not been adequately met.

Literacy rates have, of course, increased. In India the 1951 census gave a literacy figure of 15.6 percent of the total population; the Pakistani figure for 1951 was given as 18.9 percent, but this was sharply questioned. The 1961 census gave 23.7 percent for India and 15.3 percent for Pakistan. The 1971 census figure for India is 29.34 percent. There are no 1971 figures available for Pakistan (including what is now Bangladesh). In preindependence unpartitioned India the elite Muslims had shown far less interest in modern secular education than had Hindus, and Pakistan's relatively weaker position in education and literacy reflects that fact.

India and Pakistan have set themselves the goal of universal adult literacy and devised educational policies to that end. The most ambitious statements appears in clause 45 of the Indian constitution, which reads: "The State shall endeavor to provide, within a period of ten years from the commencement of this Constitution [1950], for free and compulsory education for all children until they complete the age of fourteen years." This was a bit of optimism which made Sir John Sargent with his forty-year plan look like a discouraging Jeremiah; doubtless no informed person in India dealing with education ever thought it had the remotest chance of achievement. To provide such basic education each of India's roughly 500,000 villages would have needed at least one primary school, in many cases several, amounting to three or four times the total number of schools then existing. No way was ever discovered to find the necessary teachers, buildings, equipment, and financing for such expansion in so short a period as ten years. Substantial progress, however, has been made.

Pakistan's Second Five-Year Plan (1960–1965) also made an ambitious statement. It proposed to provide "compulsory schooling for the age-group 6–11 . . . within a period of ten years, and within another five years for the age-group 11–14." Ayub Khan's government promised development in 1961 to implement recommendations of the Education Commission.

Women's education provides a serious problem in the subcontinent. In India in 1951 female literacy was given as 7.87 against 24.87 for males. In 1961 the percentages were 12.8 for females against 33.9 for males. In 1971 the percentages for the entire population (including age group 0-4 years) were 39.51 for males and 18.44 for females. In Pakistan in 1951 the percentages for all persons over 5 years of age were 3.7 for females and 21.4 for males. In 1961 the percentages for West Pakistan were 23.9 for males and 7.4 for females; in East Pakistan, which is now Bangladesh, the percentages were 31.5 for males and 10.7 for females. The Pakistan census figures for 1971 have not been published.

In India a system of "basic education" has been promoted as a matter of government policy. This supplements the usual subjects of instruction with an activity program that is correlated with the physical and social environment of the children and consists of such manual occupations as spinning and weaving, gardening, carpentry, leather work, book craft, cooking, sewing, house management, and others. This was an idea vigorously promoted by Gandhi. It has had strong official support but has not yet met with general success.

There is a pressing cry in the subcontinent for amplification of teaching facilities in the natural sciences and technological fields. But since these are notoriously expensive because of the cost of laboratory equipment and the training of instructors, India and Pakistan are still unable to expand them rapidly and have to continue sending students to western institutions. In the humanities, modern college education may be expected to make increased use of the great resources of the native Indian and Islamic civilizations in language, literature, art, speculative and analytic thought. A movement to exploit these resources was developed in Bengal in the 1920s and led to certain innovations at the University of Calcutta which have spread elsewhere. A number of studies of the position of Sanskrit have been made by state commissions dealing with educational reorganization and recommendations have been offered: United Provinces in 1938; Bihar 1939; Uttar Pradesh (formerly United Provinces) 1947; West Bengal 1948; Travancore (now mostly included in Kerala) 1948; Madras 1949; Bombay 150; Mysore 1953; Punjab; Madhya Pradesh 1955; Rajasthan 1955–1956. The culmination of the move to define and stabilize the study of Sanskrit was the work of the government of India's Sanskrit Commission 1956–1957, which submitted its interesting report in 1958 with a long series of recommendations designed to perpetuate and utilize through western-type institutions and the traditional *pathshalas* the cultural heritage of the country as this is expressed chiefly through the medium of the Sanskrit language. An international Sanskrit Conference lasting five days was convened in New Delhi in March 1972, attended by over 1500 scholars, most of them Indian. It showed that the study of Sanskrit and its literature was being pursued in all parts of India. Whether this effort will succeed or Sanskrit will share the fate which Greek and Latin have suffered in the West remains to be seen. Sanskrit can hardly have a future as a general medium of instruction, even at the highest level, as some of its partisans have hoped. The current demand is for science and technology. Pakistan has a system of education in Islamic studies, long supported mostly by private funds, centered on the Koran and the accompanying tradition (*sunna*) and law (*shari'ah*) taught by the imams of mosques or in schools (*maktab*) attached to mosques, or fostered in lower schools (*madrasah*) or in Islamic departments in colleges and universities. In both the 1956 and 1962 constitutions provision was made for an Institute of Islamic Studies supported by government funds.

Training for specialized government service and for the many development projects being executed or planned in each country requires a great expansion of the education system; institutes for such purposes have been established in each country and more are planned. Research facilities in general are poorly developed, whether for natural, social, or humanistic studies, and many distinguished scholars have publicly and vigorously lamented this fact, including Sir C. V. Raman (1888–1970), winner of the Nobel Prize for Physics in 1920. Libraries, laboratories and investigating institutes are insufficient in number and usually inadequately supported, though several of high standing and distinguished accomplishment can be mentioned (Calcutta School of Tropical Medicine, Haffkine Institute, the Gokhale Institute of Social and Economic Research in Poona, Bhandarkar Oriental Research Institute, Deccan College Oriental Research Institute, Indian Statistical Institute, the Institute of World Affairs in New Delhi, and others).

Closely related to education are the problems arising in India and Pakistan from language. The problems of education and communication associated with language center around the questions: What should be the language or languages of government and higher education? What is the way to give satisfaction to the just demands of specific language groups? The conflicts are those of Aryan with Dravidian, Indic with English, Hindi with Urdu, and each of the latter two with other Aryan tongues.

Aryan has now for more than three thousand years been encroaching upon Dravidian. More than a century ago Bishop R. Caldwell, long resident in south India, and an eminent authority on Davidian languages, spoke of Aryan contempt for Dravidian and the self-assertion of Dravidian in reaction. The conflict was intensified when the vernaculars were given a place in the public education system. Before then, when the British introduced English as both subject and medium of instruction in the first half of the nineteenth century, they did so as the preferred alternative to Sanskrit and Persian, the classical languages, not to the vernaculars, which at that time were disesteemed. The prestige of the modern Indian languages began to rise when Sir Charles Wood's dispatch of 1854 instituted instruction in them in government lower schools. Extending this principle, nationalistically minded elements of the population promoted use of the vernaculars as the medium of instruction on higher levels of education starting in the late nineteenth century and gaining momentum in the first half of the twentieth. Modern language literatures started to develop and a press grew up using them. The most striking development was the establishment at Ahmedabad, under Gandhi's inspiration, of the Vidyapith at the time of the first noncooperation movement. There the medium of instruction was Hindi and the cultural material studied was Indian. Rabindranath Tagore, too, in the institution which he founded at Shanti Niketan in Bolpur, Bengal, now become the Vishva Bharati ("Universal Indian") University and operating under the central government, used Indian languages as the medium of instruction and their literature as material for study. The Osmaniya University of Hyderabad, at the stimulus of the Nizam of Hyderabad, a Muslim, employed Urdu.

Nationalism was intent on displacing English both as the official language and as the medium of instruction, but the question was what to replace it with. Here Hindu-Muslim communalism, as well as Aryan-Dravidian rivalry, created an issue. The Indian National Congress wanted Hindi, or, when it listened to Gandhi, Hindustani. Muslims wanted Urdu. The terms Hindi, Hindustani, and Urdu, as scientifically used, represent varieties of the same language. Hindustani is the current spoken form, providing the phonology, grammatical structure, and basic vocabulary. Hindi and Urdu are literary forms of Hindustani, and are differentiated from each other in the learned or highly cultivated vocabulary and in script. Partisans of the two also apply the names to colloquial, nonliterary speech, and refer to them as separate languages. Literary Hindi borrows words freely from Sanskrit, is generally written in an indigenous script known as Nagari (or Devanagari), and as so written is current chiefly among Hindus. Literary Urdu borrows copiously from Persian and Arabic, usually is written in the Perso-Arabic script, and is largely current among Muslims. Hindi and Urdu came to be rival symbols of Hindu-Muslim communalism. Gandhi tried to resolve the language quarrel by advocating Basic Hindustani written in both scripts, and continued to do so as late as January 1948, shortly before his assassination. The Congress ministries during their period of power (1937–1939) were not always thoughtful of Muslim susceptibilities and sometimes promoted

Hindi rather than Hindustani, thus leading Muslims to react by affirming claims for Urdu.

The attack which nationalism has made upon English therefore, has also induced communal controversy over what is to be substituted, Hindi or Urdu. It has also aroused regional linguistic jealousy among Dravidians, who live in south India and are proud of their own literary tongues. Further, in various parts of India where Aryan languages are current there is now jealousy of Hindi. The Bengalis, who consider themselves the intellectual leaders of India, have thought that their language should be second to none; to a less extent speakers of Marathi in western India have had a similar feeling; to a still less extent have Gujaratis, also in western India.

Just as in India the choice of Hindi as the replacement for English is unpopular in southern, eastern, and to some extent western parts of the country, so in Pakistan the once proposed choice of Urdu, though agreeable to West Pakistan, was opposed in East Pakistan, a Bengali region. In July 1969 the Ministry of Education and Scientific Research of the military government announced that English was to be eliminated as an official language within six years, though its study and use were to be encouraged Both Urdu and Bengali were to remain as official languages and were to be required languages in both wings of the nation, while all government employees were to know both Urdu and Bengali by 1973. The language quarrel contributed to the ill feeling between East and West Pakistan that finally led to the revolt of East Pakistan and the creation of the new nation of Bangladesh, which may be expected to promote Bengali.

India has committed itself to Hindi, and the constitution in article 351 prescribes that the state should promote the development of Hindi, as against Urdu or any other, saying: "It shall be the duty of the Union to promote the spread of the Hindi language, to develop it so that it may serve as a medium of expression for all the elements of the composite culture of India and to ensure its enrichment by assimilating without interfering with its genius, the forms, style, and expressions used in Hindustani and in the other languages of India specified in the Eighth Schedule, and by drawing, whenever necessary or desirable, for its vocabulary, primarily on Sanskrit and secondarily on other languages."

The decision for Hindi, which was adopted by a single vote, did not solve the problem of finding a suitable national language. Hindi is, first of all, not at present a feasible substitute for English. That fact is revealed by the constitution itself. This says in section 343(1): "The official language of the Union shall be Hindi in Devanagari script." But after giving this acknowledgment to national cultural aspirations, it goes on to say in section 343(2): "Notwithstanding anything in clause (1), for a period of fifteen years from the commencement of this Constitution, the English language shall continue to be used for all official purposes of the Union for which it was being used immediately before such commencement." And still further in the same section it states in 343(3): "Notwithstanding anything in this article, Parliament may by law provide for the use, after the same period of fifteen years, of—(a) the English language . . . for such purposes as may be specified in the law." More stringently and specifically the constitution, dealing with a field where the use of language may be administratively critical, provides in section 348 that "until Parliament by law otherwise provides—(a) all proceedings in the Supreme Court and in every High Court, (b) the authoritative texts— (i) of all Bills . . . (ii) of all Acts passed by Parliament or the Legislature of a State and of all Ordinances promulgated by the President or the Governor or Rajpramukh of a State, and (iii) of all orders, rules, regulations and bye-laws issued under this constitution or under any law made by Parliament or the Legislature of a State, shall be in the English language." (There are certain modifications of a minor character.) In accordance with this provision the official text of the constitution is in English.

In Pakistan the constitution of 1962 deals with the question of language with great brevity. Article 215 states: "(1) The national languages of Pakistan are Bengali and Urdu, but this Article shall not be construed as preventing the use of any other language and, in particular, the English language may be used for official and other purposes until arrangements for its replacement are made. (2) In the year One thousand nine hundred and seventy-two, the President shall constitute a Commission to examine and report on the question of the replacement of the English language for official purposes." This attitude is realistic and indicates a reluctance to displace English.

Government in the subcontinent is greatly dependent upon English. It is the only medium through which legislative representatives and officials from different regions can communicate with one another. In education and business the situation is the same. The courts, except on the lower levels where small cases are handled, could not proceed today in any language other than English. The basis of modern law in the subcontinent being English jurisprudence, the English language has been and still is the vehicle of the law. Decisions are rendered and precedents established and quoted in English. The legal vocabulary is that of English law; none of the native languages, not even the classical literary languages of Sanskrit and Persian, which once were court languages, is equipped to express the necessary concepts of modern legal practice. The same considerations apply in framing legislation. Indian languages can, however, be used for many administrative procedures, and are beginning to get such usage. On November 1, 1952, for example, Uttar Pradesh replaced English with Hindi as the official language, but the change has not proved fully workable. It is evident that Hindi still lacks the vocabulary to supersede English. For international communication neither Hindi nor Urdu is usable, nor would Bengali be satisfactory.

Though the constitution of India prescribes Hindi as the goal for national language, it recognizes in section 345 that separate regions within the nation need to use their local languages internally in public affairs. But (by section 346) for communication between one state and another and between a state and the union the language shall be that authorized as the official language of the Union, unless two or more states agree to use Hindi (in place of the present official English). To prevent a majority language from dominating unfairly in a state, the president of the Union may, by section 347, on demand, if he is satisfied that a substantial portion of the state's population desires the use of a language spoken by them to be recognized by that state, direct that it be recognized in all or part of the state. The end result could well be, in theory, that in the government of a state where Hindi is not a local language officials might need to use several languages in their interstate and intrastate affairs; for example, in Madras at least English, Hindi, and Tamil would be required. In practice, however, it might equally well be that English would remain the sole official language for any but the lowest administrative levels, and a good many realistic citizens say so.

A three-language proposal (Hindi, English, and the local language) has been proposed and is hotly argued, so far without acceptance, though no better solution seems to have any backing. In some areas, for example, in Tamil Nadu, where this proposal is vigorously opposed, many are in favor of having only the local language and English as recognized means of communication for official purposes. In December 1967 the Lok Sabha voted 224 to 75 for a bill to retain English as a national language until each of the states that now oppose Hindi is willing to accept it. Public reaction to this arrangement was mixed. The action was essentially equivalent to an announcement by Home Minister Lal Bahadur Shastri in May 1962 that the government of India meant to introduce in Parliament a bill to maintain the existing position of English.

With respect to the question of which language should be the medium of instruction in the education system, cultural nationalism again urges use of a native language instead of the still prevailing English, but an issue remains as to which one to employ. In India Congress has demanded Hindi; in West Pakistan there has been sentiment for Urdu and in what was East Pakistan, now Bangladesh, for Bengali, which is native there, but again there are potent objections. The issue arises only on the higher levels of education, that is, in colleges, technical and professional institutions, and graduate schools—possibly to a limited extent in high schools. For education below these levels the local vernaculars are necessary and satisfactory. On the higher levels, however, the vernaculars lack the scientific vocabulary to replace English. But the nationalist sentiment that demands the ouster of English insists that the native literary languages can supply a terminology of new words made from their own lexical resources. That is, English terms could be translated into forms made from Hindi or Sanskrit or Urdu or Persian or Arabic elements by a process of derivation and compounding. Such proposals to manufacture a vocabulary, though fair in the hearing of cultural chauvinism, are a delusion. The meaning of scientific terminology depends largely upon usage by scholars, and newly fashioned terms with no scientific history or context have little meaning or chance to acquire any.

The language question involves a subsidiary problem of script. The various modern languages of the subcontinent employ different local systems of writing, though the different systems, with the exception of the imported Perso-Arabic, are all indigenous and derived from the Brahmi script, which was current by the third century B.C. The most widely used script is Nagari, or Devanagari, cited in article 343 of the constitution of India, which is employed for Hindi and Marathi and is used optionally for some others such as Gujarati and Kashmiri. All the scripts, whether indigenous or imported, are alphabetic but are complicated to write and difficult to learn. The symbol for any one sound may vary in appearance according to its position in the word, whether initial, medial, or final, or when combined with other symbols in ligatures, which are numerous. Hence, while our own roman script with its small and capital letters (some of which are duplicates) requires a learner to master only about forty shapes, these scripts, though having no capitals, may present literally hundreds of forms. The Perso-Arabic script is less complicated than the Devanagari, but still more complicated than roman.

The central and several state governments of India and Pakistan have been concerned with the problem of simplifying scripts so as to ease the learning process and fit them for typewriting and modern printing. Newspaper publishers and other printers have also been so concerned, and to a less extent so have business interests. Some newspapers, publishing in Bengali, Hindi, Tamil, or Urdu, have experimented with script reform so as to adapt the local scripts to mechanical type-composing machines (linotype, monotype). Such adaptation requires changes in the appearance of some symbols. Since independence the government of India and the governments of Uttar Pradesh, Bombay, Madras, and Orissa have had active script reform committees; some other states have had less active committees. The government of Pakistan seems willing to use the Naskh form of the Perso-Arabic (instead of the Nastalig now used in Iran and India), which is common in western Islamic countries and has been adapted to printing, but a change to this script has made slow progress. The problem is to simplify the scripts in such a way that, though the writing is made easier, the appearance of the symbols is kept near enough to the accepted traditional forms to be neither ambiguous nor offensive to public taste, which is extremely sensitive on the subject.

The easiest and most successful method of script reform would be to use the roman script with modifications, as was done in Turkey. With the aid of simple diacritical marks it is possible to adapt it to the phonetic demands of any language used in India. Scholars do so successfully now. Another method might be to devise a few additional symbols. Roman would have the advantages of being simple to learn, easy to use on the typewriter, in printing, and on teletype, and of being widely employed elsewhere in the world. Some of India's leading linguistic scholars proposed change of this kind in the 1920s and 1930s, and Nehru spoke in its favor at various times, as in February 1949, when he said, "It would be desirable to explore the possibilities of the roman script," but such advice has not been welcome. Nationalism continues to assert native cultural prestige, and script is an item deeply cherished in that connection. No language group in the subcontinent is eager to see its language written in a European script.

Indian newspapers—including dailies, triweeklies, biweeklies, weeklies, fortnightlies, monthlies, quarterlies—total something like 7000, many of which are inconsequential. The most important dailies are published in Calcutta, Bombay, Madras, Delhi, Allahabad, Lucknow; some are English-language publications, while some are in modern Indian languages. More dailies are published in English than in any other language; then come Hindi, Urdu, Bengali, and Gujarati. Pakistan's chief newspaper publishing centers are Karachi and Lahore; Bangladesh's is Dacca. India's first newspaper was *The Bengal Gazette* founded in Calcutta in 1780, and often known after its founder, William Hicky (1749–1830), as *Hicky's Gazette* or *Hicky's Journal*. Other newspapers in English were established shortly afterwards in Bombay and Madras, and in 1816 a vernacular press was born in Bengal. Up to the present the leadership has consistently remained with the English-language press. It had, and has today, the best newspapers, gets the best and freshest news service, publishes the best editorials and columns, gives the fullest commercial and other specialized coverage. The vernacular press draws upon the English-language press for news and ideas; contains as a rule inferior editorials, being less responsible and less original; and, with few exceptions, is poorly printed. By American standards both English-language and vernacular newspapers have small circulation. A maximum of 100,000 is considered good.

Freedom of the press has always been a critical issue since Governor General Warren Hastings suppressed *The Bengal Gazette* in 1782, two years after its founding, for various offenses, including attacks upon his wife. For the first forty years of its life the Indian press was subject to rigid control, in the beginning (until 1799)

303

by penalties such as stoppage of circulation or deportation of editors, after 1799 by regulations promulgated by Lord Mornington (Marquis Wellesley, Governor General 1798–1805) and then by a series of further restrictive rules imposed from 1823 to 1827. In 1853 these were repealed in a Press Act, which was adopted contrary to the presentiment of the far-seeing Sir Thomas Munro, governor of Madras, that a free press and an autocratic government were incompatible. "What is the first duty of a free press?" he asked, and himself answered, "It is to deliver the country from a foreign yoke." He predicted that the freeing action would come about through the Sepoy army, which later, in 1857, did revolt. A part of the press protested Lord Dalhousie's (governor general 1848–1856) annexations in Oudh, which led to the Indian (Sepoy) Mutiny, and during the time of the Mutiny Lord Canning (governor general 1856–1862) imposed severe censorship, which afterwards lapsed. In 1867 a Press and Registration of Books Act was passed. At the time of the second Afghan War, in 1878, Lord Lytton (governor general 1876–1880) imposed a Vernacular Press Act, which aroused violent protest and was repealed shortly afterwards in 1882 under Lord Ripon (governor general 1880–1884). From then until 1907, the government dealt with journalistic sedition under sections of the Penal Code.

In 1908 a Newspaper (Incitement to Offenses) Act was passed to curb the anti-British acts accompanying the growth of nationalism. In 1910 a still more stringent Indian Press Act was adopted. The reaction to this was so strong that in 1922 the acts of 1908 and 1910 were repealed and instead certain modifications were made to the Act of 1867. The result was a law less harsh than the repealed legislation but nevertheless restrictive. But in 1930, when the second civil disobedience campaign was launched, the government imposed a strict press ordinance, which in 1931 was put on the statute book as the Indian Press (Emergency Powers) Act. The various press restrictions were constantly attacked by nationalists, and when the constitution of India was adopted in 1950, it included a guarantee in section 19(1)(a) of "freedom of speech and expression," subject, however, to the modification that nothing should "affect the operation of any existing law in so far as it relates to, or prevent the State from making any law relating to, libel, slander, defamation, contempt of court or any matter which offends against decency or morality or which undermines the security of, or tends to overthrow, the State."

Part II of the Pakistan constitution of 1962, in specifying principles of law-making, dealt with freedom of expression, as follows: "1. No law should impose any restriction on the freedom of a citizen to give expression to his thoughts. 2. This Principle may be departed from where it is necessary so to do–(a) in the interest of the security of Pakistan; (b) for the purpose of ensuring friendly relations with foreign states; (c) for the purpose of ensuring the proper administration of justice; (d) in the interest of public order; (e) for the purpose of preventing the commission of offences; (f) in the interest of decency and morality; (g) for the purpose of granting privilege, in proper cases, to particular proceedings; or (h) for the purpose of protecting persons in relation to their reputation."

After independence the Indian press, which had been encouraged by Congress, the Muslim League, and many other interested parties during the nationalist struggle to extreme kinds of utterance, felt free to attack the new rule as well and to attack foreign countries, the United States being the most frequent target The most violent periodicals were organs of Communism and communalism, both of which were at times guilty of sedition and incitement to public violence and murder by almost any definition. Security of the national government seemed threatened. Action through the courts proved ineffective as a curb, because of the constitutional guarantees. The Supreme Court held that in suppressing certain such papers, the government action was unconstitutional.

The government, therefore, in the person of Prime Minister Nehru, in May 1951, introduced an amendment to the constitution to permit severe restraint upon public expression and the freedom of the press. The country's press opposed it unanimously, or so nearly so as to make any exceptions negligible, and many Congress members of the Indian Parliament privately questioned it too. It was felt that genuine cases of treason, slander, obscenity, incite ment to violence, and other crimes could be controlled through existing penal law. After heated public argument, Nehru agreed to modification of the original proposal. At last on June 1, Parliament, acting under party discipline, by a vote of 228 to 19, amended the section of the constitution mentioned above to read that nothing in the guarantee of freedom of speech and expression should affect the operation of any existing law "in so far as it imposes or prevents the State from making any law, or imposing restrictions in the interests of the security of the State, friendly relations with foreign states, public order, decency or morality . . . and in particular nothing . . . as it relates to or prevents the State from making any law relating to contempt of court, defamation or incitement to an offense." The government then introduced a bill of enforcement of wide coverage which was enacted October 6, 1951. When President Prasad made his opening speech to the newly elected Indian Parliament on May 16, 1952, he listed a new press bill as part of the government's legislative program; it was duly enacted.

The situation was admittedly a bad one, but it is doubtful if the solution was good either. Certain organs, such as the weekly *Blitz* (Bombay), which followed the Communist line, had been unscrupulously irresponsible, and its deputy editor was arrested on March 11, 1952, for attacking the impartiality of the Uttar Pradesh assembly's speaker. The editors of this same weekly and of another called *Current* were indicted in the fall of 1952 for conspiracy of forgery in publishing an alleged letter of United States Ambassador Chester Bowles. The government felt that it should be able to prevent or punish publication of "objectionable matter." But it is hard to see what advantage India now has over preindependence British-ruled India with respect to freedom of speech and expression, and the fears of the bill's opponents that it may in the future come to be used repressively by an overzealous executive seem valid. Responsibility of the press, being based upon public standards of judgment and therefore of slow growth, seems likely to be a product of patience in any country, including India, and not capable of creation by a law that the entire press opposes and with which it is therefore reluctant to cooperate.

The press in Pakistan has generally expressed itself less freely than that of India in opposing the government. After the promulgation of martial law in 1958, it became an offense, punishable by imprisonment for as much as ten years, to make a speech prejudicial to "good order or the public safety." Since then the press has been scrupulously guarded in its columns. In April 1959 the government amended the Security Act to empower the government itself to take over the management of an offending newspaper. It promptly took over Progressive Papers, Ltd., of Lahore, publisher of the English-language newspaper *Pakistan Times,* then one of the most widely read newspapers in the country; *Imroz,* the leading Urdu daily; and an Urdu weekly, *Lail-o-Nahar.* These all had a Communist slant. The chairman and largest shareholder was Iftikhar ud-Din, who had previously been in trouble with the Pakistan government because of his leftish sentiments.

The development of the motion picture industry in India, which is said to be the world's second largest, has been one of the surprises of its modern life. Unfortunately most of the productions are inferior in plot, acting, and photography, tiresomely long, and filled with debased imitations of traditional Indian music and dancing, though a few internationally outstanding films have been produced, notably the trilogy by Satyajit Ray called *Pather Panchali, Aparajito,* and *The World of Apu.* There is a small motion picture industry in Pakistan.

Broadcasting by radio has also assumed large proportions in India. There are some 66 broadcasting centers in the country, which give news coverage and a great deal of public educational material and entertainment, including excellent programs of Indian music. Since this is under government ownership and operation it is not cursed with commercials as in the United States. The number of receiver licenses in India on December 31, 1969, was over 10 million. In Pakistan and Bangladesh radio has far less use than in India. Television has still to establish itself in the subcontinent.

Public health remains a problem of overwhelming size. Throughout India, Pakistan, and Bangladesh undernourishment is widespread because of insufficient or inferior diet, accentuated by frequent food adulteration. In India in 1951 only 128 towns with a population of 50,000 or more, 60 towns with a population of 30,000 to 50,000 and 210 smaller towns with a population between 5,000 and 30,000 had a protected water supply. Only 25 percent of the urban population had access to such a supply; that is, about 45 million urban residents lacked it. About 50 million had no sewage facilities. Much progress was made in India under the Second Five-Year Plan. Some 660 city water-supply projects were started; about two thirds were completed by 1962. Some 2,800 small health centers were established under the Community

Development Program; hospitals and dispensaries were increased in the decennium from about 9,500 to about 13,000, and hospital beds from about 124,400 to about 186,000. The number of medical colleges increased from 30 in 1951 to 57 to 1961. There were in 1970, according to *India, A Reference Annual, 1970,* "95 medical colleges, 15 dental colleges, and 11 other institutions for training in the modern system of medicine. Establishment of new medical colleges and expansion of existing ones under the Plans have raised the admission capacity of these institutions from 3,660 in 1955 to over 12,000 in 1969 . . . The total number of doctors, nurses, and auxiliary non-medical personnel during 1969–70 was estimated at 109,000, 66,000, and 50,000 respectively."

In Pakistan protected water supply and sewage systems exist in the largest cities; there are few elsewhere. Pakistan in 1959 had one physician for about every 8,250 persons, one nurse for about every 38,000, 9 medical colleges (as against 3 in 1950).

It is an accepted policy of government in India to support schools and hospitals which teach and practice the antiquated Hindu (Ayurvedic) and Muslim (Unani or Yunani) systems of medicine, and to support a variety of homeopathic medicine popular in India, and to foster "research" in these. In 1948 the director of public health, Dr. Jivraj N. Mehta, endorsed this policy on the ground that any system is better than none at all. A year later the health ministers of India's states outlined a plan to put traditional medicine on a parity with western allopathic medicine, a plan which has been successful so far as number of teaching institutions is concerned, since there were in 1962 more than fifty of them, supported in whole or in part by public funds.

The chief killers among diseases in the subcontinent have been malaria, smallpox, cholera, tuberculosis. Programs have been developed for eradicating them, in many cases worked out with the World Health Organization or with foreign aid, notably from the United States. Tuberculosis and cholera have been radically reduced, especially in India. It is considered by medical authorities in India that malaria and bubonic plague have been virtually eradicated.

One of the subcontinent's curiosities among its social problems is that of holy men, Hindu *sadhus* and Muslim *faqirs*. Hundreds of thousands of these wander about the country, begging bowl in hand, ostensibly seeking some spiritual goal. Sometimes they are, but all too often they have had a reputation in both ancient and modern times of being vagabonds and rascals, known for loose living, fraud, liquor and drug addiction, and crime including murder. By the practice of asceticism they are popularly thought to acquire magic powers. Most people, though suspicious of holy men as a class, treat the individual with respect, filling his begging bowl, buying the nostrums he sells to cure disease or bring offspring to the childless, for, of course, one never knows whether he is dealing with a fraud or the real article, who if offended can put a grievous curse on the disrespectful. In modern times such a leader as Nehru has denounced them or else has endeavored to use them constructively, for example to propagandize for the five-year plans or to preach honesty to income tax dodgers. There is a Bharat Sadhu Samaj (Indian Holy Men's Association) that has government support. The government sent a special train on tour carrying *sadhus* and their devotees for three months in the spring of 1960, starting at Amritsar in the northern Punjab, going in the far south to Ramesvaram opposite Ceylon, and returning to Delhi, making over a hundred stops altogether, and bringing back 20,000 written assurances from businessmen to abjure black marketing, from government officials to perform their duties more efficiently and honestly, from students to show more obedience to teachers and respect to elders, and from other assorted sinners to mend their ways. There has never been an assessment of these pious promises.

The noble experiment of prohibition that failed in the United States is being pursued in India under a constitutional injunction of the state to end the consumption of intoxicating drinks and drugs throughout the country. By 1962 all but two states of the union (West Bengal and Kashmir) had some degree of prohibition of alcoholic drinks or were devising a program to reduce consumption; in Madras (now Tamil Nadu) and Gujarat there was total prohibition, which was hard to enforce in both rural areas, where the toddy palm makes the manufacture of illegal liquor easy, and in large cities like Bombay, where smuggling and sale of foreign and domestic liquor alike is common. In 1967 it was estimated that 300,000 organized bootleggers were operating in big cities. By that time liquor was completely banned only in Madras and Gujarat, but many of the other states had "dry regions" or "dry days." Tax revenue from liquor is prized to help out public budgetary needs. Muslim law as well as traditional Hindu Brahmanical law forbid the use of alcoholic liquor. Yet Pakistan has launched no such program as India's, perhaps because no one with the zeal and prestige of Gandhi has been at hand to push it. The use of drugs has diminished in India, partly through reduction in number of licenses issued for selling opium, hemp, and their derivatives, partly by increase of their cost, and partly by total prohibition in some areas.

There is a special problem in the subcontinent concerning the status of women. The censuses record a general sex disparity in favor of males: 1000 to 934 in unpartitioned India (1941 census); 1000 to 943 in India in 1951 and 1000 to 940 in 1961 and 1000 to 932 in 1971; 1000 to 888 in Pakistan in 1951 and 1000 to 901 in 1961. These figures contrast with the disparity in favor of females in more developed countries. Of women of reproductive age in the subcontinent an unusually high percent are married or widowed; less than 5 percent are unmarried. Both the Hindu and the Muslim communities traditionally impose disabilities upon women, but of different sorts, and both give the disabilities religious sanction.

Hindu traditional law permitted plural marriage for males, though financial consideration usually made it impracticable. A Hindu woman, however, by Brahmanical law, could marry only once, and after her husband's death had to remain a widow and be subject to lowered status in the family and constricted social privileges. Since a Hindu marriage was a religious sacrament and not a contract, divorce was permitted to neither party, and a husband might not discontinue support of his wife.

Among Hindus child marriage was common in the past. Some ancient legal authorities required marriage of girls before first menstruation. Such a marriage relieved a family of the need to support a daughter and gave the husband's family her maximum service in raising children and so perpetuating the line. The traditional Hindu joint-family system, by which all males share the family income, encourages early marriage of sons. The young husband does not need to earn the support of his wife and children; the family provides it as an accepted obligation.

Legally the Hindu woman's position has been inferior to the man's. By traditional Hindu law a woman did not share in the inheritance of family property. The Hindu joint-family system is coparcenary; property belongs to the family; but that means to the males. Inheritance is by survivorship, not by succession; each male of the family has a right in it by birth. When a woman marries, she enters the family of her husband and departs from her father's family, having no property rights in either. She has property rights only under certain conditions and only to certain kinds of property, specifically her dowry. These various provisions, codified by Brahmans, applied to only a portion of the Hindu community. Many other portions permitted divorce, remarriage of widows, and sometimes female inheritance of property, though there was a constant tendency for groups coming into the Hindu system or rising in it to accept a Brahmanical code.

Some improvement in women's status came about in preindependence times through nationalism. One of the impressive features of nationalism was the participation of women from the time of the first noncooperation movement (1920–1922) when they were arrested by thousands. Muslim women have taken less part in public affairs than have Hindu women, yet in the 1930s and since, a few have been politically prominent. Nowhere in the subcontinent is the right of suffrage a sex perquisite—the vote for women became a reality in the different provinces by legislation beginning in 1921 in Madras and Bombay. Since independence, India especially has had women holding high public office. For a long period the minister for health was a woman (Rajkumari Amrit Kaur) and so for long was India's ambassador to the United States, later the high commissioner to the United Kingdom (Madame Vijaya Lakshmi Pandit). Most impressive of all is Mrs. Indira Gandhi as prime minister.

Muslim tradition does not regard marriage as a sacrament and therefore allows divorce and remarriage for both sexes. It also allows polygamy for men. Islamic law permits four wives at once; in the subcontinent Muslim public opinion disapproves the practice, though for centuries and down to within the present century Muslims of some prominence have published heated defenses of polygamy. A Muslim woman, however, may have only one husband at a time.

Islamic law permits wives and daughters to inherit property. Among Muslims in the subcontinent segregation of women has been common, though nowadays many outstanding Muslim leaders oppose or ignore it as being intellectually narrowing and physically harmful. A conspicuous example was the former prime minister of Pakistan Liaquat Ali Khan, whose Begum ("Lady") exercised the same freedom in her country that Hindu women leaders do in India.

Various kinds of reform measures were adopted in undivided India. An Age of Consent Bill (Sarda Bill), designating minimum age of marriage, was enacted in 1930 and later was revised, but for lack of proper implementing provisions and the support of public opinion could not be enforced. A good many years before independence, advanced Hindu opinion was in favor of revising and codifying the traditional Hindu laws concerning marriage, divorce, succession to property. The central legislature adopted a Hindu Women's Rights to Property Act in 1937, and in 1941 a legislative committee headed by Sir B. N. Rau (later head of India's permanent delegation to the United Nations) was appointed to consider wider reform of Hindu law. After some years of study and investigation in all parts of India, it recommended a wide program which dealt with intestate and testamentary succession, marriage and divorce, minority and guardianship, and adoption. It provided for inheritance by daughters and control by wives and daughters of their inheritance, admitted civil marriage, prohibited both sacramental and civil marriage of anyone who had a living spouse (this would compel monogamy), recommended divorce under certain conditions (adultery or insanity) on the initiative of either husband or wife.

After independence the government of India pursued this kind of reform. The Indian constitution of 1950 provided for an Indian civil code, and a commission headed by Sir B. N. Rau drafted a Hindu Code. In 1955–1956 a series of reforms was enacted in four bills: the Hindu Marriage Act, the Hindu Minority and Guardianship Act, the Hindu Succession Act, and the Hindu Adoptions and Maintenance Act. The traditional privileges, distinctions, and differences based upon caste and custom were removed as far as law was concerned. Marriage was made monogamous for both men and women, though existing plural marriages remained legal. (Not all Indian anthropologists agree that monogamy is desirable.) A concubine's rights were severely reduced (again some anthropologists and sociologists think this unwise). Divorce was made possible on specified grounds such as adultery or incurable insanity. Guardians of minors were required to get court approval for many types of disposal of property. Rules were established defining adoption that ignore caste and also give women the right of adoption as well as men. These reforms were enacted in the face of a good deal of opposition: conservative Hindus had organized hostile meetings, inspired speeches and press articles, and instigated protest demonstrations by women before Parliament; even some within the government doubted the code's justification—certainly its political expediency. The Hindu Code applies alike to Hindus, Buddhists, Jains, Sikhs—the religions that are indigenous to India —under a law passed in 1951.

There exists in Pakistan a Marriage and Family Laws Commission, which made a report that had the support of the All-Pakistan Women's Association (organized in 1949). In 1955, when Prime Minister Mohammad Ali contracted a bigamous second marriage, various women's organizations protested though without securing any concrete results. Questions of women's status, however, are in ever increasing discussion.

Of all of India's social problems the one that has aroused the greatest attention in India and the most comment outside during the late nineteenth and the twentieth century has been that of the Untouchables. The group to which this term refers is part of a larger section of the population called in India the Backward Classes. The Backward Classes constitute about one third of the total population. Included under this category are those designated as the Scheduled Castes, so called because the constitution requires them to be listed in separate state schedules; they are otherwise referred to as Untouchables, Exterior Castes, or Harijans (Gandhi's term, meaning God's folk). The 1961 census gave their number as 64,417,366. Besides the Scheduled Castes the Backward Classes include the Scheduled Tribes, reported in the 1961 census as 30,172,21; these are also known as Adivasis or Adibasis (Aboriginals) or Girijans (Hill People). The Denotified Tribes (Vimukta Jati), before 1924 known as Criminal Tribes, estimated at more than 4 million, are also included among the Backward Classes. Finally, there are the Other Backward Classes, a vague and heterogeneous category of "socially and educationally backward classes," never satisfactorily defined.

The constitution of India says "untouchability is abolished," but the definition of untouchability is a complex and difficult problem. The term is, speaking generally, applied to castes considered by upper caste Hindus to be so impure ceremonially that they convey ceremonial pollution by touch or proximity; hence contact with them "entails purification on the part of high caste Hindus." In consequence of this fact the rest of society has acquired a set of practices to protect itself against these people. The polluting castes also are generally at the economic and educational bottom in society, and their debased position is rationalized in traditional Hinduism as the deserved consequence of actions (*karma*) in previous existences. Alleviation of their poverty, ignorance, exploitation, psychological degradation, therefore, has to counter orthodox religious prejudice, recalling to Americans the pre–Civil War sermons thundered out in the South against the sacrilege of freeing the Negro who had been put under God's curse for his ancestor Ham's inexcusable conduct toward his father.

It can be seen that the generalities in which untouchability is conceived are not easily reduced to clearly defined criteria for identifying the Scheduled Castes, and five pragmatic tests were devised by the 1951 census for that purpose, consisting of disabilities suffered by Untouchables. These were denial of temple entry, inability to obtain the ritual services of "clean Brahmans," inability to have the services of barbers and others serving "high caste Hindus," restrictions upon the acceptance of water from their hands, refusal of certain public facilities such as roads, wells, and schools. Even these criteria did not meet all the conditions.

To remedy these socio-religious disabilities the government has made political, educational, and economic concessions to the Scheduled Castes. Thus there have been special government expenditures in their behalf for livelihood, housing, well-digging, educational scholarships; reservation of political seats, namely, 76 for Scheduled Castes and 31 for Scheduled Tribes in the Lok Sabha (out of a total of 500), and 470 seats for Scheduled Castes and 221 for Scheduled Tribes in state legislatures (out of a total of 3,202); and reservation of government jobs and admissions to academic institutions. Besides such special treatment the Lok Sabha in 1955 unanimously adopted the Untouchability (Offenses) Act, which in strong words outlawed discrimination but has not been effectively applied. The purpose of the legislation and other government activity—for example, propaganda—are therefore double, to remove untouchability, that is to remove the social or socio-religious disabilities suffered by Untouchables, and to improve economic and social qualifications.

The remedies employed are not without potential liability. When does special treatment cease to be a stimulus and become a debilitating crutch? Should the policy be to abolish it and reduce concessions or to expand it so as to include a wider group as the beneficiaries of concessions? Will palliation such as is now being applied provide a cure or create a new disease? Will untouchability die out or will it become a vested interest perpetuated through the political power of the Untouchable electorate? At present there is a premium as well as a liability to untouchability. There is sentiment in favor of eliminating concessions to Scheduled Castes defined by socio-religious criteria and instead granting them only to groups defined by economic need. In this way, it is argued, if need is satisfied and the number of the needy is reduced, the socio-religious disease of untouchability will also automatically disappear. And, besides, all economically depressed people, not just a selected group, should in justice, and for the greatest benefit of the nation, be given economic and welfare assistance. The shift from caste to economic need as a criterion for assistance will lead, it is maintained, to elimination of the specific political reservations for a favored social community and the political dangers inherent in such representation. Herein we touch one of the basic problems of all India. How can the degradation of so large a backward segment of the population, something like one third of the whole, in a country with an underdeveloped economy and rapidly increasing population, be prevented from spreading and be removed, so that the dangers of an antidemocratic revolution can be obviated?

In recent years, from 1956 on, there has been a movement among the Untouchables, especially in the state of Maharashtra, to renounce Hinduism and become Buddhists. The leader of this movement was the late Dr. B. R. Ambedkar, himself born an Untouchable, who had been the chief architect of the Indian constitution. The catch in becoming a Buddhist is that once an Untouchable has done so, he is liable to lose some of the benefits available to him by law.

Those members of the upper castes who are unwilling for Untouchables to be relieved of social disabilities occasionally resort to physical violence against them, such as by attacking them with

315

sticks. This is becoming sufficiently rare that a case is newspaper copy.

The entire institution of caste has come to be recognized in progressive Indian circles as an evil, all but unmentionable in polite society. Nevertheless, except in the large cities, it remains a stubborn fact, and the great urge toward equality, coupled with the political opportunity provided the lower castes by India's democratic institutions, has made it possible for a particular caste to control local elections and political preferment in many areas. Thus is being fulfilled in part the prediction made a half century ago by Sir Herbert H. Risley, who looked upon political democracy for India as destined to produce political groupings defined by caste lines. In spite of the modern Indian government's concern, caste continues to be one of the nation's most threatening divisive forces.

15 Population, Production, and Prosperity

At the time of independence both India and Pakistan were faced with economic problems. These were immediately magnified after independence by the fact that the two nations went on a war footing. India lost by partition areas producing exportable commodities (cotton, jute, hides) and in consequence of that and of the need to purchase food lacked sufficient exchange to procure steel and other metals, capital goods, railway equipment, oil, chemicals, dyes, vehicles. At that time India began an ever increasing program of curtailing luxury imports. Pakistan, too, had similar problems and others resulting from loss of Indian manufactures and the coal needed to operate its railroads.

Though India was faced with such a prospect even as it gained independence, the government did not at first meet it squarely. It relaxed food controls in December 1947, which was too soon. At that time, with the public blessing of Gandhi, it completely removed the controls on food grains and sugar, and shortly afterwards began to ease the controls on cloth. This action was contrary to the judgment of Nehru but represented the will of the right wing of Congress, that is, prominent industrialists, among whom were Birla, Dalmia, and others, whose businesses all profited. Prices rose, inflation was rapid. By July 1948 the wholesale price index had reached nearly 390 against a base of 100 in 1939, and in 1949 and 1950 it exceeded 400 for many commodities. In July 1950 food grains and cloth were returned to control. Inflation then decelerated temporarily, but not permanently. In July 1951 prices had advanced again until they stood at over 4½ times the prewar figures.

At the time of putting food and cloth back under control, the Indian government liberalized its import policy. To finance the increased amount of imports, it drew against the sums available from the sterling balances due it in London. These were a debt to prepartition India accumulated by Britain during World War II, when India liquidated all the obligations incurred for railroad building and other forms of British capital investment, and Britain, reversing its role, became India's debtor.

It had not been easy for Britain and India to reach an agreement on what size debt should be acknowledged and how it should be repaid. After a number of conferences, not always free of acrimony, it was agreed just before partition that the sum should be set at £1,160,000,000 (at the exchange rate then this was $4,640,000,-000) for India and Pakistan jointly. Against this amount Britain received credits for military installations left in the subcontinent and annuities for British civil and military officers who had served the government of India. India ended up in August 1948, when these had been deducted, with a share of about £800,000,000. Of this sum a certain amount was made available as credit for immediate use. To this were added sums that India had earned. For the year 1948–1949 the amount to be available was fixed in July 1948 at £81,000,000; for each of the next two years (1949–1951) it was to be £40,000,000. But India quickly exhausted the first amount, and in August 1949 the sum for the ensuing two years (1949–1951) was increased to £50,000,000, while an additional £50,000-000, was made available to meet outstanding obligations. India was at the same time getting from the Sterling Pool more than twice the amount of dollars agreed upon. In 1949 India had to restrict imports from dollar areas. Devaluation in September 1949 led to an increase of exports and an improvement in the balance of payments situation, which had become alarming.

The country's economic position was worsened by poor rains and consequently poor crops in south India during the years 1947–1951 and in much more acute form in north India in 1950–1951, when too much rain in some areas and flooded rivers in some others produced what would have been famine but for large imports of grain. India utilized all funds available to meet this emergency and in 1951 received from the United States as loan a credit for the purchase of up to 4,000,000 tons of wheat at $190,000,000. Further, defense, which meant mostly the Kashmir action, every year was taking more than half the central government's revenue, expenditures having each year exceeded the estimates.

Pakistan, too, found itself in economic difficulties, but not so rapidly as did India. It had cotton and jute to export, especially jute, for which the world demand suddenly increased at the time of the

Korean War in 1950, and Pakistan relied upon these exports to bolster her economy. However, Pakistan was organized on a war footing. In addition to its revenue budget, it carried a second (capital) budget which got its receipts from the floating of loans, issuance of treasury bills, and similar methods. When these two budgets were considered together, it was clear that Pakistan was going further and further in debt, largely because of military expenditures.

From the beginning Pakistan had seemed economically shaky and had had indifferent credit standing. Foreign suppliers would sometimes demand advance deposits in foreign banks to guarantee payment when due. She gained foreign credit by supplying foreign demands for cotton and jute in other markets than the Indian. By May 1952, however, the market for those commodities seemed threatened by glut, Pakistan was seeking wheat abroad, and its economic prospects were darkening.

While Pakistan at first had raw materials to export to salvage her economic situation, India, being deprived of some of her most important ones, could not get exchange to import the raw materials needed to produce exportable manufactures. The situation might have been helped by industrial expansion, for which India has many resources. There was some small private capital in the country for investment, but this was frightened by the Congress plan for economic development issued early in 1948, which proposed nationalization of public utilities, defense, and heavy industries, and conversion of private enterprise in these fields within five years' time. Profits in industry were to be shared between owners and workers.

After industrialists had protested such a program, the government adopted an industrial policy resolution in April 1948, designating certain government monopolies (armament, atomic energy, railways, any industry vital for defense or in an emergency), and fields in which it would initiate all new undertakings (coal, iron and steel, aircraft manufacture, shipbuilding, communication equipment, mineral oils). In these latter it would not take control for at least ten years, at which time it would review the situation. Many industries were to be left to private enterprise, provided they advanced satisfactorily; but certain others, since they required government capital, were to be developed under government planning and regulation.

In 1949 the government introduced the Industries (Development and Control) Bill, embodying its 1948 plan, but held it in abeyance for two years. In the meantime Patel had died, and the right wing had no leader of equal influence. On September 4, 1951, shortly after Nehru, with elections coming up, had got his way on Congress policy, Harekrushna Mehtab, Minister for Industries and Commerce, again presented the 1949 bill to Parliament which enacted it in October, providing wide powers to nationalize industry and applying controls to all private enterprise. Said he, "the old free economy system, irrespective of social planning, has gone." This program, like that of Congress in 1948, seemed drastic, being more thoroughgoing than that of the Labour party in Great Britain. Industry considered it as undesirable as the earlier one, and therefore private capital was still not forthcoming for development.

Neither did foreign capital offer itself for investment in India, as Indians had confidently expected it to do at the close of the war. Private foreign investors thought the climate unfavorable. The government had prescribed that at least 51 percent of the stock of any company formed in India would have to be Indian-owned and the management would have to be Indian-controlled. These limitations voiced the Indian fear of western economic imperialism; they were afterward lifted when it was clear that western capital would not enter when so restricted.

India and Pakistan both came to the decision to undertake economic planning, though India was the first to make a plan. Even before independence it was obvious that economic planning would be needed for the subcontinent to achieve its needed growth. Hence, during the immediate postwar period, and for some years before, economic planning had been an Indian preoccupation. Big business had led off in 1944 with the "Bombay Plan." Following this, the government, Congress, and the provincial governments all produced plans. India became for a time the planners' never-never land. Few of the plans took a realistic view about the amount of domestic and foreign capital that would be available for economic development. Analysis not beclouded by wish-fulfillment generally showed that investment capital was only a fraction of what the plan would need for implementation. In 1950 and 1951, however, two plans were produced that were in the realm of financial reality. The first was the Colombo Plan for Co-operative Economic Development in South and South-East Asia, jointly devised by the various Commonwealth governments. It called for a total expenditure of

£1,868 million (about $5.23 billion) in six years, of which about two thirds would be for India, and something more than one seventh would be for Pakistan. The cooperating governments were to provide the money by contributing some of it and securing the rest from outside sources.

The other plan was prepared under the auspices of the government of India by its Planning Commission. This was established in March 1950 to develop means of implementing the aims, expressed in the constitution, of giving the population social justice up to the capacity of the country's resources. The commission had prepared India's proposals for the Colombo Plan. It then cooperated with the central and states ministries and issued a draft outline of the First Five-Year Plan in July 1951. This called for the expenditure of Rs. 1,793 crores (about $3.77 billion), of which the commission expected India to raise from its own resources and the Colombo Plan Rs. 1,493 crores (about $3.14 billion), while the remaining Rs. 300 crores (about $620 million) would have to come from outside. The plan received some fairly sharp criticism in India, but was nevertheless generally regarded as offering concrete and feasible means to assist in solving India's development problems.

In Pakistan no general overall plan was produced until 1955 but a variety of projects were devised for both the eastern and western parts of the nation.

It is now in order to consider the nature of the problems in population, production, and achievement of prosperity that were to be attacked with the aid of economic planning.

Before the gaining of independence commentators in India and Britain used to disagree loudly on whether or not the subcontinent was overpopulated. Nationalists during the struggle for independence often claimed that it could support a greater population if it reformed its agricultural structure and acquired a better industrial development than that permitted under British imperialism. So reformed, they held, it could accommodate a vastly increased population on its then current scale of living or a moderately increased one on an improved scale. Communist-oriented writers took a similar line. But defenders of British rule pointed out that mere increase of production would not be the answer. In the past century any such gain had always been absorbed by an increase in the population, which bred up to the full capacity of the greater production to give support on a subsistence basis. Areas newly opened to agriculture by irrigation were promptly filled with settlers who were shortly living no better than before they migrated from their old homes. Newly created industry led to the formation in cities of labor colonies, whose members lived in the most desolate poverty. The end result was not an advance of living standards, only a multiplication of the millions submerged in want.

The argument about overpopulation got nowhere, because the subject was not viewed in the whole except by a small number of sociologists and economists, whose misgivings seemed like whispers against the roaring blasts of political propaganda and rejoinder. But not long before independence the pressing evils of the population problem rudely crashed into the consciousness of politicians, who had formerly been only critics without authority but had now become responsible administrators.

The rapid expansion of population in the subcontinent is now an undenied reason for alarm. It grew by more than 48 million or 12.3 percent in the decade 1941–1951. In the half-century 1901–1951 the increase was 153 million, about 54 percent. In the decade 1951–1961 the population of the subcontinent grew from about 433 million to about 533 million, an increase of approximately 23 percent. An official estimate for India in April 1971 gave a figure of 547 million, an increase since 1951 of 190 million, or 53.2 percent. The population of Pakistan in 1970 was 114 million, an increase since 1951 of 39.5 million, about 52.3 percent. For an area with high standards of living and a rapidly expanding industrialism such rates might not be excessive, but they are ominous for an agricultural region with intensive use of land resources and reliance upon the fickle annual monsoon, and with traditional handicrafts and high density of population, an area still economically underdeveloped. Demographers make varying projections of population increase for the next fifteen or fifty years, but whatever the figure given, it always alarms political leaders. For example, Nehru, speaking in Parliament on August 21, 1961, quoted the Indian Planning Commission as estimating the country's population in 1976 as 625 million, an increase of 187 million or about 43 percent in fifteen years. His estimate was probably a little high, since the increase in the decennium 1961–71 was only from 439 million to 547 million, that is, the amount of growth was 108 million, which gives a percentage of 24.6. To reach his figure by 1976, the increase for the quinquennium 1971–1976 would have to be 78 million, a percentage for the half decade of more than 14.2 percent.

Since there has been no equally rapid increase of food production and no growth of industry sufficient to finance the needed importation of food, the average individual seems to some students to be more poorly fed now than in 1901, or at best only slightly better fed. Housing and clothing conditions have possibly deteriorated. Individual poverty is therefore said by some analysts to be worse now than ever before in this century; this is contradicted by others. Estimates of annual per capita national income in India and Pakistan are all admittedly unreliable, but as a whole they indicate a grim situation—for example, Dr. V. K. R. V. Rao's estimate for 1931–1932 of Rs. 65 (then equivalent to about $19.50) for undivided India; the United Nations figures for 1949 (issued in 1950) of $57 for India and $51 for Pakistan; the Indian Planning Commission's estimate of $69.30 in 1961; or a government of India estimate for 1966–67 of Rs. 481.5 ($64) or for 1969 of $76—for the apparent gain is offset by worldwide inflation. In Pakistan the per capita income for 1961 was given as Rs. 28.40 per month ($8.52) or $102.24 a year (the Pakistani rupee was valued at U.S. 30¢); in 1968 at $116. Even after allowing for the difficulty of translating these money figures into terms of real goods consumed, the reality is inconceivable to most Americans.

The immensity of the food problem in the subcontinent can be gauged from a comparison of food consumption with the standard of nutrition. It is usually calculated that daily food needs of an adult vary between 2,400 and 3,600 calories depending on his size, his physical exertion, and the climate in which he lives. The average intake in India was estimated by the Food and Agriculture Organization of the United Nations in 1958 to be 2,050 calories, and this was ill-balanced, since it consisted almost wholly of cereals and contained little of proteins, fats, and minerals, except for some relatively slight additions of pulses, vegetables, fruit, sugar cane, and milk and its products. To maintain even this low diet India produced in 1966–1967 about 74.2 million metric tons of food grains, in 1967–1968 about 95.6 metric tons. Variation in annual production of food grains depends chiefly upon the uncertainty of the monsoons. Because of poor monsoons the 1966 and 1967 food grain yields were low, but in 1968 there was a bumper crop. India imports about 8 to 11 million metric tons to help make up the deficit. Pakistan produces from 11.7 to 13 million tons of food grains annually. To make up the deficit Pakistan in a poor year had to put as much as 27 percent of its import expenditures into food grains and flour. The production of oil seeds and sugar cane must also be increased to meet the demands of the increasing population. The actual feeding of the population is then the first economic problem of the subcontinent. Besides solving the staggering problem of finding mere food the subcontinent must increase its production of commercial crops—cotton, jute, tea, tobacco, nuts, pepper and other spices—some needed for local consumption, but much for export.

Throughout the subcontinent, housing, sanitation, and health services are hopelessly inadequate and the death rate is high. In spite of the fact that many of the usual population controls, such as internal war, famine, and pestilence, have been checked during the past century and a half, the death rate still remains one of the highest in the world. For the decade 1931–1941 Kingsley Davis figured it at 31.2 per 1000, which, though high, was nevertheless a reduction from that of previous decades. For the decade 1941–1951 the Indian government's estimate was 27.4; for 1951–1961 it was 22.8 percent. Birth and death rates in India cannot be completely reliable because, it is conceded in official reports, the registration figures are always much below the facts. Yet the clear decline here is a cause of satisfaction. On the other hand the declining rate carries an obvious threat when viewed in relation to the food supply. So many people living in so much misery and yet steadily increasing in number are a menace, not only to the progress of their own nations but to world stability and peace as well.

The crudest manifestation of the subcontinent's population and food problem has been its repeated appeals in the past three decades for help in finding food. Concretely this has meant procuring food grains, which make up the bulk of the subcontinent's diet. The first occasion was in 1943 before India was partitioned, when a famine in Bengal was estimated to have killed three million persons. In 1945–1946 natural calamities—two droughts and a tidal wave—produced serious food shortages and led (then unpartitioned) India to seek help from abroad. In 1949, at the time of another food crisis, the government of the new India was again in difficulty. In 1950–1951, when there was still another desperate shortage after droughts and floods in 1950, India asked the United States for four million tons of wheat, and after prolonged discussion Congress approved a long-term low-interest loan of $190 million for purchases as needed up to that total tonnage. Another famine, caused by drought, followed in 1952, worse than that of 1951, and after this came another bad year in 1953. In the years 1951–1953 (inclusive) India imported about 10.6 million tons of food grains. In 1957, another bad year, India imported about 3.6 million tons. In September 1959 India's Food Minister S. K. Patil asked the United States for 5 million tons of grain a year for five years to build a reserve. In 1960 he was granted 17 million over four years.

A project to increase production by 57 percent in seven years was launched in 1960 with the help of the Ford Foundation; this was to raise the annual production to 110 million tons. The years 1966 and 1967 saw subnormal crops, and India was in great need of outside help to feed her population. The United States in the spring of 1966 began shipping wheat to India at the rate of over 700,000 tons a month for a period of nine months. In December it made an additional emergency provision of 500,000 tons. In February 1967 the United States Congress authorized shipment to India of up to 3 million tons of wheat "provided it is appropriately matched" by contributions from other industrialized countries. The Aid-India Consortium of ten nations (including the United States) later arranged to send India one million tons a month. Having been tided over these two bad years, India had a bumper year in 1968. Similar aid was provided to Pakistan also during that same period. In the year 1967–1968 the production in India, by the Indian government's final estimate, reached 95.588 million metric tons.

Besides producing poverty, semistarvation, a high mortality rate, and a low life expectancy, a rate of production that is insufficient for the growing population precludes adequate expenditure on education and helps to create group rivalries that prevent united action to achieve national ends. The subcontinent thus has a serious basic problem.

India's Planning Commission has drawn up overall economic and social five-year plans, the fourth of which went into operation in 1966. Pakistan drew up its First Five Year Plan for 1955–1960, but this proved disappointing in execution, largely because political instability disturbed its operation. Pakistan launched its Second Five-Year Plan in July 1960. To meet their needs the two countries planned to increase both agricultural and industrial production and

at the same time take steps to ensure that the increase would produce social gains for their citizens and not be unprofitably swal-
lowed up by a mere increase of population. This double aim seemed
to require a rapid rate of economic advance and an accompanying
check upon the rate of population increase.

One phase is a direct attack upon the birth rate. This has two
parts. The first is to create a desire for higher standards of living,
on the general theory that poverty, rather than prosperity, leads to
a high birth rate. There are many aspects of the national life
which, when improved, may be expected to lead to family planning.
With better health, better education, more material comforts, more
intellectual interests, the people of the subcontinent, like Americans and Europeans, will themselves limit the size of their families.

The second part is the spreading of information about birth control. The Indian Planning Commission has sponsored a program for
the state to establish family limitation clinics, provide facilities for
sterilization, furnish advice about contraception, and establish research centers to study family limitation and the means of providing inexpensive, safe, and efficacious birth control through contraceptives or otherwise. This program in India and similar meas..res
in Pakistan have not met marked religious opposition. Traditional
Hinduism and Islam, though both condemn abortion, seem to have
no scriptural injunction against contraception, and neither has developed an organization to oppose it. Each, however, endorses the
birth of many children. Hinduism does so to guarantee that a man
has a son to perform the prescribed death rites for him, his father,
and his grandfather; both communities regard many children as
an assurance of lineage and of support in old age in an environment where the mortality rate is high. There is also a great deal of
social inertia which a birth control program has to meet. The subcontinent, since it lives predominantly by an agricultural economy,
has the usual attitude of a peasantry, which looks upon offspring
as an immediate aid to the family by furnishing additional labor
and does not see the long-term implications.

The government of India began an experiment in the winter of
1951–1952 in cooperation with the World Health Organization employing the "safe period" method, which, since it involves part ab-
stinence, would to that degree be consonant with Gandhi's attitude
on sex. But by 1955 it was becoming clear that the method was un-

popular, and the project was curtailed. Experiments were then tried in various centers under the control or with the support of state governments to popularize the use of contraceptives by women, especially to use the intra-uterine contraceptive device (IUCD) or "loop," seemingly the cheapest and most effective contraceptive, although there are difficulties with the device, such as bleeding or expulsion. In recent years another approach has become increasingly favored: vasectomy. This method of sterilization is simple and quick (a ten-minute operation, painless, and consistently successful), and newspaper reports describe "mass vasectomy camps" with sterilization of great numbers (63,000 at one such fair) in a few days. The operation is usually performed upon men who have already had three or more children; these receive a small subsidy for undergoing sterilization. By October 1968 about 5 million sterilization operations had been performed and 2.6 million loops inserted. By 1969 the department of Family Planning said that there was a family planning center in urban areas for every 50,000 people and 5,080 centers in rural areas.

Pakistan made a small provision for family planning in its First Five-Year Plan, but only some pilot work was undertaken. The program under the Second Five-Year Plan was primarily designed to influence social attitudes and practices in favor of family planning. It also sought to provide the necessary medical and other facilities. Clinics were to be established in all general hospitals, dispensaries, and maternity centers.

In a program to increase production the first point of attack has to be the agrarian problem. Here it is necessary to find more acreage for crops, introduce improved farming techniques, employ improved strains of food grains so as to obtain larger crops, promote good animal husbandry, develop irrigation and other aids, eliminate the evils of the land tenure system, give the villages a better standard of living, encourage the peasantry to develop healthy political activity.

In India the net sown acreage has been increasing. In 1950–1951 it was 293.4 million acres; in 1955–1956 it was about 320 million acres; in 1964–1965 it was 340.7 acres; further acreage has been added since. Waste land has been converted to productive land by irrigation projects, by eradication of the deep-rooted destructive kans grass, and by restoring fallow land to cultivation. Pakistan increased its 52 million sown acres of 1962 to about 54.5 million acres and improved 7 million acres of its sown acreage by 1964–1965.

In part the subcontinent's low agricultural productivity comes from uneconomic distribution of the land and inferior farming practices. Holdings are small and often fragmented. The average acreage used by the individual cultivator declined from 2.23 acres in 1891–1892 to 1.90 in 1939–1940, and this generally consisted of tiny scattered parcels. Considerable soil deterioration has taken place through erosion, deforestation, overgrazing, and waterlogging in irrigated areas. Use of cow dung, which is abundant and would be the subcontinent's source of natural fertilizer, could repair some of the damage, but it is instead mixed with straw and used for cooking fuel, which otherwise would be insufficient. Hence, crop yield per acre is low: according to the Indian Planning Commission in 1961 the rice yield (807 lbs. per acre), was less than one fourth that in the United States (3411 lbs.); the wheat yield (795 lbs.), a little more than one half that in the United States (1554 lbs.); the cotton yield (108 lbs.), about one fourth to two fifths (448 lbs.). Better fertilizers and new improved varieties of rice, wheat, maize, and other food grains that give a larger yield than the old strains and require less moisture have been helping to ease the food situation. Scientific breeding experiments conducted under the government of India, and with American technical assistance, as at Etawah and Faridabad, have produced encouraging results. In some cases crop yields were reported as 30 to 40 percent more than before through the use of fertilizer, good seed, simple machinery adapted to Indian conditions, control of insects and diseases, and other modern agricultural helps. Mechanization of agriculture is hardly developed in India. Kusum Nair, in her excellent discussion of farming in the United States, Japan, and India in *The Lonely Furrow* points out that with the use of modern machines instead of the traditional tools, with the use of the combine in place of the sickle, India could easily feed its present population and a good deal more at lower total cost and need many less persons in doing so. The employment feature of modernization is the catch in the remedy: How would the discarded laborers live? Provision must be made for them, but what would the provision be?

An integral part of an agricultural development plan has to be improvement in animal husbandry. This affects particularly cattle, which are used not only to produce milk but also as agricultural draught animals. Without bullocks a farmer is helpless. Nevertheless the breeds are usually poor, the bullocks being also underfed, while milch cows have low yield. Experiments in breeding and feeding have been made over a period of years by both government and private agencies and notable results have been obtained, but a way is needed to apply them on a general scale. The magnitude of the problem is illustrated by the fact that India produces about 750 pedigreed bulls a year and with the present breeding methods could use a million. Mass castration of scrub bulls is being developed. Artificial insemination is practiced scantily in each country but the two governments are extending it. Scientific dairying is rare, but it is also being extended with impressive results, as at the Aarey milk colony outside Bombay. Veterinary hospitals and dispensaries are being multiplied.

The removal of useless cattle is complicated by the traditional Hindu religious prepossession of the inviolability of the cow. This is now enshrined in the Indian constitution, which directs the government to prevent the slaughter of cows. Old and decrepit cattle may not be slaughtered in some states; consequently *gosadans* (sanctuaries for aged cattle) exist, some operated on public funds, some on private. Cow-protection societies and organizations to prohibit slaughter of cattle are active in many parts of the country, demonstrating by parades and sometimes clashing with the police, and getting a good deal of public sympathy and financial support. (Disillusioned opponents of cow protection believe some of this support is contributed by dealers in beef to keep the price up.) In 1955 when an effort was made in Parliament to enact national legislation prohibiting the slaughter of cattle, Nehru opposed it on the ground that such a prohibition would be uneconomic and he threatened to resign if the bill passed. It was defeated by 99 votes to 12, but most of the members of the Lok Sabha were absent, not wanting to cast an affirmative vote and so risk reprisals from the Congress leadership, or to cast a negative vote and so risk offending the electorate.

Another item recognized as a necessary part of an agricultural development program is encouragement of rural cottage or village industries. Gandhi zealously promoted such a program as a part of the struggle for independence, and it has been continued ever since. The peasantry have certain off-seasons when they could profitably engage in weaving, leather and wood working, and other occupations to supply needed articles. Such occupations could also provide employment for some of the population likely to be released as agricultural methods improve. An effective cottage industry program requires organization to give instruction, provide raw materials, furnish credit and financing, and take care of marketing. The Third Five-Year Plan aimed to help both the traditional handicrafts and the new small-scale industries.

Since 1952 an extensive rural program planned and operated by the government in many parts of India has included both animal husbandry and cottage industry. The program has attempted, in addition, to advance village education, improve public health, and initiate community social projects such as adult education and amusements. Village workers have been trained; materials provided, such as fertilizer, improved seed, pedigreed animals; sanitation taught; and the building of roads and digging of wells stimulated. Labor contributions (*shramdan*) have been asked from the villagers to do the necessary work. These various undertakings heighten peasant interest, raise his morale, and give him a goal of higher standards of living. Such community development programs can help, in the words of the Planning Commission, "to change the character of Indian agriculture from subsistence farming to economic farming." They can go further and give the village a richer life. Many such projects have been launched or supported with the aid of public or private funds from the United States. Many critics, however, think the development program's coverage of the country is superficial.

Pakistan started an analogous program called "Village Aid" in 1953, which Pakistan's Second Five-Year Plan said worked fairly well in East Pakistan but not in West Pakistan.

Increase of yield and inculcation of social incentive, however, are not enough. There is another side to the agrarian problem: to reform the system of land tenure and remove peasant indebtedness. As peasant landholders were crowded out by the change in the system of tenure instituted by the British in the eighteenth and early nineteenth centuries and the resulting conversion of revenue collectors to landlords, and village artisans were forced out of their occupations by the influx of foreign machine-manufactured articles, both classes fell back on the land for support, and there was an alarming rise in the number of agricultural laborers owning no land but working for hire or occupying as tenants a minute holding. The number amounted to 14 percent of all agricultural workers in 1881; in 1931 it was 38 percent; it was 30.4 percent of the total rural population in 1951. The *Provisional Population Totals of the Census of India, 1971* report that in 1961 agricultural laborers comprised 16.71 percent of India's total working force; in 1971 the percentage is given as 25.76 of the total working force. The problem of tenancy is compounded in many places by subtenancy. The landlord or proprietor who pays the taxes to the government, especially in areas where land ownership lies with a landlord rather than the peasant, frequently does not deal directly with the cultivator but may be separated from him by a number of subproprietors as intermediaries. In Bengal cases have been reported of as many as seventeen echelons from tiller to landowner.

With the shift in land ownership has gone a great increase in peasant indebtedness. Often the landowner was the moneylender. So dear did the land become and so cheap the worth of a peasant's labor that the peasantry, whether owner or tenant, became heavily encumbered with debt, on which, because a peasant has only low-grade security to offer, the interest rates are high. Studies made in limited areas of relatively high productivity and prosperity—Gujarat (1930), the Punjab (1925), United Provinces (1932)—showed that somewhere around two thirds to three fourths of agricultural families were in debt and the size of the debt varied from about three fifths of the annual income to 110 percent of it; or, as M. L. Darling put it, about three times the annual net income. In the Punjab, he noted, the rural indebtedness was more than seventeen times the land revenue of the province. Interest rates ranged from 9 to 300 percent. Cooperative credit societies were not able to cure the evil; the peasants who form a society can provide only meager capital to operate it, and the society cannot afford to accept any but very good risks.

One of the uneconomoic results of the system of land tenure that developed in the nineteenth century is that the basic payment which the peasantry makes, whether for tax or rent or both, is excessive in relation to his resources. Land hunger following the changes in the tenure system made in the nineteenth century induced peasants to overbid for the use of land, and landowners took full advantage of them. The British introduced regulatory Tenancy Acts. Nevertheless, in dealings with landlords (*zamindari* system, under which the landlord collected government revenues from the peasants), peasants were paying out in the twentieth century for revenue or other charges connected with use of the land, "from a maximum of one-fifth or one-sixth down to one-tenth or less of the gross produce," W. H. Moreland, a profound student of the subject, said in 1911. In the case of direct dealings with officials (*ryotwari* system) they were paying "between one-eighth and one-twelfth of the gross produce." This condition left the peasant impoverished, and he grew more so as the pressure upon the land continued to increase. In successive decades of the twentieth century the landowner in one way or another got more and more of the crop. The Indian Planning Commission said in the First Five-Year Plan that "in several parts of the country today as much as one-half of the produce goes to the landlord. He makes no return to the peasants in the shape of improvements; he deals with them mercilessly in auctioning his lands for rental; he confuses his accounts so as to get more than is due; he becomes a moneylender charging excessive interest." Hence the peasant's margin of profit for "better farming" and "better living" steadily shrank until he was in the eyes of many analysts practicing poorer farming and enduring poorer living than his ancestors in the second half of the nineteenth century.

Agrarian reform got its greatest impetus when the peasants themselves began to form associations for their advancement. A number of peasant societies came into existence from about 1920, especially in the heavily settled regions of Bengal, Bihar, the United Provinces (now Uttar Pradesh), and the Punjab, that is, in the highly productive and densely populated northern plain. Here the landlord system of tenure prevailed. The reform organizations went by various names, of which one of the most widely used was Kisan Sabha (Peasants' Association), while another was Krishak Proja (Agriculturist Masses). They hoped to get relief through reduction in the amount of rent paid or abolition of landlordism and reversion of the land to peasant proprietorship. They wanted curtailment or removal of the landlord's right of eviction and establishment of cooperative credit and marketing systems.

When Congress launched its first noncooperation campaign (1920–1922), Gandhi, who was deeply concerned by peasant problems, won over the existing peasant organizations. It was a kind of paradox for him to do so, for Congress was getting its financial support and administrative direction from the middle classes, who were likely to be landowners. At that time Congress had no constructive policy on either agrarian or industrial labor problems. Gandhi's own attitude was that no one class should benefit at the expense of another but all should unselfishly work together. Landlords and industrialists, peasants and workers, should not treat each other as enemies but should practice mutual forbearance and tolerance. The one should not withhold rent or go on strikes; the other should provide good living and working conditions, take only a just amount in rent, and pay fair wages. Under the application of this teaching the landlords lost nothing and the peasants gained nothing.

Other elements in the Congress, however, headed by Nehru, felt that a stronger Congress policy was needed for effecting agrarian reform. They were spurred on, too, in the late 1920s when the Communists sought political leadership of the peasants and workers. The Draft Program of Action of the Communist Party of India published late in 1930 included a section of peasant demands, which called for "confiscation without compensation of all lands and estates, forests, and pastures of the native princes, landlords, moneylenders, and the British Government, and the transference to peasant committees for use by the toiling masses of the peasantry . . . immediate confiscation of all plantations . . . immediate nationalization of the whole system of irrigation, complete cancellation of all indebtedness and taxes . . . the peasantry and agricultural proletariat to engage in all kinds of political demonstrations, and collective refusal to pay taxes and dues . . . refusal to pay rent . . . refusal to pay debts and arrears to government, the landlords, and the money-lenders in any form whatsoever." This sweeping program was a challenge to both government and Congress.

When Congress as a whole still would not adopt a clear agrarian program, a number of liberal and left-wing Congress members, including Jawaharlal Nehru and Jayaprakash Narayan, in 1934 formed the Congress Socialist Party. Functioning as a group within Congress, this subparty cooperated with the peasant associations, for a time controlled them, and urged Congress to admit them as a unit, but the more conservative elements in Congress defeated this.

In 1936, when the first elections under the 1935 constitution were coming up, many of the separate peasant groups came together as the All-Indian Kisan Sabha. This adopted a resolution

stating, "The Kisan movement stands for the achievement of ultimate economic and political power for the producing masses
through its active participation in the national struggle for winning
complete independence," and demanded a series of reforms including abolition of landlordism, cancellation of arrears of debt, rent
reduction, and many other changes similar to Communist party demands. It also adopted the red flag, but not the hammer and sickle,
as its emblem.

Nehru and his associates persuaded Congress to include in its
manifesto for the 1936 election a statement which, as Nehru has
described it in his *Unity of India*, advocated "a reform of the system of land tenure and revenue and rent, and an equitable adjustment of the burden on agricultural land, giving immediate relief
to the smaller peasantry by a substantial reduction of agricultural
rent and revenue now paid by them and exempting uneconomic
holdings from payment of rent and revenue."

This was a commitment, but when Congress set up its ministries
in 1937 it was slow in fulfilling it. Congress did, however, introduce
legislation which effected some reforms in tenancy, limited the
rights of landlords, and abolished forced labor. These were still far
from satisfying the peasantry. Between 1942 and 1944, when the
British were suppressing the Congress by jailing its leaders but letting the Communist party have free rein, Communists gained control of the Kisan Sabhas.

In India after independence and partition Congress again took
up the agrarian question and had acts passed in many states (especially in Uttar Pradesh, Bombay, Madhya Pradesh) that were designed to effect further reforms. In areas where the zamindari system prevailed, under which the land was owned by landlords and
worked by tenants, the landlords were ousted, and provision was
made for recompensing them, usually through payments by the
peasants among whom the land was distributed. Limitations were
put upon the size of future acquisitions (50 acres in Bombay, 30 in
Uttar Pradesh), and restrictions upon the eviction of tenants at
will. Intermediaries were abolished and the zamindari system was
eliminated, though the zamindars continued to hold lands which
they personally cultivated. In the ryotwari (peasant proprietorship)
areas the new laws gave protection to peasants against eviction and
regulated rents. In both zamindari and ryotwari reforms, the laws
proved to have many loopholes. Some provisions have been severely

criticized, especially that requiring compensation of the landlords by the tenants, who have few resources. Forced labor, as in *begar* (forced uncompensated labor) or in other forms, has been eliminated.

An idealistic approach to the agrarian problem was promoted after 1951 by Acharya Vinoba Bhave, inspired at that time by his observations in the Telingana districts of the then state of Hyderabad (now Andhra). He was one of Gandhi's close followers, a man perhaps of less imagination and persuasiveness but as devoted in his spiritual aims, and equally ascetic in his manner of life. The essence of the problem, as he saw it, was to distribute the land among the landless laborers working on it. He undertook a campaign to induce landowners, especially those with large holdings, and absentee landlords to donate land for distribution to the landless. He called his program *bhoodan* (land gift). Where whole villages were given, the term used was *gramdan* (village gift). Vinoba toured on foot in many parts of India, but especially in Bihar, attended by volunteer workers, who prepared the way for his arrival, assisted in persuading potential donors, and later in some cases went out on their own to solicit donations. The pressure which Vinoba himself applied was purely religious, but often landowners would find themselves subjected to social pressure also, a community sentiment that was hard to resist. It was commonly said that large landowners prayed he would not come to their villages and groaned when he did. In the first few years the campaign had a good deal of apparent success: by 1955 he had had gifts of about 4 million acres and the movement seemed to be growing. But by June 1955 only about 5.5 percent of the land donated had been distributed (212,721 acres). The Indian Planning Commission said in 1961 that about one million acres of voluntary gifts of land and of whole villages had been distributed.

There were some catches in the *bhoodan* and *gramdan* program. The basic one was that the appeal was to the rich and landed and to their generosity rather than to the poor and landless themselves, who were to receive charity rather than to enforce their rights. Moreover, much of the donated land was inarable by present methods and was of questionable title. Vinoba looked upon the land gift as part of a wide program of general religious, moral, and social benefit called *sarvodaya* (universal uplift), Gandhi's term. For a time bhoodan had a considerable following and even interested some elements of the Congress, which gave Vinoba a public and official welcome at the annual session at Avadi in January 1955. In March of that same year U. N. Dhebar, president of the Congress, himself a person of strongly idealist motivation, attended the Sarvodaya Convention and lauded Vinoba and the movement. By 1962 the campaign was much less vigorous and seemed to have suffered the moribund fate that so often befalls well-intentioned, idealistically conceived, but fundamentally unrealistic movements. Today it seems dead.

The ultimate goal of agrarian reform as viewed by the Indian Planning Commission in the First Five-Year Plan was to be Village Cooperative Management. The entire holdings of a village were to be treated as a single farm; individual owners were to receive annual harvest dividends according to the extent of their ownership. Workers were to receive compensation according to the amount of work they contributed. A management body was to assign cultivation to individual families or groups of families, working on blocks of land of appropriate size, as local circumstances might suggest. Such cooperative village management was to be available to any village on demand of two thirds of the owners or permanent tenants holding not less than one half the cultivated area of the village, whereupon the system would apply to the entire area of the village including the holdings of the minority. A limited program was put into effect in various parts of India.

By 1958, after various studies, it was agreed by the Indian government that the program of community development should be decentralized and pursuaded under a system called *Panchayati Raj* (Control or Rule by Village Panchayats or Councils). Each village would elect its own Panchayat or Council. The elected heads of the villages in each community development block would constitute a *Panchayat Samiti* (Panchayat Association). The elected heads of the various Panchayat Samitis in a district would constitute a *Zila Parishad* (District Assembly). The exact organization and operation of the system would be determined by each state. By 1961 seven states had enacted legislation to implement this system. The Panchayat (literally, Council of Five) is an old Indian institution, which conducted much of the petty administration of villages in pre-British India. It offered possibilities of renewed and enlarged duties in independent India and the constitution of 1950 includes "the fostering of village panchayats" among the directive principles of state policy. Use of them is viewed very hopefully by the government of India. There is, as can be seen, some similarity between Panchayati Raj in India and the system of Basic Democracies that Ayub Khan devised for Pakistan, though the role of the Panchayat System is much more limited.

In Pakistan some ameliorative measures were taken in the Punjab in the early 1950s, but the Pakistan Planning Commission in its Second Five-Year Plan remarks. "No significant action was taken until October 1958 [the time of the Military Revolution], when the government appointed the Land Reforms Commission to examine the problems relating to the ownership and tenancy of agricultural land, and to recommend suitable measures for ensuring social justice, security of tenure for the tenant and better production." In February 1959 a Martial Law Regulation applicable to West Pakistan imposed a ceiling on holdings, forbade partition of economic and subsistence holdings, abolished state land grants (*jagir*) and any other form of intermediary between tiller and government, made the consolidation of holdings compulsory, assured tenants of security in their holdings, and conferred the right of ownership upon certain types of existing tenants. To take over land in excess of the maximum holdings permitted, the state recompensed the owners and sold the land to new owners. In East Pakistan provisions had been made by the East Bengal Estate Acquisition and Tenancy Act of 1950 to eliminate intermediaries and to fix ceilings on the size of holdings for all but certain types of holdings. Little happened. In 1958 the East Pakistan government appointed a Land Revenue Commission, which reported in July 1959. The commission reformulated the ceiling (upwards), reviewed what had already been done under the Act of 1950, revised the rights of ownership, and provided for consolidation of holdings.

Closely allied to the agrarian problem is the development of irrigation and power schemes, somewhat like the Tennessee Valley Authority. In undivided India about 24 percent of the total cultivated area was irrigated (72 million acres out of 298). In independent India by 1961 an estimated 70 million acres were under irrigation. The Third Five-Year Plan set a target of adding another 20 million acres. Since irrigation is the surest way of providing water, it needs to be extended. Many multiple-purpose projects, large and small, have been considered for utilizing the rivers, and the government of India has been developing four that are very large: the

Bhakra-Nangal Project on the Sutlej River in the northeastern Punjab; the Mahanadi Project (Hirakud Dam) in Orissa; the Damodar Valley Corporation scheme in Bihar; and the Tungabhadra Project (Harike) for Andhra and Mysore. Besides these there are a number of smaller schemes, as well as many irrigation works which were completed before independence in the nineteenth and twentieth centuries. In 1966–67 India had 27,478,000 hectares (about 68 million acres) under irrigation. Irrigation schemes have not always had full usage by agriculturists, and the terms of usage have therefore been reconsidered by the government of India. Sometimes, also, mere inertia of the peasantry, as Kusum Nair records in her book *Blossoms in the Dust,* stultifies the government's best efforts.

The area included in West Pakistan made extensive use of irrigation in preindependence time. Some scholars think the use of the Indus system water for irrigation is as ancient as the Harappa civilization in the third millennium B.C.; they base the opinion on the archaeological evidence of old canals. Possibly they are right, but it must be admitted that the canals could be of later origin than in Harappa times. In the nineteenth and twentieth centuries, in any event, cultivation by irrigation was the main reliance for agriculture there. Hence in Pakistan's First Five-Year Plan further irrigation works were planned, some by inundation canals, some by tube wells. Also, irrigation projects were undertaken in East Pakistan. In this respect, as in most others, the First Five-Year Plan's achievements fell far below hopes. Under the Second Five-Year Plan Pakistan continued the program of the first plan and expanded it. The allocation of funds for water and power development was the largest segment of the plan, involving an expenditure of 3.14 billion rupees ($659.4 million), which was about 32 percent of all the expenditures planned in the private sector (Rs. 9.75 billion). With some supplement expected from the semipublic and public sectors the planned expenditure was Rs. 3.39 billion, about 18 percent of the plan's contemplated total (Rs. 19 billion). The various works planned for East Pakistan (now Bangladesh) were meant to regulate river flow, protect tidal lands against sea water, drain wet swampy areas after the monsoons, determine ground water potential and the use of ground and surface waters, and develop electricity. In West Pakistan the works involved building storage facilities, remedying waterlogging, salinity, and alkalinity, revamping canals, channeling of rivers and protecting Indus delta lands from sea encroachment, and generating electricity. The need for water and power works in Bangladesh is of high importance; in Pakistan such works are at the very basis of human existence itself. In Bangladesh the largest schemes are the Karnafuli hydroelectric project and the Ganges-Kabadak development project. In Pakistan the principle schemes are the multipurpose Warsak project on the Kabul River in the northwest, the Kurram Garhi power and irrigation scheme, three major barrage works meant to put 6.5 million acres of land under irrigation, and a tube-well project at Rasul. All these and some others were under construction in the 1950s. Pakistan, it has been estimated, has to bring under cultivation 45 million acres of cultivable land out of an estimated cultivable total of 75 million acres.

India's problem of feeding her population now seems to some planners to have a solution in sight. Improved seed and breeds of grain, use of fertilizers and pesticides, increase of irrigation, crop planning, better marketing facilities, and improved laws of land tenure have been producing encouraging results. People even speak of "India's Green Revolution."

Forest conservation, development of use of forest products, soil conservation, and checking of desiccation are other important problems in the subcontinent.

The extension of fisheries—fresh, brackish, and marine—could increase food resources. It has been estimated that the present consumption is around 3.5 pounds per capita a year, as against 16 in Ceylon and 70 in Burma. The fishermen would have to be organized and helped to obtain supplies and market the catch. Seagoing mechanized fishing craft must be multiplied. Modern nets and other fish-catching devices are needed.

The extraction of the subcontinent's mineral resources, most of which lie in India, needs development. India, with the cooperation of the United States, inaugurated a minerals survey in 1967, searching primarily for copper, zinc, and lead deposits. India produces coal, iron ore, manganese ore, mica, gold, ilmenite, building materials, bauxite, industrial clays, steatite, chromite, atomic energy minerals, refractory minerals, and abrasives. For any large industrial production these need to be supplemented by imports of sulphur, copper, tin, nickel, lead, zinc, graphite, cobalt, mercury, and liquid fuels. The search for petroleum, which the subcontinent badly needs, has not located any great reserves, but Pakistan found large natural gas fields in West Pakistan, the best known being at Sui, where the reserves are estimated to be 6 million cubic feet, and at Mari, where they are estimated to be 3.5 million cubic feet. Production began in 1955. Pakistan produces a small amount of crude oil, about 82 million imperial gallons a year. India also has a small production. Both countries import petroleum produlcts. The Indian mining industry is poorly organized and methods still need modernizing. Nevertheless there was improvement during the period of the First and Second Five-Year Plans, and production of coal, iron ore, and other metals increased. Iron ore production began in Pakistan in 1956.

Industrial development in the subcontinent has to proceed side by side with agricultural. If for no other reason, this is necessary to give employment to the increasing surplus labor force. It is also necessary to put the subcontinent on a more nearly self-sufficient basis and give it commodities for export trade. Almost all the subcontinent's existing industry is located in India. It is still lopsided in producing more consumers' goods than producers' goods, though under the First and Second Five-Year plans the discrepancy was reduced. The greatest strength is in cotton textiles: 1.67 to 1.8 billion pounds of yarn and 4.9 to 5.35 billion yards of cloth are produced annually. India had a production for 1967–1968 of about 6.3 million metric tons of steel ingots; about 6.9 million metric tons of pig iron, ferro-alloys, and direct castings; and about 3.4 million metric tons of finished steel. India was expanding its steel industry, but had to contract the expansion in 1967 under the pressure of an economic recession brought on by the bad crop years of 1966–67. But plans for continuation of the expansion already in progress were not abandoned. India produces over 8 million tons of cement. It produces sugar (in the neighborhood of 3 million metric tons annually), paper, cigarettes, soap, matches, bicycles, radios, automobiles, electric fans, domestic appliances. It raises over 55 million metric tons of coal annually (increase from 34 million in 1951). There is a shipbuilding yard at Vizagapatam on the east coast with a production capacity of three ships of modern design per year. Under the Fourth Five-Year Plan it was hoped to raise this to six ships. A second shipbuilding yard is being developed in Cochin with Japanese cooperation. Since the war India has been developing the manufacture of machine tools,

Diesel engines, textile machinery, locomotives. It has been developing a nuclear fission industry for nonmilitary purposes. India began plans in 1948 for the development of atomic power. The Atomic Energy Act was passed in 1948 and the Indian Atomic Energy Commission was set up on August 19, 1948, with the late Dr. H. J. Bhabha as its chairman. India's first nuclear research reactor was operational on August 4, 1956. Now there are three nuclear research reactors, and a nuclear fuel complex is being established at Hyderabad to meet the fuel requirements of power reactors. The Minister of State in the Department of Atomic Energy stated in May 1967 that nuclear power will be produced by 1974. Under the Third Five-Year Plan India hoped to expand basic metallurgical, chemical, mechanical, and electrical engineering industries, as well as textile and food industries.

The growth of industry generally since independence has, of course, been unprecedented in India's history. In this period the country has made greater industrial progress than in the entire preceding century. The total industrial labor force employed in registered factories seems to have increased from around less than two million to about three million. (The total industrial labor of India in 1961 was stated by the Planning Commission to be 7.5 million out of a total labor force of 165 million.)

At the time of independence Congress had talked of nationalization of industry, but business would not cooperate on these terms and the government therefore announced in 1948 that nationalization would be postponed for at least ten years, perhaps longer, as indeed has been the case. The government also had to ease the terms it had first announced for the investment of foreign capital. The government reserved for itself control over munitions, atomic energy, railways, communications, transportation, electric power. It has promoted new iron and steel plants, seeking financial assistance from abroad (the United States, West Germany, the Soviet Union). But private industry has also expanded greatly in the fields of iron and steel, textiles, and others mentioned above. Large industries and small have had a part in the development, the private sector in the Third Five-Year Plan being assigned a greater part than in the preceding plans.

As objectives of industrial development, the Indian Planning Commission sees production of the tools and materials needed for agriculture, irrigation, and power; increase of the supply of consumers' goods; expansion of heavy industries (pig iron, steel, heavy chemicals, and others); and the filling in of gaps in the existing industrial structure. The supply of raw materials needs to be increased—this is in part a function of an agricultural program. These aims have been furthered by both planning and legislation. The Fourth Five-Year Plan, though holding to these aims, looked forward to "self-reliance" as a goal even though this would mean less borrowing and therefore less development.

Pakistan has had some industrial progress since independence, almost entirely in West Pakistan, but is still nearly unindustrialized. From producing no cotton yarn in 1948 it moved to a production of around 380 million pounds in 1959. Cotton cloth yardage rose from about 88 million yards in 1948 to about 576 million yards in 1958. In 1959–1960 Pakistan exported yarn and cloth valued at Rs. 200 million ($42 million). The cotton textile interest employs more than one third the total labor force in large-scale industries.

In the jute industry in what is now Bangladesh mill production grew from nothing in 1948 to an estimated 232,000 tons (not a large amount) in 1959–1960, with 14 mills in operation. This industry was the second largest employer of industrial labor in Pakistan.

A cement industry in Pakistan grew from 324,000 tons in 1948 to a capacity in 1960 of 1.22 million tons annually. Before independence in 1947 the area later included in West Pakistan produced about 35,000 tons of sugar (1947); by 1958 this had increased to about 1.6 million tons. Pakistan's resources for foreign exchange were chiefly raw jute (now in Bangladesh and so lost to Pakistan) and raw cotton, which accounted for over three fourths of the nation's exports. Pakistan looked for private investment in its proposed development under the Second Five-Year Plan; the plan said, "Private investment in industry is to be given maximum encouragement." It was expected under the plan that of the total of Rs. 19 billion the plan called for, the government would supply Rs. 11.5 billion and private sources Rs. 7.5 billion.

Bangladesh has an extensive jute export business—indeed has almost an international monopoly. It also exports tea.

After World War II the railways of the subcontinent needed extensive rehabilitation—an expensive proposition, involving the purchase of modern equipment. India's railway system has about

35,000 route miles and is the longest in Asia; Pakistan and Bangladesh together, 7,000 miles. The highway system also needs modernization. In India it is about 400,000 miles in length, an estimated 144,000 of which has hard surface. Pakistan and Bangladesh together have about 65,000 miles of highways, of which about 10,500 are all-weather roads. In each country the present system can be tolerated only because the bullock cart is still the prevailing form of rural transport in the initial stages of getting agricultural surpluses to market, that is, in conveying them to the railways.

Port facilities have been expanded since independence. India has seven so-called major ports, the newest being Kandla in the section of Gujarat formerly known as Cutch, which was opened in 1961. The others are Calcutta, Bombay, Madras, Cochin, Marmagaon in Goa, and Vizagapatam. All of them together are able to handle about 37 million tons per year (as against 20 million tons at independence). India also has 225 minor ports, of which 150 are working ports, such as Calicut, Pondicherry, Verawal, handling about 5 million tons. Pakistan has a first-class port in Karachi, handling over 4 million tons annually (against 2.18 million in 1942–1948). Bangladesh has a port at Chittagong, in 1959–1960 handling 2.6 million tons (against 322,000 in 1947); it has a second port at Chalna-Mangla Anchorage, which was opened in December 1950 and in 1959–1960 handled 1.06 million tons. At the time of independence India had shipping of 391,000 gross registered tonnage; this has been increased to about 900,000. Indian registry ships carry all India's coastal trade, about 40 percent of India's trade with Burma, Ceylon, and other adjacent countries, and about 6 percent of the trade with distant countries. Pakistani shipping companies own 26 cargo ships, which are used for coastal trade. Each of the three nations has its own government-owned aviation line, though that of Bangladesh was reported in early 1972 to consist of only one airplane. The Indian and Pakistani lines operate domestic and international services and, especially in India, are undercutting upper-class railway travel.

Just as industrial production in the subcontinent is far below needs or potentialities, so the condition of industrial labor is substandard. The labor force is small in numbers, poorly paid, compelled to accept inferior working conditions, provided few if any chances for training; the workers are ill-housed and underfed, and inefficient. At present the work force displays diverse political allegiance. It was long drawn not from a settled industrial population but chiefly from agricultural workers, usually landless and belonging to the Backward Classes, who at times of seasonal unemployment or other economic distress migrate to urban areas for temporary jobs. In recent decades an urban industrial population has been coming into existence. It includes many women and children as well as transients—male workers who have left their families behind in the villages and will return to them when conditions improve. Turnover is high, unit productivity low. Many families live in perpetual debt. India has a statutory limitation of of 54 working hours to the week; in certain seasonal factories 60 hours are allowed. There is a good deal of labor legislation (in Pakistan especially since 1959) that is difficult to implement A Code of Discipline in Industry was put into effect in India in 1958. A scheme of Joint Management Councils, to give labor a sense of participation in industry, has been launched in India. There are two social security schemes, so far of very limited coverage, open to perhaps 4.5 million workers. Some employers, both private and government, have improved working conditions, provided better housing, furnished welfare amenities, but such improvements are by no means universal. Most industrial cities have labor camps. The usual evils of a developing urban life have indeed fallen upon the subcontinent's industrial workers.

Labor conditions being what they are, it is no wonder that the subcontinent has had a good deal of industrial dispute and that political parties have endeavored to get control of the labor organizations. Trade unionism began in India about 1920, though before that time there had been a few strikes and as early as 1887 the Indian National Congress had recognized that India had labor problems to solve. In 1918 the Madras Textile Union was formed and Gandhi led a nonviolent strike of textile workers in Ahmedabad, which was successful and resulted in the birth of the Ahmedabad Textile Labor Association. Gandhi rejected the class struggle in favor of cooperative solution of problems, but Indian trade unionism has not accepted this principle generally. In 1920 the All-India Trade Union Congress (AITUC) was formed with the cooperation of Congress, which made use of it in the first noncooperation movement (1920–1922). Several leading Con-

gressmen at various times in its early years held its presidency:
Jawaharlal Nehru, C. R. Das, Subhas Chandra Bose. But it was
dissatisfied when Gandhi and Congress called off the noncooperation campaign in 1922 with objectives unattained. The Communists, who had been active in the Indian labor movement since
1920, in 1927 tried and in 1929 succeeded in getting control of the
AITUC. In 1931 they lost control, and in the 1937 provincial
elections Congress won a majority of the seats reserved for labor.
Labor, however, was disappointed with its few gains under the
Congress ministries in 1937–1939, and in 1942, when the Congress leaders were in detention and the Communists at large,
the Communists again won so much power in the AITUC as practically to control it and they still do.

Various splits and realignments have occurred in the labor
organizations since 1929 and besides the AITUC there are now
three other important national labor organizations in India. Of
these the Indian National Trade Union Congress (INTUC),
founded in 1947, is formally an independent body but it was
organized under Congress leadership by Vallabhbhai Patel and
Acharya Kripalani. The INTUC accepts the Gandhian principle
of cooperation between management and labor and a certain
degree of government leadership. In return the government nomi-
nates members of it to the International Labor Organization, considering it the most representative Indian labor group.

In 1948 the Hind Mazdoor Sabha (Indian Labor Association,
HMS) was founded chiefly at the inspiration of the Socialist party,
at that time newly become an independent successor to the
(former) Congress Socialist party, and headed by Jayaprakash
Narayan. Another labor organization was founded in 1949 under
the name United Trades Union Congress (UTUC) by nonparty
Socialists, including the well-known economist K. T. Shah.

There is also an All-India Railwaymen's Federation (AIRF),
which is not a trade union congress, but a federation of unions
aligned with various parties; its most influential element seems
to be the Socialist.

The membership of the four trade union congresses is hard to
determine, since requirements are loose and the figures each
group issues are challenged by its rivals. *India, A Reference
Annual 1970* gives the following figures.

	Number of unions affiliated			Membership		
	1958	1960	1966	1958	1960	1966
INTUC	727	860	1,305	910,221	1,053,386	1,417,533
AITUC	807	886	808	537,567	508,962	433,564
HMS	151	190	258	192,948	286,202	436,977
UTIC	182	229	170	82,001	110,034	93,454
Total	1,867	2,165	2,541	1,722,737	1,958,584	2,381,528

Trade unions in India are poorly financed and provided almost no hardship benefits for workers. They are set up by industry or locality, rather than by craft, and get much of their direction from middle class leaders. Nevertheless, they have promoted labor's sense of solidarity and have organized large strikes, as in the Bombay textile industry in 1928 and 1950.

In Pakistan trade unions are controlled by the Trade Unions (Amendment) Ordinance of 1960. Trade unionism is little developed on the national scale because industry is small and the workers few. One organization was the Pakistan Trade Unions Congress, Communist-controlled, whose president until his arrest on charges of complicity in a revolutionary conspiracy case, March 1951, was Faiz Ahmed Faiz, editor of the Pakistan *Times* (Lahore). Another is the non-Communist All-Pakistan Confederation of Labour organized in 1950 by the merger of two already existing labor organizations.

The improvement of living conditions in the subcontinent, whether rural or urban, requires a great increase in low-cost housing. The total task of providing adequate housing would take so much in building materials, architectural designing, city and town planning, and financing that it can be accomplished only by minute and slow stages. Beginning in 1961 long-term studies of various cities were undertaken starting with Calcutta.

Solution of the subcontinent's social and economic problems requires large expenditure of money, that is, large for the subcontinent. The government of India has an annual ordinary revenue of only about $4.34 billion, the government of Pakistan including what is now Bangladesh, had a revenue of about $1.67 billion. None of the three nations can obtain from its own resources the amount needed to raise the living standards of its population, but must get much assistance from outside. Both must rely upon careful planning for economic growth and both have undertaken it.

The government of India started its Third Five-Year Plan on

April 1, 1961, and on August 7, 1961, announced that its total expenditure under that plan was to be about $24.36 billion. Of this $2.52 billion was to be for "current outlays" for extending social services and for certain administrative overheads on plan projects and programs while "the figure for total private and public investment was $21,840 million (Rs. 10,400 crores) [at 1960–1961 prices], about 50 per cent more than in the second plan, allowing for the increase in prices."

The First Five-Year Plan had originally called for an expenditure of Rs. 2,069 crores (a crore = 10,000,000), which was later raised to Rs. 2,356 crores, but the amount that actually became available and was spent was Rs. 1,960 crores ($4.12 billion).

The government regarded the First Five-Year Plan as a success. National income was estimated to have been raised above the expected level, and so too was per capita income. On the basis of the expected achievement and during the years 1954 and 1955, when harvests were unusually good, the Planning Commission drafted the Second Five-Year Plan, calling for total expenditures of Rs. 4,800 crore ($10.08 billion).

The great contrast between the first and second plans lay in the greatly increased expenditure contemplated for expansion of industry, and in the matter of financing, that is, in the great increase expected from nongovernment and private investment. Before execution of the plan was half over it was evident that the cost of the planned developments had been greatly underestimated, and the amount of private and foreign aid had been greatly overestimated. The Planning Commission could devise no way to meet these conditions and the plan had to be cut back severely.

The Third Five-Year Plan, even as reduced, called for a program more than twice as expensive as the Second Five-Year Plan when it was adopted, since it involved Rs. 10,400 crore ($21,840 million) of capital investment. Per capita annual income, even with the expected population growth to 492 million by 1966, was to rise from $69.30 to $80.95. Self-sufficiency in food grains was to be achieved, and 14 million new jobs were to be created. The Plan was democratically conceived, reaffirming the government's aim of achieving a socialistic pattern of society, and conceded a large place to the private sector in the development of India. Two weeks after announcement of the projected amount of expenditure under the Third Five-Year Plan, that is, on August 21, 1961, Nehru announced in Parliament that austerity would have to be India's program to finance it.

India was encouraged in June 1961 to count on heavy foreign assistance when the so-called Aid-to-India Club made a substantial pledge toward the first two years' operations under the Third Five-Year Plan. This was a consortium of six nations: the United States, Great Britain, Canada, France, West Germany, Japan. The United States agreed to match the sums made available by the other nations up to $500 million a year. The total amount pledged by the consortium was $2 billion. To this was added $225 million from the International Bank of Reconstruction and Development and $45 million in United States loans made earlier. The United States subscription totaled $1.045 billion. All subscriptions were subject to approval of the nations' legislatures. The nations met the first year's subscriptions but fell short in the second year. However, four new nations joined the consortium in 1962— Austria, Belgium, Italy, and the Netherlands—contributing among them $79 million, which was matched by the United States, and the International Bank added $50 million.

Pakistan's planning was at a less advanced stage and on a less ambitious scale than India's. The First Five-Year Plan (1955–1960) was never really backed by the Pakistan government until 1958, as the Second Five-Year Plan pointed out, and it cannot be considered to have been implemented, though progress was made toward economic growth. The plan called for a total outlay of Rs. 10,800 million ($2,269 billion), of which Rs. 7,500 million were to be in the public sector and Rs. 3,300 million in the private sector. It appears, according to the Second Plan, that total expenditures were Rs. 9,715 million, of which Rs. 6,315 million were in the public sector and Rs. 3,400 million in the private sector.

The Second Five-Year Plan proposed an expenditure of Rs. 19,000 million ($3.99 billion). Supplementary to the amount of the plan budget were the sums the Pakistan government receives from the United States under the Mutual Security Act and Public Law 83-480, without which during the years since 1953 Pakistan's economy might well have collapsed. In January 1962 the same consortium that gave India a loan in 1961 set aside a credit to Pakistan of $945 million for the first two years of its development program under the plan, including $320 million allocated in

June 1961. Of the total the United States provided $500 million.

These plans represent the hopes of India and Pakistan for bringing prosperity to their citizens within the framework of their existing economic, social, and political systems. If the plans succeed, the two countries may be expected to continue within the ideological environment of the western democracies; if the plans fail and prosperity fades into an illusion, the nations may become open to counsels of desperation and violence and turn to some form of radical left philosophy or be captured by the radical right.

There has been a slowly accelerating economic growth in the twentieth century that can hardly fail to impress one who has been a recurrent visitor. Electricity is now common not only in cities but in many towns, and even in some villages; air travel is general for long distances; good roads are available between most of the large cities; airconditioning and refrigeration are abundant for the economically fortunate in the large cities (the masses still do not know them). Industrial plants have sprung up unexpectedly in many regions previously devoid of industry, and every day it seems that some new one is announced in the press. Education expands rapidly too. Some small progress has been made toward satisfying the needs of the people. Demand, however, increases more rapidly than the economy, and the deprived do not so resignedly accept their deprivation as half a century ago. Notable as economic growth has been, it lags far behind the rising expectations of the people, and the subcontinent is in a potentially explosive situation. United States interests are involved in the advancing movement of the subcontinent's economy. When the United States supports it, it invests in its own future as well as in the subcontinent's.

The prospects of economic development in India were seriously affected by the undeclared war with China in 1962. The country's material resources and manpower were diverted from the much needed development of agriculture, industry, transportation, and especially education and cultural activities; instead the country had to go on a war footing. This was a situation which could appall any nation, however rich; for India with its poverty it was a disaster. Pakistan at that time was spared the need to face a war, but its time came later with the revolt and secession of East Pakistan in 1971. Further, Pakistan could not fail to suffer when its greater neighbor in the subcontinent had to retrogress economically.

India has not ceased planning for prosperity. In 1971, after her sweeping victory in the national elections in that year, Mrs. Gandhi in a statement of policies prepared by her and read by President V. V. Giri on March 23, 1971, announced plans to reorganize the Planning Commission, wage war on poverty and unemployment, stimulate investment in economic undertakings, reform the system of land tenure, impose limitations on urban property holdings, abolish the tax-free pensions of the former princes (the privy purse), and other privileges, extend credit to agricultural workers, improve housing, both urban and rural, simplify licensing procedures for industry, and expand the family planning program. This was her program of advancement. She had no illusion of suddenly achieving the millennium. She will be satisfied to have her country just make some progress.

Pakistan has now, since the secession of Bangladesh, to reorganize its whole economy, a problem of staggering proportions. Bangladesh has an even more difficult problem, for besides the need to construct a national economy it has a scarcity of personnel experienced in public finance and national budgeting and planning. Both nations will need foreign advice and aid.

16 Foreign Relations

In the realm of international relations India and Pakistan have had to deal with two types of problems; Bangladesh will now have to deal with some of them. One kind consists of those in which one or the other of the nations is immediately concerned as a contesting party. These are such problems as their relations with each other, or disagreements of Pakistan with Afghanistan or of India with Portugal or China. Problems of the other kind are of less immediate concern to either nation but are of wider international range, in the widest sense matters in which the world at large is involved, above all the clash between the western democracies and the Soviet Union or China. These include such questions as thermonuclear arms testing, the status of Berlin, the composition of the United Nations. Problems of the first category are not sharply separated from problems of the second catgeory. For example, Pakistan's quarrel with Afghanistan has become associated with the efforts of both the Soviet Union and the United States to make an ally of Afghanistan, and India's quarrel with China over their Himalayan border impinges upon China's general concern about boundaries and immediate borderlands in Asia. On issues concerning which either India or Pakistan is a contestant that country naturally aims to promote its own interests as it views them. On larger questions of international significance India especially has avoided partisanship and has sought to act as an intermediary and assist in bringing about a peaceful solution. Led by Nehru, who must surely be regarded as one of the great constructive statesmen of the mid-twentieth century, India obtained a position of international prestige and influence quite out of proportion to its military or economic resources.

In considering the foreign relations of India, Pakistan, and Bangladesh we should look first at matters near at hand, treating them with some brevity, and we may begin with Pakistan's dispute with

Afghanistan, which was the only nation to vote against Pakistan's admission to the United Nations. In the largest sense this is a manifestation in the twentieth century of the ancient and continuing pressure from Central Asia through the mountainous and barren regions of Iran and Afghanistan into the northwestern section of the Indian subcontinent. In the nineteenth century British efforts to check the threat to India from Russia by way of Afghanistan led to wars with Afghanistan (1839–1842, 1878–1879, 1879–1880) and the drawing of the "Durand Line," which set a limit to British influence inside territory that Afghanistan regarded as its own. Since Pakistan attained independence the Pashtu-speaking people —inhabiting an area consisting of eastern Afghanistan, the western part of the old North-West Frontier Province, and the no-man's land between those two areas—have aspired to be a separate nation-state to be called Pakhtunistan, Land of the Pathans. Such a state would presumably incline more to Afghanistan than to Pakistan, which claims that Afghanistan supports the movement. Afghanistan repudiates the old Durand Line, which Pakistan has insisted on maintaining. Added to disputes over Pakhtunistan and delimitation of the border is the fact that Afghanistan is landlocked and has relied upon Karachi as its seaport. After independence Pakistan made transit of imports difficult, delaying the movement of Afghanistan imports, and in 1955 closed its border with Afghanistan for a few months. In July 1955 the two nations signed an agreement guaranteeing reciprocal transit rights.

Meanwhile the United States had signed its military and economic aid pact with Pakistan. Afghanistan, aiming at neutrality, accepted economic assistance from the United States as well as military and economic aid from the Soviet Union. By mid-1968 the United States grants amounted to $340 million, mostly for agricultural development in the Helmand valley, where years before the Morrison-Knudtsen Company had done a great deal of irrigation work and road-building. The Soviet grants to Afghanistan for similar purposes are estimated to have about equaled the United States grant. In addition the Soviet Union supplied arms.

Actual shooting took place between Afghanistan and Pakistan at various times, as in May 1961, each side claiming that the other was using arms supplied by the United States or the Soviet Union. In September 1961 Afghanistan broke off diplomatic relations with Pakistan. The Shah of Iran offered his services as mediator in 1962, but the two nations could not then agree to accept them. In July Ayub Khan remarked that Pakistan, Iran, and Afghanistan would do well to fuse into a greater political entity, a project that hardly seems realizable. In 1963 diplomatic relations were restored.

The simmering Pakhtunistan issue continues to prevent the achievement of good relations between Pakistan and Afghanistan. Meanwhile both the Soviet Union and China seem to stand by ready to intervene if a good excuse should offer itself.

At the time of independence both France and Portugal had small enclaves in India inherited from the sixteenth and seventeenth centuries. Almost immediately after gaining independence India opened negotiations about the surrender of these. France saw what had to be done and accepted the necessity of the situation, realizing that the most it could hope for was treaty rights with India. Not so Portugal.

France gave up one of her five possessions in 1952 after a referendum. This was Chandernagore, which in modern times has been a suburb of Calcutta. In November 1954, following an agreement with France, India took over the administration of the four other French establishments in India, 196 square miles in area, and on May 28, 1956, a treaty was signed in New Delhi by which France formally ceded the territories to India. The treaty was not finally ratified by the French National Assembly until July 12, 1962, but in the meantime India was in possession of the territories involved. The chief of these was Pondicherry, an inferior port on the east coast, south of Madras. India and France have remained on good terms and France is a member of the international Aid-to-India consortium.

Portugal, however, remained obdurate about its possessions, which consisted of Goa on the west coast south of Bombay, the island and anchorage of Diu at the southern end of the peninsula of Kathiawar, and the small fishing port of Daman (Damão) in Gujarat north of Bombay, which had a tiny landlocked outpost Nagar Aveli (or Haveli). The total area of these possessions was 1,615 square miles, of which 1,301 constituted Goa, and the total population was about 685,000, most of whom lived in Goa. Goa was a notorious channel of smuggling into India, and the profits from this trade restrained the ardor of those who practiced it for annexation by India. Goa is also a stronghold of the Roman Catholic church in India and was once a seat of the Inquisition. The vested church interests therefore opposed annexation. In spite of these two interests, a great deal of sentiment favoring a merger showed itself in Goa. The discussion between India and Portugal over the Portuguese possessions was acrimonious. In June 1953 India withdrew its mission to Lisbon, though it did not then sever diplomatic relations. In July 1954 some Indians took possession of a village named Dadra in Damão. By July 1955 there was agitation in India for "peaceful invasion" of Goa along the lines of *satyagraha,* but this was opposed by Nehru, though the government of India ordered Portugal to close its embassy in India by August 8, as a protest against Portugal's refusal to negotiate on Goa. An unarmed "invasion" finally took place in August; in this 21 Indians were reported killed and 120 wounded. On August 19, 1955, India broke off her last diplomatic relations with Portugal.

While the quarrel over Goa was progressing, N. A. Bulganin and Nikita Khrushchev, visiting India, issued strong pro-Indian and anti-Portuguese statements. Thereupon United States Secretary of State Dulles and Portugal's Foreign Minister Cunha, after a conference, issued a formal statement in which they jointly spoke of the Portuguese possessions in India as a "province" of Portugal. This was how the Portuguese described them, having passed an amendment to the Portuguese constitution (June 12, 1951) converting Portuguese overseas possessions to territories. As was bound to be the case, this was understood to put the United States on the side of Portugal, and the consequent reaction in India was intense and bitter, quite likely bringing more harm to American prestige there than it did good to the NATO alliance which it seemed meant to further.

In 1954 India refused to allow Portuguese troops to cross Indian territory to get from Damão town to Dadra and Nagar Aveli to quell revolts there. Portugal was angered by this and, after being admitted to membership in the United Nations in 1955, took the matter to the World Court at The Hague, which in April 1960 decided in India's favor. In October 1960 India announced its intention to administer the two villages and in August 1961 Parliament passed an act to integrate them. The issue of Goa itself lay dormant while in 1961 sentiment was developing in many parts of the world against Portugal over its administration of Angola. It was obvious that India could take the Portuguese territories with only a slight military operation but was restrained from doing so by other considerations.

In 1960, after the World Court's decision in favor of India, the United Nations Trusteeship Committee, unimpressed by the Portuguese claim that Goa was a Portuguese province rather than a possession, had adopted a resolution offered by the Afro-Asian nations that Portugal should transmit to the United Nations information concerning the territories it administered. On December 14 the General Assembly adopted an Afro-Asian resolution "solemnly proclaiming the necessity for bringing to a speedy and unconditional conclusion colonialism in all its forms and manifestations." The next day the General Assembly, rejecting Portugal's claim that its overseas possessions were provinces, listed them, including Goa, as nonselfgoverning territories, and demanded that Portugal transmit reports on them without further delay. Portugal would not comply and in 1961 took brutal measures in quelling a terrorist movement in Angola, for which the Security Council censured it (June 9, 1961). On November 31 the Trusteeship Committee adopted a 33-nation resolution reproving Portugal for not transmitting information about overseas territories.

These developments were watched with close attention in India, where tension over Goa became extreme. The press, the political parties, and a strong pro-Indian element in Goa itself were active on the issue, while Nehru was under considerable attack in Africa as being only a hypocritical proponent of anticolonialism. Then occurred disorders in Goa itself and reports circulated that Goa was building up military defenses. Indian vessels were fired on from Portuguese island fortifications. Late in December 1961, therefore, India moved into Goa, and in twenty-six hours took possession, with practically no bloodshed. The official Indian figures gave the Indian casualties as 22 dead and 53 injured, and the Portuguese as 17 dead, 38 injured, and one missing.

The Portuguese had lost the hold they had had in India for four and a half centuries, without so much as having treaty rights to protect their future interests, which Nehru had indicated were open as late as December 14, 1961. But presumably if Portugal had acceded to India on Goa, it would logically have had to make concessions to international, especially African, sentiment regarding Angola, a possession of vastly greater economic importance to her.

On taking possession of Goa India instituted military rule, which it terminated in May 1962 with the establishment of civil government. By an ordinance promulgated March 5, 1962, Goa and the other Portuguese areas became a federally administered territory with a civil service of 3,000 Goans, created in the time of Portuguese rule and retained by India, headed by a few top officials from India. In August 1962 the government of India began to institute land reform in the former Portuguese areas.

Closely related to India's domestic affairs are its relations with Nepal, Sikkim, and Bhutan, all strategically located in the Himalayas (map, page 202). Nepal is a sovereign independent state, about 500 miles in length. Bhutan is completely autonomous with respect to its internal affairs, but has entrusted its foreign relations to India and to that extent accepts Indian control. During the period of British rule, after making a treaty with Britain in 1910, its ruler tendered homage to the King-Emperor at the Delhi Darbar in 1911, and at the time of the transfer of power in 1947 it was regarded as an Indian State, but in a special category that excluded its territory from being considered Indian. Sikkim is a "protected state," having given India control of its foreign affairs, defense, communications, and currency, and thus is not fully autonomous, yet has not acceded to India.

India's concerns about Nepal, Bhutan, and Sikkim rise from China's forward policy in the Himalayas. After the Chinese began to move into Tibet, India occupied Sikkim (1949) to prevent "bloodshed" and executed a treaty with it (1950) gaining the right to conduct Sikkim's defense. Sikkim has a Congress party which urges accession to India and Indians hold important appointments under the government, while there is a demand among the people for liberalized institutions. The state lies athwart the route from India to Lhasa in Tibet and Chinese Communists have been active in the area, though China has made no territorial demands upon it. During India's brief war with Pakistan in 1965 China charged that Indian troops in Sikkim had fired across the boundary between Sikkim and Tibet, and demanded that India withdraw her troops. India denied the charge and did nothing. China too did nothing, but claimed that India had withdrawn. Today India keeps 25,000 troops in Sikkim (some say the number is 40,000).

Bhutan is more remote than Sikkim. Nehru visited it in 1958—having to do part of his traveling by pony, mule, and yak—to promote Indian interests against the Chinese claims to Bhutanese territory. India has since given Bhutan economic aid for development along modern lines and for defense, including some modern roads.

Nepal, long known to many westerners as the home of the famous Gurkha soldiers, whom the British and later the Indians recruited for the Indian army, emerged into world politics in consequence of Chinese Communist efforts to penetrate the country. After signing the treaty with Sikkim of 1950 India began to take a strong part in Nepal's affairs, stimulating reconstitution of the Nepal government and sending troops across the border to quell local uprisings. Nepal had long been ruled by a family named Rana, which had acquired hereditary possession of the premiership and kept the titular rulers in virtual imprisonment. In 1951 King Tribhubana managed by a coup to overthrow the Ranas and assume power himself and he instituted some reforms. He died in 1955 and was succeeded by his son Mahendra Bir Bikram Shah Deva, who continued the policy of gradual political reform. Prime Minister Nehru in November 1959 guaranteed to defend Nepal against aggression, obviously meaning aggression by China. India has given economic aid to Nepal—as has the United States—and has assisted with road-building. Nepal's own position in world affairs was stated by King Mahendra before the United States Congress on April 28, 1960, to be one of "nonalignment and nonentanglement." Nepalese politics, once the reconstitution was effected, have revolved chiefly around the issue of pro-India versus pro-China. Nepal's policy has been an effort to stand uncommitted to either, not unlike India's effort to stay neutral between the Soviet Union and the West. This policy is not acceptable to India, whose security interests require something more than complete neutrality on the part of Nepal.

The country has been developing industry. India purchases 90 percent of Nepal's exports and permits Nepal to ship the rest from Indian ports. This is under a trade agreement of 1960. When the agreement was expiring, the two nations could not agree on renewal terms and while they were negotiating the agreement ran out on December 31, 1960. There followed in Nepal shortage of gasoline and some other necessities, leading to anti-Indian demonstrations before trade was resumed. India gives financial aid to Nepal, which is a very poor country, and so does China, which has built a road from Katmandu, the capital of Nepal, to Lhasa in Tibet. The entire Himalayan area bordering China (that is, Tibet) is an unceasing worry to India, lest China should move through it into India as it did in 1962.

An important category of foreign relations concerned India and Pakistan as members of the British Commonwealth of Nations. This includes questions of relationship with the United Kingdom as the core of the Commonwealth and relations with other member nations. These questions now relate to Bangladesh, which was admitted to membership on April 18, 1972. Pakistan, however, withdrew from the Commonwealth on February 4, 1972, offended by Great Britain's recognition of Bangladesh.

During the latter phases of the nationalist struggle the Indian National Congress more than once formally committed itself to severing its political tie with Britain when it should win power. There were, of course, bound to be certain disadvantages in such an action. India would lose protection from the British navy and the trade preferences it enjoyed with other Commonwealth members. Some Congressmen conceded these points, but Congress as a whole felt that other features of the British association, which it considered offensive, should be decisive. It wanted to eliminate every form of foreign domination and even the appearance of it. It was influenced also by the general Indian resentment against discrimination based upon color which humiliated Indians in South Africa, Canada, Australia, New Zealand.

It is possible that if in 1947 India had obtained dominion status as a single unpartitioned nation, it would have exercised its right to secede from the Commonwealth. At the time of independence and partition, when the costly results of partition were only dimly foreseen and nationalist resentment against Britain still flamed high, most politically conscious persons in the subcontinent thought that of the two dominions India at least would leave the Commonwealth. Without doubt most of the British public thought so too. There was less apprehension in Britain concerning Pakistan, whose weaker position made her less likely to break away. Severance of relations by India was sure to be a serious blow to the Commonwealth. It would deprive it of nearly two thirds of its population and a large part of its area, diminish its economic power, and impair its prestige in Asia and the world. During the first year of dominion status there seemed to be an omen in the decision of Burma, which formally severed all ties with the Commonwealth when it became a republic early in 1948. One of the first resolutions of the Indian Constituent Assembly preparatory to framing a constitution, taken on January 22, 1947, six months before the British Parliament had passed the Indian Independence Act and while the Assembly still expected India to be an undivided nation, had asserted that India was to become an "independent sovereign republic." The situation was still delicate after independence and partition. Britain deplored the prospect of secession, but could only state, as it had stated previously in the Cabinet Mission's proposals in 1946, that it hoped the two new nations would maintain the connection.

It seems to have been Prime Minister Nehru who devised a solution continuing the association. In a conference of the eight Commonwealth prime ministers, April 1949, he agreed to a declaration, promptly ratified by the Indian Constituent Assembly in May, containing the words: "The Government of India have informed the other Governments of the Commonwealth of the intention of the Indian people that, under the new Constitution which is about to be adopted, India shall become a sovereign independent republic. The Government of India have, however, declared and affirmed India's desire to continue her full membership of the Commonwealth of Nations and her acceptance of the King as the symbol of the free association of its independent member nations and, as such the head of the Commonwealth."

This decision was a matter of great gratification to the rest of the Commonwealth. It was a relief to all parties in Britain, and Conservatives and Liberals, as well as Labourites, had worked to achieve it. In spite of some differences of opinion with India and Indians since, Britain and the British generally have stood well with Indians.

Pakistan did not redefine its position with respect to the Commonwealth after receiving dominion status in 1947. In various public statements high government officials from time to time expressed their country's satisfaction with the relationship, agreeing essentially with the sentiments of former Prime Minister Liaquat Ali Khan, speaking before the Canadian House of Parliament on May 31, 1950, when he said: "If the Commonwealth does nothing more than give the world a lead in establishing the brotherhood of man, irrespective of race, creed or colour, it will still have made a notable contribution to the cause of human welfare . . . the Commonwealth has great opportunities for raising the hopes of mankind by outlawing war and aggression and the use of coercion as a method of settling disputes amongst its own members. We sincerely believe that in this way the free association of free nations can set the world an inspiring example and can give greater reality and efficiency not only to itself but also to the charter of the United Nations, to whose aims we are all pledged and whose success we all pray for." By the constitution of 1962 the Republic of Pakistan proclaimed itself a sovereign state, but the membership in the Commonwealth was not cancelled at that time.

There has been a certain amount of anti-British sentiment in Pakistan, partly resulting from dissatisfaction with the Radcliffe award demarcating the partition lines with India in 1947, and partly created by a feeling that Britain has not stood at Pakistan's side in the disputes with India before the United Nations. Britain's disputes with other Islamic nations—Iran, Egypt, Iraq—over oil, the Suez crisis in 1956, and its presumed favoritism to Israel have intensified the situation because Pakistan has strong sympathy for them as Muslim kin.

The European Common Market has caused some apprehension. Membership by Britain in it will, in the opinion of many leaders in India—as in some other Commonwealth nations—impair their own economic interests, since the Commonwealth countries would lose their preferential treatment. About 15 percent of India's exports go to the United Kingdom, and so this is a very real concern.

In the relations of India and Pakistan with Commonwealth states before the withdrawal of Pakistan from the Commonwealth in 1972 the thorniest issues concerned the treatment of emigrants from the subcontinent and their descendants. There are around three million such persons in Ceylon, Malaysia, Fiji, Mauritius, Jamaica, Trinidad, British Guiana, Kenya, Tanzania, Uganda, and the Union of South Africa (since May 1961 no longer a member of the Commonwealth). In Fiji, Trinidad, and British Guiana Indians constitute from one third to nearly half of the population, in Mauritius about two thirds. There are negligible numbers in Canada, Australia, and New Zealand, but the smallness of the numbers is the result only of strict exclusion policies (modified in Canada in 1950 to permit a small number of immigrants). A million more live in Burma, which was a member of the Commonwealth until 1948, and the status of Indians there was a Commonwealth problem.

Indians first went to most of these regions as unskilled cheap labor, eagerly desired in undeveloped areas, such as South Africa (especially Natal) and the British West Indies. Often they went under indenture, being recruited from uneducated and economically underprivileged groups. They had low standards of living and were looked down upon in their new homes. When their terms of service were completed, they usually remained in the country, having few or no ties to draw them back to India. They did not, however, become assimilated. They retained an Indian language, adhered to their native religion, married almost exclusively among themselves, and observed many of their traditional social practices. Sometimes they were joined by other Indians, who came unbound by indenture, to make their living either as laborers or traders. A few Indians came for the professions, mostly for law; Gandhi won his first fame in South Africa by being a legal champion of his fellow Indians.

In various parts of the Commonwealth Indians have been and still are subjected to disabilities of domicile, which make them second-class citizens. These include denial or elaborate restriction of franchise, limitation upon ownership of property and rights of trading, restriction of intermarriage with non-Indians, segregation of residence on "sanitary" grounds without any accompanying provision of sanitary facilities, denial or severe limitation of entry to public eating and amusement places frequented by "whites"—in short, some form or other of legal Jim-Crowism.

Indians abroad look back to the government of India for protection of their civil rights and the government of preindependence undivided India accepted the responsibility. One might say that Indians living in foreign countries, even unto the third and fourth generation, are still looked upon in India as Indians. In their interest the government of preindependence India conducted negotiations, frequently unprofitable, with the dominions and the British Colonial Office. The feeling in India was one of resentment, especially toward the dominions where color prejudice was a factor. In the then colonies or possessions where the population, like that of India, was dark-skinned, agreements were worked out to protect Indian laborers and at the same time to keep emigration from India within limits satisfactory to the receiving country. Some of these agreements have at times proved insufficient, for example, those with Ceylon (then a British possession) concerning voting regulations and labor conditions.

The dominions and colonies with higher living standards than India's wanted protection from India's inexhaustible reservoir of unskilled, undernourished, cheap labor, and many Indians and Pakistanis since independence have seen justice in this desire. They have also concluded that protection of their country's own good name abroad requires control of emigration. Hence they have modified their bitterness at being excluded as a group. They remain firm, however, in demanding just civil status for Indians legally in Commonwealth states. In recent years, therefore, they have fought hard in the United Nations for a full and extensive code of human rights.

The longest and most bitter quarrel was with the Union of South Africa, where the Boers have been more race-conscious than the British ever were. As a dominion South Africa had a long history of discrimination against Indians. After Indian independence the first real crisis came in March 1951, when South Africa put into operation a Group Areas Act, imposing segregation and a series of other restrictions. By it no one could live, acquire property, or conduct business in any area except one designated for his own racial group. India and Pakistan had already objected to this law and had laid a complaint before the United Nations General Assembly. Periodically from that time on South Africa has had to meet almost universal world criticism for its policy of apartheid or racial segregation imposed by the 3,000,000 whites who rule the total population of about 12,000,000. In May 1960 Nehru raised the question of South African apartheid in the conference of Commonwealth prime ministers, which criticized South Africa. In consequence Prime Minister Verwoerd conducted a campaign for withdrawal from the Commonwealth which was effected May 31, 1961. The issue between India and Pakistan on one side and the Union of South Africa on the other remains unresolved with no evidence to show that the governing group in South Africa is minded to adapt itself to the attitude of the modern world on racism.

Race discrimination in South Africa and exclusion policies in current members of the Commonwealth have thus damaged Commonwealth solidarity and help foster an inter-Asian or Asian-African alignment that might disrupt it. If the Commonwealth is to continue, those members in which the rulership is white will have to gain and hold the confidence of those where the population is dark. The nationalist revolutions in Asia and Africa, those already achieved and others still in progress, demand the removal of racism.

In Kenya there has come into existence a social situation concerning Asians domiciled there that has deeply disturbed Indians and Pakistanis and has produced a paradoxical and embarrassing consequence in Britain. The Asians in Kenya—as also in Uganda and Tanzania, which with Kenya were formerly British East African possessions—are mostly Indian and Pakistani emigrants from prepartioned India and their descendants. When Britain gave Kenya its independence in 1963, the Independence Act gave these persons the option of being British citizens or, for two years, taking Kenyan citizenship. Most Asians seem not to have taken Kenyan citizenship, perhaps not having thought about future developments. The Kenyans had, it happened, become unhappy about the Asians in their midst, most of whom were small merchants, not wealthy but living in at least modest comfort, having marked ability in business—more of such ability than the Kenyans showed. Indeed, the Asians dominated small trade and, thus the Kenyans felt, blocked Kenyans from profitable employment. Early in 1968 the Minister of Commerce and Industry in Kenya announced that "within the next six months the Government estimates that about 3,000 noncitizen traders will have been refused licenses. This is a conservative estimate. There could be more."

The Asians, recognizing that their livelihood was imperiled, began to emigrate from Kenya, most of them going to India or to Britain. Neither country really wanted them. India felt that it could not repatriate some 90,000 British citizens of Indian origin living in Kenya, when it was already repatriating many Indians who had been living in Ceylon and Burma, and might be called upon to receive back in India some five million Indians living in other countries. Those with British passports might better go to Britain, which was in a better economic position to provide for them than was India. But Britain already had been accepting a great many Indians and Pakistanis since the war, and a problem of color prejudice was developing there. When a flood of Indians and Pakistanis began coming to Britain from Kenya, the matter of Asian immigration was debated in the House of Commons, and the Labour government introduced a bill to permit only 1500 heads of Asian families with British passports and their dependents to enter Britain annually. On February 27, 1968, this bill was approved in principle by a vote of 372 to 62, with about 180 abstentions. The inconsistency of denying entry into Britain of British citizens with valid passports was, of course, a shock to the British ideals of justice and there were demonstrations against the bill.

The British Parliament's action alarmed India, which feared an influx from Kenya, and in March India's Minister of State for External Affairs announced in the Indian Parliament that British citizens in Kenya wishing to enter India would have to apply for visas, an unprecedented ruling in India, which until then had been admitting freely all Commonwealth citizens except Pakistanis. It was reported that Indians had begun to leave Uganda and Tanzania in similar circumstances.

By March of 1969 the government of Kenya had checked its purge of Indian traders, presumably because the loss of the Asians' business efficiency was proving detrimental to the nation's economy.

Ceylon and India have for decades discussed the question of the South Indians, mostly Tamil-speaking, in Ceylon, who migrated there over the past hundred years or more to work on the tea and rubber plantations. These migrant laborers came at first without protection of their civil rights; later the government of India, feeling a responsibility for them, succeeded in getting, bit by bit, some recognition of their rights. In recent years, when Ceylon's tea and rubber exports have been declining, the government of Ceylon has found these Indian Tamils more a burden than an asset. Besides the Tamil laborers there is another Tamil section of the Ceylonese population, which is of long standing in the island, a thousand years or even longer, with fully established citizenship, living in and controlling the northern part of the island and enjoying social esteem. The civil rights of these people, referred to as Ceylon Tamils, have not been at issue; in any event since they are Ceylonese, not Indian, the government of India does not consider them its responsibility.

The latest agreement between India and Ceylon concerning the immigrant Tamil laborers was reached in 1964. This provided for the repatriation during a period of fifteen years of 525,000 of these Tamils with their dependents, and for the recognition of 300,000 as Ceylonese citizens. The fate of 200,000 of the group was left undecided. The fulfillment of the provisions of the agreement has been slow. In August 1969, when five of the fifteen years had expired, the Indian High Commissioner's office in Ceylon reported that only 9,792 of the Tamils covered by the agreement had left for India, while the Ceylonese government reported that only one thousand had received Ceylonese citizenship. Since the signing of the agreement Ceylon has altered its provisions for granting citizenship to aliens, limiting the number to twenty-five in any one year. Also the government of Ceylon had imposed foreign exchange controls which made it difficult for Indians to take their assets out of the country, but these regulations were being eased by 1969. Nevertheless it seems very doubtful that the provisions of the 1964 agreement can be fulfilled in the specified period of fifteen years.

With Canada India's relations have been good in spite of the limitation on immigration. Canada has given aid to India for various purposes including the development of an atomic power plant at Rana Pratap Sagar, and has established a Shastri Indo-Canadian Institute of Indian Studies (1968) for service to the growing field of Indian studies in Canada. The Shastri Institute has purposes analogous to those of the American Institute of Indian Studies founded in 1961.

Membership in the Commonwealth was for a time in the 1950s felt by many thoughtful Indians and Pakistanis to be of less importance than association with other Asian nations. With Asians they argued, India and Pakistan had the prospect of more productive relations than with Commonwealth areas. With them, too, they could have more mutual understanding, because they have similar problems to solve and a similar dearth of resources to use in the solution. They also have a common affinity in that they themselves are Asians and constitute a group that is marked off from white-skinned western groups.

To appreciate the position the nations of the subcontinent have taken in their relations with other Asian nations and with African nations it is necessary to recall two important features of their history in the nineteenth and twentieth centuries and their present internal situation. One is the pressing poverty and population problem, which demands each nation's primary attention and the use of all available material resources to relieve it. For India and Pakistan, with their weak economies, involvement in full-scale war would bring obliteration of the very basis of life. In dealings with other Asian nations they have therefore had the fundamental and compelling motive of maintaining peace between themselves and those nations and between those nations and European and American nations.

Secondly, because they themselves emerged from a colonial status only in 1947 and many of their people are still on the defensive with regard to the western industrialized powers, they have been keenly sensitive to any infringement upon the independence of other Asian nations and, as African nationalism has developed, of African nations as well. These nations, they often maintain, when in dispute with one another, should reach a settlement without interference from western nations and in such a dispute other Asian or African nations would be the most interested external parties and the natural go-betweens and arbiters. This assertion of intra-Asian and African autonomy has been buttressed by resentment of western racism and an unswerving promotion of their own modernizing economic, political, and social revolution. It has not been accompanied, however, by general Asian and African solidarity; rather, disputes and jealousies exist among those various nations themselves.

The feeling against western imperialism explains the lukewarm support India gave the western powers in World War II when the Japanese had occupied Indonesia, Indo-China, Siam, Malaya, and Burma, had bombed Calcutta, and stood poised at the Burma frontier to invade eastern India. Similarly, after the war was over, westerners were astounded at the intense sentiment which arose in India on behalf of those Indians who had collaborated with the Japanese in Malaya and Burma to form the Indian National Army. Their resentment forced the government to abandon prosecution of that army's leaders for treason. To Indians there was after all not much difference between imperialist Japanese and imperialist westerners. What India's eyes were fixed upon was the common element of both, namely, the imperialism.

The conviction that Asian nations should work together with common international aims led India to convene the Asian Relations Conference in New Delhi during March and April 1947 (before partition). Twenty-eight countries participated, from the Near East, Southern Asia, Southeastern Asia, Central Asia, and the Far East. Some of these were Asian republics included in the Soviet

Union. The topics discussed at the conference were national movements for freedom, intra-Asian migration, transition from colonial
to national economy, agricultural reconstruction and industrial development, labor problems and social services, cultural problems,
the status of women and women's movements. In connection with
the conference there was an Asian art exhibition, a science exhibition, and an archaeological exhibition. An Asian relations organization was set up to provide for future meetings, but this never
came to much. It was clear from the discussions that these Asian
nations felt they had common interests of political, economic, and
intellectual development, and faced social problems that required
united action. It was also clear that they felt they must preserve
their independence against any political or economic encroachment from the West. Some years later, India, Pakistan, and other
Asian nations created the Asian-Arab bloc, which for a time was a
strong force in the United Nations. But neither the Asian Relations
Conference nor the Asian-Arab bloc showed the existence of Asian
solidarity or created the "third force" in international affairs that
some observers feared. Nor did either show that India was dominant in Asian affairs or wishful to become so.

As time has passed Indian and Pakistani suspicion of the western powers has diminished markedly, especially as these powers
have given friendly assistance to the two countries in meeting their
pressing economic problems.

In their relations with other Asian nations India and Pakistan
have tended to cast their glances in opposite geographical directions. Though each has had a concern with all of Asia, India has
looked more toward Southeast and Eastern Asia while Pakistan has
looked prevailingly toward Western Asia, the Near and Middle
East.

This divergence has a basis in history. From India's indigenous
traditional culture, much of religion, literature, drama, language,
folklore, script, architecture, sculpture, dance, proper names—family, personal, and place—and law has gone out by sea to Ceylon,
Thailand, Burma, Malaysia, Singapore, Cambodia, and Indonesia,
even to Vietnam. By land it has gone to Central Asia. It was carried by colonizers and merchants and occasionally by conquerors.
From some of these areas items have gone still farther, by sea
from Southeast Asia to the Philippines and the Pacific, by land
from Central Asia to China and Korea, and from China and Korea

still farther by sea to Japan. India has been one of the great contributors to civilization in Southeast and Eastern Asia, and is well
aware of her contributions. Those regions on their side are for the
most part aware of their borrowing, and ties have therefore been
created.

Pakistan, as a Muslim nation adhering in large measure to a
nonindigenous culture, looks back to the lands where Islam was
born and became great. This is natural enough. Indian Islam has
had an uneasy stance in the subcontinent and has sought to steady
itself by leaning upon the Muslim West. Part of the motivation has
been a still larger desire to see all Islamic nations working together. When a conference of Muslim divines from all Islam was
held in Karachi in February 1952, Prime Minister Khwaja Nazimuddin said that Pakistan's "existence has brought the unification
of the Muslim world and the cohesion of the *Millat* [Faith] within
the pale of possibility." Shortly afterwards Pakistan proposed a
conference in Karachi of the prime ministers of twelve Muslim
countries (Afghanistan, Egypt, Indonesia, Iran, Iraq, Jordan, Lebanon, Libya, Saudi Arabia, Syria, Turkey, and Yemen) besides itself.
The purpose was to consult on questions of common interest. Pakistan has sought to be a part of Western Asia, though itself uncher-
ished by the classical lands of Islam. Hence it would forget geography and normal economic relations, ignore the natural associations it should have with India, and cultivate instead new links,
supplementing the existing connections of spiritual culture with
fragile and illusive transmontane threads of political and economic
intercourse.

India's relations with the nations of Southeast Asia were for a
decade or more basically determined by opposition to Western imperialism. The war was hardly over before the Indian National
Congress, through its Working Committee, adopted (September 21,
1945) a resolution asking for freedom from "imperialist domination" of India, Burma, Malaya, Indo-China, and Indonesia.

The first reference of this resolution outside India was to Indonesia. To Indian leaders there was only one just solution of that
situation: the Indonesians themselves should prescribe their own
form of government and should not be compelled to accept any
arrangement that would perpetuate Dutch control. Shortly after
Nehru and the other nationalist political leaders of India had been
released from jail on June 15, 1945, they paid visits to Indonesia

and Singapore. Thereafter they indicated that they expected Indonesia to be self-governing now that the Dutch had been expelled and an Indonesian republic had come into existence. They were disappointed that the British had condoned, even helped, the restoration of Dutch power in Java. In 1947, when the Dutch failed to adhere to the terms of agreements they had made with the Indonesian republic, the Indians again expressed their keen disapproval.

After the Dutch in December 1948, in a "police action," had moved by force of arms against Djokjakarta, then the capital of the Republic of Indonesia, and put President Sukarno and other leaders in detention, India convened a conference on Indonesia (sometimes called the second Asian Relations Conference). It consisted of representatives from fifteen nations (Afghanistan, Australia, Burma, Ceylon, Egypt, Ethiopia, India, Iran, Iraq, Lebanon, Pakistan, the Philippines, Saudi Arabia, Syria, and Yemen) with observers from four others (China, Nepal, New Zealand, Thailand). No constituents of the Soviet Union were invited. In issuing the call to the conference Nehru had spoken of the Dutch attack on the Indonesian Republic as "the most naked and unabashed aggression," and in opening the conference he remarked, "Asia, too long submissive and dependent and a plaything of other countries, will no longer brook any interference with her freedom." Three days after its organization, the conference adopted a series of strong resolutions which it presented to the United Nations Security Council, and following the conference some of the nations (Burma, Ceylon, India, Pakistan, and Saudi Arabia) represented at it imposed sanctions against the Dutch by denying facilities of transit by land, sea, or air. The immediate subsequent action of the Security Council was disappointing to India and the other participants; nevertheless, the final winning of Indonesian independence, by the terms of an agreement with the Netherlands on November 2, 1949, may be considered a result in part of this united stand by Asian nations. After Indonesia gained independence India and Pakistan both stood with Indonesia in its quarrel with the Netherlands concerning ownership of West Irian (Dutch New Guinea), finally settled in Indonesia's favor in 1962.

India and Pakistan did not take so forceful an attitude with respect to the Viet Minh League's nationalist movement in Indo-China. Nehru said specifically in March 1950, "in regard to Indo-

China we have not interfered in any way and we intend keeping apart." He gave as his reason that countries emerging from colonialism do not like outside interference. He did, however, use his good offices with China in 1954 to get a joint declaration that Vietnam, Laos, and Cambodia should be "free, democratic, unified, and independent states" not to be used for aggressive purposes or be subject to foreign intervention. Developments in Malaya, Laos, Cambodia, and Vietnam in 1961–62, and still more after the heavy American military movement in Vietnam, starting in 1965, have been the cause of much worry to India, which has hoped and worked for a peaceful solution.

In every case there was nothing equivocal in India's unsympathetic attitude toward the position of the western nation involved in the disputes. The French, the British, and the American positions were considered indefensible by Indian, and to a less extent by Pakistani, public opinion, as expressed in newspapers, editorials, and many speeches of political and cultural leaders. As time has gone on and the French and British have withdrawn, the onus of imperialism in those countries has been transferred from Britain and France to fall upon the United States.

With Burma India has consistently maintained good relations, standing in the position of Burma's best friend. She promoted economic aid to Burma for recovery from wartime losses suffered during the Japanese occupation, and offered to mediate between the government and the various unreconciled groups that have kept Burma's politics in violent confusion. India's leaders have been conspicuously friendly on such occasions as Burma's assumption of independence, and the prestige of India has been high there. Such troublesome issues as that of Indians in Burma and the restoration of property rights to Indian moneylenders, who owned vast areas of Burma rice land before the war but were dispossessed by the Burmans during the war, did not impair the general goodwill.

Pakistan has had a less amicable relationship with Burma. Rice-smuggling from Burma into East Pakistan created friction. So too have the aspirations of the Muslim community that lives on the Arakan coast and speaks a kind of Hindustani. This community has felt itself insufficiently represented in Burma government affairs, considered itself discriminated against by the majority Buddhist community—as did the Muslims of India in relation to the Hindus—and some of its members have indicated a desire to be a part of Pakistan. But the Pakistan government wisely stood apart from this situation. Another aspect of the same situation, however, has been that Arakan Muslims emigrated into East Pakistan, where they were not cordially received. Possibly they will now wish to secede from Burma and unite with Bangladesh.

India was one of the leaders convoking the Asian-African Conference at Bandung in Indonesia in April 1955. Twenty-nine countries were represented, of which Communist China and India were the largest. The conference reaffirmed the principles of anti-colonialism, so often stated and by that time almost universally accepted in Europe and America as well as in Asia and Africa, and anti-racism, not quite so widely accepted in the West. It expressed its confidence in the United Nations as the agency for handling international disputes. India seemed intent upon improving China's position in the eyes of other "uncommitted" Asian nations, not too successfully, since most of the smaller Asian nations were fearful of Chinese imperialism. The issue of colonialism by 1961, six years after that conference, seemed to be a dead horse, and when efforts were made at the conference of uncommitted or neutral nations in Belgrade in 1961 to resurrect it Nehru characterized it as worn out, and instead emphasized the use of thermonuclear power and testing in space as live issues.

Toward Japan the Indian attitude since the war has not been one of animosity, but rather one of increasing friendship. Indians still have considerable admiration for the Japanese as the first Asian people of modern times to defeat a western power (in the Russo-Japanese War, 1904–1905). Subhash Chandra Bose, who collaborated with the Japanese during World War II and was "Leader" (*Neta, Netaji*) of the Japanese-organized Indian National Army in Singapore and Burma, was widely popular in his native Bengal and other parts of India as well. In September 1951, when the Japanese peace treaty was signed in San Francisco, India stayed away, not signing the treaty. Among her reasons for staying away was the fact that the treaty deprived Japan of the Ryukyu and Bonin islands, the inhabitants of which have strong historic affinities with Japan. India later separately terminated her war with Japan, formally signing a treaty in June 1952.

India's solicitude for Japan on general Asian nationalist grounds outweighed, apparently, the potential economic rivalry between the two countries. Before the war Japan had large markets in Southeast Asia and her cotton textile industry sent its products not only there but to India as well, which protected itself by imposing prohibitive import duties. When the United States began to rebuild the Japanese economy, Indian industry was alarmed lest its own budding aspirations to win the Southeast Asia market some day would be thwarted. It even feared that Japanese industry might again invade the Indian market. Yet the government, the newspapers, and public opinion were practically unanimous in opposing the San Francisco treaty. In Pakistan there was also doubt about the treaty, but not enough to sway the government, which gave it hearty endorsement at San Francisco. To Pakistan the case of Japan was hardly worth a quarrel with western nations when the issue of Kashmir, much more important to her, was still undecided. Pakistan had been developing its trade with Japan, which helped to replace its diminished trade with India.

In August 1967 Morarji Desai, then Deputy Prime Minister of India and Minister of Finance, went to Tokyo for several purposes: to promote closer relations between India and Japan as a counterweight to China; to oppose the proliferation of nuclear weapons, which China was developing; and to promote enlargement of a number of organizations in Southeast Asia and the Pacific concerned with economic development and security problems and at the same time remaining nonaligned in the world's ideological division.

India and Japan have indeed been working out bit by bit a policy of mutual accommodation by which each helps to repair some of the other's economic deficiencies. Japan exports inexpensive manufactures to India under an agreement signed in 1958, and various agreements have been signed since then for the development by Japan in India of industries to produce consumers' goods, such as watches, clocks, and other products that Japan manufactures at a financial cost more commensurate with Indian purchasing power than does the West. Japan had been purchasing iron ore in India since 1958 at 1.4 million tons a year; in 1960 India signed an agreement to supply Japan with 4 million tons or iron ore annually for fifteen years starting when a new iron producing project at Baliadila should become operative. Japan is the one Asian member of the international Aid-to-India consortium.

India's relations with the People's Republic of China were until 1959 based primarily upon the principle that as an Asian nation and the world's most populous country, China should have all the status enjoyed by any western nation. This consideration of abstract justice, though weakened, still seemed in 1962, before the undeclared Indo-Chinese War of that year, to outweigh for India the vigorous military, economic, and political advance of Communist China during the 1950s into Tibet, over which China has long claimed suzerainty, the reassertion of the ancient Chinese claim to parts of northern Burma and a corner of Assam—as in maps published in pre-Communist China, later by the Communist government in 1951, and since—and the Chinese claims in eastern Kashmir and Nepal and in the Indian Himalayas, all of which aroused alarm, resentment, and indignation in India, and even the demand for resistance by force. The situation led to notes of protest from each country to the other, military preparations, shooting; finally in the late summer and fall of 1962 it grew into outright war. After penetrating into northern India, and having established military supremacy, China unexpectedly withdrew its forces. Negotiations have still not taken place, but there has been no further fighting. Ill feeling in India toward China, and presumably in China toward India, has become great. The ancient friendship the two nations had somehow convinced themselves had once existed —though history does not confirm the assumption—quickly dissolved. China's support of Pakistan in the India-Pakistan War in 1971–1972, followed by the unfriendly attitude expressed in a communiqué issued by Chou En-lai and President Nixon in Peking in February 1972 increased the Indian mistrust of China, and amity may never be restored.

Another kind of rivalry, chiefly commercial, between Indians and Chinese has existed in Malaysia, Singapore, and Indonesia, where migrants from both countries have gone in the nineteenth and twentieth centuries. In these areas the Chinese are the more numerous. Both groups are also represented in Burma, where the Indians outnumber the Chinese, and in Thailand, where the Chinese outnumber the Indians. The whole area where these Chinese and Indians are settled is a natural market for both India and China, whenever they get to the point of developing a large foreign trade. Militarily neither nation has endeavored to establish itself in the area. Competition has not yet, and perhaps never will, produce armed conflict. Actually, Japan seems more likely to capture the market than either China or India.

It might seem that the two great nations of China and India, the one possessing a Communist political philosophy and government and the other a democratic political philosophy, might easily find each other insufferable. India until 1962 had not seemed to be hostile to China. The Indian view, as expressed by Nehru, was that China, after passing through a great revolution, had freely chosen its present government. This is a fact, Nehru maintained, that should be faced, and India was therefore the second nation outside the Russian orbit and Yugoslavia to give China recognition. India maintained an active embassy in Peking, continuously advocated the admission of China to the United Nations from July 1950, and opposed the branding of China as an aggressor in January 1951. India led the Asian-Arab group in seeking the reconciliation of the United Nations and China, regretted that Communist China was not represented at the Japanese peace treaty conference in San Francisco, and repeatedly requested the United Nations to take up the question of Taiwan, which it has stated should be put under the existing mainland China government.

This was all done in spite of former close relations between the Kuomintang and the Indian National Congress, between Chiang Kai-shek and Nehru, dating from 1925. At that time Congress supported the Kuomintang and Chiang as leader of a unified China. During the time of Japanese aggression against China in the 1930's the Indian National Congress continued to support Chiang's government, and in August 1939 Nehru visited him in Chungking. Early in 1942 Chiang visited India, seeking India's support for the war, aid for China against Japan, and an endorsement of his own unsteady government. Nehru, writing in jail in 1944, characterized the visit as "a great event in India," and he and other nationalist leaders considered that through it "the bonds that tied India and China grew stronger." But Nehru's primary desire respecting China was to see it united and strong, and when Chiang's government could not make it so, but the Communists under Mao Tse-tung and Chou En-lai could, he supported the Communists.

Another point that interested India in regard to Communist China was its program of agricultural, social, and administrative reform. China's basic problem is agrarian, as is India's, and the Communist government focused its attention upon it. This has been the most significant feature of the new Chinese revolution in Indian eyes, not the degree of affiliation with the Soviet Union, while it existed, nor the hostility between China and the Soviet Union which exists now. India never expected China to become a Russian tool or to become like Russia, and the correctness of this opinion seemed to be substantiated by the differences between China and the Soviet Union that became apparent by 1960. Even Indian industrialists for a time, at least, did not seem to be alarmed. G. D. Birla, one of the most influential of them, said (November 1951), "Our knowledge of the Chinese makes us believe they can never become narrow-type communists. We know that the Chinese capitalists in Malaya, Siam, and Burma take the side of the Chinese government, which strengthens us in this belief. Therefore we hope that through our friendship China will play an important role for world peace." China was long popular in independent India, and the two nations exchanged cultural missions, with frequent references to cultural exchanges in the millennia of antiquity, and assertions of ancient and modern friendship alike.

In spite of all this friendliness, India was never entirely free of apprehension about her Himalayan border. When China, after various preliminary threatening announcements and moves, invaded Tibet in October 1950, India formally protested, but the Chinese government stated flatly that "Tibet is an integral part of Chinese territory," called relations between itself and Tibet, "a domestic problem of the People's Republic of China," and brusquely rejected the Indian protest. The then Deputy Prime Minister Vallabhbhai Patel called the Chinese move "aggression," but had no way to check it.

Few, if any, persons in India foresaw then the vigorous advance China was to make toward India in the late 1950s and the 1960's, culminating in an undeclared war in September 1962. From 1959 on, as the Chinese policy in the Himalayan borderlands became clearly a policy of taking by force what it had been claiming, Indians were surprised, shocked, enraged, and completely astounded. They found themselves at war with a determined and powerful enemy, who easily forced them back.

Alas, the ancient friendship between India and China was little more than myth, never mentioned explicitly in the records of antiquity, and the modern amity of the early 1950s had no substantial basis in spite of Chou En-lai's goodwill visits to India in

1956–1957 and in 1960, to try to win back some of the esteem for China that by then had been lost in the China-Indian border dispute. This dispute, which had been building up for many years, burst in August 1959 when Chinese troops raided some Indian posts in the extreme north of Uttar Pradesh in the Himalayas. In October Chinese attacked an Indian force in Ladakh in Kashmir, where the international border had never been properly delimited, killing seven Indians and taking ten prisoners, and followed this by claiming a fairly large area there that India had considered Indian for over a century. The acrimonious diplomatic interchanges that followed led Nehru at one point to declare (November 10) that Indians "cannot allow China to keep a foot on our chest," but he continued to rely upon negotiation and to abstain from force, which would probably not have been effective anyhow. China also repudiated the McMahon Line in the eastern Himalayas, which was drawn by agreement of Britain, Tibet, and China in 1914 but never ratified by the Chinese government. In April 1960 Peking was claiming Mount Everest which had been considered to lie part in Nepal and part in Tibet. Neither India nor China was willing to relax its claims in the Himalayas. India's position was that the disputed territory was hers by treaty and agreement, while China, which regularly takes the attitude that territory once occupied by China is forever Chinese, claimed that the territory in dispute was ceded to Britain unjustly by Tibet or occupied by forces from India at a time when China was too weak to assert its rights. To Indians the Chinese claims and armed advance came as a brutal shock, for it was in conference with Chou En-lai in New Delhi in June 1954 that Nehru's long celebrated five principles (*panch shil*) of mutual respect, nonaggression, noninterference, equality and mutual benefit, and peaceful coexistence were adopted as a guide to Indian-Chinese relations. An added irritation for India lay in Chinese approaches to Pakistan in 1962 to discuss their border, that is, the border of China with Kashmir. Nehru, speaking of this in Parliament on May 7, characterized it as "interference" by China with India's "legal sovereignty" over Kashmir.

In the developing quarrel it was not clear just what territory China claimed, for as far as was reported in the news stories, the Chinese demands kept shifting and no limits were set for the area claimed. This was the Indian view of the situation leading to the

Indo-Chinese war of 1962. The Chinese view is very different, as it has since been presented to the world by various western students. China feels that it acted with full justice in the case of Tibet, ignores the violence of its treatment of the Tibetans, does not consider its moves in the western end of the Himalayas as worthy of notice nor its moves toward Nepal and Kashmir as being in any respect an occasion for alarm in India. China's apologists point out that after China had started its moves toward India in Assam and the Himalayas Nehru would never listen to Chinese suggestions that India sit down in negotiation, but instead replied to China in terms not unlike those that China had used with India concerning the Chinese takeover of Tibet, namely that the matter was strictly an internal concern and was not subject to negotiation. Whether one inclines to the Indian or the Chinese view of the affair, the result was a lamentable one that could have been avoided if the two nations had been frank with each other long before 1962.

When the attack finally came in the autumn of 1962 China struck at the northeastern corner of India and in the extreme west at Ladakh; later came movement elsewhere in the Himalayas. After making extensive and impressive advances, China suddenly announced toward the end of November that it would make a unilateral withdrawal from its advanced positions. It did execute such a withdrawal in the eastern sector but retained its advanced positions in Ladakh.

The explanation for China's withdrawal after its unchecked success was as puzzling as its intentions in attacking the Asian nation that had given it international support. The world with but few exceptions (such as Albania, Cuba, Portugal) roundly condemned China as an aggressor. Even the Soviet Union censured China, and did not withdraw its promise, given before the crisis, to supply India with some MIG jet fighter planes and to equip a plant in India to manufacture them. The United States and Britain promptly began to supply India with modern arms, the lack of which was held responsible for India's military defeat. Inside India barely a handful of people, and these a minority of the Communist party, supported China. Instead the Indian people responded with full and enthusiastic support of the war effort, and joyously welcomed the dismissal of Krishna Menon as minister of defense, who was popularly considered responsible for the Indian debacle and was held to be pro-Chinese. They contributed money and gold ornaments to the national defense fund, and vowed that the enemy must be driven from India's land. There was no indication that any or all of these facts influenced the Chinese withdrawal. Nor was there any surety in India that the Chinese had withdrawn in order to promote a peaceful settlement; rather, China was suspected of guile, but no purpose was identified.

Pakistan until recently was less wholehearted in supporting China than India had been before 1962, though popular sympathy for the new China government for a time appeared to be strong. It had generally acted with India on the issue of China before the United Nations, and like India had had an intense interest in China's agrarian reforms. Chinese moves in the Himalayan region, however, raised apprehension in Pakistan. But by the beginning of 1963 Pakistan was engaging in conversations with China that were expected to lead to a treaty. It was possibly then that an understanding of some sort was reached between Pakistan and China which led to China's support of Pakistan during and following the India-Pakistan War of 1971–1972.

At the time of the Korean crisis, India and Pakistan were slow in endorsing the first United Nations resolution of June 25, 1950, though eventually they both did. Neither nation contributed troops, but India sent a medical unit. In October 1950, India opposed the Security Council's resolution to cross the 38th parallel, and issued a warning on the basis of communications from K. M. Panikkar, its ambassador in Peking, that the crossing would bring China into the conflict. The United States newspapers and military leaders seemed rather generally to consider this a bluff, having no real conception of the feeling in China. Later, in December, India besought China not to cross the 38th parallel when its forces were advancing southward. Throughout the Korean affair, India offered its services as mediator.

The role of mediator and peacemaker which India assigned itself in the Korean War was paralleled in the breakup of the French colonial empire of Indo-China. As crises developed there India used whatever weight it had to keep the fighting from spreading and to keep the settlement along democratic lines, as far as practicable in a region where democratic institutions had at the most only an embryonic existence. Communist control was eventually established in North Vietnam in 1954. Laos, Cambodia, and

South Vietnam, after gaining autonomy within the French Union in 1949, became sovereign states in 1955. As the crisis in Laos became acute in 1961 India again tried to bring about truce and negotiation. India would not join SEATO (Southeast Asia Treaty Organization), founded in 1954 to block Communist progress into free Asia, having as its members the United States, Great Britain, Australia, New Zealand, France, Thailand, the Philippines, and Pakistan. Though SEATO, unlike NATO, was not organized on a military basis with a unified command structure, it was hostile to Communist ideology and political spread and guaranteed defense of Laos, Cambodia, and South Vietnam (but without requiring automatic commitment of its members to go to war). India felt that its own influence for peaceful solution of world problems would be lessened if it aligned itself with either side.

As the Federation of Malaysia progressed from colonial status to autonomy in 1946 and complete independence in 1957 as a sovereign state with membership in the Commonwealth of Nations, India supported the liberalizing political policy which came to prevail. It also supported the merger of Singapore with the Federation of Malaya in 1963 to form Malaysia, but did not oppose the separation of Singapore from the federation in August 1965.

India and Pakistan both disapproved the formation of Israel, though for different reasons. Pakistan, being a Muslim state created to affirm Muslim integrity as a nation, sided on religious grounds with its Arab fellow Muslims. India, whose leaders had fought the partition of the old India, objected to the partition of Palestine on principle. Nehru stated at the Asian Related Conference (March 1947) that the people of India regarded Palestine as an essentially Arab region. India was one of the countries sponsoring the minority report of the United Nations Special Committee on Palestine (September 1947) which recommended, rather than partition a federation of Arab and Jewish states, wherein the Arab states were bound to be dominant. India at last recognized Israel on September 18, 1950, but only after three Islamic countries had done so: Turkey, Indonesia, and Iran. Pakistan has continued not to recognize it, from time to time has reiterated its support of the Arab states' demands concerning Israel, and has shown its hostility, as when in January 1960 it barred an Israeli observer from a United Nations Economic Commission for Asia and the Far East scheduled for Karachi. In the Suez crisis in 1956, both India and Pakistan stood firmly with Egypt against Israel, Great Britain, and France.

The continued blocking of the Suez Canal after Israel's victory over the United Arab Republic in the brief war of 1967 has interfered with the shipment of food to India, but India seemed able to find other routes, though less satisfactory ones, for shipments, either around Africa or by the Pacific. The Indian public, including some members of the cabinet, but not Mrs. Gandhi, seemed to side with Israel. India laid before the Security Council in 1967 a resolution supporting the Arab position, but this did not have a clear endorsement by the Indian press.

Pakistan's policy of cultivating pan-Islamic friendship—possibly early in her existence Pakistan expected to become the leader of such a group—progressed well enough with all Islamic countries except Afghanistan and for a time the Hashimite kingdom of Jordan, though Pakistan effected an agreement of cooperation with Jordan in 1957, and in the India-Pakistan War of 1971–72 Jordan supported Pakistan. As Pakistan's Foreign Minister, Sir Zafrullah Khan, claimed of his nation on August 18, 1951, "It has served actively . . . in the cause of independence of Indonesia, Libya, Eritrea, and Somaliland." Though none of these nations has many ties with Pakistan other than the cultural, the promotion of Muslim culture—as Prime Minister Liaquat Ali Khan said in Washington on May 4, 1950—was one of Pakistan's national aims, and even under the largely secular administration of General Ayub Khan after 1958 seemed to rank second only to the political integrity and economic growth of the state itself, if one may judge from public attitudes and the implication of the Muslim religious clauses in the 1962 constitution. There is still much credence in what Khwaja Nazimuddin once said when he was Prime Minister (October 21, 1951), "Islam is a body, and the Muslim states represent the limbs of this body. Pain inflicted on any one part of the body gives pain and anguish to the whole body." King Hussein of Jordan visited Pakistan in January-February 1968, at which time the usual declarations of mutual friendship and support were expressed. During the India-Pakistan War of 1971–1972 Jordan served as a channel to get United States fighter planes to Pakistan.

Pakistan's closest ties are with Iran, which has been the chief channel of Islam and Islamic civilization into the subcontinent, giving it much of specifically Iranian art, literature, script, vocabulary, social customs, and dress, as well as transmitting Arabic Muslim religion and law. The two nations have exchanged cultural missions and executed the usual treaty of friendship and commerce.

With Turkey, Pakistan's relations are correct and friendly, but hardly go beyond that point into active association. Pakistan admires Turkish achievement, and Turkey respects Pakistan. The two have executed the usual treaty, but economic and political ties are few and unimportant. Turkey, as the most secular of Islamic states in the Near and Middle East, has possibly been farther removed in spirit from Pakistan than any of the others and correspondingly has been closer to India.

When Iran, then Egypt, and then Iraq exploded against Britain in the summer and autumn of 1951, Pakistan found itself in an embarrassing situation. It had a policy of close friendship with those countries; at the same time their immediate actions were prejudicial to its interests. Iran's abrogation of Britain's oil rights threatened Pakistan's essential oil supply. Egypt's effort at that time to break the treaty concerning the Suez Canal could have interfered with the flow of trade to Pakistan from the West. Further, Pakistan wanted British support in the United Nations in its quarrel with India. Hence it tried to soothe both sides.

When the Middle East Treaty Organization (METO, also known as the Baghdad Pact) was organized in 1955, Pakistan was a member, along with Turkey, Iran, Iraq, and Great Britain. This anti-Communist organization was without Egypt, which under Nasser was dickering with the Soviet Union and with Iraq. Iraq, after a change to a government under Abdul Karim Kassem friendly to the Soviet Union, withdrew in 1958. To save this alliance the United States in 1959 helped to recreate it as the Central Treaty Organization (CENTO), but did not itself become a member, since it had signed bilateral defense agreements with Turkey, Iran, and Pakistan and membership did not seem necessary.

Though India has had no policy of unity with the Muslim countries on religious grounds, it has sympathized with their nationalism, which Nehru called a "legitimate growth," and has viewed it as resistance to western imperialism in Asia. It also has not wished to offend the sensibilities of its own large Muslim population. At the same time the quarrels of Iran and the UAR with Britain have threatened Indian economic interests and might have imperiled its defense as well, since India's sea communications depended upon the Suez Canal and the supply of oil for India comes mostly from Near Eastern countries.

In both nations public sentiment as expressed in the press generally favored the anti-French position in Algeria, Tunisia, and Morocco.

Relations of India and Pakistan with western European countries other than those already mentioned have not been critical or noteworthy except perhaps that in 1968 Pakistan purchased from Italy about 100 rebuilt Sherman medium tanks, with the approval of the United States Department of State. This was said to be the first sale of American weapons to Pakistan after the United States suspended arms sales to both India and Pakistan in September 1965, when the two countries had a brief war. (Italy has an arrangement with the United States to be the source of supply of rebuilt M-47 tanks.)

Neither the people nor the governments of the subcontinent have viewed the Soviet Union and Communism with the alarm and preoccupation that have existed in the United States. The Cold War seemed to them a struggle between two great powers for world superiority, while Communism has been viewed as a political and social philosophy with features of possible application to their own countries' ills. Communism becomes an active menace in their eyes, deserving suppression, only when it employs violence. The attitude in each country toward the Soviet Union, therefore, has rarely been one of open or widespread hostility. Violent opposition may sometimes be expressed in newspaper editorials and private conversation but it is generally objective disapproval, grading off to sufferance and reserve, or mild sympathy or approval, or sometimes definite friendliness. Whenever the Soviet Union has taken the side of an Asian nationalist movement against a western power, then it has appeared to people in India and Pakistan to be on the right side. For example, when the question of Indonesia was before the Security Council, the position of the Soviet Union in supporting the Indonesian republic's demands was more satisfactory to both the governments and the press of India and Pakistan than the American position, which during a large part of the discussion appeared to them unduly favorable to the Netherlands. In the Vietnam War that the United States has fostered, the Indian position as expressed in the press and in speeches by Prime Minister Indira Gandhi is strongly against the American intervention.

The Soviet Union long seemed to these nations better qualified to appreciate their problems than any of the world's great nations except Communist China. They felt that Russia at the time of her revolution was in an economic state not greatly unlike theirs at the time of gaining independence, while her progress since has not yet carried her to a point so far from that earlier condition that the Russians could no longer grasp the character and importance of the subcontinent's present problems. The Soviet Union's advance in less than half a century, with the accompanying improvement in public education and health and increase of world power, has stimulated Indians and Pakistanis to think that there may be profitable lessons for them in Russian techniques. India and Pakistan have felt too that racial discrimination does not exist in the Soviet Union, as in western Europe and America. The Soviet Union has also generally maintained a neutral position in India-Pakistan quarrels, though since Pakistan began accepting military aid from the United States, starting in 1954, the Soviet Union has tended to take India's side, and the Russian support of India in the India-Pakistan War of 1971–1972 has naturally estranged Pakistan. Bangladesh started its life with cordiality toward the Soviet Union, which helped it to win freedom and nationhood and was one of the first nations to give it diplomatic recognition.

The relations of the Soviet Union with India have been helped by the Communist propagandists throughout the villages and in the urban industrial centers. Those who make this unceasing day-to-day campaign are of the same economic and social groups as the villagers and industrial workers to whom they address it. They speak primarily of food, shelter, wages, that is, they deal with the basic question of poverty; then they relate these subjects to political institutions. No other foreign power has such an approach to the people.

Relations between India and the Soviet Union have been well cultivated on both sides, though until August 1971 not so much by India with the Soviet Union as with the United States. Bulganin and Khrushchev visited India (and Burma and Afghanistan) in November and December of 1955, receiving a warm and enthusiastic welcome wherever they went, though it was reported that Nehru resented the harsh terms Khrushchev used in speaking of the West. Khrushchev visited India again in 1960 and again was cordially received. The various trade agreements that India and the Soviet Union have signed since 1953 have led to trade expansion, but the volume has been much less than that with the United States. The three nations that have the greatest amount of trade with India are the United States, the Soviet Union, and the United Kingdom. According to the *Statistical Abstract for India, 1969* (published in 1970 and at this writing the latest such *Abstract* in print), the value of imports in 1968–1969 from the United States was Rs. 5,750,569,000; from the Soviet Union, Rs. 1,855,-033,000; from the United Kingdom, Rs. 1, 278, 654,000. The value of exports of merchandise (Indian produce and manufacture) for 1968–1969 was as follows: to the United States, Rs. 2,333,978,000; to the Soviet Union, Rs. 1,481,708,000; to the United Kingdom, 2,008,337,000. (One rupee = USA 13.7376 cents.)

The Soviet Union made an agreement in 1960 to sell petroleum products to India at less than the world price, whereupon the western-owned refineries in India refused to refine the Soviet oils. India arranged in 1960 to purchase turboprop transport airplanes from the Soviet Union, and in May 1962 India was negotiating for the purchase of MIG fighter planes—to the alarmed protest of the United States backed by Great Britain. In 1962 India entered into an agreement with the Soviet Union for manufacturing supersonic aircraft engines, thus starting to rely in part upon the Soviet Union for arms. The growth of this military reliance has been continuous and was one of the principal reasons for India's easy defeat of Pakistan in the war of 1971–1972.

The major item in India-Soviet political relations is the friendship Pact the two nations signed in August 1971, when the revolt of East Pakistan was growing and it seemed likely that India would be drawn into the quarrel. This Pact was possibly a deterrent to China, which was backing Pakistan and giving it military assistance.

In the cultivation of good relations with India, the Soviet Union has fostered within its borders the study of modern Indian languages, especially in Moscow and Tashkent, and the study of Sanskrit in Leningrad, where it has flourished from tsarist times. Some important Indian literary works, both ancient and modern, have been translated into Russian. Such translations are well reported by the Soviet agencies in India and used as propaganda material.

The study of Indian history has also been promoted, almost invariably from the point of view of Marxian economic and political doctrine. Sometimes this has led to critical, even scornful, comments on Gandhi, which have been resented in India. To what extent the Soviet Union has contributed funds to the support of Communist political parties in India is not publicly known.

There have been three political items damaging to Soviet prestige in India. The first was the suppression of Hungarian nationalism in 1956. Nehru did not at first censure the Soviet Union for this. Later as indignation mounted in the Indian press and among Indian leaders he expressed disapproval, though India abstained from the United Nations General Assembly vote (55 to 8) condemning the Soviet Union. Later, in January 1957, the Indian National Congress, at its annual session, adopted a resolution condemning the Soviet checking of democracy in central Europe as well as the British attitude concerning Egypt and the Suez Canal issue. In 1958 Nehru criticized the execution of Imre Nagy.

The second item was the Soviet Union's unilateral resumption of nuclear testing in the atmosphere in 1961. Public opinion in India was severely shocked. Nehru tried to avoid being drawn into the quarrel, merely saying at the Conference of Nonaligned Countries in Belgrade in August–September 1961 that the renewed testing brought nearer the danger of nuclear war. He did not press for condemnation of the Soviet Union in the conference report. The resumption of testing by the United States, especially the high-altitude space testing in the Pacific in 1962, produced strongly unfavorable reaction in India.

The third item was the Soviet suppression of Czechoslovakian efforts to exercise political independence, starting under Stalin and continuing until late in 1968.

In the undeclared war between India and China in 1962 the Soviet Union gave some moral support to India but little material aid. India, however, was glad to have the Soviet Union essentially unaligned. Indians felt that if India had taken sides in the Cold War, the Soviet Union would almost automatically have been aligned with China. The situation was quite different from the one that developed ten years later, in which the Soviet Union supported India in the India-Pakistan War of 1971–1972 at the time of the East Pakistan revolt that led to the creation of Bangladesh.

Pakistan, as a member of the anti-Communist Middle East Treaty Organization (METO) and its successor the Central Treaty Organization (CENTO) has been uniformly opposed to the Soviet Union, going so far in 1956 as to refuse proffered Russian economic aid.

Though the Indian and Pakistani public both started out by giving a full hearing to Soviet propaganda, in the long overall view the governments and the leaders must be considered to have been hardening against Russia. Nehru's case is illustrative. In 1927 on the tenth anniversary of the Russian Revolution, he visited Moscow at the invitation of the Society for Cultural Relations with Foreign Countries. While there he wrote a number of newspaper articles and on his return published (1928) a book based on them, *Soviet Russia*. His position is summarized, when he says (page 54), "the impressions I carried back with me from Moscow were very favourable and all my reading has confirmed these impressions, although there is much that I do not understand and much that I do not like or admire."

A few years later in his autobiography, written in 1934–1935 while in jail, he said (*Toward Freedom,* page 348): "As these pages will show, I am very far from being a communist. My roots are still perhaps partly in the nineteenth century, and I have been too much influenced by the humanist liberal tradition to get out of it completely. This bourgeois background follows me about and is naturally a source of irritation to many communists. I dislike dogmatism, and the treatment of Karl Marx's writings or any other books as revealed scripture which cannot be challenged, and the regimentation and heresy hunts which seem to be a feature of modern communism."

A few more years later in *The Discovery of India,* written during 1942–1945, when he was again in jail, he said (page 528): "I know that in India the Communist party is completely divorced from, and is ignorant of, the national traditions that fill the minds of the people. It believes that communism necessarily implies a contempt for the past. So far as it is concerned, the history of the world began in November 1917 and everything that preceded this was preparatory and leading up to it. Normally speaking, in a country like India with large numbers of people on the verge of starvation and the economic structure cracking up, communism should have a wide appeal. In a sense there is that vague appeal, but the Communist party cannot take advantage of it, because it has cut itself off from the spring of national sentiment and speaks in a language which finds no echo in the hearts of the people. It remains an energetic but small group with no real roots." In an interview in March 1951 (Norman Cousins, *Talks with Nehru*), he said, "In recent years . . . the communist tendency has come into conflict with the nationalist tendency in many countries—India, Indonesia, Burma, and some other countries . . . Today in India communism is definitely opposed to nationalism." And on May 22, 1952, he remarked that India "will never pay the price that the Soviet Union and China have paid to achieve progress." He described the activities of the Communist Party of India (CPI) as "counter-revolutionary and completely out of date."

When in the summer of 1952 several private organizations in the Soviet Union and China offered food for famine relief in India to be distributed through Communist-front organizations there, the government of India refused the gift, insisting that it should be distributed only by itself or by the Indian Red Cross.

Both India and Pakistan for some seven years tried to maintain nonpartisanship toward the Cold War, and India has continued to do so. Pakistan allied itself with the West in 1954, accepting United States military aid. India's policy, however, is for independent action, often described in the West as "neutralism," motivated by a desire to avoid "entangling alliances." Even before partition, at the time of the interim government on August 31, 1946, Nehru voiced this policy as leader of the government. He affirmed it on December 4, 1947, in his first full-dress statement of India's foreign policy after the attainment of independence: "We have proclaimed during the past year that we will not attach ourselves to any particular group. That has nothing to do with neutrality or with passivity. If there is a big war there is no particular reason why we should jump into it. Nevertheless, it is a little difficult now-a-days in world wars to be neutral. We are not going to join a war if we can help it and we are going to join the side which is to our interest when the choice comes to it." He went on to say that India wished to cooperate with both the United States and the Soviet Union, but "neither of these big blocs looks with favor on us. They think we are undependable because we cannot be sent a writ to vote this way or that way." A little later, in April 1948, he affirmed India's desire to be friendly with every country but follow its own line on all questions.

That policy has consistently remained India's international aim ever since.

It is widely felt in India that the country's destiny would be best served if she could act as a peacemaker between the two great powers, provide a bridge between them. This type of thinking has been official government of India policy. Speaking before the Indian Parliament on March 8, 1949, Nehru said: "Nevertheless, it is true that the background of Europe is not completely the background of India or the world and there is absolutely no reason why we should be asked to choose between this ideology and the other in toto." He added: "Our main stake in world affairs is peace, to see that there is racial equality and that people who are still subjugated should be free. For the rest we do not desire to interfere in world affairs and we do not desire that other people should interfere in our affairs. If, however, there is interference, whether military, political, or economic, we shall resist it."

It might have been thought in 1962 that the Indo-China War was pushing India toward the West, toward Great Britain and the United States, for India turned to the United States for aid, and the Indian press seemed to think that the country was being allied to the West. Nehru, however, did not abandon the policy of nonalignment. But there exists now a question whether Mrs. Gandhi did not abandon it in signing the Pact of Friendship with the Soviet Union in August 1971 and receiving military aid from that country during the 1971–72 war with Pakistan. It might also be said that the United States, in supporting Pakistan in that war, took a position that amounted to alliance with Pakistan and repudiation of friendship with India. The United States official position, it must be recognized, was not that of the United States people, who were not frankly informed of the United States policy. This fact is well known in India—thanks to Jack Anderson, who got possession of the minutes of the policy committee's meetings in Washington and published them in his newspaper column—and Indians were as warmly friendly to visiting nonofficial Americans in March and to assess. The official American position in the creation of Bangla-April 1972 as before the India-Pakistan war.

Bangladesh's attitude toward the United States is more difficult desh was definitely calculated to frustrate the movement there for self-rule. Perhaps aid to Bangladesh for restoring the economy and rebuilding the area will counteract the suspicion that quite naturally came into existence there when the official United States position was recognized by the Bengalis.

The Soviet Union's support of India in the war of 1971–72 left Pakistan hostile. At the same time Pakistan was disappointed that the United States did not do more in Pakistan's support than it did. In 1972 the government in Karachi seemed to feel friendless.

17 Relations with the United States

The official relations of the United States with unpartitioned India began only during World War II. Before then India's foreign affairs were handled by the British Foreign Office. The United States maintained in India only a few consular offices, lightly manned, to care for trade relations and the interests of the few hundred American citizens living in the country. The officers, conforming to the usual practice of the United States foreign service, stayed only a brief period in India before being transferred to some other country. The State Department received and transmitted most of its political communications concerning India through the British Foreign Office in London or the British embassy in Washington. It received also a few direct reports from its own officers on social, political, and general economic conditions.

Unofficial relations between the United States and the subcontinent were also poorly cultivated. Each side lacked a substantial body of knowledge about the other, each had only the slenderest tradition of careful study about the other; in each, scholars, experts, and competent journalists to interpret the other were scarce. Public attitudes of both, therefore, were chiefly based on ignorance and subject to rapid fluctuation.

For most Americans at that time India had an ill-defined interest as a land of romantic color, ancient splendor, present poverty, and varied religions characterized as debased, curious, or profound, according to the commentators' prepossessions. A number of Americans had a vague opinion of Indians as cruel, rising from distant reports of the Black Hole of Calcutta (1756) and the Sepoy Mutiny (1857–1858). India had an economic interest to a few Americans for its trade, though in this respect it was vastly more important to Great Britain. There were also Americans who knew that certain Indians with nationalist aspirations were seeking their country's freedom from Britain, but these usually had little if any knowledge of the origins, aims, and problems of Indian national-ism, and their views were determined almost entirely by either an unreasoning Anglophobia or an uninquiring Anglophilia.

American contacts with India had started before the American Revolution through soldiers and seamen who had lived both in the American colonies and in India. After the Revolution, during the remainder of the eighteenth century and the early part of the nine-teenth, many American ships visited Indian ports, trading within the limits permitted by the East India Company's monopoly. Some decades later, when the clippers were sailing from Atlantic ports around Cape Horn to the Far East, a few made the full passage to India, to return with tea, spices, and other commodities for the American market, textiles, curios made of wood, metal, and ivory, and even now and then a sculpture or miniature painting, such as can still be found in New England in old homes and local mu-seums. The persons engaged in this enterprise were realistic busi-nessmen and knew about trading conditions, but they had little curiosity about India's intellectual life, history, or politics. America learned nothing of India from them nor did they leave any impres-sion of America in India.

American missionaries started to go to India in 1810. The great development of American missions in India under Congregational, Baptist, and Presbyterian missionary societies started in the 1830s; many other denominations followed in succeeding decades. India was a major field for Protestant missions, and the American pub-lic's conceptions of India to a large extent were influenced by the reporting of returned missionaries. This was not always happy. Too often missionaries were ardently evangelistic and at the same time untrained in the scientific study of religion, uninformed about their own and Indian religions, and unappreciative generally of the civilizations existing in India. Such persons would be in-clined to picture America's superior economic culture as attributa-ble to superior religion and morality, thus confusing the material and the spiritual. Back in the United States they disparaged India for poverty, lack of sanitation and education, and addiction to re-ligious notions which they regarded as irrational and reprehensible, though most of these could be matched in character, if not in spe-cific form, in the United States. The higher culture of India they did not know and could not describe. The reports of this type of missionary were not counterbalanced by the reports of those educational and medical missionaries who had intellectual curiosity and endeavored to learn about India. On returning to America these more receptive sojourners were likely to speak with knowledge and sympathy, but they did not get the audiences that the others did.

The intellectual side of Indian culture was brought to the attention of America in the 1820s in connection with Unitarianism. The American interest in that doctrine was preached by William Ellery Channing (1780–1842) in New England, who was closely associated with the Unitarian movement in Great Britain. The British Unitarians had become aware of the Brahmo Samaj movement in Bengal in the early part of the nineteenth century and of Ram Mohun Roy who was prominent in the Brahmo Samaj. This was an Indian variety of unitarianism, quite unrelated in origin to the Christian. The two varieties had much in common in belief, and on discovering each other entered into communication both by letter and by a visit of Ram Mohun Roy to England. Channing also became involved in these contacts.

More enduring than the contact through Unitarianism was the wider introduction of Indian thought to America through Emerson and the Transcendentalists a little later in the nineteenth century, especially through Emerson, who had become acquainted with Indian thought in translations by European scholars. Emerson and his associates contributed Indian ideas to American thought, but in the successive generations of transmission Americans lost sight of the Indian source.

There was a very small number of distinguished American scholars in the nineteenth century who worked on India but never got a large public audience. Their field was the traditional language and culture and they held chairs in American universities, where they carried on research and taught their few students. The first great Indic scholar in America was William Dwight Whitney (1827–1894) of Yale. Four others whose activities bridged the nineteenth and twentieth centuries were: Charles Rockwell Lanman (1850–1941) of Harvard; Maurice Bloomfield (1855–1928) of Johns Hopkins; E. Washburn Hopkins (1857–1932) of Yale; and A. V. Williams Jackson (1862–1937) of Columbia. These five scholars together with their pupils in the twentieth century and a few additional scholars from abroad, such as Ananda K. Coomaraswamy (1877–1947) at the Museum of Fine Arts in Boston, estab-

lished a distinguished tradition of productive humanistic scholarship concerning India. But the number of American institutions
willing to shelter such work was small. Only eight universities
maintained chairs of Sanskrit or Indic studies in the interwar period: Harvard, Yale, Columbia, Princeton, Pennsylvania, Johns
Hopkins, Chicago, California. Only one museum (Boston) had a
full-time curator of Indian art.

The high achievements of American humanistic scholarship concerning India were not matched in the social sciences. Before
World War I there was scarcely an American economist, sociolo-
gist, modern historian, political scientist, geographer, or anthropologist who was trained in the Indian aspect of his science or
knew his way around in it. In the interwar period a very small
number of social scientists, less than a dozen all told, came to qualify as competent on India. The dearth was felt during World War
II, when government agencies needed social scientists to work on
India and could find barely a handful. In the first ten years after
the war a few American universities, aided by philanthropic foundations or other benefactors, began to provide specialized training
on a systematic basis at the graduate level. Some other Americans
by direct contact with India or Pakistan and with the use of Indian
or Pakistani materials had trained themselves. By 1952 there were
in American academic institutions, government agencies, and jour-
nalism possibly sixty or seventy Americans with an authoritative
knowledge of some one of the humanities, social sciences, biologi-
cal, physical, or technical sciences in relation to India or Pakistan.
A few foreigners living in America were qualified specialists on India or Pakistan, possibly fifteen or twenty excluding official representatives of the two countries.

Distinguished Indian visitors to the United States were few until
after World War II. Occasionally there had been such guests as Tagore or the poetess and nationalist leader Sarojini Naidu. They did
not draw large audiences. Besides the few outstanding figures, other
Indians came to the United States to present India on the propa-
gandist or journalist level. Sometimes these were well versed in
their own culture and disinterested, sometimes less well motivated.
The most celebrated was Swami Vivekananda (born Narendranath
Datta, 1862–1902), who was a kind of reverse missionary. Following him there was a continuous stream of swamis, some of them
worthy and dignified men preaching in the best tradition of devo-

tion, courtesy, and tolerance. Others, however, too often came to America for mercenary purposes masked by religion, preying upon the credulous and bringing ridicule and discredit upon India. Frequently the Indian who received the most public attention was some playboy prince whose escapades made good newspaper copy.

Thoughtful books about India had small sale. E. M. Forster's *Passage to India* was read less for what it said about India than for its literary quality. Gandhi was admired by a few for his devotion to nonviolence, which they hoped could be applied universally, but to most Americans who heard of him he was a curiosity whose notions seemed fantastic and costume ludicrous, though he was conceded to have a fascinating skill in twising the British lion's tail.

Of improperly qualified Americans who wrote on India for other Americans the most conspicuous was the anglophile Katherine Mayo. Her sensational *Mother India* (1927) had a wide audience. It shocked Americans, aroused loathing of India, and discredited that country before tens of thousands who would never hear another presentation. It offended Indians grievously, inspired a number of retaliatory attacks on America, and probably did more to create ill feeling between India and America than any other book ever published.

From these different sources developed various American stereotypes about India, some of them mutually contradictory, which appeared in the remarks of legislators, editorial writers, columnists, public speakers, and thereafter lodged as accepted truth in the minds of numerous readers or listeners. A large number of Americans, therefore, had a picture of India as a land of soul-seeking yogis sunk in meditation, hypnotic swamis, naked ascetics, bejeweled princes of fabulous wealth and incomparable harems, gross superstition, bare-skinned, poverty-stricken, famine-ridden masses, where most of the people were beggars and caste was more important than life, the countryside terrifying with Bengal tigers, the houses and fields infested with hooded serpents, a land where disease and depravity were rampant. It added up to an unreal and shoddy India, for which Americans might feel wonder, envy, pity, loathing, ridicule, patronage, the urge to charity, but not the sympathy born of knowledge that Indians were the same kind of beings as themselves, creators of civilizations deserving the highest respect, capable of giving as well as receiving, a people with whom

America should plan to cooperate on terms of moral and intellectual equality.

In India before World War II the sources of information about America were as unreliable as those about India in America. It is doubtful if there were as many Indians competent in any American field at that time as there were Americans competent in an Indian field, small as that number was. Few Indians had come to the United States to study American civilization and institutions; students who came usually came for one of the sciences. Back in India they interpreted America in terms of their personal experiences. If they had been successful in their studies, made agreeable social contacts, been able to live in something better than constricting poverty, and found good jobs on returning home, they would speak well of America. But if they had had unpleasant experiences because of their skin color, they might be soured. If it had been difficult for them to adjust to the western world, so different from their own, they might leave America confused, frustrated, unfriendly.

The few Americans in prewar India did not do much to create a favorable public impression. This was particularly the case with the more illiberal type of evangelistic missionary, who was contemptuous of India's civilization. Educational and medical missions were better appreciated. Until World War I American missionaries usually stood behind the British on the issue of nationalism, but the opposition to Indian nationalism began to change in the interwar period, as did also the strong American home control over the Indian mission churches.

Every winter a few round-the-world shiploads of American tourists rushed through the country from Bombay or Calcutta to Banaras, Agra, Delhi, perhaps a few other cities, dispensing their dollars freely, showing little discrimination in their purchase of curios, and revealing small understanding of Indian architecture, sculpture, and ideas, but usually expressing friendliness to Indians personally. Unconsciously they served to confirm the frequent Indian opinion of Americans as good-humored over-age children with too much spending money.

Certain isolated instances of contact left strong impressions upon Indians. One was American relief during the famines of 1896–1900. Gandhi's sympathetic press in America at certain periods pleased Indians. On the negative side was the United States exclusion law, which prohibited Indians from immigrating and acquiring citizenship. When the Supreme Court confirmed this in 1922, Indians were humiliated and puzzled, and called American democracy hypocrisy. Though Congress in 1946 passed the India Immigration and Naturalization Bill which mitigated the situation, the memory of the years of exclusion continued to rankle, and was associated in the Indian mind with color prejudice, or with any unpleasant experience which an Indian might have had in America, like Tagore when the West Coast immigration authorities in 1929 were conspicuously discourteous to him.

The stereotypes in India concerning America were like the American concerning India, often false and conflicting. They began with a cliché which contrasted the spiritual East, represented best by themselves, and the material West, whose foremost illustration they considered to be the United States. The dollar they spoke of as the American god, the safe-deposit box as the American soul. We were all rich, they thought, beyond an Indian's dream, and engrossed in getting richer. We disdained the teachings of India's religious thinkers; we gave only lip service to those of western Asia whose names we celebrated—like Christ's. We boasted of our great and well-built cities, our comforts of life, our high standard of living, the size, elegance, speed, efficiency of everything American—all of which, it was clear, they envied deeply. We were a young nation, crude, bouncing, full of the new graduate's self-conceit. Our city streets were assumed to swarm with feather-hooded wild Indians and gun-toting gangsters. We had no sex morals, no idealism, but we were easygoing, democratic in our behavior, and free spenders. American movies seemed to them to confirm it all.

Many of the old stereotypes in the United States concerning India and in the subcontinent concerning America still exist. But since Indian and Pakistan independence there has been progress toward truer mutual appraisal.

The United States and India began to have more and closer contacts during World War II. In the years 1939–1941 President Roosevelt apparently saw that India would be important in the war, that the western democracies would need Indian physical and moral support, and that Britain was alienating India. In the summer of 1941, therefore, the United States agreed with India and Britain for exchange of diplomatic representatives. The United States placed a commissioner with the rank of minister in New

Delhi and India sent an agent general with the same rank to Washington, to act under the British embassy. The American press, too, began to recognize the importance of Indian news, and in due time several large newspapers stationed full-time correspondents there; the most sustained service has been that of the *New York Times.*

After American entry into the war in December 1941, the question of India created a delicate situation between the United States and Britain, or more specifically between Roosevelt and Churchill. The British war cabinet either could not or would not satisfy Indian leaders so as to win their cooperation in the war effort. Churchill had a long record of anti-Indianism, which was now obstructing the Indian aspirations for self-rule. We do not know what Roosevelt thought when Churchill denied that the Atlantic Charter of August 1941 presaged freedom for India, but allusions in R. E. Sherwood's *Roosevelt and Hopkins* make it clear that whenever throughout the war Roosevelt felt it opportune to do so he urged that steps be taken to settle the Indian question.

In the spring of 1942 Roosevelt sent Colonel Louis Johnson to India as his personal representative with the rank of ambassador. A technical mission headed by Henry F. Grady, formerly assistant secretary of state and in 1947–1948 first United States ambassador to India, was also dispatched to survey industrial potential for the war effort. Johnson was in India when the British war cabinet's mission headed by Sir Stafford Cripps arrived in March 1942, and he talked unofficially with many of the Indian leaders and with Cripps, creating the impression that Roosevelt hoped for a liberal political settlement. This gave the United States prestige in Indian eyes. When the Cripps Mission failed, however, the American press was unreserved in denunciation of the Indian leaders for refusing the proposals and for failing to cooperate in the war. Like the lady in a Helen Hokinson cartoon of the period, it had become "tired of being patient with India." It assessed all Indian actions according to their assumed harm or good to American war purposes, and British propaganda contributed to producing this result. Indians resented the reaction as unfair in not taking Indian necessities into account and on their side judged the United States in relation to their own nationalist aspirations rather than war strategy. At the same time a number of Indians suspiciously saw the Grady Mission as an American effort to get a foot in the door so that after the war America could establish an economic imperialism over India to succeed that of the British, which was obviously declining.

Two factors, however, regained much of Indian goodwill for the United States. One was the strong democratic world leadership of Roosevelt, expressed in his speeches, his policies, and his sponsorship of material aid to all the United Nations including India. He already had appeared to Indians before the war as the protector of the oppressed, a champion in our time of freedom and democracy. They hoped for much from him, and his prestige increased steadily as he threw America's resources unreservedly and successfully into the war. When he died, grief in India was general and sincere. Through him the United States acquired a stature in Indian minds never achieved before or since. Specifically much was due in this respect to the activities of William Phillips, Roosevelt's second personal representative in India, who served in New Delhi with the rank of ambassador from December 1942 to 1943. He endeavored to bring the government of India and the Indian political parties into a working relationship but without success, in part because of the government of India's reluctance to let him be a go-between: it refused him permission to see Gandhi, who was then in detention Phillips strongly urged Roosevelt to press for a settlement of the Indian problem, and his views, though not officially revealed, were well known and appreciated in India. Afterwards some of his correspondence, published by a journalistic leak, confirmed the Indian presumptions.

The second factor was the presence of American troops in India. The G.I.s were liked for their informality and easy social relations with Indians, so different from those of the British, and they helped smooth out some of the old misconceptions about Americans. When the war ended United States stock stood high; indeed, it was idealized as a nation.

After the war this warmth began to cool as the United States disappointed Indian expectations and criticized Indian actions. Indians were offended when Washington gave moral support to the reestablishment of Dutch and French rule in Indonesia and Indo-China, though the policy in the Phillippines commanded high approval. The net result was equivocal: suspicions that American policy would be imperialist were both aroused and allayed.

The first major postwar disappointment in India came from the failure of Americans to provide capital for industrial expansion. During the latter war years Indian industry had begun to draft plans for postwar development. Indians thought their country an ideal field for investment, and expected to be besieged by offers of funds that they could accept on favorable terms. These were not forthcoming for a variety of reasons, including the unsettled political condition resulting from the Hindu-Muslim conflict, the still unresolved nationalist issue, and the disadvantageous terms India prescribed for the entry of foreign capital. Many Indians were also disappointed that the United States did not help India recover promptly her blocked sterling balances in London, which Britain was obviously in no position to make over with any rapidity.

During the final stages of the British-Indian and Hindu-Muslim settlements the United States played a part not very clear to the public, but one which seemed on the outside to imply that any settlement at all would be satisfactory to Washington if only it avoided civil war. Thus in February 1947 the Department of State welcomed the then expected federal solution for an undivided India, applauding the Labour government's decision that month. But when in June the Labour government reversed itself and announced that the solution would be by partition, the State Department applauded this too. It appeared to many Indians that the United States' primary interest was Anglo-American concord rather than India's welfare. The United States was, they felt, promoting its alliances in the Cold War, which had developed in 1946, rather than considering the needs of Asian nations. India—and after partition India and Pakistan—and the United States, each in its own way, thought its position unappreciated by the other.

Relations of the United States with India reached a low point in the spring of 1951, but after Chester Bowles was sent as ambassador they improved. In Pakistan attitudes were generally good in the early years after independence except for critical moments when Pakistan felt the United States was biased against her on the Kashmir issue and discriminating against her on technical aid. Pakistan at first got far less of this, even proportionally to her size and population, than did India.

Both India and Pakistan have been responsive to the personalities of American ambassadors as well as to the policies they were promoting. Besides Bowles, India has reacted favorably to Senator John Sherman Cooper when he was ambassador and to J. K. Galbraith. Visiting personalities have also made a valuable impression in each country—Mrs. Roosevelt, President Eisenhower, Vice President Johnson, Mrs. John Kennedy. So, too, visits to the United States of Prime Minister Nehru, Prime Minister Liaquat Ali Khan, and President Ayub Khan aided materially in helping American officials and the American public to understand Indian and Pakistani problems and policies. The ambassadors these two countries have sent to the United States have also usually made a good impression for their country, especially those who were kept at the post long enough to become well known, as in the case of Mrs. Vijaya Lakshmi Pandit, G. L. Mehta, Justice M. C. Chagla, B. K. Nehru.

A very serious situation arose concerning military aid to Pakistan provided under the United States Mutual Security Act in an agreement signed in 1953 to bolster the American worldwide defense system against the Soviet Union, but which India saw only as giving arms to Pakistan which could, and very well might be, used against India. India itself would not ask the United States for similar aid, since it wished to retain its neutral position in the Cold War. The United States stipulated expressly that these arms could not be used to support any Pakistani aggression, but India was not satisfied and Indian officials, the Indian press, and the Indian public have continuously expressed resentment against the United States for giving Pakistan such resources. Pakistan used some of this equipment in September 1961 in clashes on the Afghan border. President Ayub Khan was reported to have resented United States inquiries about this use and to have stated in January 1962 that Pakistan would use these arms in the event of any threat to itself, having specific reference to speeches by Indian leaders that Pakistan officially described as threats to the nation's integrity. These arms were used against India in the India-Pakistan War of December 1971. Conversely, when the United States started to give arms to India in late 1962 to repel the Chinese attack in the Himalayas, Pakistan voiced strong resentment on the ground that India would be likely to use these arms against her.

The wisdom of giving arms to Pakistan in the 1960s was severely questioned by many Americans, including Ambassador Chester Bowles at the time the agreement was being negotiated. The same amount of money given to Pakistan for economic aid might have been more useful in the long run and would not have created anti-American feeling in India. Whether the gain to the United States security system was great enough to offset the harm to relations with India was a matter of considerable doubt. The economic aid that accompanied the military aid was, however, an important element in preserving Pakistan's national existence.

In 1971 when Pakistan was ferociously trying to crush the East Pakistan revolt and the United States was shipping arms to Pakistan that were used to support the West Pakistan cause against East Pakistan, the United States was severely criticized in India, while no convincing reason was given the American people for supplying those arms.

A political issue that created a good deal of misunderstanding between the United States and India was the annexation of Goa in 1961 (see Chapter 16). The American press almost without exception, and Adlai Stevenson as head of the United States delegation at the United Nations, strongly condemned India on the ground of practicing aggression, especially a kind of aggression that India through the voice of Nehru had always denounced in others in high-sounding moral terms. Emotion was surely stronger than reason in this reaction. India had long and patiently tried to get Portugal to discuss the Goan situation; the United Nations had tried to bring Portugal to reason; nothing was successful. Both the Indian and the Goan public were restive about Portuguese retention of this enclave in India. The annexation was bound to take place at some time. When it took place, it was practically bloodless, and Goa has now been peacefully and considerately assimilated to India. Leaving aside the obvious malice in much of the reaction, the rest of the emotion in the United States response perhaps stemmed from an idealization of Nehru as a man of peace, peace perhaps at any price, a proponent of nonviolence along complete Gandhian lines, as the American press understood those lines. Nehru himself had never taken such a position. He vigorously supported all efforts to solve problems peacefully but he did not renounce the use of force, as is illustrated in Hyderabad, in Kashmir, or on the Himalayan frontier. He regarded force as the last resort. Few, if any, other nations and leaders would have abstained so long. But to the American public an image, however flimsily molded, had been shattered and the nation and personality that image symbolized were not to be forgiven.

In 1962 India was reported to be negotiating with the Soviet Union for the purchase of MIG jet fighter planes and the building of a jet plane factory in India. This naturally aroused apprehension in the United States. It should probably be understood as at least partly motivated in India by a desire to align the Soviet Union with India in the dispute with China. Since such negotiations were also opposed by the British, it is possible that they might have been calculated to affect British moves respecting the European Common Market, which seemed to be an economic threat to India.

An issue of wider human importance wherein India has been critical of the United States is that of nuclear testing. India was shocked when the Soviet Union in 1961 broke the moratorium on such tests and its leaders and its press expressed strong disapproval. Nehru expressed that disapproval at the Belgrade conference of nations unaligned in the Cold War but did not press for a resolution of condemnation, thus disappointing the United States. When the United States was considering resuming its own tests, India urged that it not do so, and when it decided to make the tests the Indian reaction was strongly disapproving. The issue in the Indian view transcended the interests of any state or group of states. Rather it was one concerning universal humanity, which Indians felt, along with many western scientists, would eventually be completely destroyed if such tests were continued and even more destructive weapons than were then known were developed. The testing and devising of weapons, they felt, only brought war and inevitable world annihilation nearer. The American reaction was, of course, that the initiative had been taken by the Soviet Union and that India should have condemned that country in round and ringing terms and should have had no reproach for America, which was only pursuing a necessary policy of national security. It was not possible to get India and the United States to accept each other's point of view. Leading Indians have continued to press this issue on moral and humanitarian grounds. India herself is developing nuclear power, but for peaceful purposes only. Indian opinion is very strong on this point.

In connection with the dispute of India and Pakistan over the Jammu and Kashmir state each country has charged the United States with favoring the other in the Security Council. India feels that she needs to have the state for her own security against the possibility of renewed Chinese encroachment upon her territory in the Himalayan region. When the United States and Great Britain urge Pakistan to settle this quarrel with India Pakistan suspects them of being willing to sacrifice her rightful claim to Jammu and

Kashmir merely to pacify India, having no thought of promoting justice. India fears that the United States and Great Britain are willing to sacrifice her security if by doing so they can keep Pakistan happy.

When President Nixon and Premier Chou En-lai, in their joint communiqué in Peking on February 27, 1972, urged India and Pakistan to withdraw their forces to their own sides of the cease-fire line in Jammu and Kashmir, India regarded that admonition, coming from the two nations that had given aid to Pakistan, as a bit of officiousness.

Americans have often been irked by a tone of self-righteousness which they have thought lay in the remarks made by Indian leaders on international relationships—especially some made by Nehru—and have been resentful of the charge that the United States acts "imperialistically." Americans have therefore pointed out inconsistencies in Indian—and sometimes in Pakistani—arguments. For example, they point out that there has been no simple struggle in progress between western colonialism and Asian democratic aspirations. Instead Asia itself has been full of internal conflicts—interregional strife in the Near East, in the Far East, even in South Asia between India and Pakistan. With regard to Korea, India's attitude of first supporting and then not supporting the United Nations was characterized in America as illogical and indefensible. Americans have maintained that mere economic aid to Asia is not enough. They have thought the area must become militarily strong and must forestall subversion lest as it prospers it tempts aggression by some powerful and expansionist neighbor, that is, the Soviet Union or China.

Neither the Indians and the Pakistanis on one side and the Americans on the other seem to have grasped the other's point of view. Americans have considered their international motives and policies clear and unexceptionable. They have looked upon the world as engaged in a gigantic ideological struggle and as divided into two camps of Democracy versus Communism, of individual freedom versus suppression of individual rights, of liberty versus slavery, of the United States and the other western democracies versus the Soviet Union and its satellites and as against China. Many Americans have felt that the United States has a duty as the world's richest and most powerful nation to lead the world, even to direct it.

India and Pakistan, on the other hand, are engaged in a great social, economic, and political revolution, which is the most important phase of their national life. The birth of Bangladesh in 1971–1972 shows that this revolution is still vigorously in process. It has been more important in the subcontinent than the struggle between the western democracies and Soviet Communism, and the character of political institutions.

In the light of their own interests and aspirations, how has the United States appeared to India and Pakistan? The United States is, first of all, economically and militarily the world's leading nation and to that extent the heir of nineteenth and early twentieth century Great Britain. The sins of Britain which Indians complained about fifty or even thirty years before were in 1947 feared as possible dangers from the United States, for it seemed to them that the United States had all the potentialities of committing them. Britain was then in India's view an imperialist power, upholding reactionary regimes, denying to India and other parts of Asia and Africa their democratic rights. America, too, despite its own opinion of itself, sometimes seemed so to many Indians. They said America tolerated fascist aggression in Ethiopia in 1935 and in Spain in 1936–1938, Japanese aggression in China in the 1930s, British and French imperialism in the Near East. But the Indian National Congress during those various decades was in every case denouncing the aggressors and denouncing Britain for perpetrating or tolerating the aggression.

Secondly, Americans still appear to Indians and Pakistanis as race conscious. They used to assail the United States perennially for its treatment of blacks. Those attacks have diminished since the United States Supreme Court began its series of desegregation decisions in 1954. In connection with the race issue they used to point out also that when the atom bomb was employed at the end of World War II, America used it on the Japanese, not the Germans, on Asians, not Europeans—they ignored the fact that it was available too late for use in Europe. When President Truman in December 1950 spoke in terms taken to imply that America might use it in Korea or China, again to annihilate Asians, there was an outburst in all Asia, which was particularly violent in India and Pakistan.

Thirdly, Indians and Pakistanis subject the American profession of democracy to criticism in the light of situations in Asia. Respecting China, America was censured as opposing that nation's unification. India and Pakistan officially regarded the People's Republic as the regime which the Chinese wanted. The United States, too, should recognize it, they maintained, or at least admit it to membership in the United Nations, whether liking it or not. The press in each country and the public interested in international affairs generally have expressed the same sentiment. When China was admitted in 1971 that matter appeared to be settled.

The United States in supporting Chiang and trying to keep him in power in Taiwan was, in Indian and Pakistani eyes, supporting a wrong—because a repudiated—government. That attitude, how-ever, was considerably modified in the Indian press in consequence of the Chinese advance in the Himalayas in 1962.

In respect to the Korean War, the press and public of these two nations again questioned the American position, which they saw as blocking Korean freedom. They referred back to the end of the Russo-Japanese War when the United States and Britain approved the Treaty of Portsmouth (1905) and the delivery of Korea to the Japanese and commented that American interest in checking Communism there in 1950 was not based on a concern for the Korean people but a desire to promote power politics.

The United States is not considered by Indians and Pakistanis to have had a clear record on the issue of colonialism. Though Ameri-can actions respecting the Philippines were commended, America appeared to them for a long time to be of two minds about Indo-nesia. They saw America helping the French retain Indo-China and supporting a political head, Bao Dai, in whom the people had no confidence, and helping France to hold Tunisia. They re-proached America for supporting first one regime that had no support from the people and then another that was without a democratic base. They maintained that America's policy had been determined only by a desire to retain the aid of France against the Soviet Union in Asia and Europe, and, when that goal proved im-possible, to get a foothold so as to strike down North Vietnamese Communism. The United States did not act, they said, with a de-sire to meet the aspirations of the people in Indo-China, but out of concern for its own interests. In respect to Algeria the United States position appeared to them to be better; at least it was less criticized.

The United States was also charged with helping the British maintain their position in Malaya, where with large resources of men and arms they were not able to crush an opposition, small in numbers but strong through the moral support of the Chinese minority, not the majority of the people who greatly feared the Communist movement in Malaya. The American motive was considered to be maintenance of an Anglo-American alliance against Communism at the expense of Malay nationalist goals.

In respect to Goa, the United States attitude was viewed as motivated by a desire to keep Portuguese support for NATO, whatever the rights or wrongs of the Goan situation. Whenever the United States has voted with the colonial powers in the United Nations against the Asian-Arab and Latin American countries, it has usually lost in Indian and Pakistani estimation.

The United States position with respect to Southeast Asia has steadily moved from bad to worse in the view of India and Pakistan. America sided with the Netherlands in the revolt of Indonesia against Dutch rule. It sided with the French when the Vietnamese were driving the French out. Later it complacently let North and South Vietnam remain divided into two nations contrary to the Geneva agreement of 1954, which ended the Indochina war and anticipated general elections and reunification of North and South. The United States attitude was interpreted as being based on a desire to keep the strong Communist government of North Vietnam under Ho Chi Minh from winning the election and getting control of South Vietnam. The United States in supporting the incompetent and corrupt government in South Vietnam seemed in India merely to be carrying the Cold War with the Soviet Union into a region where it had no right to intrude.

At that time United States policy in Southeast Asia was motivavated by the "Domino Theory"—that if an area should become Communist, its immediate neighbor would next be sure to fall, and then the area adjacent to the latter, and so on. India did not subscribe to the Domino Theory. On the contrary India considered that when the United States gave military aid to South Vietnam in 1961 she was unjustifiably intruding in Southeast Asian affairs. India's view has not changed, and the United States interference in Vietnam continues to be viewed as entirely gratuitous and increasingly pernicious. The confidence that in the late 1940s India had in United States' wisdom and disinterested motives in Asian relations has been steadily corroded by the United States' increased involvement in Vietnam and the accompanying devastation of that land, destruction of its economy, and slaughter of its population. The expansion of the Vietnam war into Laos and Cambodia, with the possibility that Thailand too may become the victim of war, seriously disturbs India. It all seems to Indians—at least to many Indians—to confirm the old suspicion that America is imperialistic. The American involvement in Vietnam has been, and still is, a most serious liability to the American position in South Asian public opinion. The American motives are considered to be a desire for power and control of natural resources in the area, such as mineral wealth.

Muslims in Pakistan have frequently claimed that the United States opposes the unity and economic development of Islamic nations in the Near East, being concerned, they say, to procure oil, support the British, and check Russian influence and Communist progress. They have interpreted American support of Israel in the same way.

The United States, in the early years after India and Pakistan won independence, was often charged by the Indian and Pakistani press with being indifferent to their countries' real economic and social welfare and moved to give such help as it did only to "use" them for anti-Russian purposes. Indians and Pakistanis would complain that America asked support and affirmed that it would be to their advantage to side with America, but allotted them only a fraction of the economic aid it bestowed upon Europe, though their necessity was greater. America was charged, along with Britain, with doing nothing to remove racial discrimination throughout the world. It influenced the Security Council, people in India and Pakistan would say, to act promptly where its own interests were affected, as in the case of Korea in June 1950, but let their affairs drag along interminably, as in the quarrel over Kashmir.

As the years have passed and the Indian and Pakistani public have become more sophisticated in world affairs, they have lost their fear of imperialism and have come to see more clearly into the complexity of international problems. While each has been receiving continuous and substantial economic aid from the United States, suspicion of the United States has declined, while disillusionment with respect to the Soviet Union, and especially mistrust and positive fear of Chinese aggression have mounted.

Nevertheless, the opinion of many Indians and Pakistanis long remained in large terms that the United States has a single dominating motive in all its international relations, and that is to check the Soviet Union. Their comment was that this aim was not primary in their own eyes, that having been drawers of water and hewers of wood for the West in the nineteenth century they do not propose to become cannon fodder for it now in the second half of the twentieth. The United States is still viewed as playing its own game and making little effort to see the viewpoint and needs of nations it tries to win as allies. Yet an observer visiting South Asia frequently must surely see an improved understanding in India and Pakistan of American policies.

The largest contributing element to improved relations between the United States and India and Pakistan has come from what is, speaking largely, an increase of the positive element in American dealings with them during the years from 1947. There has been less of unskilled contentious propaganda against the Soviet Union and Communism and more of constructive economic approach and cultural understanding toward Indian and Pakistani needs and institutions.

On the economic front the United States has become increasingly aware that the friendship of India and Pakistan can be won by helping them solve their problems of population and production. It was a mistake to ask only: Are you for America or Russia? Are you for democracy or totalitarianism? The problem is not so simple, and there are other questions more immediate and more relevant. The basic questions of the subcontinent have been and still are: How do we eat? Do we govern ourselves? Are we as good as other people? How can we become strong? Who will help us?

The United States made a start in helping with the $190 million wheat loan to India in 1950. On January 5, 1952, an agreement was signed with India by which each side contributed $54 million to a pool called the Indian-American Technical Cooperation Fund. This was to be used chiefly for increasing food production and rural community development. The American contribution came from the fund set up under the Mutual Security Act of 1951. An additional sum of $45.4 million was made available later. This was only a small portion of what was needed and only a beginning; assistance has been granted from United States public funds continually ever since, whether as low-interest loans, gifts, or in other ways.

Pakistan received $10 million of economic aid early in 1952 under the Point Four program, and in September 1952 effected a

$15 million loan through the Export-Import Bank. That was only a fraction of what it could use and has since had. In addition Pakistan has received military assistance—India did not ask for this kind of aid—to an amount which is not publicly known.

The loans for economic assistance have been made on generous terms. Interest and repayment of principal is made in rupees which are not convertible into dollars and must be used in the countries themselves. Eighty percent of these payments are returned to the governments of those countries under United States Public Law 83–480 with its various amendments to be used by them for economic development through schemes approved by the United States. The other 20 percent is retained by the United States government to be expended at its discretion in the two countries, partly in support of its diplomatic missions there, partly in support of cultural and educational projects.

Assistance has not always been rendered in the most graceful manner. In the early days there was a tendency in Congress to try to attach anti-Communist and pro-American strings. This was resented, notably in India, starting with the wheat loan bill. The tendency has cropped up repeatedly since but has fortunately not often been allowed to go too far. An illustration of this occurred on May 12, 1962, when the Senate Foreign Relations Committee by a vote of 8 to 7, in dealing with an authorization bill for economic and military aid to underdeveloped countries, cut the administration's request for economic aid to India for 1962–1963 by 25 percent (or more than $200 million). On May 21 the Committee, this time by a vote of 9 to 7, rescinded that action but nevertheless still denied the administration's request that aid to India in 1962–1963 should be increased by $90 million over the amount made available in 1961–1962. Statements by various senators indicated that the adverse voting reflected displeasure over India's seizure of Goa, the attitude of India's sharp-spoken Minister of Defense Krishna Menon, who had alienated American sentiment by unfriendly remarks, by his policies in international affairs, and by an uncooperative posture in the United Nations in favor of Soviet Union policies. India's unwillingness to put the status of Kashmir to a plebiscite was mentioned as another reason, and also the prospect that India might purchase Russian MIG jet fighter planes and build a plant to manufacture them under Russian license. This public spanking of India aroused a great deal of bitter comment in India.

Economic assistance helps the subcontinent answer the most immediate and most critical of its questions, those of self-preservation and the acquisition of national self-sufficiency and security. Private philanthropic agencies, too, notably the Ford Foundation and the Rockefeller Foundation, have been helping find the answers to some of the subcontinent's questions by fostering medical and agricultural research, supplying technical advice, conducting pilot development projects. Much more moderately financed, but well appreciated, have been other private endeavors, such as those undertaken by the American Friends Service Committee and Peace Corps projects.

The Indian attitude toward the United States suddenly improved when the Indian-Chinese (undeclared) war broke out, but the attitude of Pakistan toward the United States worsened. The prompt response of the United States to India's desperate appeal for military aid won India's immediate and deep gratitude. India even failed to notice—very much—the relish with which the American press greeted the failure of India's policy of nonalignment, the disaster into which military unpreparedness had propelled it, the acknowledgment of the unrealistic policy toward China which Nehru confessed, and most of all the toppling of Krishna Menon. Rather, Indians felt the United States to be their friend, much more of a friend then than the Soviet Union, which equivocated, too embarrassed to face a choice between a Communist, if ideologically opposed, nation and India, which it had so long courted. Pakistan, however, resented the supplying of arms to India. With these arms India might become as modernized militarily as Pakistan, and many Pakistanis feared that India might use the newly acquired weapons against Pakistan itself. The United States had a problem to meet in having at the same time to build up Indian strength to resist China and to allay the fears of its ally Pakistan. As part of its answer to the total complex of problems the United States, with the help of equally vigorous efforts by Britain, used its good offices to bring India and Pakistan into negotiations about the future of Kashmir. The interests of India and Pakistan were not all that was involved; United States policy toward all the problems stemming from conflict between the United States and China were affected as well.

Possibly the most far-reaching effect upon relations between the United States and the Subcontinent will stem from educational and cultural developments in process. The United States has been conducting exchange of persons by providing funds under the Fulbright, the Fulbright-Hayes, and the Smith-Mundt Acts to send American scholars and students to India and Pakistan and to bring Indian and Pakistani scholars and "leaders" to America, sometimes for short tours, but often for extended stays. In India and Pakistan the United States Information Agency maintains free public libraries in the large cities, which are well, one might sometimes say enthusiastically, patronized; publishes periodicals, which are not confined to articles about America but include articles about India and Pakistan; finances translations of novels and other works of nonpropagandistic character into local languages; arranges local exhibitions by Indian and Pakistani artists; provides movies and public lectures; brings American artists and athletes to the subcontinent for public performances; and in other ways presents aspects of American and also Indian and Pakistani culture. Further, the United States Technical Cooperation Administration and now the Agency for International Development, with the aid of American institutions of learning, has been inaugurating and staffing technical teaching programs in India and Pakistani universities. It now has become in order for the United States to establish cultural relations with Bangladesh.

Most likely to have long-range effects are academic developments that have been inaugurated in the United States and are now being started in India and Pakistan. The educational picture in America with respect to India and Pakistan is far different today from what it was before World War II, when eight universities had chairs of Sanskrit and that was practically the total extent of American study of India. The war showed the inadequacy of such a meager treatment of India; experts on India were badly needed but were not available in anything like the number wanted.

After the war was over, when India achieved independence and became the two nations of India and Pakistan, the importance of the modern South Asian area (India, Pakistan, Ceylon, Nepal, Afghanistan) became even more evident. The same sort of situation became obvious with regard to the countries in Eastern Asia, Southeast Asia, Western Asia, Africa, Eastern Europe, and Northeastern Asia, and there was a general problem of how to introduce

411

the necessary instruction in American universities and promote accompanying research. Here the great philanthropic foundations led the way by helping to finance graduate programs of "language and area" studies in the universities. The Carnegie Corporation of New York, the Rockefeller Foundation, and the Ford Foundation, as soon as it was established, supported such teaching, research, and fellowship programs, including programs to deal with India and Pakistan. In 1949 under the provisions of Public Law 79–584 (Fulbright Act) United States government funds available in India and Pakistan were opened to use for American faculty and student grantees to study in those countries. In 1959 the United States government also began to give support to such studies in America, acting through the Office of Education under Public Law 85–864 (National Defense Education Act). In 1961, under authorization of Congress and administration by the Library of Congress, Public Law 83–480 funds were made available to provide American university libraries with publications from India and Pakistan. That same year fifteen American universities joined in a corporation to establish an American Institute of Indian Studies located in India, supported by contributions by these institutions, a grant from the Ford Foundation, and Public Law 83–480 funds.

In the South Asia field the first modern language and area program was established at the University of Pennsylvania in 1947. Later, support was given to similar programs in other institutions, until now they also exist at these universities: California (Berkeley), Chicago, Columbia, Cornell, Duke, Hawaii, Illinois, Kansas State, Michigan, Minnesota, Missouri, Rochester, State University of New York, Syracuse, Texas, Washington, Wisconsin. Area courses on South Asia are offered in each of the programs in one or more of the following fields: geography, economics, anthropology, sociology, history, political science, government, history of art, music, dance, drama, philosophy, religions, public health. Many of these institutions offer classical languages: Sanskrit, Pali, Prakrit, Persian. Modern teaching materials for courses in language and area subjects have been developed, chiefly with the assistance of funds provided by the United States Office of Education under Public Law 85–864.

The number of Americans with specialized professional training and knowledge has increased progressively every year since 1947.

All this is an index of American appreciation of South Asia's greatness in the development of civilization and its contemporary importance in Asian and general world affairs.

Clearly, this kind of developing interest in the United States about South Asia calls for a corresponding development of studies about the United States in those countries. An organized program for such a development was begun about 1960. Arrangements were made to inaugurate chairs in American history or political institutions or literature or even total programs of American studies on the graduate level in various universities, such as the Osmania University at Hyderabad, the University of Bombay, the Jadavpur University in Calcutta, supported by Public Law 83–480 funds and operated by those institutions with staff assistance from American universities. After a few years these programs are to be staffed and operated by the Indian and Pakistani institutions.

Gratifying as it is to interested persons in both America and the Indian subcontinent to view the economic and technical aid programs and the great development of educational offerings that have been described, this is not all that is needed. India and Pakistan want certain psychological assurances as well. One of these is that Americans look upon them and other Asians as equals. Indians and Pakistanis have often complained of an arrogance of wealth in official American dealings with their countries and a self-righteousness in the attitude of American representatives at the United Nations. These include uncivil remarks that on occasion have been made on the floor to representatives of India and Pakistan and reported in their press. More serious is their feeling that the smaller or the less powerful nations are slighted. President Prasad, speaking at the opening of the new Indian Parliament on May 16, 1952, complained of this situation and added, "Gradually the noble aims of the founders of the United Nations and the Charter they framed appear to be getting blurred." Such a view naturally reduces the success of United States policies in the United Nations.

It is doubtful, of course, that the United States will ever fully succeed in winning the confidence of India, Pakistan, and Bangladesh, and of other Asian nations, until color discrimination is eliminated in the United States itself. Though this issue seems to many Americans to be purely domestic, it has serious connotations for international relations. It is one on which the Soviet Union has been frequently viewed in Asia as having a clear advantage over America.

One of the most damaging blows to American prestige in the subcontinent was self-inflicted in 1971–72 in connection with the revolt of East Pakistan, which led to the India-Pakistan War of December 1971 and the birth of the new nation Bangladesh. The reports in the American and European press of West Pakistan's effort to suppress the revolt had been hard to believe; nevertheless they had to be believed, for they were on-the-scene accounts submitted by competent correspondents of the most prestigious and reliable daily newspapers and weeklies. No effort was made to refute or discredit those accounts except a few weak and half-hearted denials by the Pakistan government.

But the government of the United States exhibited no concern about Pakistan's repudiation of democratic procedures, the horrors of its method of suppressing the revolt, the pitiable plight of the refugees. Though claiming to maintain even-handed neutrality toward India and Pakistan in the war that ensued when India moved troops into East Pakistan in support of the insurgents, Washington definitely aligned itself with Pakistan, and that too, according to news reports, contrary to the advice of Ambassador Kenneth B. Keating in New Delhi, who was urging a policy of genuine neutrality. The climax came on December 4, 1971, when President Nixon authorized a public statement by the Department of State that "India bears the major responsibility for the hostilities that have ensued." On December 5 the United States introduced a resolution in the Security Council calling for an immediate cessation of hostilities, and withdrawal of armed personnel of India and Pakistan present on the territory of the other to their own sides of the India-Pakistan borders. This would have brought the war—which was already going badly for Pakistan—to a close. Other nations submitted resolutions. The United States resolution was voted by the Security Council, but was vetoed by the Soviet Union. On December 6 the United States suspended $87.6 million of development loans to India, and George Bush, the United States delegate to the United Nations, after stating in the Security Council that India was the main aggressor, said in reference to India, "There is quite clear aggression. It is obviously quite clear." Charles W. Bray, 3d, spokesman for the Department of State,

414

confirmed that Mr. Bush's statement represented the views of the United States administration. A resolution for a cease-fire and withdrawal of forces was introduced in the United Nations General Assembly on December 7; it was approved by a vote 104 to 11 with 10 abstentions, but India would not accede to the resolution since compliance was not obligatory. The United States position remained unaltered, and in the debates in the Security Council and the General Assembly Bush maintained that India was mainly responsible for the outbreak of fighting between India and Pakistan. In comments to newsmen he talked of aggression by India. The reaction in New Delhi and throughout India was one of outrage.

The United States government's postion against India was clear and it put the United States squarely on Pakistan's side, thus supporting genocide, military incompetence, and recklessness in incurring international shame.

The genocide and military incompetence were lapses by Pakistan. The one was unqualified immorality. The other, consisting of division of its armed forces in two parts with no communication with each other and with 900 miles of India in between them so that neither could support the other, was an elementary and inconceivable strategic blunder.

The recklessness of the American administration in relations with the world's largest democracy—and a natural ally of America—seems beyond explanation. Not even the secret minutes of the high-level Washington planning group, which the columnist Jack Anderson got hold of and published, reveal any basis for the action. They merely show that the President, though claiming to be even-handed, was really "tilting" his policy in favor of Pakistan. This was deeply resented in India and, of course, destroyed much of India's confidence in America. It may also have diminished the confidence of other Asian—and African—nations in America and in America's professions of democracy and support of democracy throughout the world. If for no other reason than expediency, the American policy was unwise. But since there was a clear moral issue involved in the Pakistan government's treatment of the revolutionary part of Pakistan, which was seeking a democratic process in Pakistan's administration and political procedures, the American policy of supporting Yahya Khan and his government was a major mistake.

No explanation of the American policy of supporting Pakistan has been offered by the United States administration. Possibly, by some devious process of reasoning, it was expected to deter the spread of communism. Pakistan is a member of the Central Treaty Organization (CENTO), an anti-Communist association which the United States, though not a member, helped to create as a successor to the Middle East Treaty Organization (METO), also known as the Baghdad Pact, which had disintegrated in 1958 when Iraq, on establishing a government friendly to the Soviet Union, withdrew from it. Also President Nixon and his advisers in a vague way may have been apprehensive that Bangladesh might some day fuse with West Bengal (in India), where communism is strong but by no means dominant.

As Asian countries learn from and about America, they increasingly feel that there are things that it is worthwhile for Americans to learn from and about them. The process, they think, should be two-way. The United States will have and retain the respect for India, Pakistan, and Bangladesh that those countries deserve only when it has acquired a large body of knowledge about them spread throughout its citizenship. Such knowledge is not to be gained easily or cheaply. American efforts, though now progressing, must be intensified still more if they are to meet the national need in respect to South Asia.

Knowledge of the history, culture, aspirations, and problems of South Asia will help Americans take a genuine and intelligent interest in the people of the subcontinent for their intrinsic human worth rather than as so many millions of bodies to stand in support of American international policies. The people of the subcontinent have for some four and a half or five millennia been developing and practicing the arts of civilization, and they have been one of the great civilizers throughout that period. They have the ability to lead their region themselves and the pride and self-respect to do so. This point is one that Mrs. Gandhi has made at various times during the period of her leadership of India. She expressed it in New Delhi on April 24, 1972, when inaugurating a five-day Asian Trade Union Seminar: while Asian countries, she said, follow different systems of government and ideologies, one sentiment is common to the majority of peoples in the Asian continent, "and that is revulsion against outside presence. We do not want any foreign presence." What self-respecting nation would?

Appendices / Suggested Reading / Index

Appendix 1. Population and Literacy Rate in India, by Political Subdivision

| | Population, 1971 | | | Growth rate of population, 1961–1971 | Percentage of literates to total population (including 0–4 age group) | | Rate of growth of literacy rate over 1961 |
	Persons	Males	Females		1961	1971	
India	547,367,926	283,252,214	264,115,712	+ 24.66	24.03	29.34	+ 22.10
STATES							
Andhra Pradesh	43,394,951	21,944,826	21,450,125	+ 20.60	21.19	24.56	+ 15.90
Assam	14,952,108	7,863,725	7,088,383	+ 34.37	27.47	28.81	+ 4.88
Bihar	56,332,246	28,797,238	27,535,008	+ 21.26	18.40	19.79	+ 7.55
Gujarat	26,687,186	13,787,240	12,899,946	+ 29.34	30.45	35.72	+ 17.31
Haryana	9,971,165	5,317,149	4,654,016	+ 31.36	19.93	26.69	+ 33.92
Himachal Pradesh	3,424,332	1,735,106	1,689,226	+ 21.76	21.26	31.32	+ 47.32

Jammu and Kashmir	4,615,176	2,162,515	+ 29.60	11.03	18.30	+ 65.91
Kerala	21,280,397	10,741,524	+ 25.89	46.85	60.16	+ 28.41
Madhya Pradesh	41,650,684	20,211,820	+ 28.66	17.13	22.12	+ 29.13
Maharashtra	50,335,492	24,281,260	+ 27.26	29.82	39.08	+ 31.05
Mysore	29,263,334	14,322,673	+ 24.07	25.40	31.54	+ 24.17
Nagaland	515,561	240,202	+ 39.64	17.91	27.33	+ 52.60
Orissa	21,934,827	10,906,791	+ 24.99	21.66	26.12	+ 20.59
Punjab	13,472,972	6,280,667	+ 21.00	26.74	33.39	+ 24.87
Rajasthan	25,724,142	12,282,086	+ 27.63	15.21	18.79	+ 23.54
Tamil Nadu	41,103,125	20,330,576	+ 22.01	31.41	39.39	+ 25.41
Uttar Pradesh	88,364,779	41,441,907	+ 19.82	17.65	21.64	+ 22.61
West Bengal	44,440,095	20,951,851	+ 27.24	29.28	33.05	+ 12.88
UNION TERRITORIES AND OTHER AREAS						
Andaman and Nicobar Islands	115,090	45,085	+ 81.11	33.63	43.48	+ 29.29
Chandigarh	256,979	110,058	+114.36	51.06	61.24	+ 19.94
Dadra and Nagar Haveli	74,165	37,216	+ 27.95	9.48	14.86	+ 56.75
Delhi	4,044,338	1,800,048	+ 52.12	52.75	56.65	+ 7.39
Goa, Daman and Diu	857,180	426,154	+ 36.78	30.75	44.53	+ 44.81
Laccadive, Minicoy and Amindivi Islands	31,798	15,736	+ 31.90	23.27	43.44	+ 86.68
Manipur	1,069,555	530,454	+ 37.12	30.42	32.80	+ 7.82
Meghalaya	983,336	479,985	+ 32.02	25.71	28.43	+ 10.58
North East Frontier Agency	444,744	211,590	+ 32.14	7.13	9.34	+ 31.00
Pondicherry	471,347	234,497	+ 27.71	37.43	43.36	+ 15.84
Tripura	1,556,822	754,313	+ 36.32	20.24	30.87	+ 52.52

Source: *Census of India 1971, Provisional Population Totals*, published by A. Chandra Sekhar, Registrar General and Census Commissioner, India (New Delhi, May 31, 1971), pp. 1 and 2.

Appendix 2. *Population Estimates of Pakistan and Bangladesh, 1951 to 1970*

	East Pakistan (now Bangladesh)	West Pakistan (now Pakistan)
1951 Adjusted Census figure	4,20,62,610	3,37,79,555
1951	4,24,23,185	3,43,85,325
1952	4,32,33,341	3,51,95,100
1953	4,40,58,968	3,60,23,945
1954	4,49,00,362	3,68,72,309
1955	4,57,57,824	3,77,40,652
1956	4,66,31,661	3,86,29,444
1957	4,75,22,186	3,95,39,167
1958	4,84,29,717	4,04,70,314
1959	4,93,54,579	4,14,23,390
1960	5,02,97,103	4,23,98,911
1961 January 31 Census figures	5,08,53,721	4,29,78,261
1961	5,12,49,479	4,33,97,617
1962	5,22,19,888	4,44,19,848
1963	5,32,08,672	4,54,66,158
1964	5,42,16,178	4,65,37,113
1965	5,52,42,761	4,76,33,295
1966	5,62,88,783	4,87,55,297
1967	5,73,54,611	4,99,03,728
1968	5,84,40,621	5,10,79,210
1969	5,95,47,194	5,22,82,381
1970	6,06,74,720	5,35,13,892

Source: *Pakistan Statistical Yearbook 1968* (latest edition published), issued by Central Statistical Office, Government of Pakistan (Karachi 1970), page 2.

Note on computation.
1. 1951 Census figures have been adjusted for 5 percent under enumeration of urban population of Pakistan. Population of Gwadur (13,000) and that of Mohmand Agency (24,000) were also added to the actual of 1951 Census figure of West Pakistan for necessary adjustment.
2. All estimates refer to July 1 of the respective year. The estimates from 1961 to 1965 were revised on January 28, 1966. The estimates from 1961 onward are provisional.
3. The estimates from 1951 to 1970 have been computed on the basis of constant Geometric Rate of Growth derived from 1951 and 1961 Census figures separately by provinces and the rates are given as under:
   (a) East Pakistan 1.8935 percent per annum.
   (b) West Pakistan 2.3555 percent per annum.
4. Non-Pakistanis and the population of the Frontier Regions are included in the base figures.

Party	1951–52	1957	1962	1967	1971
Congress	362	371	361	283	
Congress (R)				(221*)	350
Congress (O)				(63*)	16
Socialist Party	12	7	6		
Praja Socialist Party		19	12	13	2
Samyukta Socialist Party				23	3
Kisan Mazdoor Party	9				
Revolutionary Socialist			2		
Jana Sangh	3	4	14	35	22
Swatantra			18	44	8
Communist Party of India	27	27	29	23	23
Communist Party (Marxist)				19	25
Dravida Munnetra Kazhagam		2	7	25	23
Forward Bloc (Marxist)		3	2		
Ram Rajya Parishad	3		2		
All-India Scheduled Castes Federation	2				
Hindu Mahasabha	4	2	1		
Jharkhand Party	3	7	3		
Peasants' and Workers' Party		4			
Ganatrantra Parishad		7	4		
Bangla Congress				5	1
Akali Dal	4		3	3	1
Bharatiya Kranti Dal					1
Muslim League	2	1	2		
Hill Leaders					
Republican Party of India		7	3	1	
Other parties	21	8	1	46	40
Independents	37	25	24		
Total	489	494	494	520	515

* Seats held by Congress (R) and Congress (O) at dissolution.

Appendix 4. *Election Results for Pakistan National Assembly, 1970*

Awami League	167
Jama'at-e-Islami	8
Pakistan Muslim League (Qayyum)	9
Pakistan Muslim League (Convention)	2
Pakistan Muslim League (Council)	7
Pakistan People's Party	87
Pakistan Democratic Party	1
All Pakistan Jamiat-e-Ulema-e-Islam (Hazarvi)	7
National Awami Party (Wali Khan)	6
Markazi Jamiat-ul-Ulema-e-Pakistan	7
Independents	12
Total Seats	313

The following political parties contested the elections but won no seats·
All Pakistan Markazi Jamiat-e-Ulema-e-Islam and Nizam-e-Islam
Sind-Karachi-Muhajir Punjabi-Pathan-Muttahida Mahaz
Jatiya Gana Mukti Dal
Islamic Ganatantri Dal
Krishak Sramik Party
Pakistan National Congress
Pakistan Masihi League
Markazi Jamiat-e-Ahl-e-Hadis
Khaksar Tehrik
Baluchistan United Front
Sind United Front
Pakistan Darodi Sangha

The following parties nominated candidates but boycotted the elections:
National Awami Party (Bhashani Group)
Pakistan National League

Suggested Reading

The literature on India and Pakistan is voluminous and I have therefore selected for mention here only works in English which, as far as I know, are either in print and purchasable or available in good libraries. Even within those limits I have omitted many that would be pertinent to the subject matter of this book. The most glaring omissions are the numerous publications by the governments of the two countries, including such basic materials as their censuses; the five-year plans; their educational, health, and other administrative reports; and the reports of special investigating commissions and committees. These are essential for specialized study; this bibliography is intended as a guide to acquiring a more general understanding.

General Works

A brief survey, but one not too highly compressed to be authoritative and useful, is *India, Pakistan, Ceylon,* 2nd edition (Philadelphia, University of Pennsylvania Press, 1963). This consists of a series of articles appearing as "India" (vol. XV), "Pakistan" (vol. XXI), and "Ceylon" (vol. VI) in the 1962 edition of *The Encyclopedia Americana,* prepared by American, European, Indian, Pakistani, and Ceylonese scholars under the joint direction of the *Encyclopedia's* editors and W. Norman Brown. The separate articles deal with political divisions, the people, the land and its resources, economic development, way of living, education, architecture and art, dance, music, drama, languages, linguistic science in ancient India, literature, science, religion and philosophy, law, government, prehistory, history (in three sections) from the sixth century B.C. to 1958. There are brief bibliographies. A short book on modern India is Ved Prakash Mehta, *Portrait of India* (New York, Farrar, Straus and Giroux, 1970). On the problem of the subcontinent's security, there is a book by D. E. Kennedy, *The Security of Southern Asia* (London, Chatto and Windus, 1965).

For the use of college classes an exceedingly valuable help is Leonard A. Gordon and Barbara Stoler Miller, *A Syllabus of Indian Civilization* (New York and London, Columbia University Press, 1971).

Histories

There are other general treatments of greater length though less scope. In the field of history the most authoritative for long has been the *Cambridge History of India* (Cambridge, Engl., Cambridge University Press, 1922–1937), planned in six volumes although the second has never appeared. A supplement to the first volume of this is *The Indus Civilization* by R. E. Mortimer Wheeler (first published in 1953, reprinted in 1960); revised edition published with the title *Early India and Pakistan to Ashoka* (New York, Praeger, 1968). Two other encyclopedic treatments of Indian history are *The History and Culture of the*

Indian People in eleven volumes, a composite work prepared by Indian scholars under the direction of R. C. Majumdar (Bombay, Bharatiya Vidya Bhavan, 1951–1960). The chapters in these volumes vary much in quality. The other lengthy treatment is *A Comprehensive History of India,* another compilation of articles by Indian scholars, this time edited by Nilakanta Sastri, planned in twelve volumes. Only the second volume of this, dealing with the Mauryas and Satavahanas, has been published (Bombay, Orient Longmans, 1957), and it is again uneven in its quality. An informative historiographical work is *Historians of India, Pakistan and Ceylon* edited by C. H. Philips (London, Oxford University Press, 1961). A pamphlet by Robert I. Crane, *The History of India: Its Study and Interpretation* (Washington, D.C., American Historical Association: Service Center for Teachers of History, publication no. 17, 1958), is a guide for nonprofessionals.

Of single-volume histories the standard work for many years was Vincent A. Smith's *The Oxford History of India* (London, Oxford University Press), first published in 1919. This has had several revisions, first by S. M. Edwardes in 1925, later under the editorship of Percival Spear: Part I: "Ancient and Hindu India" revised by Sir Mortimer Wheeler and A. L. Basham; Part 2: "India in the Muslim Period" revised by J. B. Harrison; Part 3: "India in the British Period" rewritten by Percival Spear (London, Oxford University Press, 1958). The most recent revision is by the same scholars (Oxford, Clarendon Press, 1968). Though this work is still useful, it has been difficult to bring its point of view up to date, however good as historians the various revisers have been. *The Cambridge Shorter History of India,* edited by H. H. Dodwell (New York, Macmillan, 1934), remains valuable after nearly forty years. A second edition of this work was published in Delhi by S. Chand and Company in 1958 and has additional chapters on "The Last Phase (1919–1947)" by R. R. Sethi. A more thought-provoking work than either of these two one-volume histories is *A Short History of India* by W. H. Moreland and A. C. Chatterjee, fourth edition (London, Longmans Green, 1957). A still more valuable work is R. C. Majumdar, N. C. Raychaudhuri, and Kalinkar Datta, *An Advanced History of India,* (New York, St. Martin's, 1951; second edition, London, Macmillan, and New York, St. Martin's Press, 1965).

Historical works accenting particular periods are C. H. Philips, *India* (London, Hutchinson's University Library, 1949), a most reliable study concerned almost wholly with India since the arrival of the Europeans; Romila Thapar, *Asoka and the Decline of the Mauryas* (London, Oxford University Press, 1961); Romila Thapar's first volume of *A History of India* (Hermendsworth, Penguin Press, 1966); Percival Spear, *Twilight of the Mughals* (Cambridge, Engl., Cambridge University Press, 1951); Holden Furber, *John Company at Work* (Cambridge, Harvard University Press, 1948), an objective study of the East India Company's operations; Holden Furber, *The Bombay Presidency in the Mid-eighteenth Century* (New York, Asia Publishing House, 1965); Stanley A. Wolpert, *Morley and India, 1906–1910* (Berkeley, University of California Press, 1967); Ram Gopal and Digvijaya Singh, *Indian Politics, from Crown Rule to Independence, 1858–1947* (Aligarh, Bharat Publishing House, 1967); P. E. Roberts, *History of British India* (London, Oxford University Press, 1952); Pratipal Bhatia, *The Paramaras, c. 800–1305 A.D.* (New Delhi, Munshiram Manoharlal, 1970); Donald F. Lach, *India in the Eyes of Europe in the Sixteenth Century* (Chicago, University of Chicago Press, 1965); Vincent A. Smith, *Akbar: The Great Mogul* (Oxford, Clarendon Press, 1917); Michael Edwardes, *British India, 1772–1947* (New York, Taplinger Publishing Company, 1967); Percival Griffiths, *Modern India* (London, Ernest Benn, 1957); Percival J. Griffiths, *The British Impact on India* (London, Cass, 1965); Edward Thompson and G. T. Garratt, *Rise and Fulfillment of British Rule in India* (New York, A Magazine Service Press, 1971); Percival Spear, *India: A Modern History* (Ann Arbor, University of Michigan Press, 1961; second edition, 1964); and T. Walter Wallbank, *A Short History of India and Pakistan* (New York, Mentor, 1958), which is an abridged paperback revision of his *India in the New Era* (Chicago, Scott, Foresman, 1951). Some other histories of periods are: Prakash Tandon, *Punjabi Century, 1857–1947* (Berkeley, University of California Press, 1968); Durga Das, *India from Curzon to Nehru and After* (New York, John Day, 1970); Thomas L. Metcalf, *The Aftermath of Revolt; India 1857–1870* (Princeton, Princeton University Press, 1964); Sarvepalli Gopal, *British Policy in India 1858–1905* (Cambridge, Engl., Cambridge University Press, 1965). Stanley A. Wolpert has published a small book, *India*, appearing in the series "The Modern Nations in Historical Perspective" (Englewood Cliffs, Prentice-Hall, 1965).

A three-volume *History of the Sikhs* is being written by Khushwant Singh, of which the first two volumes are in print (Princeton, Princeton University Press, 1963, 1966); the same author has a one-volume work, *The Sikhs: Their Religion, Culture, Customs, and Way of Life* (Bombay, Orient Longmans, 1959). A study of the social life of the English in eighteenth century India is Percival Spear, *The Nabobs* (Oxford paperback, 1963). On the Muslims see Gopal Ram, *Indian Muslims; A Political History 1856–1947* (Bombay, Asia Publishing House, 1964).

Books on the birth of Bangladesh began appearing in India in December 1971. The titles of three are: *Bangla Desh Documents* (New Delhi, Ministry of External Affairs, 1971); Yatindra Bhatnagar, *Mujib, the Architect of Bangla Desh; a Political Biography* (Delhi, Indian School Supply Depot, Publication Division, 1971); Ajit Bhattacharjea, ed., *Dateline Bangla Desh*, reports of the beginning of the terror by news correspondents of American and British newspapers and news magazines, with translations of some dispatches published in continental European newspapers (Bombay, Jaico Publishing House, 1971).

Cultural Heritage

In the field of cultural history a first-class book, which has the additional merit of being available in a Grove Press paperback reprint, is A. L. Basham, *The Wonder That Was India* (London, Sidgwick and Jackson, 1954; New York, Macmillan, 1955; third revised edition, New York, Taplinger Publishing Company, 1968), which surveys the cultural history down to the Muslim period. A Marxist view of India's historical development appears in D. D. Kosambi, *Ancient India: A History of Its Culture and Civilization* (New York, Pantheon, 1965, paperback 1970). H. G. Rawlinson's *India: A Short Cultural History*, fourth impression revised (New York, Praeger, 1952) gives prominence to the Muslim elements in Indian civilization (reissued in London, Cresset Press, 1965). A. A. Macdonnell's short *India's Past* (London, Oxford University Press, 1927; reprinted in Banaras, Banarsidass Jain, 1956) is still a good summary down to the Muslim period, though now needing some revision. An outstanding work by two eminent French scholars is Louis Renou and Jean Filliozat, *L'Inde classique*, 2 vols. (Paris, Payot, 1947, 1953), from which selections have been translated by Philip Spratt and published as part of the series *Classical India* (Calcutta, Susil Gupta, 1957, 1962). Another good French work is by Paul Masson-Oursel, Helena Willman-Grabowska, and Philippe Stern, translated into English by M. R. Dobie under the title *Ancient India and Indian Civilization* and appearing in the History of Civilization Series (New York, Knopf, 1934). The distinguished French scholar Jean Filliozat is the author of a copiously illustrated book, *India: The Country and Its Traditions*, translated from the

French by Margaret Ledesert (Englewood Cliffs, N.J., Prentice-Hall, 1962). *The Legacy of India,* edited by G. T. Garratt (London, Oxford University Press, 1937), is a collection of essays by various scholars on different aspects of India's civilization such as religion, science, and art, including a chapter on Muslim culture in India. A general survey of Indian political and cultural history, more interesting for the author's assessment of various phenomena, events, and institutions than for scholarly research, is Jawaharlal Nehru's *Discovery of India* (frequently printed in India; American edition, New York, John Day, 1946).

For the early period of cultural history, besides R. E. Mortimer Wheeler's *The Indus Civilization* mentioned above, there is the same scholar's survey dealing with archaeological findings concerning most ancient India, *Early India and Pakistan to Ashoka* (New York, Praeger, 1959; revised edition, 1968). For prehistoric cultures there is a well-written inexpensive scholarly book by Stuart Piggott entitled *Prehistoric India to 1000 B.C.* (Penguin Books, Pelican series, 1950; second edition, London, Cassell, 1962); also D. H. Gordon, *Prehistoric Background of Indian Culture* (Bombay, Tripathi, 1958); and F. R. Allchin, *Neolithic Cattle-Keepers of South India: A Study of Deccan Ashmounds* (New York, Cambridge University Press, 1963). To these should be added E. J. H. Mackay's *Early Indus Civilizations* (London, Luzac, 1948), which describes the important Harappa culture in brief but satisfactory form. Some works on various other aspects of the early period are Vincent A. Smith, *Ashoka,* third edition revised and enlarged (Oxford, Clarendon Press, 1920); W. W. Tarn, *The Greeks in Bactria and India* (Cambridge, Engl., Cambridge University Press, 1951); Nilakanta Sastri, *A History of South India,* second edition (London, Oxford University Press, 1958).

A textbook selection of material focused on the contemporary scene is *Introduction to the Civilization of India: Emergence of India and Pakistan into the Modern World* (Chicago, University of Chicago Press, 1957).

Some good brief books on various features of the subcontinent's cultural heritage are Humayun Kabir, *The Indian Heritage* (Bombay, Asia Publishing House, 1955); S. M. Ikram and Percival Spear, *The Cultural Heritage of Pakistan* (London, Oxford University Press, 1955); S. M. Ikram, *Muslim Civilization in India* (New York, Columbia University Press, 1964) Tara Chand, *Influence of Islam on Indian Culture* (Allahabad, The Indian Press, 1954); a collection of articles appearing as *Crescent and Green: A Miscellany of Writings on Pakistan* (London, Cassell, 1955). A compact statement of native Indian (that is, Hindu) traditional values appears in a pamphlet by Sudhakar Chattopadhyaya, *Traditional Values in Indian Life* (New Delhi, India International Center, 1961), which was prepared for the Indian National Commission for UNESCO. *Traditional Cultures in South-East Asia* (Bombay, Orient Longmans, 1958), prepared by the Institute of Traditional Cultures in Madras, deals with South Asia, in spite of its title.

Geography and Economic Structure and Development

The geography of the subcontinent is well covered in O. H. K. Spate's standard work *India and Pakistan: A General and Regional Geography,* third edition (New York, Barnes and Noble, 1967). With this may be mentioned C. Collin Davies, *An Historical Atlas of the Indian Peninsula,* second edition (Oxford, Oxford University Press, 1959), and the treatment of the subcontinent in George B. Cressey, *Asia's Lands and Peoples,* third edition (New York, McGraw-Hill, 1963), and that in the long-recognized standard work by L. Dudley Stamp, *Asia: A Regional and*

Economic Geography, twelfth edition (New York, Barnes and Noble, 1966). There is a good treatment of South Asia by John Brush in *The Pattern of Asia* (Englewood Cliffs, N.J., Prentice-Hall, 1958), edited by Norton Ginsburg. An interesting book is Alastair Lamb, *Asian Frontiers* (London, Pall Mall, 1968).

A historical atlas of India is far advanced toward completion as a project by a group of scholars at the University of Minnesota under the direction of Professor Joseph E. Schwartzberg.

For the economic structure and development of India standard works are Vera Anstey, *Economic Development of India,* fourth edition (New York, Longmans Green, 1942); P. A. Wadia and K. T. Merchant, *Our Economic Problem,* fifth revised edition (London, Probsthain, 1957); G. B. Jathar and S. G. Beri, *Indian Economics,* eighth edition (London, Oxford University Press, 1947, 1949), which is presumably superseded by G. B. Jathar and K. G. Jathar, *Indian Economics* (Bombay, Oxford University Press, 1957); Jagdish N. Bhagwati and Padma Desai, *India Planning for Industrialization and Trade Policies since 1951* (New York, Oxford University Press, 1970). A well-known and valuable book is D. R. Gadgil, *Industrial Evolution of India,* fourth edition (London, Oxford University Press, 1944). An instructive work, now a classic, is M. L. Darling, *The Punjab Peasant in Prosperity and Debt,* fourth edition (London, Oxford University Press, 1947). A sharp analysis of India's most fundamental problem is Daniel Thorner's *The Agrarian Prospect in India* (Delhi, Delhi University Press, 1956), while a group of equally trenchant articles has been published by Daniel and Alice Thorner as *Land and Labour in India* (Bombay and New York, Asia Publishing House, 1962). A different type of work is C. D. Deshmukh, *Economic Developments in India 1946–56* (Bombay, Asia Publishing House, 1957). A very instructive work has been written by John P. Lewis, former director of the American Aid for International Development's operations in India, under the title *Quiet Crisis in India* (New York, Doubleday, 1963). Two other valuable studies are Ansley J. Coale and Edgar M. Hoover, *Population Growth and Economic Development in Low-Income Countries: A Case Study of India's Prospects* (Princeton, Princeton University Press, 1958); and Charles A. Myers, *Labor Problems in the Industrialization of India* (Cambridge, Harvard University Press, 1958). The Gokhale Institute (Poona) and the Indian Statistical Institute (Calcutta) publish numerous studies.

Good works on the economy of Pakistan (since partition) are J. Russell Andrus and A. F. Mohammed, *The Economy of Pakistan* (London, Oxford University Press, 1958); W. N. Peach, Mohammed Uzair, and G. W. Rucker, *Basic Data of the Economy of Pakistan* (Karachi, Oxford University Press, 1959); and S. M. Akhtar, *Economics of Pakistan,* fifth edition (Lahore, Publishers United, 1961). An important book is Gustav F. Papanek, *Pakistan's Development: Social Goals and Private Incentives* (Cambridge, Harvard University Press, 1967). The Institute of Development Economics in Karachi, a nonofficial organization established by the government of Pakistan, publishes worthwhile research material on national and international problems of economic development.

With these various economics works should be examined as fundamental studies the various five-year plans of India and Pakistan.

A most interesting study is that by Albert Mayer and associates, in collaboration with McKim Marriott and Richard L. Park, *Pilot Project India: The Story of Rural Development at Etawah, Uttar Pradesh* (Berkeley, University of California Press, 1959). A careful analysis of prospects is Wilfred Malenbaum, *Prospects for Indian Development* (London, George Allen and Unwin, 1962). Malenbaum has also published *Modern India's Economy.* Some lively observations on the working of community development programs in India are found in Kusum Nair's very readable *Blossoms in the Dust* (London, Gerald Duckworth, 1961). The same author has published a work of scholarly research of the highest sort—and at the same time most readable—with the title *The Lonely Furrow: Farming in the United States, Japan, and India* (Ann Arbor, University of Michigan Press, 1969). A good study of a basic problem is D. K. Ragnekar, *Poverty and Capital Development in India* (London, Oxford University Press, 1958). A publication by the long-time chairman of the Indian Planning Commission is V. T. Krishnamachari, *Planning in India* (Bombay, Orient Longmans, 1961). The Indian Planning Commission has issued a fairly nontechnical popular book, *Towards a Self-Reliant Economy: India's Third Plan 1961–66* (Publication Division of Ministry of Information and Broadcasting, Government of India, Delhi, 1961). A book with current appeal is Francine R. Frankel, *India's Green Revolution, Economic Gains and Political Costs* (Princeton, Princeton University Press, 1971).

Anthropological and Sociological Studies

J. H. Hutton, *Caste in India*, fourth edition (London, Oxford University Press, 1963), G. S. Ghurye, *Caste and Class in India*, second edition (Bombay, Popular Book Depot, 1957), and Louis Dumont, *Homo Hierarchicus: The Caste System and Its Implications*, a translation from the original French (Chicago, University of Chicago Press, 1970), are all at once anthropological and sociological in approach. Dr. Ghurye has also published a study of Indian social structure entitled *Caste, Class, and Occupation* (Bombay, Popular Book Depot, 1961), which is the fourth edition of his *Caste and Race in India*. Kingsley Davis, *The Population of India and Pakistan* (Princeton, Princeton University Press, 1951), is an excellent demographic study which also treats social structure and change. Another important sociological work is M. N. Srinivas, *Social Change in Modern India* (Berkeley, University of California Press, 1966). A somewhat more specialized book is Krishnan Bhatia, *The Ordeal of a Nationhood: A Social Study of India since Independence, 1947–1970* (New York, Athenaeum Press, 1971).

A reliable nontechnical and interestingly written description of village life is Gertrude Emerson, *Voiceless India*, second edition (New York, John Day, 1944). Margaret Read's *The Indian Peasant Uprooted* (Longmans Green, 1931) is a study of the factory worker population in pre-partition India. Richard D. Lambert is author of *Workers, Factories, and Social Change in India* (Princeton, Princeton University Press, 1963).

McKim Marriott has edited *Village India, Studies in the Little Community* (Chicago, University of Chicago Press, 1955; originally published as a Memoir of the American Anthropological Association). The West Bengal government has published a group of articles by various authors under the title *India's Villages* (1955). An important work is A. R. Desai, *Rural Sociology in India*, fourth edition (New York International Publication Services, 1969). A most interesting and authoritative work is M. N. Srinivas, *India's Villages*, second edition (London, Asia Publishing House, 1960). Aileen D. Ross has published a book on *The Hindu Family in Its Urban Setting* (Toronto, University of Toronto Press, 1967). S. C. Dube has a simply written study on *The Indian Village* (Ithaca, Cornell University Press, 1955). A very well-written and illuminating study is Oscar Lewis, *Village Life in Northern India: Studies in a Delhi Village* (Urbana, University of Illinois Press, 1958). *Traditional India: Structure and Change*, edited by Milton Singer (Philadelphia, American Folklore Society, 1959), is a collection of essays reprinted from the *American Journal of Folklore*, volume 71, no. 281,

1958. Singer's *When a Great Tradition Modernizes: An Anthropological Approach to Indian Civilization* (New York, Praeger, 1972) is the product of years of reading and discussion with many scholars.

A number of books have been written about the Depressed or Backward Classes, of which one is Mohinder Singh, *The Depressed Classes* (Bombay, Hind Kitabs, 1947). The Government of India's Backward Classes Commission published a three-volume report in 1956. A large and excellent bibliography has been published by Eleanor Zelliot, *The Untouchables in Contemporary India* (University of Arizona Press, Tucson, Arizona, 1972). A psychoanalytical job on upper-caste Hindus is done by G. Morris Carstairs in *The Twice-Born* (London, Hogarth Press, 1957). A psychological study is Gardner Murphy, *In the Minds of Men: The Study of Human Behavior and Social Tensions in India* (New York, Basic Books, 1953). Swaminath Natarajan has published *A Century of Social Reform in India* (Bombay, Asia Publishing House, 1959). Taya Zinkin has an interesting appraisal in *Caste Today* (London, Oxford University Press, 1962). A source book for the study of social change in the past one hundred years is D. D. Karve, *The New Brahmans: Five Maharashtrian Families* (Berkeley, University of California Press, 1963), being material selected from various personal diaries and translated into English.

Religion and Philosophy

Of the legion of books on Indian religions the briefest of overall works that has both simplicity of presentation and scholarly merit is J. N. Farquhar, *A Primer of Hinduism* (London, Oxford University Press, 1912), frequently reprinted in both England and India. Another brief work of the highest scientific quality is Louis Renou, *Religions of Ancient India* (University of London, Athlone Press, 1953).

Maurice Bloomfield's *The Religion of the Veda* (New York, Putnam's, 1908) is a short work that is at once scientific, vivid, and readable. Much longer is the standard two-volume work of A. Berriedale Keith, *The Religion and Philosophy of the Veda and Upanishads* (Cambridge, Harvard University Press, 1925). *The Thirteen Principal Upanishads*, translated by R. E. Hume, second edition revised (Madras, Oxford University Press, 1965), is the most reliable rendition of those texts into English, though not always smooth reading. The many smoother renderings, whether of single Upanishads or collections, are too often sectarian or misleading or meaningless. The best interpretation and translation of the frequently translated *Bhagavad Gita* is Franklin Edgerton, *The Bhagavad Gita*, 2 vols., comprising Sanskrit text, translation, introduction, and notes (Cambridge, Harvard University Press, 1944); without the Sanskrit text this is also available in paper in a Harvard Paperbacks edition.

On Buddhism in India a good work is the short treatment by T. W. Rhys Davids, *Buddhism: Its History and Literature*, third edition (New York, Putnam's, 1918). An authoritative book is Edward Conze, *Buddhism: Its Essence and Development* (Harper Torchbooks, 1960). Conze has also published *Buddhist Thought in India* (London, Allen and Unwin, 1962). A long and valuable general treatment of Hinduism and Buddhism is Sir Charles N. E. Eliot, *Hinduism and Buddhism*, 3 vols. (London, E. Arnold, 1921). For the legendary life of the Buddha, see A. Foucher, *The Life of the Buddha according to the Ancient Texts and Monuments of India* in an abridged translation from the French by Simone Brangier Boas (Middletown, Wesleyan University Press, 1963). A critical study is E. J. Thomas, *The Life of Buddha as Legend and History* (New York, Knopf, 1927). For Jainism see Walther Schubring, *The Doctrine of the Jainas, Described after the Old Sources*, translated from

the German by Wolfgang Beurlen (Delhi, Motilal Banarsidass, 1962);
Margaret Sinclair Stevenson, *The Heart of Jainism* (London, Milford,
1915); the article by H. Jacobi in the *Encyclopedia of Religion and
Ethics*. On the popular religion very good books are Bishop Henry White-
head's *The Village Gods of South India*, second edition (London, Oxford
University Press, 1921); and L. S. S. O'Malley's *Popular Hinduism*
(New York, Macmillan, 1935). A very interesting study in the field of
popular religion is Milton Singer, ed., *Krishna Myths, Rites, and Attitudes* (Chicago, University of Chicago Press, 1968).

Reform movements in modern Hinduism are best treated in J. N.
Farquhar, *Modern Religious Movements in India*, second edition (New
York, Macmillan, 1931). Another work of less scholarship but great enthusiasm is Romain Rolland's *Prophets of the New India*, translated
from the French by E. F. Malcolm Smith (New York, Boni, 1930). R. S.
Khare has made a study of the very interesting changes taking place
among the Brahmans: *The Changing Brahmans; Associations and
Elites among the Kanya-Kubjas of North India* (Chicago, University of
Chicago Press, 1970). Works of the well-known socialist reformer and
politician Jai Prakash Narain have been compiled by Bimla Prasad and
published under the title *Socialism, Sarvodaya, and Democracy* (Bombay
and London, Asia Publishing House, 1965).

An easily read book on the Sikhs is John Clark Archer, *The Sikhs*
(Princeton, Princeton University Press, 1946). For Christianity in India
see the pertinent sections in volumes 1 (5), 2 (5), 6 (3), and 7 (7) of
K. S. Latourette's seven-volume *History of the Expansion of Christianity*
(New York, Harper, 1937–1945). For Islam in India, see Murray T.
Titus, *Indian Islam* (New York, Oxford University Press, 1930); Wil-
fred C. Smith, *Modern Islam in India*, second edition (Lahore, Pratap
Krishna for Minerva Bookshop, 1947); Mohammed Yasin, *A Social His-
tory of Islamic India (1605–1748)* (Lucknow, Upper India Publishing
House, 1958).

In the field of Indian philosophy there are two very summary works
by Mysore Hiriyanna, both published in London by George Allen and
Unwin: *Outlines of Indian Philosophy* (1932) and *Essentials of Indian
Philosophy* (1949). There is a two-volume work by Dr. Sarvepalli Radhakrishnan, *Indian Philosophy* (New York, Macmillan, 1923, 1927);
and a work in five volumes by S. N. Dasgupta, *A History of Indian Philosophy* (Cambridge, Engl., Cambridge University Press, 1922–1955).
Possibly the average general reader would be satisfied initially with the
descriptions of the various systems in the general works on Indian civilization mentioned above. A good book on early speculative thought in
India is Franklin Edgerton, *The Beginnings of Indian Philosophy:* Selections from the Rig Veda, Atharva Veda, Upanishads, and Mahābhārata,
translated from the Sanskrit with an introduction, notes, and glossarial
index (London, George Allen and Unwin, 1965). A different sort of
work dealing with early Indian thought is W. Norman Brown, *Man in
the Universe: Some Cultural Continuities* (Berkeley, University of California Press, 1966, in both hard cover and paperback). Sarvepalli Radhakrishnan's small book *The Hindu View of Life* (New York, Macmillan, 1927, republished in 1939) is very suggestive. A readable book on
varied aspects of Indian thought is Heinrich Zimmer, *Philosophies of
India,* edited by Joseph Campbell (New York, Pantheon Books, 1951;
now available from the Princeton University Press). Another book by
this gifted writer is *Myths and Symbols in Indian Art and Civilization*
(New York, Pantheon Books, 1946, now available from the Princeton
University Press). For the thought of Islam in the subcontinent see Muhammad Iqbal, *The Reconstruction of Religious Thought in Islam* (Lahore, Civil and Military Gazette, 1944); and I. H. Qureshi, *The Pakistan
Way of Life* (New York, Praeger, 1956). Hajime Nakamura, *The Ways*

of *Thinking of Eastern Peoples* (Japanese National Commission for UNESCO, 1960), is a work of wide intellectual range. A thoughtful and thought-provoking approach to Indian philosophy is given by Karl H. Potter in *Presuppositions of India's Philosophies* (Englewood Cliffs, N.J., Prentice-Hall, 1963).

Languages and Literature

On the languages of the subcontinent a small, easily procurable, and authoritative pamphlet is Suniti Kumar Chatterji's *Language and the Linguistic Problem,* Oxford Pamphlets on Indian Affairs, No. 11, third edition (London, Oxford University Press, 1945). Another book is by Jyotirindra Dasgupta, *Language Conflict and National Development: Group Politics and National Language in India* (Berkeley, University of California Press, 1970).

The traditional Hindu, Buddhist, and Jain literature may be studied in Moriz Winternitz's distinguished three-volume work in German, of which the first two volumes have been translated into English by S. Ketkar and published as *A History of Indian Literature* (Calcutta, University of Calcutta, 1927–1933); a second edition is in progress, of which part I of volume one has been published (1959). A. Berriedale Keith's *History of Sanskrit Literature* (London, Oxford University Press, 1928) is standard for the period after the Veda. A short but now largely outdated work is A. A. Macdonell, *A History of Sanskrit Literature* (New York, Appleton, 1914). A further work is being published under the editorship of Surendra Nath Das Gupta entitled *A History of Sanskrit Literature.* The first volume of this on the *Classical Period* by S. N. Das Gupta and S. K. De has been published (Calcutta, Calcutta University Press, 1947); a second volume was planned but has not appeared. It does not seem within the scope of this essay to list works on the vernacular literatures, which for the most part are not well reported.

Much classical Indian poetry has been translated into English. Two recent translations from Sanskrit lyric poetry that give some conception of the poetic values of the originals have been made by Barbara Stoler Miller and are easily available: *Bhartrihari: Poems* (New York, Columbia University Press, 1967) and *Phantasies of a Love-Thief, the Caurapanchasika, attributed to Bilhana* (New York, Columbia University Press, 1971). A volume of Bengali tales translated in a way to reflect the literary quality of the originals is Edward C. Dimock, *The Thief of Love: Bengali Tales from Court and Village* (Chicago, University of Chicago Press, 1963).

Of contemporary literature, novels by Indians writing in English include, as examples: Mulk Raj Anand's *Coolie* (London, Hutchinson, 1947) and *The Village* (London, Jonathan Cape, 1939); Dhan Gopal Mukherji's *My Brother's Face* (New York, Dutton, 1925). R. K. Narayan, frequently characterized as India's foremost novelist, has written a number of novels, of which some are: *The Financial Expert* (East Lansing, Michigan State College Press, 1953; New York, The Noonday Press, 1959); *The Bachelor of Arts* (East Lansing, Michigan State College Press, 1954); *The Maneater of Malgudi* (New York, Viking 1961); *The Guide* (New York, Viking, 1958). Mrs. R. Prawer Jhabvala, though not an Indian by birth, is a close observer, good reporter, and satirical commentator; her novels include: *The Nature of Passion* (London, George Allen and Unwin, 1956); *The Householder* (London, John Murray, 1960). Kamala Markandaya's *Nectar in a Sieve* (New York, John Day, 1954; also a Signet paperback, 1960) has been much read. Some other novels by her are: *A Handful of Rice* (London, Hamilton, 1966) and *The Cofferdams* (New York, John Day, 1969). There is a collection of short stories by Raja Rao, *The Cat and Shakespeare* (New York, Macmillan, 1965). Of other collections of stories available a few may be noted: R. K. Narayan, *Horse and Two Goats* (New York, Viking, 1970); *Short Stories of Yashpal,* translated and introduced by Corinne Friend (Philadelphia, University of Pennsylvania Press, 1969). *Green and Gold: Stories and Poems from Bengal* is a volume of translations assembled and edited by Humayan Kabir (New York, New Directions, 1958). There is a bibliography by Dorothy M. Spencer, *Indian Fiction in English: An Annotated Bibliography* (Philadelphia, University of Pennsylvania Press, 1960). Studies of the Indian novel have been published by T. W. Clark, *The Novel in India: Its Birth and Development* (Berkeley, University of California Press, 1970); M. E. Derrett, *The Modern Indian Novel in English; A Comparative Approach* (Brussels, Université libre de Bruxelles, 1966). There is a study of the author Mulk Raj Anand by Margaret Berry, *Mulk Raj Anand, the Man and the Novelist* (Amsterdam, Oriental Press, 1971).

A literary figure of great power is Nirad C. Chaudhuri, who has written *The Autobiography of an Unknown Indian* (Berkeley, University of California Press, 1968) and *The Continent of Circe* (London, Chatto and Windus, 1965), in which he shows himself a satirist of high ability.

Art and Architecture

For architecture, sculpture, and painting inclusive works are: Ananda K. Coomaraswamy, *History of Indian and Indonesian Art* (New York, Weyhe, 1927; paperback by Dover); Vincent A. Smith, *A History of Fine Art in India and Ceylon,* third edition revised by Karl Khandalavala (London, Oxford University Press, 1961); Benjamin Rowland, *The Art and Architecture of India* (Baltimore, Penguin, 1953). On architecture specifically there is an excellent two-volume work by Percy Brown, *Indian Architecture* (Bombay, Taraporevala, 1942), of which the first volume deals with Hindu and Buddhist architecture and the second with Muslim. A quite different type of work, which analyzes the intellectual content equally with, if not more than, the structural, stylistic, and iconographic features, is Stella Kramrisch, *The Hindu Temple,* 2 vols. (Calcutta, University of Calcutta Press, 1946). For sculpture, bronzes, textiles, and painting there is *The Art of India and Pakistan* by K. de B. Codrington, John Irwin, and Basil Gray, edited by Sir Leigh Ashton (New York, Coward-McCann, 1950), a survey based upon an exhibition at Burlington House, London, 1947–1948. Stella Kramrisch has another thoughtfully analytic volume on the principles of Indian art, *The Art of India* (London, Phaidon Press, 1954; third edition, 1965), and another, *Indian Sculpture in the Philadelphia Museum of Art* (Philadelphia, University of Pennsylvania Press, 1961). A splendidly illustrated work is a two-volume production by Heinrich Zimmer, *The Art of Indian Asia* (New York, Pantheon Books, 1955; second edition, Princeton University Press, 1960).

Law and the Political System

Treatments of Indian law include first the large and scholarly five-volume work by Pandurang Vaman Kane, *History of Dharmasastra* (Poona, Bhandarkar Oriental Research Institute, 1930–1958). A scholarly one-volume work is Julius Jolly, *Hindu Law and Custom,* translated from the German (Calcutta, Greater Indian Society, 1928). Other recommended works are J. D. M. Derrett, *Hindu Law, Past and Present* (Calcutta, A. Mukherjee, 1957); and Alan Gledhill, *Republic of India: The Development of Its Laws and Constitution* (Westport, Conn., Greenwood Press, 1951).

In ancient India, law, political theory and practice, and religion were tightly meshed. Besides the works by Kane and Jolly mentioned above a standard work in this general field, but dealing more specifically with political theory, is U. N. Ghoshal, *A History of Indian Political Ideas* (London, Oxford University Press, 1959). A volume of well-chosen selections from Indian writers on political theory has been compiled by D. MacKenzie Brown, *The White Umbrella: Indian Political Thought from Manu to Gandhi* (Berkeley, University of California Press, 1953; now available as a paperback). For the British period a standard work is A. Berriedale Keith, *Constitutional History of India,* second edition (London, Metheun, 1937).

On postpartition systems there are a number of books, of which may be mentioned here: G. N. Joshi, *The Constitution of India* (London, Macmillan, 1952); Sir Ivor Jennings, *The Commonwealth in Asia* (London, Oxford University Press, 1951); Sir Ivor Jennings, *Some Characteristics of the Indian Constitution* (London, Oxford University Press, 1953). The study of the modern party system in India can well begin with Briton Martin's book *New India 1885: British Official Policy and the Emergence of the Indian National Congress* (Berkeley, University of California Press, 1969). Other pertinent books are: Norman D. Palmer, *The Indian Political System* (Boston, Houghton Mifflin, second edition, 1961); Sir Ivor Jennings, *Constitutional Problems in Pakistan* (Cambridge, Engl., Cambridge University Press, 1957); Myron Weiner, *Party Politics in India* (Princeton, Princeton University Press, 1957); Richard L. Park, *India's Political System* (Englewood Cliffs, N.J., Prentice-Hall, 1967); Myron Weiner, *Political Change in South Asia* (Calcutta, K. L. Mukhopadhyaya, 1963); Myron Weiner, *Party Building in a New Nation: the Indian National Congress* (Chicago, University of Chicago Press, 1967); Myron Weiner, *State Politics in India* (Princeton, Princeton University Press, 1968); Myron Weiner and Rajni Kothari, ed., *Indian Voting Behaviour: Studies of the 1962 General Elections* (Calcutta, K. L. Mukhopadhyaya, 1965); Rajni Kothari, *Politics in India* (Boston, Little, Brown, 1970); V. P. Varma, *Modern Indian Political Thought* (Agra, Lakshmi Narain Agarwal, 1961). A most interesting discussion of *India as a Secular State* has been written by Donald E. Smith (Princeton, Princeton University Press, 1963); the same author has written *South Asian Politics and Religion* (Princeton, Princeton, University Press, 1966). V. P. Menon has published *The Story of the Integration of the Indian States* (New York, Macmillan, 1956). Some essays on a unified theme appear as *Leadership and Political Institutions in India,* edited by Richard L. Park and Irene Tinker (Princeton, Princeton University Press, 1959). W. H. Morris-Jones has an analytical study, *Parliament in India* (London, Longmans Green, 1957). A brief analysis appears in Hugh Tinker, *India and Pakistan: A Political Analysis* (New York, Praeger, revised edition, 1968). Fuller works on more limited topics are Leonard Binder, *Religion and Politics in Pakistan* (Berkeley, University of California Press, 1961), and Myron Weiner, *The Politics of Scarcity, Public Pressure and Political Response in India* (Chicago, University of Chicago Press, 1962). A collection of essays by a number of leading scholars, most of them British, has been published by C. H. Philips under the title *Politics and Society in India* (New York, Praeger, 1963).

Other interesting books are: Lloyd L. and Susanne Rudolph, *The Modernity of Tradition: Political Development in India* (Chicago, University of Chicago Press, 1967); Donald B. Rosenthal, *The Limited Elite; Politics and Government in Two Indian States* (Chicago, University of Chicago Press, 1970); Robert W. Stern, *The Process of Opposition in India; Two Case Studies of How Policy Shapes Politics* (Chicago, University of Chicago Press, 1970); M. V. Pylee, *Constitu-*

tional Government in India, second revised edition (Bombay and New York, Asia Publishing House, 1965); W. H. Morris-Jones, *The Government and Politics of India* (London, Hutchinson University Library, 1964; second edition, 1967; third edition revised, 1971); Robert L. Hardgrave, *India: Government and Politics in a Developing Nation* (New York, Harcourt Brace and World, 1970); Eugene F. Irschik, *Politics and Social Conflict in South India,* a study of the Justice party (Berkeley, University of California Press, 1969); Craig Baxter, *The Jana Sangha: A Biography of an Indian Political Party* (Philadelphia, University of Pennsylvania Press, 1969); Mary Carras, *The Dynamics of Indian Political Factions: A Study of Factions in Four District Councils of Maharashtra* (New York, Cambridge University Press, 1972).

Values and the Active Community: A Cross-cultural Study of the Influence of Local Leadership (New York, Free Press, 1971) is a comparative study of India, Yugoslavia, Poland, and the United States by a team of scholars of those countries.

The British in India

Surveys and appraisals of British rule in India have been many, but most are either ardently pro- or ardently anti-British. A number of treatments appear in the volumes on history mentioned above. A carefully worked out description in just over a hundred pages is that by Daniel and Alice Thorner in the chapter "India and Pakistan" in *Most of the World,* a large work on the peoples of modern Africa, Latin America, and the East, edited by Ralph Linton (New York, Columbia University Press, 1949). A much longer treatment is that by Sir Reginald Coupland, published in England in three volumes and republished in the United States in a single volume as *The Indian Problem* (New York, Oxford University Press, 1944), a reasoned defense of the British position. A briefer study by the same author is *India: A Restatement* (London, Oxford University Press, 1945). A Marxist interpretation appeared in R. Palme Dutt's *India Today* issued both in short form (London, Gollanez, 1940) and in longer forms (Bombay, People's Publishing House, 1947, 1949; London, Collet, 1950). There was a still briefer form of this work entitled *The Problem of India* (New York, International Publishers, 1943); much affected by this was Kate Mitchell, *India without Fable* (New York, Knopf, 1942). An account of the terms on which British capital was attracted to invest in the Indian railways appears in Daniel Thorner, *Investment in Empire* (Philadelphia, University of Pennsylvania Press, 1950).

Memoirs of British residents in India and of Indians at all periods of the connection are innumerable; only a very few of special pertinence to the subject matter of this volume will be mentioned. One of the best by an English civil servant is Walter R. Lawrence, *The India We Served* (Boston and New York, Houghton Mifflin, 1929). Some connected with the achievement of independence are: Sir Francis Tuker, *While Memory Serves* (London, Cassell, 1950); Alan Campbell-Johnson, *Mission with Mountbatten* (New York, Dutton, 1953); Leonard Mosley, *The Last Days of the British Raj* (New York, Harcourt Brace and World, 1962), a work highly critical of both Nehru and Mountbatten; Maulana Abul Kalam Azad, *India Wins Freedom: An Autobiographical Narrative* (Bombay, Orient Longmans, 1959), a work that has aroused controversy and considerable unfavorable criticism among inflexible nationalists in India.

Nationalism and the Partition of India

The rise and development of nationalism is discussed in the books on history mentioned above. It is carefully and fully outlined up to the last part of the interwar period by William Roy Smith, *Nationalism and Reform in India* (New Haven, Yale University Press, 1938). The rise of Hindu and Muslim nationalism is discussed separately in Anil Seal, *The Emergence of Indian Nationalism: Competition and Collaboration in the Later Nineteenth Century* (London, Cambridge University Press, 1968), and Hafeez Malik, *Moslem Nationalism in India and Pakistan* (Washington, Public Affairs Press, 1963). An exceedingly helpful study of social elements in the nationalist movement is A. R. Desai, *Social Background of Indian Nationalism*, fourth edition (Bombay, Popular Book Depot, 1966). N. S. Bos has an interesting book, *The Indian Awakening and Bengal* (Calcutta, K. L. Mukhopadhyaya, 1960). Also of interest, on quite different subjects, are: David Kopf, *British Orientalism and the Bengal Renaissance* (Berkeley, University of California Press, 1967), and John Patrick Haithcox, *Communism and Nationalism in India; M. N. Roy and Comintern Policy, 1920–1939* (Princeton, Princeton University Press, 1971). Two of the most important figures in the development of nationalism are ably discussed in Stanley Wolpert, *Tilak and Gokhale: Revolution and Reform in the Making of Modern India* (Berkeley, University of California Press, 1962). The official *History of the Indian National Congress* is a two-volume work by B. Pattabhi Sitaramayya (Madras, Law Printing House, 1935, 1947). An official publication under the auspices of the government of India is by Tara Chand, *History of the Freedom Movement in India*, which is to be in three volumes, one of which has been published (Delhi, Publication Branch of the Government of India, 1961). Kanji Dwarkadas, *India's Fight for Freedom 1913–1937*, is an eyewitness story (Bombay, Popular Prakashan, 1966). There is an extensive bibliography of the nationalist movement and history of the two nations from independence to 1955, compiled and edited by Patrick Wilson, *Government and Politics of India and Pakistan 1885–1955: A Bibliography of Works in Western Languages* (Berkeley, University of California, Institute of East Asiatic Studies, 1956). An outstanding work in relation to the final achievement of independence is V. P. Menon, *The Transfer of Power in India* (Princeton, Princeton University Press, 1957).

Perhaps the most important book about the partition of India is the report of a series of conferences in the School of Oriental and African Studies at the University of London, held weekly over a long period of time, and presented by C. H. Philips and Mary D. Wainwright as *The Partition of India: Policies and Perspectives, 1935–1947* (London, Allen and Unwin, 1970). As volume IV of the series "Select Documents on the History of India and Pakistan," C. H. Philips, one of the leading historians of India and Pakistan, has published *The Evolution of India and Pakistan, 1858–1947: Select Documents* (London, Oxford University Press, 1962). Books for and against the partition are *Pakistan, or the Partition of India,* third edition (Bombay, Thacker, 1946), by B. R. Ambedkar, leader of the Scheduled Castes Federation; and *India Divided,* third edition (Bombay, Hind Kitabs, 1947), by Rajendra Prasad, afterwards President of India, 1952–1962. An interesting book that had the blessing of the Pakistan government is Richard Symonds, *The Making of Pakistan* (London, Faber and Faber, 1950), dealing with cultural as well as political matters. In relation to the consequences of partition a well-considered appraisal published shortly after the event was one by the economist S. N. Vakil and associates, *The Economic Consequences of Divided India* (Bombay, Vora, 1950). See also Hugh Tinker, *Experiments with Freedom in India and Pakistan 1947* (London, Oxford University Press, 1967).

Kashmir

The quarrel over Kashmir, which has been the most important issue between India and Pakistan, is discussed in Michael Brecher, *The Struggle for Kashmir* (Toronto, Oxford University Press, 1953); Josef Korbel, *Danger in Kashmir* (Princeton, Princeton University Press, 1954; revised edition, 1965), which gives the clearest narrative; Prithivi Nath Kaul Bamzai, *Kashmir and Power Politics from Lake Success to Tashkent* (Delhi, Metropolitan Book Company, 1966); Prem Nath Bazaz, *The Shape of Things in Kashmir* (New Delhi, Pamposh Publications, 1965); Prem Nath Bazaz, *Kashmir in Crucible* (New Delhi, Pamposh Publications, 1967); Mahomedali Currum Chagla, *Kashmir, 1947–1965* (New Delhi, Ministry of Information and Broadcasting, Government of India, 1965); S. S. R. Chari, *The Kashmir Problem* (New Delhi, M. Kalimulla, 1965); Babu Ram Chauhan, *Kashmir Problem in Constitutional and International Law*, with a supplement on Article 370 (Chandigarh, 1965); Jyoti Bhusan Das Gupta, *Jammu and Kashmir* (The Hague, M. Nijhoff, 1968); S. C. Gogia, *The Fight for Peace; the Long Road to Tashkent* (New Delhi, Hardy and Ally, 1966); Prahlad Balacharya Gajendragadkar, *Kashmir, Retrospect and Prospect* (Bombay, University of Bombay, 1967; Patel Memorial Lectures Series, 1966); Sisir Gupta, *Kashmir: A Study in India-Pakistan Relations* (Bombay and New York, Asia Publishing House, 1966; also issued under the auspices of the Indian Council of World Affairs by Asia Publishing House, Bombay and New York, 1967); K. Sarwar Hasan, *The Kashmir Question* (Karachi, Pakistan Institute of International Affairs, 1966); Muhammad Ibrahim Khan, *The Kashmir Saga* (Lahore, Ripon Printing Press, 1965); Sitaram Joshi, *The Indo-Pakistan Conflict of 1965* (Lucknow, Himalaya Publications, 1967); Alastair Lamb, *Crisis in Kashmir, 1947–1966* (London, Routledge and Kegan Paul, 1966): D. R. Mankekar, *Twenty-two Fateful Days; Pakistan Cut to Size* (Bombay, Manaktalas, 1966); Krishna Mehta, *This Happened in Kashmir* (Delhi, Publications Division, Ministry of Information and Broadcasting, 1966); Sheikh Mohammad Abdullah, *Kashmir, A Human Problem and a Moral Issue* (Delhi, Plebiscite Front of the Jammu and Kashmir State, 1965); K. C. Saxena, *Pakistan, Her Relation with India 1947–1966* (New Delhi, Vir Publishing House, 1966); Brij Lal Sharma, *The Kashmir Story* (Bombay and New York, Asia Publishing House, 1967); Satish Vashishta, *Sheikh Abdullah, Then and Now* (Delhi, Maulik Sahitya Prakashan, 1968). Many of the publications on the Kashmir quarrel listed here are very partisan in their approach, but they are mentioned to illustrate the depth of emotion that the quarrel has produced.

India and Pakistan since Partition

The character of the militant right-wing Hindu action organization Rashtriya Svayamsevak Sangh, held responsible for much of the killing at the time of partition, is described by J. A. Curran, *Militant Hinduism in Indian Politics: A Study of the R.S.S.* (New York, Institute of Pacific Relations, 1951).

Some books on various aspects of government and politics in modern India and Pakistan are the following: Hugh R. Tinker, *India and Pakistan: A Political Analysis*, second edition, revised and enlarged (London, Pall Mall Press, 1967); Michael Brecher, *Succession in India; A Study in Decision-Making* (London, Oxford University Press, 1966); Ahmad Mushtaq, *Government and Politics in Pakistan*, third edition (Karachi, Space Publishers, 1970); G. W. Choudhury, *Democracy in Pakistan* (Vancouver, Publications Center, University of British

Columbia, 1963); Ralph D. Braibanti, *Research on the Bureaucracy of Pakistan,* a critique of sources, conditions, and issues, with appended documents (Durham, Duke University Press, 1966); Donald Newton Wilbur, *Pakistan: Its People, Its Society, Its Culture* (New Haven, *Human Relations Area Files Press,* 1964); Karl von Vorys, *Political Development in Pakistan* (Princeton, Princeton University Press, 1965); Lawrence Ziring, *The Ayub Khan Era; Politics in Pakistan* (Syracuse, Syracuse University Press, 1971); Richard S. Wheeler, *The Politics of Pakistan; A Constitutional Quest* (Ithaca, Cornell University Press, 1970).

Margaret Bourke-White in *Halfway to Freedom* (New York, Simon and Schuster, 1949) describes in words and photographs vividly and trustworthily what she saw in 1947–1948, when the two nations were coming into existence. Horace Alexander in *New Citizens of India* (London, Oxford University Press, 1951) writes about the problems caused by refugees immigrating to India. Andrew Mellor in *India since Partition* (New York, Praeger, 1951) ably carried the story forward from 1947 in 150 pages. An important book is Ian M. Stephens, *Pakistan,* third edition (New York, Praeger, 1967). A British view of the nation's situation is given by Sir Percival Griffith in *Modern India,* second edition (New York, Praeger, 1958). A survey of India by a highly qualified Indian journalist is Frank Moraes, *India Today* (New York, Macmillan, 1960). A rather quick journalistic survey of Pakistan is found in H. B. Pithawalla, *Introduction to Pakistan* (London, Probsthain, 1948). Scholarly treatments are found in Wildred C. Smith, *Islam in Modern History* (Princeton, Princeton University Press, 1957; Mentor Books, 1959); in Keith Callard, *Pakistan, A Political Study* (New York, Macmillan, 1957); and in Callard's pamphlet *Political Forces in Pakistan, 1947–1959* (New York, Institute of Pacific Relations, 1959). A well-documented and keenly analytical study of divisive forces in India is Selig S. Harrison, *India: The Most Dangerous Decades* (Princeton, Princeton University Press, 1960). An estimate of new political trends is Vera M. Dean, *New Patterns of Democracy in India* (Cambridge, Harvard University Press, 1959, second edition, 1969). A small summary book by Paul Grimes, *New York Times* correspondent in India, 1959–1962, is *India: 15 Years of Freedom,* Headline Series No. 152 (New York, Foreign Policy Association, 1962). There is a survey for high school students by Emil Lengyel, *The Subcontinent of India* (New York, Scholastic Book Services, 1961). Golam Waheed Choudhury has written *Pakistan's Relations with India, 1947–1966* (New York, Praeger, 1968). *Communism in India* is the title of a long and detailed study by Gene D. Overstreet and Marshall Windmiller (Berkeley, University of California Press, 1959). A work in the same field is John H. Kautsky, *Moscow and the Communist Party of India: A Study in the Post-War Evolution of Communist Strategy* (Massachusetts Institute of Technology, Center for International Studies, 1954, cyclostyle). A personal response to postindependence India, well written and sensitive, is Margaret Parton's *The Leaf and the Flame* (New York, Knopf, 1959).

Foreign Relations

Relations between prepartition India and the West are discussed in a symposium edited by L. S. S. O'Malley, *Modern India and the West* (London, Oxford University Press, 1941). Various studies of postpartition India and Pakistan in their relations with other nations have been produced. Of special interest to Americans are the following works: Lawrence K. Rosinger, *India and the United States* (New

York, Macmillan, 1950); Lawrence K. Rosinger, ed., *The States of Asia* (New York, Knopf, 1951), in which the chapter on India was written by Rosinger and that on Pakistan by Holden Furber; Philips Talbot and S. Poplai, *India and America: A Study of Their Relations* (New York, Harper, 1958). A small and compact work is Percival Spear, *India, Pakistan, and the West,* fourth edition (London, Oxford University Press, 1967). There is a volume by Ross N. Berkes and Mohinder S. Bedi, *The Diplomacy of India: Indian Foreign Policy in the United Nations* (Stanford, Stanford University Press, 1958). Written with attention to economic relationships and issues is Barbara Ward, *India and the West* (New York, Norton, 1961). The report of a conference of considerable size with many distinguished speakers and informed scholars has been edited by Selig S. Harrison as *India and the United States* (New York, Macmillan, 1961).

Conceptions of India prevailing in America during something more than a century down to present times are identified and analyzed by Harold R. Isaacs in *Scratches on Our Minds: American Images of China and India* (New York, John Day, 1958). The effect of residence in America on Indian students is studied in Richard D. Lambert and Marvin Bressler, *Indian Students on an American Campus* (Minneapolis, University of Minnesota Press, 1956). The effect life in America has upon Indian students after their return home is the subject of a volume by John and Ruth Useem, *Western Educated Man in India* (New York, Dryden Press, 1955).

Chester Bowles gives his findings on the basis of his experience in India in *Ambassador's Report* (New York, Harper, 1954). He gives further reports in *A View from New Delhi* (New Haven, Yale University Press, 1969) and in *Promises to Keep* (New York, Harper and Row, 1970). John Kenneth Galbraith has recorded his reactions in *Ambassador's Journal* (Boston, Houghton Mifflin, 1969). Many of Nehru's views appear in *India's Foreign Policy: Selected Speeches September 1946–April 1961* (Delhi, Publications Division, Government of India, 1961).

On India's relations with China are: M. S. Rajan, *India in World Affairs* (New York, Asia Publishing House, 1964); William F. Van Eckelen, *Indian Foreign Policy and the Border Dispute with China,* second revised edition (The Hague, Nijhoff, 1967); Neville George Anthony Maxwell, *India's China War* (London, Cape, 1970).

Studies of Individual Leaders

Prominent personalities have played a large part in the development of modern India and Pakistan. Gandhi is the one most frequently written about. A few of the many books on him are the following. First, his two-volume autobiography published in India in 1927–1929 as *The Story of My Experiments with Truth,* republished in Washington, D.C., with the title *Gandhi's Autobiography* (Public Affairs Press, 1948). Of the studies about him the most illuminating to me is the trilogy of his close associate C. F. Andrews: *Mahatma Gandhi's Ideas* (1930); *Mahatma Gandhi: His Own Story* (1930); *Mahatma Gandhi at Work: His Own Story Continued* (1931), all published by Macmillan. These give a contemporary report of the spirit of his activities. A penetrating, original, and thought-provoking study of *satyagraha* is Joan V. Bondurant, *Conquest of Violence: The Gandhian Philosophy of Conflict* (Princeton, Princeton University Press, 1958; revised edition, Berkeley University of California Press, 1965). There are many biographies of Gandhi. Louis Fischer wrote *The Life of Mahatma Gandhi* (New York, Harper, 1950). A different kind of biography is that by B. R. Nanda, *Mahatma Gandhi: A Political Biography* (London, George Allen and Unwin, 1958). A number of well-chosen selections from Gandhi's writings have been published by Homer A. Jack, *The Gandhi Reader* (Bloomington, Indiana University Press, 1956), republished in paperback as *Gandhi Reader No. 1: A Source Book of His Life and Writings* (Evergreen Pocket Books, 1961). A compilation of articles by various authors appears in G. Ramachandran and T. K. Mahadevan, eds., *Gandhi: His Relevance for Our Times* (New Delhi, Gandhi Peace Foundation, and Berkeley, California, World Without War Council, 1971; also Bombay, Bharatiya Vidya Bhavan, 1964). Other books about Gandhi are Horace Alexander, *Gandhi through Western Eyes* (Bombay and New York, Asia Publishing House, 1969; Geoffrey Ashe, *Gandhi* (New York, Stein and Day 1968; Sibnarayan Ray, ed., *Gandhi, India, and the World* (Philadelphia, Temple University Press, 1970); and Penderel Moon, *Gandhi and Modern India* (New York, Norton, 1969). Three of India's greatest leaders in the fight for freedom are treated by V. B. Kulkarni in *The Indian Triumvirate: A Political Biography of Mahatma Gandhi, Sardar Patel, and Pandit Nehru* (Bombay, Bharatiya Vidya Bhavan, 1969). R. A. Huttenback, *Gandhi in South Africa: British Imperialism and the Indian Question, 1860–1914* (Ithaca, Cornell University Press, 1971), treats a different period in Gandhi's life. Still another biography is Stephen Robert Payne, *The Life and Death of Mahatma Gandhi.*

Quite different from all the books listed above, both in subject matter and in treatment, is the psychoanalytical study by Erik H. Erickson, *Gandhi's Truth, on the Origins of Militant Nonviolence* (New York, Norton, 1969).

Jawaharlal Nehru, a most articulate writer of English, has himself produced a number of books. One is his autobiography, published in the United States as *Toward Freedom* (New York, John Day, 1941). Others are his *Discovery of India,* in which he records much of his political and social philosophy, which has already been mentioned; and his *Glimpses of World History.* A small work consisting of a discussion of international problems with Norman Cousins appeared as *Talks with Nehru* (New York, John Day, 1951).

Nehru's political democracy is probed in Donald E. Smith, *Nehru and Democracy* (Bombay, Orient Longman's 1958); and in Michael Brecher, *Nehru: A Political Biography* (London, Oxford University Press, 1959). Frank Moraes, one of the leading journalists of India, has written *Jawaharlal Nehru: A Biography* (New York, Macmillan, 1956). A work written with considerable emotion is Vincent Sheean, *Nehru: The Years of Power* (New York, Random House, 1960). Note also Marie Seton, *Panditji: A Portrait of Jawaharlal Nehru* (London, Dobson, 1967); and Bani Shorter, *Nehru, A Voice for Mankind* (New York, John Day, 1970). *The First Sixty Years* presents in his own words the development of the political thought of Jawaharlal Nehru and the background against which it evolved, selected and edited by Dorothy Norman, 2 volumes (New York, John Day, 1965).

Of Jinnah there is a biography by M. H. Saiyid, *Mohammad Ali Jinnah: A Political Study* (Lahore, Ashraf Press, 1945). What is essentially an official biography is Hector Bolitho's *Jinnah: Creator of Pakistan* (New York, Macmillan, 1955). See also Saleem M. M. Quereshi, *Jinnah and the Making of a Nation* (Karachi, Council for Pakistan Studies, 1969).

Ayub Khan has written his autobiography, *Friends Not Masters, A Political Autobiography* (New York, Oxford University Press, 1967).

Rabindranath Tagore published his *Reminiscences* (latest edition,

London, Macmillan, 1946). J. Edward Thompson published a literary biography of him, *Rabindranath Tagore, Poet and Dramatist* (London, Oxford University Press, 1926). Marjorie Sykes is the author of a biography, *Rabindranath Tagore* (New York, Longmans Green, 1945). Krishna Kripalani, *Rabindranath Tagore* (New York, Grove Press, 1962), is a biography prepared for the centenary of his birth. A study of his thought is Stephen N. Hay, *Asian Ideas of East and West: Tagore and His Critics in Japan, China, and India* (Cambridge, Harvard University Press, 1970).

On Iqbal there is a work by A. Anwar Beg, *The Poet of the East: the Life and Works of Sir Muhammad Iqbal, the Poet-Philosopher* (Lahore, Islamic Publications, 1956).

There is a three-volume biography by L. J. L. D. (Earl of) Ronaldshay, *The Life of Lord Curzon* (New York, Boni, 1928). Another study of Lord Curzon is by Leonard Mosley, *Curzon: The End of an Epoch* (London, Longmans, 1960).

Selected speeches by important figures, besides those mentioned above, are: Lord Mountbatten, *Time Only To Look Forward* (London) N. Kaye, 1949); Vallabhbhai Patel, *On Indian Problems* (Delhi, Publications Division, Ministry of Information and Broadcasting, Government of India, 1949); Jawaharlal Nehru, *Independence and After* (New York, John Day, 1950); Liaquat Ali Khan, *Pakistan: Heart of Asia* (Cambridge, Harvard University Press, 1951).

Newspapers

For current news of India and Pakistan the best service in America is furnished by the *New York Times,* which for a number of years has kept correspondents in New Delhi and for part of the time in Karachi. *The Christian Science Monitor* has frequent good articles; *Time,* the Baltimore *Sun,* and other dailies and weeklies have stationed correspondents in India and carried special articles.

Index

NOTE on pronunciation of words transliterated from Oriental languages. Speakers of English should stress the next to the last syllable when it is long, otherwise the first long syllable before it. A long syllable is one containing a long vowel (*ā, ī, ū*) or a diphthong (*e, o, ai, au*) or a vowel followed by more than one consonant (but note that usually *h* following a consonant indicates aspiration of the consonant and does give length to the syllable). The sounds of the vowels are roughly as follows.

a like *u* in English up	*ū* like *oo* in English soon
ā like *a* in English bar	*e* like *a* in English take
i like *i* in English sin	*ai* like *ai* in English aisle
ī like *ee* in English sheen	*o* like *o* in English so
u like *u* in English pull	*au* like *ow* in English how

Pronounce *c* like *ch* in English chin; *g* like *g* in English gun. The aspirate sounds *th, kh, ph* are much like the sounds of *t, k,* and *p* in English tin, kin, pin (as distinguished from the sounds in English stun, skin, spin). The aspirates *dh, gh, bh* are like the combinations in English roundhouse, doghouse, clubhouse. In Arabic words the sound ' is the glottal stop; the sound ' is a deep laryngeal, which is not pronounced in India but lengthens the adjacent vowel.

The following abbreviations are used: Skt. for Sanskrit, Ar. for Arabic, Pers. for Persian. Diacritical marks have been omitted throughout for typographical reasons.

447

457

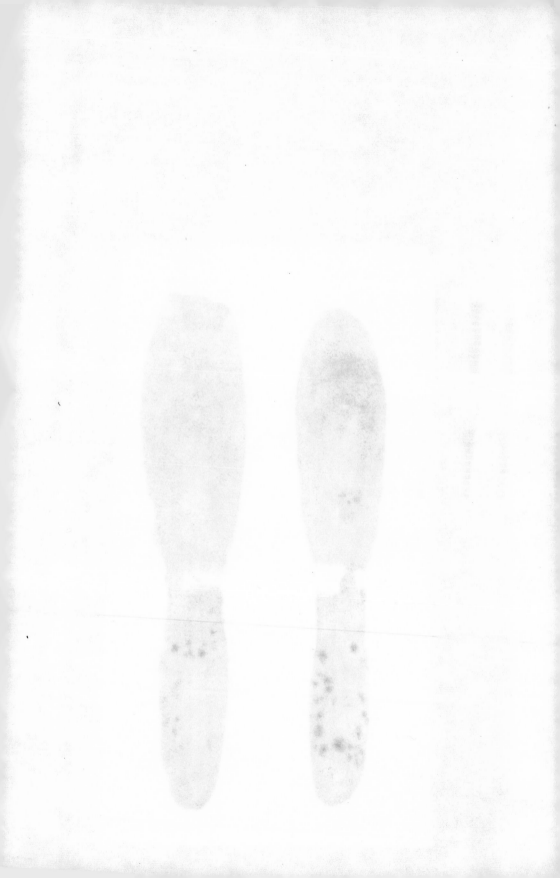